Introductory Economics
Sixth edition
G F Stanlake and S J Grant

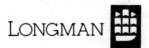
LONGMAN

Longman Group Limited
*Longman House, Burnt Mill, Harlow, Essex CM20 2JE, England
and Associated Companies throughout the World*

First published 1967
Second edition 1971
Third edition 1976
Fourth edition 1983
Fifth edition 1989
Sixth edition 1995

ISBN 0 582 24614 8

Produced by Longman Singapore Publishers Pte Ltd
Printed in Singapore

Acknowledgements

We are grateful to the following for permission to reproduce copyright
material:

The Economist Newspaper for fig. 'Official Reserves' *The Economist*
26.10.85, © *The Economist* 1985; The Financial Times Ltd for the
graphic 'Balancing the books 1994–5' in *The Financial Times* 1.12.93;
the Controller of Her Majesty's Stationery Office for fig's. 'Public
Expenditure 1994–5', 'Public Revenue 1994–5', 'Public Sector Borrow-
ing Requirement' from *The Budget in Brief*, pubd. H.M. Treasury,
November 1993. and fig. 'Treasury Bill'. all Crown Copyright; Times
Newspapers Ltd for fig's. 'Decline in union membership' from *The
Times* 5.9.94, 'Gatt & Industrial tarrifs' in *The Sunday Times* Dec. '93,
'Percentage of People' in *The Times* 8.6.94. and drawing only from
'Unions: the members and their leaders' in *The Times* 5.9.94. © Times
Newspapers Ltd. 1993/1994.

Contents

Part One: Introduction

1   The nature, scope and methods of economics   1
2   Production possibility curves   8
3   Economic systems   14
4   The move to market economies: recent events   22

Part Two: Factors of production

5   Economic resources   27
6   Specialisation   37
7   Combining the factors of production   47

Part Three: The organization and scale of production

8   Costs of production   56
9   The scale of production   64
10   Growth of firms   78
11   UK industry – size and structure   87
12   The finance of industry   97
13   Influences on the location of industry   104

Part Four: Price determination

14   Demand   113
15   Elasticities of demand   127
16   Supply   143
17   Market price   153
18   Relationships between prices   161

Part Five: Market structure

19   Perfect competition   168
20   Monopolistic competition   179
21   Oligopoly   184
22   Monopoly   189
23   Comparisons of market structure   202

Part Six: Market failure and government response

24 Costs and benefits   214
25 Causes of market failure   221
26 Government response to market failure   225
27 Other forms of government intervention   237
28 Ownership of industries   244
29 Marginal revenue product   250
30 Profit   255
31 Rent   258
32 Interest   264
33 Labour markets   277
34 Wage determination   287
35 Labour market failure   297
36 Government action to correct labour market imperfections   304
37 Distribution of wealth and income   309

Part Seven: National income determination

38 Measures of living standards   316
39 Models of national income determination   329
40 Aggregate demand and supply   339

Part Eight: Changes in national income

41 Changes in injections and leakages   350
42 Growth   358
43 Business cycles   365
44 Unemployment   371
45 Money   382
46 Financial institutions   388
47 Assets and liabilities of the banking sector   395
48 The value of money   405
49 Inflation   416
50 The relationship between inflation and unemployment   425

Part Nine: International trade

51 The nature of international trade   431
52 Protectionism   440
53 Trade blocs   448
54 The terms of trade   458

55 The balance of payments   461
56 Exchange rates   470
57 International liquidity   480
58 Development economics   490

Part Ten: Government policy

59 The nature of government policy   499
60 Fiscal policy   503
61 Monetary policy   521
62 Balance of payments policies   527
63 Measures to reduce unemployment   532
64 Anti-inflationary policies   539

Index   547

Preface to the sixth edition

George Stanlake's *Introductory Economics* has proved to be deservedly popular with students for its comprehensive coverage, clarity of language and use of real world examples. In this new edition I have sought to retain these features whilst taking into account the philosophy and coverage of the new A Level syllabuses and developments in the economy, government policy and economic theory. This has involved editing chapters, rearranging some of the material, updating tables, facts and figures and including more diagrams and new material.

The traditional Keynesian approach is still covered in this edition, but more use is made of aggregate demand and aggregate supply curves. The coverage of the relationship between markets, comparisons of market structures, market failure, labour markets, the relationship between inflation and unemployment and government policy has been increased. There are new chapters on the move to market economies, externalities, the causes of market failure and business cycles. A number of new topics are also covered including the peace dividend, games theory, contestable markets, buffer stocks, the Human Development Index, the costs of unemployment, the question of independence for the Bank of England and government failure.

The aims of this new edition are to cover the syllabuses of all the examining boards and to assist students to develop a clear and critical understanding of economic concepts, theories, how the economy works and current economic issues.

My work on this edition has been greatly assisted by the very useful comments of Tim Mason who also contributed Table 38.3 on page 324.

S.J.G.
May 1995

1 The nature, scope and methods of economics

The individual and society

Most introductory textbooks of Economics begin by posing the question, 'What is Economics about?' Although Economics is a vast subject and precise definitions are usually very complex, it is not a difficult matter to give a simple and sensible answer to this basic question. Economics is essentially a study of the ways in which humankind provides for its material wellbeing. Economists are concerned with the study of 'human behaviour as a relationship between ends and scarce means which have alternative uses'. (Lionel Robbins).

Micro and macroeconomics

Economics can be divided into microeconomics and macroeconomics. Microeconomics is the study of individual markets. (A market is an arrangement which links buyers and sellers.) For instance, an economist may study the market for compact discs. This will involve looking at the decisions and behaviour of people who buy compact discs, the firms that sell the compact discs and any other groups which influence the price and availability of compact discs, such as the government.

While macroeconomics is the study of the whole economy, it includes looking at unemployment, overseas trade and government policy.

Wants and needs

Economics, both macro and micro economics, is about the satisfaction of material wants. It is necessary to be quite clear about this; it is people's *wants* rather than their *needs* which provide the motive for economic activity. We go to work in order to obtain an income which will buy us the things we want rather than the things we need. It is not possible to define 'need' in terms of any particular quantity of a commodity, because this would imply that a certain level of consumption is 'right' for an individual. Economists tend to avoid this kind of *value judgement* which tries to specify how much people *ought* to consume. It is assumed that individuals wish to enjoy as much well-being as possible, and if their consumption of food, clothing, entertainment, and other goods and services is less than the amount required to give them complete satisfaction they will want to have more of them.

Scarcity

Resources are scarce when they are insufficient to satisfy people's wants. Scarcity is a relative concept. It relates the extent of people's wants to their ability to satisfy those wants. Neither people's wants nor their ability to produce goods and services are constant. Most countries productive potential is increasing but so is the appetite of their citizens for material goods and services. When a certain living standard is reached, people strive for even better living conditions. A good example of this is health care. As medical science advances, people expect more ailments to be treated. So scarcity is a feature of all societies from the poorest to the most affluent.

Choice

The resources available to satisfy our wants are, at any time, limited in supply. As most people cannot have all the goods and services they want, they have to make choices. With no rise in income, if someone wants to buy, for instance, a new coat they may have to spend less on eating out for a while. Similarly with limited resources, if a country wishes to devote more resources to health care it will have to reduce the resources it devotes to defence.

Opportunity cost

In considering scarcity and choice economists make use of opportunity cost. This is a very important concept in economics. It makes clear the true resource cost of any economic decision. For instance, building a new hospital may mean that the construction of a stretch of motorway has to be postponed so opportunity cost is the cost in terms of the best alternative forgone. If one buys a watch it may cost £30 but what is more significant is what has to be given up to make the purchase. This may be the opportunity to purchase a pair of shoes or the opportunity to have extra leisure instead of working to earn the £30.

Economics as a social science

Normative and positive statements

It may be useful to begin this section on the scientific approach by distinguishing between positive and normative statements. An understanding of the difference between these two types of statement will help us to appreciate the scope and limitations of economics.

Positive statements are those that deal only with facts. 'Britain is an island', 'British Coal employs *x* thousand workers', 'Jane Smith obtained a grade A in Economics', are all positive statements. If a disagreement arises over a positive statement it can be settled by looking at the facts and seeing whether or not they support the statement. Positive statements must be either true or false, where the word 'true' is taken to mean 'consistent with the facts'.

Normative statements usually include or imply the words 'ought' or 'should'. They reflect people's moral attitudes and are expressions of what some individual or group thinks ought to be done. 'Britain should leave the European Union', 'we ought to give more aid to under-developed countries', 'income should be distributed more equally', are all normative statements. These statements are based on value judgements and express views of what is 'good' or 'bad', 'right' or 'wrong'. Unlike positive statements, normative statements cannot be verified by looking at the facts. Disagreements about such statements are usually settled by voting on them.

Scientific method

Scientific enquiry, as the term is generally understood, is confined to positive questions. It deals with those questions which can be verified or falsified by actual observations of the real world (i.e. by checking the facts).

One major objective of science is to develop theories. These are general statements or unifying principles which describe and explain the relationships between things we observe in the world around us. Theories are developed in an attempt to answer the question 'Why?'. Tides rise and fall at regular intervals of time, a city is afflicted by smog at certain times of the year, the price of strawberries falls sharply during the summer months. When some definite regular pattern is observed in the relationships between two or more things, and someone asks why this should be so, the search for a theory has begun.

In trying to produce an explanation of observed phenomena, scientific enquiry makes use of procedures which are common to all sciences. These procedures are called scientific method.

The first step is to define the concepts to be used in such a way that they can be measured. This is necessary if we are to test the theory against facts. If the task is to discover a relationship between 'income' and 'consumption', these terms must be defined in a clearly understood manner.

The next step is to formulate a *hypothesis*. This is a tentative untested statement which attempts to explain how one thing is related to another. For example, an economist asked to say why prices vary over time, might offer the hypothesis that changes in prices are caused by changes in the quantity of money. Hypotheses will be based on observation and upon certain assumptions about the way the world behaves. These assumptions may themselves be based upon existing theories which have proved to have a high degree of reliability. In economics, for example, many theories are based upon the assumption that people will behave in such a manner as to maximise their material welfare. Using observed facts and making use of certain assumptions, a process of logical reasoning leads to the formulation of a hypothesis. This must be framed in a manner which enables scientists to test its validity.

It is now necessary to think about what would happen if the hypothesis is correct. In other words, the hypothesis is used to make predictions (or the hypothesis itself may be framed as a prediction). If the hypothesis is correct, then if certain things are done, certain other things will happen. If the general level of prices is causally related to the supply of money, we might deduce that an expansion of bank deposits would be followed by an increase in prices.

The hypothesis must now be tested – are the predictions of the hypothesis supported by the facts? In the natural sciences the testing of hypotheses can be carried out by controlled experiments in the laboratory, but this, as explained later, is not possible for the social scientist. If the hypothesis is supported by the factual evidence we have a successful theory which may be formulated in the form of a scientific 'law'. It must be noted, however, that, since the number of tests which can be carried out is limited, we can never say that a theory is true for all times and in all places. A successful theory is one which *up to now* has not been proved false. If, at some future time facts emerge which confound the theory and its predictions become unreliable, it will be discarded and a search for a better theory will begin. A successful theory is extremely useful because it helps us to predict with a high degree of probability the outcome of certain events.

The nature of economics

Economics is defined as a social science. A social science is a subject which is concerned with human behaviour. Social sciences, which include for instance politics and sociology as well as economics, differ from the natural sciences in a number of ways.

The most obvious limitation experienced by the social scientist is that he cannot test his hypothesis by laboratory experiment. His laboratory is human society; he cannot put a group of human beings into a controlled situation and then see what happens. The predictions of economic theory must be tested against developments in the real world. Economic activities must be observed and recorded and the mass of resulting data subjected to statistical analysis. Modern statistical techniques help the economist determine the probability that certain events had certain causes. He can assess from recorded data, for example, the probability that some given increase in consumption was caused by an increase in income.

The fact that 'all people are different' is not such a handicap to the social scientist as might appear at first sight. The economist is interested in group behaviour. He is concerned with the total demand for butter rather than the amount purchased by any one individual. While the behaviour of any one person may be unpredictable, this is not necessarily true of the large group. When Arsenal score a goal at Highbury we can predict with a high degree of certainty that there will be a roar from the crowd, although we cannot forecast how this or that individual will react. The economist is able to make generalisations about economic groups (consumers, workers, shareholders) which are quite dependable guides to their expected behaviour.

Another problem facing economists is the complexity of the world they are studying – so many things are changing simultaneously. Natural scientists in their laboratories can 'hold other things constant' while they study the effects which changes in X have on Y. Economists cannot do this. They cannot vary the quantity of money in the economy, hold everything else constant, and then see what happens. What they have to do is to *assume* that other things remain constant. Many propositions in economics begin with the phrase 'If other things remain equal' (or the Latin equivalent *ceteris paribus*).

Economic models

From the vast array of facts observed, economists (and other scientists) must isolate those things which are important and study them in isolation. They have to *abstract* from reality in order to build a simplified model of a small part of the real world which will help them to see how things are related one to another. In fact, the influences surrounding real-life situations are so many and so varied that we cannot take them all into account. All that economists can do is to try to get close to the real world by extending their model to include more and more 'other influences' – but no one can construct or understand a model which includes everything.

Indeed economic models vary from very simple models of economic reality to more and more sophisticated ones which include more data. These models are constructed by the government, by international organisations and by groups of economists working in universities and for financial institutions. It is also possible for students to develop their own computerised models of how the economy works.

Economic models are used to help understand how the economy works and to make forecasts. For instance, economists will use models to predict how a change in the rate of income tax will affect inflation and the balance of payments position.

Why economists disagree

It is often said that economics cannot be a science because no two economists agree on any economic problem. This is an exaggeration, but it is certainly true that economists disagree. Disputes among economists often arise from problems of definition and from the inadequacy of statistical data. For example, the statement 'The unemployment rate in the USA is much higher than that in the UK' may be based upon the official figures issued by the authorities in these countries, but that does not mean that the statement cannot be disputed.

The numbers unemployed may refer to those people who actually register themselves as available for work, or it may represent all those who would take a job if one became available. This latter group would include a large number of people (e.g. married women) who do not normally register themselves as unemployed. In fact, the figures for the UK and the USA are collected on these very different bases so that *official* unemployment rates are not strictly comparable and the real differences between them may be disputed.

Although statistical information on economic affairs is now available to a far greater extent than ever before, there are still many deficiencies. Such information often takes a long time to become available in processed form, and often it is too late to be used in current analysis. It may often be presented in a form which is not very convenient for analysis, as the example above demonstrates. These deficiencies therefore leave room for disagreement among economists.

Economics is a very young science, and although economic analysis has made great strides in recent years, there is still a great deal about the workings of the economic system that is imperfectly understood. There are many aspects of existing theories which have not yet been tested, either because insufficient time has elapsed to provide adequate data, or because no one has found a satisfactory way of testing them. Technical and economic changes also bring about changes in economic behaviour so that assumptions about human behaviour which served as useful bases for predictions at one period of time may become increasingly unreliable as the social and economic environment changes. Economists, then, will be in dispute over the adequacy of certain existing theories – but it is these very disputes which lead to improvements in existing theories and the development of new ones.

The main area of disagreement among economists is on matters of economic policy. This is exactly what one would expect because policy recommendations are influenced by both economic and political analysis.

The skills of an economist

The famous British economist, John Maynard Keynes wrote

> ... the master economist must possess a rare combination of gifts. He must reach a high standard in several different directions and must combine talents not often found together. He must be mathematician, historian, statesman, philosopher – in some degree. He must under-

stand symbols and speak in words. He must contemplate the particular in terms of the general, and touch abstract and concrete in the same flight of thought. He must study the present in the light of the past for the purposes of the future. No part of man's nature or his institutions must lie entirely outside his regard.[1]

This is an ambitious list. Economists need to know what has happened in the past, have a keen interest in and knowledge of current affairs, understand human behaviour and appreciate the role of the key economic institutions including the Treasury and the Bank of England. They must be able to think logically, write clearly, be able to use and interpret statistics, basic algebra and graphs. You will develop these skills gradually. They are well worth acquiring. They will enable you to analyse current problems and issues and to consider how the quality of people's lives can be improved.

NOTE 1. 'Essays in Biography' *The Collected Writings of John Maynard Keynes*, Vol X, Royal Economic Society. Published by Macmillan Press Ltd 1972).

2 Production possibility curves

Production possibilities and opportunity cost

We can examine scarcity, choice and opportunity cost in some detail, by looking at what a society is capable of producing with its existing supplies of land, labour, capital and technical knowledge. With this limited supply of economic resources, a society has a wide variety of options as to the quantities and varieties of goods and services it may produce. It might produce fewer ships and more aircraft, less wheat and more barley, fewer tanks and more motor cars and so on. In an advanced economy capable of producing thousands of different commodities the range of choices is clearly enormous, but the basic problem can be illustrated by greatly simplifying the situation and assuming that the economy can only produce two types of good, say agricultural products and manufactured products. Table 2.1 illustrates such a situation.

The extreme possibilities are that the economy devotes all its resources to agriculture and produces 6 million tonnes of food and no manufactured

Table 2.1 Production possibilities

Agricultural products (millions of tonnes)	Manufactured products (millions of units)	Opportunity cost of one tonne of agricultural products (expressed in units of manufactured products)	Opportunity cost of one unit of manufactured products (expressed in tonnes of agricultural products)
0	60		
		2	$\frac{1}{2}$
1	58		
		3	$\frac{1}{3}$
2	55		
		5	$\frac{1}{5}$
3	50		
		8	$\frac{1}{8}$
4	42		
		12	$\frac{1}{12}$
5	30		
		30	$\frac{1}{30}$
6	0		

goods or all the resources are put to work in manufacturing industry and no food is produced. These are very unrealistic possibilities. The economy will choose to produce some combination of the two commodities.

The third and fourth columns illustrate the important point mentioned in Chapter 1 that the production of one thing involves the sacrifice of another thing; it has an opportunity cost. In the third column we can see the opportunity cost of producing one tonne of agricultural produce measured in terms of manufactured products forgone. If this community increases its food production from 3 million tonnes to 4 million tonnes, the opportunity cost of the additional output is 8 million units of manufactured goods. The fourth column shows the opportunity cost of manufactured products measured in terms of the output of agricultural products which have to be forgone when more resources are allocated to manufacturing.

Production possibility curves

The combination of goods that a country can produce can be illustrated by a production possibility curve. This can also be referred to as an opportunity cost, transformation curve or production possibility frontier. Figure 2.1 is based on the information contained in Table 2.1. Notice that as the production of food increases so does the opportunity cost of the food. This is partly because some resources will be more suited to

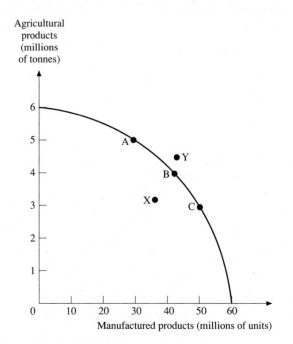

Fig. 2.1   Production possibility curve

agriculture and some more suited to manufacturing. It is also due to the law of diminishing returns (see Chapter 7). As food production increases, the resources being moved into the industry will be less and less suited to agriculture. The same reasoning can be applied to attempts to increase the output of the manufacturing industries; as resources are transferred from agriculture to manufacturing, the cost in terms of the forgone agricultural output will steadily increase.

Points on the production possibility curve such as A, B, and C show the maximum possible combined outputs of the two commodities. The economy can produce any combination *inside* the curve, but this would mean that some resources are unemployed or that inefficient methods of production are being used. Point X illustrates this type of situation. In this case the economy could produce more of *both* goods by moving to a point such as B. Points outside the production possibility curve (such as Y are not attainable with the country's present productive capacity).

Shifts in production possibility curves

A country's production potential is constantly changing. If its capacity to produce goods and services increases the production possibility curve will shift outwards to the right as shown in Fig. 2.2.

A country's ability to produce more goods and services of all types depends upon changes such as an increase in the labour force, an increase in

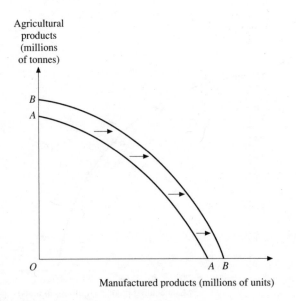

Fig. 2.2

the stock of capital goods (factories, power stations, transport networks, machinery etc.) and/or an increase in technical knowledge.

The production possibility curve can also shift inwards to the left if a country's production potential declines. This could occur due to war or a natural disaster which reduces a country's resources.

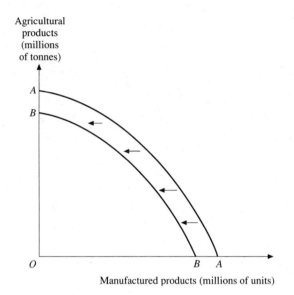

Fig. 2.3

The shape of the production possibility curve

Figures 2.1, 2.2 and 2.3 show the usual shape of the production possibility curve. They show that as more of one good is produced the opportunity cost rises. They are concave to the origin of the graph, that is, they are bowed outwards.

If we are examining two products which use similar methods of production there may be a constant opportunity cost. In this case the production possibility curve will be a straight line as illustrated in Fig. 2.4. Here resources are able to switch easily from producing wheat to producing linseed oil and are equally good at producing each crop. To move from producing 3 million tonnes of wheat to 4 million tonnes of wheat, 2 million tonnes of linseed oil have to be forgone. The opportunity cost of 2 million tonnes of linseed oil remains the same when the output of wheat is raised from 6 million tonnes to 7 million tonnes, and at any other level of production. If a decreasing opportunity cost is experienced the production possibility curve will be bowed inwards (convex to the origin of the graph) as shown in Fig. 2.5.

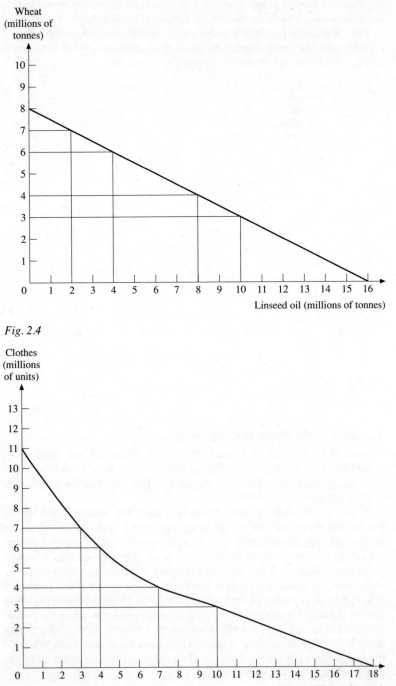

Fig. 2.4

Fig. 2.5

To increase the output of clothes from 3 million units to 4 million units, 3 million tonnes of food have to be forgone whereas to increase the output of clothes from 6 million to 7 million units, the opportunity cost falls to 1 million units of food. This may be because resources initially being used to produce food are more suited to producing clothes. This situation can be referred to as increasing returns since as more resources are devoted to producing clothes their output increases by larger quantities.

3 Economic systems

To an economist, economic society presents itself as a mechanism for survival – a means whereby people are able to carry out the tasks of production and distribution. There are a variety of economic systems operating in the world but these can be categorised into command economies, market economies and a combination of the two, mixed economies.

Two key features distinguish economic systems; who owns the land and capital, and who decides what is produced.

The questions facing all economies

All societies face three fundamental questions and how these are answered will depend on the type of economic system being operated. These questions are:

Which goods shall be produced and in what quantities?

This problem concerns the composition of total output. The community must decide which goods it is going to produce and hence which goods it is *not* going to produce. Having decided the range of goods to be produced, the community must then decide how much of each good should be produced. In reality the choices before a community are rarely of the 'all or nothing' variety. They usually take the form: more of one thing and less of another. The first and major function of any economic system is to determine in some way the actual quantities and varieties of goods and services that will best meet the wants of its citizens.

How should the various goods and services be produced?

Most goods can be produced by a variety of methods. Wheat can be grown by making use of much labour and little capital, or by using vast amounts of capital and very little labour. Electrical appliances can be made by using large and complex machines operated by relatively few semi- or unskilled workers. Alternatively they might be produced in hosts of small workshops by highly skilled technicians using relatively little machinery. Different methods of production can be distinguished from one another by the differences in the quantities of resources used in producing them. Economists use the terms capital-intensive and labour-intensive to describe the alternative methods just outlined. The total output of the community depends not only on the total supply of resources available but on the ways in which these resources are combined. A community must make decisions on the methods of production to be adopted.

How should the goods and services be distributed?

This is the third question which an economic system has to answer. The total output has to be shared out among the members of the community. The economic system has to determine the relative sizes of the shares going to each household. Should everyone be given an equal share? Should the division depend upon the individual's contribution to production? Should the output be shared out in accordance with people's ability to pay the price, or should the shares be decided according to tradition and custom?

Command economies

A command economy is one in which the government makes the decisions on what to produce, how to produce it, and who gets it. The communist regimes in Cuba and North Korea can be described as command economies, although this type of economic structure is not peculiar to communism. It is applicable wherever the economic resources of a nation are directly controlled by some centralised authority. The UK became very much a command economy during the years of the Second World War when the government took control of all important economic affairs.

It is more usual to refer to the present-day command economies as *planned* economies although, strictly speaking, leaving the economy to run itself (i.e. *laissez-faire*) may be described as a kind of economic 'plan'. Nevertheless, in line with general usage, we shall use the term 'planned economy' to refer to an economy which is subject to a high degree of direct government control.

Ownership and control of economic resources

Although economic planning may be employed in societies where property is privately owned, it seems realistic to assume that a fully planned economy means one in which all the important means of production are publicly owned. In communist and socialist societies (which are the most important examples of planned economies) all land, housing, factories, power stations, transport systems, and so on are usually owned by the state.

The logic of public ownership in these societies is based upon the desire for a more equitable distribution of income and wealth. Private ownership of property leads to great inequalities of wealth, and this, in turn, means that the wealthier groups are able to exercise great economic power. Such a situation implies great inequalities of opportunity. The better-off members of society are able to use their greater wealth to obtain superior education, better health services, more effective training, and better business opportunities. The elimination, or severe limitation, of private ownership is seen, therefore, as the most effective way of removing these inequalities of opportunity. It is also argued by the supporters of the planned economy that only the direct ownership of the means of production can give the state the full control that it needs in order to carry out its economic plan.

Forms of collective control

Although land and capital may be owned *collectively* rather than individually, it does not follow that control of these resources must be centralised. In some planned economies the state keeps a tight control on the use of economic resources and all important economic decisions are taken by powerful central committees. They decide what should be produced, how and where production should take place, and how the output should be shared out among the people. This is described as *bureaucratic* organisation, because the running of such an economy will require large numbers of planners and administrators to draw up and operate the national plan.

Alternatively, although the ultimate ownership of resources may be vested in the state, the control and day-to-day running of the farms, factories, and shops may be handed over to cooperative groups of workers and consumers. These organisations are usually described as *workers' collectives*, as opposed to the state enterprises which are controlled directly by the government.

One important feature of a society in which property is publicly owned is that there will be no form of personal income which is derived from the ownership of property. In the capitalist system incomes take the form of wages, interest, rent, and profits – the last three of which arise from the ownership of various types of property.

Production decisions

The administrators in a planned society face a most complex task. They must begin by making a survey of the productive potential of the economy. This involves looking at the resources of workers, machines, factories, etc., the country has and what can be produced with these. First, assessments must be prepared showing the outputs which might be produced by the mines, farms, factories, etc., together with some estimates of the carrying capacities of the transport networks and the capacities of the other service industries. The decisions on the quantities and varieties of goods to be produced must then be made and each unit of production (e.g. farm or factory) will be given a target output for the period of the plan – normally five years. The next task will be to allocate the necessary supplies of materials, equipment, and labour to the various units of production.

A modern economic system is exceedingly complex. The output of any one factory is dependent upon supplies from many different sources. The fitting together of all these planned outputs into one huge national plan is a formidable task. In fact it is virtually impossible for central planners to fix targets and resource allocations for every single farm, factory, and shop. The planners are more likely to give directions (orders) to whole industries. Whilst the ways in which the targets set down in these orders may be left to local decisions at the industry and factory levels, it is most probable that the allocations to various industries of the more vital resources (e.g. new capital) will be centrally controlled.

Distribution decisions

While it is possible, although very difficult, to subject the outputs of goods and services to complete control by planners, it is much more difficult to use these methods in the markets for labour and consumer goods. In respect of industrial investment (i.e. capital goods), defence requirements, and social investment (e.g. schools, hospitals, housing) the necessary allocations of resources can be directly controlled and the outputs firmly determined. In the case of consumer goods, however, there are restraints on the planners' ability to use direct controls.

Ideally, the complete planning of production should be accompanied by the complete planning of distribution. What had been produced could then be allocated to consumers by some kind of physical rationing scheme. Workers could be paid in kind, receiving vouchers which entitle them to various quantities of different goods and services. In this manner the pattern and volume of consumption could be matched exactly to the planned output. Such a system might operate perfectly well in a poor country where all resources are committed to the bare necessities of life. In a more developed economy, however, consumers are likely to demand a large measure of freedom of choice in the disposal of their income. Allowing for freedom of choice in the consumers' market makes the planners' problems much more difficult. It is very unlikely that the spending plans of consumers will exactly match the production targets of the planners. This does not mean that direct planning will not work; it means that the plan must contain some flexibility so that production can respond to the various surpluses and shortages as they appear in the consumer markets.

There are various ways in which planners can test consumer demand – assuming, that is, that they wish to respond to it. They might conduct a continuous poll or carry out surveys of public attitudes and preferences. Alternatively they could allow the goods to be sold in free markets. Goods which are in short supply will rise in price while those in surplus will fall in price. These price movements could then be used as indicators to producers as to which industries should expand their outputs and which should contract output. Planners may, however, regard such price movements as an inequitable means of testing the market (e.g. a shortage of bread might cause its price to rise beyond the means of the poor). The state may, therefore, fix prices, and where shortages arise the good may be physically rationed. In this case it would be the movements in retail stocks which act as indicators to the planners.

Labour market decisions

There are similar problems to be dealt with in the market for labour. Whilst iron ore, wool, machines, lorries and so on can be distributed directly to the different industries, workers will not usually continue to accept such direction. They will demand some degree of freedom in choosing their jobs and the part of the country in which they wish to work. Getting the right amounts of labour in the right places to meet the production targets cannot normally be achieved by the direction of labour; it must be done by inducement. As is the case with consumer goods, it means that some limited use must be made of the price mechanism.

Plants which are short of labour will have to be given permission to offer higher wages in order to attract labour from other sources. In the longer run the state can influence the supplies of the different types of labour by providing more and better training facilities for those skills which are in short supply and reducing the intake of trainees for occupations where demand is declining.

Market economies

A society may attempt to deal with the basic economic problems by allowing free play to what are known as *market forces*. The state plays little or no part in economic activity. Most of the people in the world earn and spend in societies in which market forces play a significant role.

The market system of economic organisation is also commonly described as a *free enterprise* or *laissez-faire*, or *capitalist system*. We shall use all these terms to stand for a market economy. Strictly speaking the pure market or *laissez-faire* system has never existed. Whenever there has been some form of political organisation, the political authority has exercised some economic functions (e.g. controlling prices or levying taxation). It is useful, however, to consider the way in which a true market system would operate because it provides us with a simplified model, and by making modifications to the model we can approach the more realistic situations step by step. The framework of a market or capitalist system contains six essential features.

- private property
- freedom of choice and enterprise
- self-interest as the dominating motive
- competition
- a reliance on the price system
- a very limited role for government.

Private property

The institution of private property is a major feature of capitalism. It means that individuals have the right to own, control, and dispose of land, buildings, machinery, and other natural and man-made resources. Man-made aids to production such as machines, factories, docks, oil refineries and road networks are known as capital.

Private property not only confers the right to own and dispose of real assets, it provides the owners of property with the right to the income from that property in the form of rent, interest, and profits.

Although all non-human resources can be privately owned, labour cannot be bought and sold in the same way. Except in slave societies, labourers own themselves, whilst land, buildings, and machinery are owned by others. Owners of land and capital purchase *the services of labour* in order to operate their factories, farms, shops, and so on.

Freedom of enterprise and choice

Freedom of enterprise means that individuals are free to buy and hire economic resources, to organise these resources for production, and to sell their products in markets of their own choice. Persons who undertake these activities are known as *entrepreneurs*. These people are risk takers and such people are free to enter and leave any industry.

Freedom of choice means, as we have seen, that owners of land and capital may use these resources as they see fit. It also means that workers are free to enter (and leave) any occupations for which they are qualified. (This is a rather meaningless freedom when there is large-scale un-employment.) Finally it means that consumers are free to spend their incomes in any way they wish. This freedom of consumer choice is usually held to be the most important of these economic 'freedoms'. The consumer is regarded as being sovereign since it is the way in which he chooses to spend his income which determines they ways in which society uses its economic resources. In the model of capitalism, producers respond to consumers' preferences – they produce whatever consumers demand. This feature of capitalism is discussed more fully in the section on markets and prices.

Self-interest

Since capitalism is based on the principle that individuals should be free to do as they wish, it is not surprising to find that the motive for economic activity is *self-interest*. Each unit in the economy attempts to do what is best for itself. Firms will act in ways which, they believe, will lead to maximum profits (or minimum losses). Owners of land and capital will employ these assets so as to obtain the highest possible rewards. Workers will tend to move to those occupations and locations which offer the highest wages. Consumers will spend their incomes on those things which yield the maximum satisfaction.

Advocates of the market system such as Adam Smith argued that the individual pursuit of self-interest would lead to the maximum public good. 'By pursuing his own interest he [the individual] frequently promotes that of society more effectually than when he really intends to promote it'.[1]

Competition

Economic rivalry or competition is another essential feature of a free enterprise economy. Competition, as economists see it, is essentially *price competition*. The model of the market economy envisages a situation where, in the market for each commodity, there are large numbers of buyers and sellers. Each buyer and seller accounts for an insignificant share of the business transacted and hence has no influence on the market demand or market supply. It is the forces of total demand and total supply which determine the market price, and participants, whether buyers or sellers, must take this price as given since it is beyond their influence or control. In theory at least, competition is the regulatory mechanism of capitalism. It limits the use of economic power since no single firm or individual is large enough or strong enough to control a market and exploit the other buyers or sellers.

Markets and prices

Perhaps the most basic feature of the market economy is the use of the *price mechanism* for allocating resources to various uses. The price system is an elaborate system of communications in which innumerable free choices are aggregated and balanced against each other. The decisions of producers determine the supply of a commodity; the decisions of buyers determine the demand. The interactions of demand and supply determine the price. Changes in demand and supply cause changes in market prices and it is these movements in market prices which bring about the changes in the ways in which society uses its economic resources.

Let us take a simple example. A particular product proves to be increasingly popular with consumers. Increasing demand outstrips supply at the existing price, a shortage develops and price increases. This rise in price makes production more profitable. Existing firms will tend to expand their outputs and new firms will be attracted to this industry. More and more resources will move into the industry because the greater profitability will enable firms to offer higher rewards in order to bid labour and capital away from other uses. The opposite process will apply when the demand for a commodity is declining. Price movements act as

NOTE 1. Adam Smith, 'The Wealth of Nations'.

indicators and provide an essential link between consumers' preferences and producers' profit-seeking decisions.

In a free enterprise society, price has another important function – it acts as a rationing device. We have seen that economic goods are scarce goods. Price serves to ration these scarce goods among the people who are demanding them. Where the supply of a good or service is insufficient to meet the demands of prospective buyers at the existing price, the market price will rise and continue to rise until the quantity demanded is just equal to the existing supply. Those unable to pay the higher prices will be eliminated from the market. Price rations scarce goods to those who can afford to pay the price. If supply exceeds demand, the price will fall bringing in more buyers (and expanding the purchases of existing buyers) until a price is established which equates the quantities being demanded and supplied. Note that price rations goods and services, not on any basis of need or want, but on the basis of the ability to pay the price.

The price mechanism allocates resources to different uses on the basis of consumer 'votes'. The act of purchasing a commodity is, in effect, a vote for the production of that commodity. Under this system those with the greater purchasing power have more votes. This might be regarded as an inequitable system especially where there is great inequality in the distribution of income.

Mixed economies

We have seen that there is some use of the market mechanism in planned economies. Likewise there is some measure of state control in free market economies. Indeed, there are no pure command or pure market economies in the world. Where there is both a public (i.e., a state) sector and a private sector (where non-government firms and individuals decide what is produced), the economy is called a mixed economy. It has features of both a command and a market economy.

As we shall see in the next chapter many economies are moving towards greater reliance on the market system. Nevertheless, all economies have some degree of state intervention and are essentially mixed economies.

4 The move to market economies: recent events

1989 witnessed the collapse of the communist regime in Poland. Solidarity, the trade union movement, pressured the government into holding free elections and won most of the seats. This was the start of the change in the political and economic systems in a number of East European countries, including Hungary, East Germany, Romania and, probably the most famous, the former Soviet Union. The role of the price mechanism in allocating resources has also increased in many African, and Asian countries. China, whilst still a communist country, has undertaken a number of economic reforms including introducing a stock market.

Reasons for the move towards market economies

Increased information about living standards in Western Europe and the USA increased the dissatisfaction felt by people in Eastern Europe with the goods and services on offer to them. They were unhappy about the poor quality of many goods, including housing and the lack of other goods such as cars, telephones and CDs. Shortages and rationing also meant that people wasted much of their time standing in queues.

The shortages and poor quality arose largely due to be problems of planning and co-ordination. Information proved difficult and expensive to obtain and it often quickly became out of date. It was also found to be easier to set targets for and monitor quantity rather than quality. Indeed, producers often sacrificed quality and environmental concerns in order to meet quantity targets. High levels of pollution occurred in all the Eastern European countries. For instance, more than 90% of rivers in Poland were heavily polluted.

The absence of the profit motive meant that inefficient firms continued in production whilst efficient firms did not always expand. (It was also usually not possible for new, non-government firms to set up to meet expanding consumer demand.) Producers of state-run industries, unable to benefit from profits, were not encouraged to introduce new techniques and products.

Although there were differences in wages, there was a lack of incentives for workers since wage differences were nevertheless limited and many workers had almost complete job security. So those workers who were most skilled often earned little more than those who were unskilled and those who did not work as hard.

In the 1970s and 1980s Eastern Europe experienced problems in exporting goods and services. This was largely due to increased competition from the newly industrialised countries including Singapore, and South Korea. To make up for the fall in export revenue Bulgaria, Hungary, Romania and other Eastern European countries borrowed heavily from the West. Paying off the debt meant that the countries had less to spend on improving living standards within their own countries.

Problems of transition

In moving towards a market economy, countries are experiencing a number of problems.

Inflation

Command economies usually keep prices below those changed by non-government producers so when government production is replaced by private-sector production prices will usually rise. In 1994 inflation in Russia was above 400% and in Romania it was above 150%.

Industrial unrest

Workers will press for wage rises to enable them to pay the higher prices. They are also likely to try to maintain job security. In the early 1990s a number of strikes occurred in key Russian industries, including mining.

Changing pattern of employment

There is likely to be large-scale structural change, with some industries expanding, some contracting and some going out of business. This will require workers and machines to move from one job to another. However, not all workers and machines may be able to do this. They may be geographically and occupationally immobile (see Chapter 35). Indeed workers are unlikely to be accustomed to changing jobs or to retraining. Many former soldiers in Eastern Europe are finding it difficult to get jobs in civilian life.

Fall in living standards

Much of the machinery may be out of date and resources may have to devoted to making more up-to-date replacements. These resources could alternatively be used to make consumer goods, for example, TVs, dish-washers, etc., so living standards may have to fall in the short term at least. In Russia output fell from 1990 to 1995 thereby reducing the quantity of goods and services Russians could enjoy.

Advantages of a move to a market economy

It is possible that a number of advantages may be gained from moving from a command to a market economy. These include:

- Consumers can influence what goods are produced directly by their purchases, i.e., they can exercise consumer sovereignty and greater use of the price mechanism will provide an automatic and quick way to signal to producers what consumers want.
- The market system provides incentives to entrepreneurs in the form of profits and to workers in the form of higher wages. This should encourage entrepreneurs to produce high-quality products and to innovate, and workers to work hard.
- Consumers will have a greater choice of producers. Instead of having to buy from one government firm they may have a choice of a number of private-sector producers. This increased competition may increase the quality of products since rival producers will seek to attract new customers by improving the standard of their goods.
- Foreign investment may be encouraged since overseas producers may expect a higher return on their investment and be less fearful of government intervention.
- Efficiency may increase since those firms which do not produce what people want at low cost (and hence low prices) may go out of business.

Disadvantages of a move to a market economy

There are also potential disadvantages of making greater use of market forces:

- Private-sector firms may try to reduce their costs by, for example, dumping waste materials in rivers. As private-sector firms are concerned primarily with profits they may not take into account the effects their production has on the environment.
- Some people will not be able to earn high incomes. These people include the sick, the elderly, and those with skills that are not in high demand. These people may fall into poverty.
- Those with the highest purchasing power will have the most influence on what is produced and so goods wanted by the poor may be under-produced.
- Goods and services that are difficult to make consumers pay for directly may not be produced, e.g., defence.
- Whilst people may buy less of some product, for example, seat belts, than is desirable they may buy more of other products, for example, cigarettes and alcohol, than is beneficial. The first type of goods are

called merit goods and the second type are referred to as demerit
goods.
- It is a feature of the market economy, especially in more recent times,
that firms tend to increase in size and power. Modern technology has
made it possible for large-scale producers to obtain great advantages
in the form of lower production costs. This tendency towards market
domination by giant firms reduces, or removes, the limiting role of
competition and gives the large firm power to exploit the consumer by
charging prices well above costs.
- Advertising may persuade people to want products they would not
have naturally chosen. In this case it will be producers rather than
consumers who will be determining what is produced.
- There is no guarantee that everyone who wants a job will be able to
find one.

The role of government

Even in market economies governments have a role to play. They must
seek to offset the problems outlined above by implementing various
measures.

Creating a framework of rules

Most of the rules and regulations under this heading are designed to see
that there is 'fair play' in the competition between producers and in the
relations between producers and consumers. Most of the regulations are
necessary if the freedom to compete is not to be abused. There are laws
which protect property rights, and which enforce contractual obligations
(e.g., people are legally obliged to pay their debts.). The public is protected
from fraud by regulations such as those which oblige firms to publish
adequate financial information so that investors will not be misled, and
which prevent the dishonest labelling of goods. Regulations which insist
on adequate standards of hygiene and on minimum safety standards in
manufacture protect the public from unnecessary dangers and health
hazards. To ensure a reasonable degree of competition the state may pass
laws forbidding restrictive trade agreements between producers (e.g.,
agreements between firms to limit output so as to maintain high prices).
Workers are protected by regulations which govern the conditions of
work in factories, offices, and shops. In most modern economies, industrial
and commercial behaviour is closely regulated by the state.

Supplementing and modifying the price system

It has long been recognised that certain services, regarded as essential to
civilised existence, will not be provided by private enterprise, or, if

provided, will not be made available on a scale which society thinks desirable. Such things as defence, internal law and order, education, roads, and health services, are typical of the kind of services which have become accepted as suitable subjects for public enterprise. These services may be purchased by the state but provided by private firms. In most cases however the state takes over the responsibility for the supply of such services. The government may also influence the pattern of production by making use of taxes and subsidies. The output of goods subject to taxation is likely to fall, while subsidies generally lead to an increase in output.

Redistributing income

It is now a major objective of governments to promote the general economic welfare of the citizen. One means towards this end is a more equitable distribution of income and wealth. Governments may aim to achieve this by a system of taxation which bears more heavily on the richer members of society, together with the provision of benefits for the needier groups. These benefits may take the form of money grants such as child benefit but in other cases the government may attempt to ensure greater equality by providing the services directly at zero market prices. Education and health services are the best examples of the universal provision of essential services financed from taxation.

Stabilising the economy

The Great Depression of the inter-war years and the prolonged nature of the large-scale unemployment during that period forced governments in almost every country to accept the responsibility for the maintenance of a high and stable level of employment. This responsibility has obliged governments to take wider powers to influence the level of economic activity. We shall see later in this book that governments in mixed economies now have policy instruments which enable them to influence the volume of money, the level of spending, the amount of investment, the location of industry, the levels of imports and exports, and most of the important economic variables.

5 Economic resources

The meaning of production

Production consists of all those activities which provide the goods and services to satisfy wants. The complete cycle of production in a modern society can be a very long-drawn-out process. It is a process which is not complete until the commodity is in the hands of the final consumer. The production of a shirt may begin in the cotton fields of Alabama, but it will not be complete until a consumer makes a purchase in a retail store. The making of a shirt will engage the efforts of thousands of workers in fields, factories, offices, ships, docks, railways, road transport, banks, insurance companies, warehouses, and shops. Nearly three-quarters of the working population of the UK is now engaged in producing services.

Output

Economic activity results in the output of an enormous variety of goods and services. The composition of total output is usefully classified into consumer goods, producer goods, and services.

Consumer goods are those commodities which satisfy our wants directly – we want them for their own sake. This group of commodities is usefully sub-divided into non-durable and durable consumer goods.

Non-durable consumer goods are items such as food, heating, lighting, cigarettes, etc. They are consumed or destroyed in the very act of being used. Some of them are good only for a single use while others, such as soap, can be used up a bit at a time.

Durable consumer goods include such things as books, furniture, television sets, motor cars, and domestic electrical appliances. Such goods produce a steady stream of satisfaction while their values diminish relatively slowly through age and use.

Producer goods, which can also be called *capital goods*, do not satisfy wants directly. They are not wanted for their own sake, but for the contribution they make to the production of other goods (both consumer and producer goods). Lathes, lorries, bulldozers, cranes, factory buildings, and blast furnaces are examples of capital goods.

Services are intangible goods, i.e., goods which cannot be touched and include banking, dentistry, accountancy, and education.

The structure of industry

The many different activities which lead to the production of goods and services can be grouped into three broad categories.

Primary production

Primary production is carried out by what are generally known as the *extractive industries* because they extract the gifts of nature from the earth's surface, from beneath the earth's surface, and from the oceans. Primary industries, therefore, include farming, mining, oil extraction, forestry and fishing.

Secondary production

This includes those industries which process the basic materials into semi-finished and finished products. They are generally described as *manufacturing and construction industries*. They include such obvious examples as engineering and building, and the manufacture of vehicles, furniture, clothing and chemicals.

Tertiary production

Industries in the tertiary sector do not produce goods, they produce *services*. These services are supplied to firms in all types of industry and directly to consumers. In developed countries, production could not be carried on effectively without such services as banking, insurance, law, administration, transport and communications.

Some economists identify a fourth sector which they call the quartenary sector. It consists of those services which are concerned with the collection, processing and transmission of information (e.g. microtechnology), with research and development (e.g. higher education) and with administration and financial management (e.g. accountancy).

Figure 5.1 shows the proportions of the UK working population employed in each of the three main sectors.

The factors of production

Production cannot take place unless the necessary resources are available. We are all familiar with these resources. Factories, railways, farms, mines, human skills, offices, and shops – these are the kind of things we identify as economic resources. Again, for purposes of analysis, economists resort to a broad classification of these resources or *factors of production* as they are usually called.

Primary production

Extractive industries
examples: mining, quarrying,
farming, fishing,
forestry, oil extraction

1.2%

Secondary production

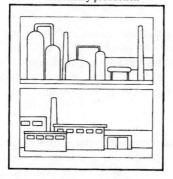

**Manufacturing, processing,
and construction industries**
examples: chemicals,
engineering, vehicles,
food processing, building

28%

Tertiary production

Service industries
examples: banking, insurance,
law, transport, communications,
wholesaling, retailing,
administration

70.8%

Source: *Department of Employment Gazette*

Fig. 5.1   Distribution of the employed population, 1992

The factors of production are usually divided into three main types, land, labour, and capital. Land is the term used to stand for natural resources; labour represents all human resources; and capital is the term used for all man-made resources. Economists often identify a fourth factor – enterprise. This is discussed later.

This classification is not completely satisfactory because it is sometimes difficult to allocate the real-world resources into these neat categories. For example, land which has been fertilised, drained, and fenced is really a combination of land and capital. We shall also find that within each broad category there are very wide divergencies. Nevertheless the classification is still the one most commonly used and it does serve to assist analysis.

Land (natural resources)

The term 'land' is used to describe all those natural resources over which people have the power of disposal and which may be used to yield an income. It includes, therefore, farming and building land, forests, mineral deposits, fisheries, rivers, lakes – all those resources freely supplied by nature which aid people in producing the things they want.

The supply of land

Economists have always emphasised one particular aspect of land – the fact that its supply is strictly limited. Now this is true of the total supply of land in the world in the sense of the surface area available to man. Although reclamation work has tended to increase the supply in some areas, this is offset by erosion of various kinds so that changes in the total area are probably relatively insignificant.

If, however, we are considering the supply of land for some *particular use*, this strict limitation on supply is not applicable The amount of land used for growing wheat can be increased by growing less of some other crop (e.g. barley). The supply of building land can be increased at the expense of farmland, and the area of *cultivated* land may be increased by drainage, irrigation, and the use of fertilisers. The use of land can therefore be changed; however, land cannot be moved from one area of the country to another. No matter how high the price may rise for sites fronting the High Street, the supply cannot be increased. This particular feature of land has important economic implications which are discussed later.

Conservation

In recent years we have become dramatically aware of the fact that the supply of many natural resources is strictly limited. This is most obviously true of the mineral resources and especially of those which man relies upon for his sources of energy. Present-day civilisation is based upon a massive utilisation of non-replaceable minerals and fuels. Some raw materials such as cotton, wool, timber, and foodstuffs are replenishable, but others such as coal, iron ore, oil, and natural gas cannot be replaced.

A rapidly rising world population together with insistent demands for higher standards of living have led to a growing awareness of this problem. It has been calculated that the American standard of living requires an annual consumption per head of about 20 tons of fuels, metals, other minerals, and non-metallic building materials – most of it coming from non-replaceable resources. The more obvious consequences of present trends are rising prices as these things become more scarce and a more energetic search is made for substitutes.

The most pressing immediate requirement is for an effective policy for the *conservation* of natural resources. This does not mean that we should refrain from using them, but that we should use them much more efficiently and less wastefully. Every effort must be made to get a greater value of output per unit of input of these depletable resources, and more attention must be paid to schemes for the recovery of such materials for future use – recycling as it is called. While such resources are abundant and cheap there is little financial incentive to embark upon relatively costly projects of research and recovery, but as fuels and minerals become more scarce and more expensive such projects become more profitable and hence more attractive to profit-seeking enterprises. It is doubtful, however, if conservation can be left entirely to market forces and governments are increasingly becoming involved in this matter.

Unique characteristic

A further characteristic of land is that it has no costs of production. It is already in existence – there are no costs involved in creating it. In this respect it differs from labour and capital. Labour has to be reared, educated, and trained. Capital has to be created by using labour and other scarce resources. From this it follows that any increase in the value of natural resources due to rising populations and rising incomes accrues to the owners of these resources as a windfall gain – it does not arise from any efforts on their part.

Labour

Labour is human effort – physical and mental – which is directed to the production of goods and services. But labour is not only a factor of production, it is also the reason why economic activity takes place. The people who take part in production are also consumers, the sum of whose individual demands provides the business person with the incentive to undertake production. For this reason when we are considering real-world economic problems it is necessary to treat labour somewhat differently from the other factors. There are social and political problems which have to be taken into account. For example, the question of how many hours per day a machine should be operated will be judged solely in terms of efficiency, output, and costs. The same question applied to labour would raise additional considerations of individual freedom and human rights.

It must be borne in mind that it is the *services of labour* which are bought and sold, and not labour itself. The firm cannot buy and own labour in the same way that capital and land can be bought and owned. See also chapters 33, 34, 35 and 36.

Capital

Capital is a man-made resource. Any product of labour-and-land which is reserved for use in further production is capital, for example, machines, factories and delivery vans. It might be helpful at this stage to deal with the confusion which commonly arises over the meanings of three important terms: capital, money, and wealth.

Capital, as already indicated, means any produced means of production.

Wealth is quite simply the stock of all those goods which have a money value. Capital, therefore, is an important part of the community's wealth.

Money is a claim to wealth. From the standpoint of the community as a whole, money is not wealth, since we cannot count both the value of real assets *and* the value of the money claims to those assets. From the point of view of the individual citizen, however, money represents a part of his *personal* wealth since he sees it as a claim on assets held by other people. To the individual business person, therefore, any money he possesses he regards as capital since it gives him a claim on resources now possessed by others. We must be quite clear, however, that money is not part of the *national* wealth. Capital is usually divided into two broad categories, working and fixed.

Working capital

Working capital is capital that is used up in the course of production. It consists of the stocks of raw materials, partly finished goods, and finished goods held by producers. These stocks are just as important to efficient production as are the machines and buildings. Stocks are held so that production can proceed smoothly when deliveries are interrupted, and so that unexpected additional orders for finished goods can be met without changing production schedules. This kind of capital is sometimes called *circulating capital* because it keeps moving and changing. Materials are changed into finished goods which are then exchanged for money and this in turn is used to buy more materials.

Fixed capital

Fixed capital is not used up in production. It consists of equipment such as buildings, machinery, railways and so on. This type of capital does not change its form in the course of production and move from one stage to the next – it is 'fixed'.

A large part of a nation's stock of capital, particularly its fixed capital, consists of houses, schools, hospitals, public baths, and other types of

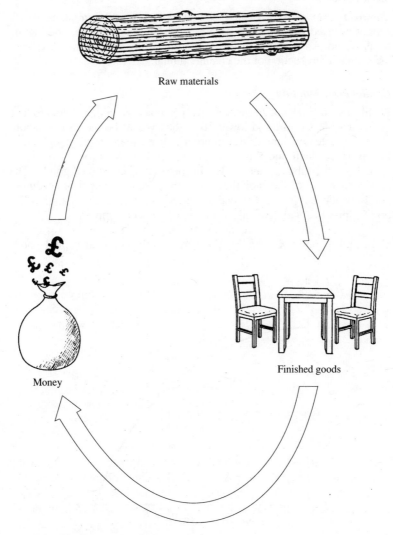

Raw materials

Money

Finished goods

Fig. 5.2   *Working or circulating capital*

property which are not *directly* concerned with the production of goods. The term *social capital* is used to describe this type of asset. Such property is part of the capital stock because it assists people in the production of their material wants, but it does so indirectly. We can verify this by asking ourselves the question, 'Would the nation be more or less productive if it did not have its present stock of houses, schools, hospitals, and so on?'

Sunk capital

This is a form of fixed capital. It consists of capital equipment which cannot be used for any purpose other than the current one, and has no resale value. An example of this is the tunnelling equipment which was used in the construction of the channel tunnel.

Capital accumulation

People use capital not to satisfy any personal craving, but to produce goods with less effort and lower costs than would be the case if labour were unassisted by capital. But in order to use capital goods people must first produce them and this calls for a sacrifice. While it is producing capital goods, labour cannot also be producing consumer goods. The *opportunity cost* of the capital goods is the potential output of consumer goods which has to be forgone in order to produce that capital. The production of capital demands *abstinence* from consumption.

Figure 5.3 shows an economy making full use of its resources, producing at point X initially. To increase the output of capital goods

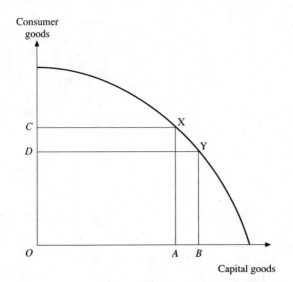

Fig. 5.3

from OA to OB and produce at point Y, CD amount of consumer goods have to be forgone so the creation of capital means forgoing some *present* consumption for the prospect of a much higher level of *future* consumption. People are prepared to make this sacrifice because the use of capital equipment greatly increases labour's productivity. This is the reality of capital accumulation and it is as true of the complex society as it is of the less developed society. The machines, factories, houses, and roads we are building today involve the use of resources which could be used to make more consumer goods.

Two things make possible the creation of capital: (*a*) saving, and (*b*) a diversion of resources. *Saving* is the act of forgoing consumption. It means that a claim on the resources required to produce consumer goods is not being exercised. By choosing not to buy consumer goods with some part of our income, we refrain from buying the services of the factors of production required to make those goods. The factors of production might, therefore, remain unemployed. But these savings might be borrowed (by entrepreneurs) and used to finance the construction of capital goods. This is the second step – the *diversion of resources* from the production of consumer goods to the production of producer goods. Saving makes possible capital accumulation – it does not *cause* it.

Capital consumption

A modern economy produces a large output of capital every year, but all of this does not add to the national stock of capital. Capital goods are continually wearing out or becoming obsolete. Repairs and replacements are required as capital depreciates. In any one year some proportion of the total output of producer goods is required for replacement. The value of this part of the total output is known as *depreciation*. The total production of capital is termed *gross investment*, and any addition to the capital stock is *net investment*. Hence,

Gross Investment – Depreciation = Net Investment

It could happen that the rate of depreciation exceeds the total output of capital so that net investment is a minus quantity. A nation which finds itself in this position is said to be consuming capital; it is not making good the wear and tear and obsolescence of its capital stock. If this should continue, output in the future is bound to decline. Capital consumption is most likely to occur during a war when a country is obliged to devote a large part of its economic resources to the production of military equipment.

The entrepreneur

As mentioned earlier, economists sometimes identify a fourth factor of production – enterprise. It is held that, left to themselves, land, labour, and capital will not produce anything. There must be some person or persons, who will organise these three factors so that production can take place. Someone must take the decisions (*a*) what to produce (i.e. the type of good or service and the quantity); (*b*) how to produce (i.e. the methods of production); (*c*) where to produce (i.e. the location of the enterprise).

Whoever takes the decisions, and the consequent risks, is known as the *entrepreneur*. There is no really suitable English word to describe such a person; perhaps 'enterpriser' is the nearest we can get. The entrepreneur is the person who undertakes production with a view to profit. In a capitalist society, production would not take place unless someone was prepared to buy and organise economic resources for production on the basis of expected profits.

The entrepreneur is a *risk-bearer*. This is the key, defining role of the entrepreneur.

Most production is undertaken in anticipation of demand. Firms will produce those things which they *believe* will yield a profit – they do not *know* that they will do so, because the future is unknown. Entrepreneurs must bear the costs involved during the time that elapses between the decision to produce and the eventual marketing of the commodity. They must pay rent for their land, interest on the money borrowed, wages to labour, and meet the costs of materials. These payments must be made without any certainty that such costs will be covered by receipts. If the sales revenue exceeds their expenses, the entrepreneurs will make a profit – if not, they must bear the loss. The risks borne by entrepreneurs arise from uncertainty. Economic conditions are always changing and past experience is not necessarily any good guide to future prospects.

Many economists do not accept that the functions just described represent those of a factor of production which is clearly distinguishable from labour. They argue that the entrepreneurial function is no more than that of a particular and specialised form of labour. They point out that risk-bearing is not peculiar to the entrepreneur. Many types of labour take risks – the steeplejack and the miner run the risk of personal injury, and most forms of labour cannot avoid the risk of unemployment.

Intrapreneurs

Economists are now beginning to distinguish between entrepreneurs and intrapreneurs. Entrepreneurs are people such as Richard Branson and Anita Roddick who start their own business whilst intrapreneurs are people such as David Jones, Chairman of Next, who work their way to the top of existing companies. In a 1994 study into 'Business Elites' conducted by Cary Cooper, professor of organisational psychology, entrepreneurs were found to be loners, innovative but people who found growth of their companies difficult to handle because of the need for more structure and greater decentralisation. In contrast intrapreneurs were found to be better at handling detail, more methodical and more efficient.

6 Specialisation

The division of labour

By far the most striking feature of production in a developed economy is the fact that a worker almost never makes a complete product. By the time a product reaches the retail store few can say 'I made that'. People's daily work does not consist of providing for their own wants directly. The food we eat, the clothes we wear, the furniture we use, are all made by hands other than our own.

All this emphasises the fact that workers *specialise*. They contribute but a small part to the production of some article or the provision of some service. Labour is *divided* in the sense that the production process is split into a very large number of individual operations and each operation is the special task of one worker. This principle of the division of labour is now carried to remarkable lengths and the production of relatively simple things may be broken down into hundreds of separate operations.

The development of the division of labour

At a very early stage in human development, people realised the gains to be obtained by applying this most important principle. The earliest people must have attempted to provide all their daily wants by their own efforts. They would have been obliged to provide food, clothing, shelter, and protection for themselves. In doing so they could have produced little more than the barest essentials for survival. By living in communities where some degree of specialisation was practised they learned that the total output of any group was much greater than the sum of the individual outputs of independent producers. One person might specialise in hunting, another in making cloth, another in making tools, and so on. Each would exchange his or her surplus for the goods made by other specialists. From these earliest times the principle of the division of labour has been progressively extended. The process is still going on, and a visit to any modern factory making motor cars, television sets, or clothing gives a vivid picture of the extent to which production is now specialised.

Adam Smith, writing in the latter part of the eighteenth century, provided what has now become the most celebrated account of specialisation. On a visit to a factory engaged in making pins he observed: 'One man draws out the wire, another straightens it, a third cuts it, a fourth points it, a fifth grinds the top to receive the head; to make the head requires two or three distinct operations; to put it on is a peculiar business; to whiten it is another; it is even a trade in itself to put them into paper. The important business of making pins is, in this manner, divided into about 18 distinct operations.'

He estimated that production per day in this factory was about 5000 pins per person employed. If the whole operation had been carried out from start to finish by each employee, Smith estimated that he would have been able to make only a few dozen each day.

Advantages of the division of labour

Why should specialisation lead to such great increases in productivity? Smith followed up his description by an analysis which attempted to discover the reasons for the improved performance.

- A person who spends his or her time performing one relatively simple task becomes extremely proficient at that particular operation. Constant repetition leads to great dexterity, or, as most people would say, 'practice makes perfect'.
- No time is wasted in moving from one job to another. The necessity of moving from station to station, putting down one sets of tools and picking up another is eliminated.
- There is a saving of time in the training of operatives. A man or woman can be trained very quickly for the performance of a single operation.
- There is a saving of skill. Specialisation means that many different occupations are created, each one of which calls for some particular aptitude. It is possible, therefore, for each worker to specialise in the job for which he or she is best suited.
- One of the most important advantages of the division of labour is that it makes possible a much greater use of machinery. When a complex process has been broken down into a series of separate, simple processes it is possible to devise machinery to carry out each individual operation. It would be extremely difficult, for example, to construct a machine which would carry out the whole business of making a chair, but, once this has been reduced to a series of separate operations, it becomes possible to use electric saws, planing machines, power-driven lathes, etc.

An example

It might be thought that if a person is more efficient in all tasks than another person specialisation will not be beneficial. However it can be shown that specialisation of labour might still be advantageous. A simple arithmetical example will make this point clear. Let us suppose that there are two leather workers, A and B, each producing shoes and handbags.

In 1 week A can make *either* 10 pairs of shoes, *or* 10 handbags
In 1 week B can make *either* 8 pairs of shoes, *or* 4 handbags

In the absence of any specialisation we will suppose that each week,

A makes 5 pairs of shoes *and* 5 handbags
B makes 4 pairs of shoes *and* 2 handbags

Total: 9 pairs of shoes *and* 7 handbags

A is more efficient in both activities, but the fact that he is *relatively* more efficient in producing handbags (10:4) than in producing shoes (10:8) means that specialisation will result in a greater total output.

We can assume that B specialises completely in shoes while A partially specialises in handbags. Thus each week,

A makes   2 pairs of shoes and 8 handbags
B makes   8 pairs of shoes and 0 handbags

Total: 10 pairs of shoes and 8 handbags

This is a very simple account of the important principle of *comparative advantage* which is discussed in detail in Chapter 51.

The disadvantages of the division of labour

There are a number of reasons why the development of specialised production has not been an unmixed blessing. The drawbacks of the system are mainly concerned with the loss of 'job satisfaction' which results from the constant repetition of simple operations.

Monotony

A cycle of simple movements which is repeated every few minutes is all that is demanded of large numbers of workers in factories. This undoubtedly makes for monotony and boredom; there is no opportunity for the worker to exercise initiative, judgement, manual skills, or responsibility. Whilst there are operatives who may prefer to have daily tasks which make very limited calls upon them and who do not wish to have a job which carries any great responsibility, it must be the case that large numbers of workers do find such jobs rather frustrating.

Loss of craftsmanship

The extension of specialisation has been accompanied by a great increase in the use of machinery which, in turn, has tended to become more and more automatic. Basic skills have been transferred from the hands of the worker to the machine; it is the machine which now controls the design, the quality, and the quantity of the product, and not the person tending the machine. All this has led to a marked decline in the degree of craftsmanship required of the average industrial worker. The satisfaction to be derived from 'making something' – the pride in creation – is denied to the machine minder.

While much of this criticism is well founded, we must not overlook the fact that mechanisation has produced many new types of craftsmen – the designers and creators of the machines themselves – and many new occupations which call for a high degree of skill and applied knowledge (e.g. the computer has created a demand for systems analysts). The use of machines has also abolished much of the heavy manual labour associated with hand methods of production. Imagine the work involved in reducing the trunk of a tree to a dining table without the use of power-driven tools.

Increased risk of unemployment

Specialisation means that workers do not have the wide industrial training which would make them adaptable to changes in the techniques of production. Their specialised functions can become obsolete when new machines are invented, and their particular skills will be useless elsewhere. Such workers, it is held, are especially liable to unemployment in a rapidly changing world.

In answer to this argument it has been pointed out that the division of labour, by simplifying tasks, makes jobs in one industry very similar to those in another. Since the operation is easy to learn, retraining is easily and quickly accomplished and workers can, without great difficulty, move from one job to another.

Interdependence

A specialised system of production increases the extent to which different sectors of the economy depend upon one another. It is not simply a question of workers specialising, factories, firms and even whole industries specialise. Many modern industries consist of a large number of firms each concentrating on the production of one, or very few, components which are brought together in what is in effect a large assembly plant. This is most clearly typified by the motor car industry where many hundreds of different parts are manufactured by relatively small specialist firms. These components are brought together on the assembly line. This is a very efficient, low-cost method of production, but it is extremely vulnerable to a breakdown in any one of the large number of links in the chain. Delays in the supply of any one component may cause massive hold-ups throughout the industry.

Modern technology allied to the extensive use of the division of labour has made possible enormous increases in the output of goods and services. It has transformed the living standards of millions of people, removed much of the back-breaking toil from people's daily labour, made possible a great reduction in working hours and by providing for more leisure, has given people the opportunity to lead fuller and richer lives.

Nevertheless the loss of job satisfaction, particularly in manufacturing industries, is raising some serious social problems. In many industrial

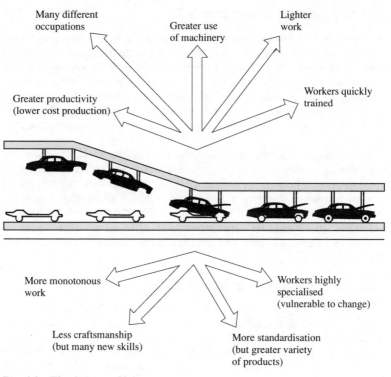

Many different
occupations

Greater use
of machinery

Lighter
work

Greater productivity
(lower cost production)

Workers quickly
trained

More monotonous
work

Workers highly
specialised
(vulnerable to change)

Less craftsmanship
(but many new skills)

More standardisation
(but greater variety
of products)

Fig. 6.1   The division of labour

countries, managers are seriously considering various projects aimed at
'*job enrichment*'. These are attempts to reverse recent trends by
enlarging the role and responsibilities of the workers. Several factories
have tried to abolish the assembly line by reorganising production so that
teams of workers are responsible for assembling the entire product (or a
major component of it). Each team is free to decide how the various
tasks will be allocated and the speed with which the job is carried out.
Within each team the jobs may be rotated so as to increase the element of
variety in the work.

Moves away from specialisation

A number of firms, for example Volvo, have moved away from
specialisation in order to increase the quantity and quality of output.
Allowing workers to undertake a number of different tasks may increase
workers' enjoyment of their jobs, identify their strengths, increase their
ability to make suggestions for improving production methods and the
product, enable workers to cover for colleagues who are sick or
undertaking training and increase labour flexibility.

Specialisation and exchange

A system of specialised production, no matter how simple, cannot exist without exchange. When people become specialists they are dependent upon some system of exchange to provide them with the variety of goods and services required to satisfy their wants. Without some means of exchange, the farmers would have too much corn for their personal needs, but would have no coal, oil, electricity, or machinery. There must be some means whereby the outputs of specialist producers can be exchanged.

In addition to this need for a highly developed mechanism for carrying out exchanges, there is another important factor governing the degree of specialisation. The principle of the division of labour can only be applied extensively when there is a large market for a standardised product. Automatic and semi-automatic machinery and highly specialised workers are equipped to produce large outputs of identical products. Specialisation, therefore, is limited by the extent of the market.

Specialisation and the size of the market

The work of engineers and scientists continues to provide increasing scope for wider applications of the principle of the division of labour. The most striking evidence of this fact is the increasing use being made of modern, computerised technology. These methods of production are worth while only if there is a market (i.e. a potential demand) large enough to keep the equipment fully employed. However, as micro technology becomes cheaper, it becomes possible for firms to cater for smaller markets. Desk-top publishing means that now even relatively narrow interests, such as parrot keeping, have specialist magazines produced for them.

Specialisation and economic change

We live in a world of specialists. Many people are trained for highly specialised roles in the economic system. Doctors, lawyers, accountants, physicists, chemists, surveyors, civil engineers – the list of specialised occupations seems endless. All of these people may be extremely productive in their particular fields, but the fact that each of them concentrates on a narrow range of skills makes them *occupationally immobile*. They can do one thing very well, but they cannot do much else. A shortage of labour in one profession cannot be overcome by moving people from another profession; a chemist cannot do the work of an accountant.

But it is not only labour which is highly specialised. Capital equipment is usually designed for a specific task. A modern blast furnace is a very effective means of producing iron, but it cannot be used for any other purposes; a petrol tanker cannot carry coal, and a combine harvester cannot dig ditches. Much of our capital equipment, therefore, is also occupationally immobile.

These may be very obvious points but they have important economic implications. These are times of rapid economic change and economic progress depends very much on the community's ability to adapt quickly and smoothly to changes in consumer demand, in technology, in world trade, and so on. When economic resources are highly specialised (i.e. *specific* to a particular task), it may be extremely difficult to transfer such resources from one use to another. The mobility of the factors of production is clearly an important economic problem. Let us now examine some of the causes of economic change.

Wars

Modern wars completely disrupt the economic life of a country. They increase the pace of economic and social change and in particular they speed up the rate of technological progress. Some industries undergo great expansion (e.g. chemicals, electronics, engineering), while many industries are forced to change the nature of their outputs. Large numbers of workers change their jobs and learn new skills. The structure of world trade is distorted and the pattern of exports and imports which develops after a major war is sometimes very different from that which existed before the war. The British economy has been particularly affected by export markets lost during wars (e.g. in cotton and coal).[1] While the prosecution of the war itself calls for a high degree of mobility of labour and capital, so does the need to adjust to the very different economic situation which emerges after the war.

The peace dividend

The fall of communism in Eastern Europe and budget pressures have resulted in a fall in defence expenditure in most European countries and in the USA. This provides the opportunity to increase the output of non-military goods and services. However, to reap this benefit there must be civilian job opportunities and workers and machines must be able to switch from making weapons or driving tanks to making ice cream or selling insurance. For some workers and machines this may not be too difficult. For instance an RAF pilot should not find it too hard to adjust to flying civilian aircraft. However, it may prove less easy for a paratrooper to find another job and particularly for a tank to find an alternative use.

Population changes

Emigration, immigration and movements in birth and death rates bring about changes in both the size and age composition of the population.

NOTE 1. This was only one of many reasons for the decline of these industries.

Such population changes call for changes in the allocation of resources to different industries. A rapidly increasing population will have a large proportion of younger people and there will be increasing demands for schools, schoolteachers, and those commodities consumed mainly by the young. A declining population will have an increasing proportion of older people. There will be a decreasing demand for social capital such as houses and schools and increasing demands for those things which meet the needs of older people.

Technological changes

Man's ingenuity produces a constant stream of technological inno-vations, and these in turn call for new methods of production, new types of capital equipment and changes in the skills required of the labour force. A good example is provided by recent developments in secretarial work where the microchip revolution demanded a new range of skills including word processing.

Political changes

The economy of a country is affected by political changes both at home and abroad. Changes in the structure of taxation and in the volume and distribution of government spending are important instruments of government policy which affect all sectors of the economy. Where industries are nationalised, the government, by varying the development programmes of these industries, can directly influence the allocation of resources. Policies on privatisation will alter the way industries are run. External political changes and changes in the policies of international trade bodies are also important, especially where a country is dependent upon export markets.

Changes in taste and fashion

Changes in taste and fashion can influence the demands for most consumer goods to some extent, but they are particularly important to producers of such things as clothing, furniture, footwear, and domestic appliances. Advertising, of course, is a powerful agent in stimulating changes in demand of this type. Changes in income too play an import-ant part. Rising incomes tend to bring about different patterns of consumption. A typical example would be the movement from public to private transport in recent years.

Occupational and geographical mobility

Changes in the character of the national output can only take place if the factors of production are mobile. There are two aspects of mobility: occupational and geographical.

Occupational mobility concerns the movement of a factor of production from one occupation to another. Most of the examples considered so far have referred to occupational mobility.

Geographical mobility describes the movement of a factor from one location to another. This is an important matter when new industries establish themselves in locations different from those in which the older industries were established.

Land

Land, quite obviously, is not mobile in the geographical sense, but a great deal of land has a high degree of occupational mobility. In the UK, for example, a large proportion of the land has many alternative uses. It might be used for farmland, for roads, railways, airports, parks, residential housing, industrial development, and so on. Some of the land, for example, the mountainous areas, has an extremely limited degree of occupational mobility, being useful perhaps for sheep grazing, or as a centre for tourism.

Capital

Capital is mobile in both senses, although some types of capital are extremely immobile. Such things as railway networks, blast furnaces, and shipyards are virtually immobile in the geographical sense. It may be physically possible to dismantle them and move them to different sites, but the cost of doing so will almost certainly outweigh any advantages of the new location. Neither is such equipment mobile in the occupational sense; it can only be used for a specific purpose – it is sunk capital. Many buildings, however, can be effectively adapted to other uses. Many of the former cotton mills in Lancashire are now housing a variety of industrial activities. Former schools, churches and railway stations are used as private houses.

Some capital equipment is mobile both geographically and occupationally. Electric motors, machine tools, hand tools, and lorries, for example, can be used effectively in a wide variety of industries and are capable of movement from one location to another without great cost.

Labour

Theoretically we should expect labour to be the most mobile of the factors of production both occupationally and geographically. Economic history does indeed provide abundant evidence of great movements of labour from one industry to another and from one region to another. During the nineteenth century and the early years of this century, millions of people left Europe to settle in North America, Canada and Australia.

Occupational mobility concerns the movement of a factor of production from one occupation to another. Most of the examples considered so far have referred to occupational mobility.

Geographical mobility describes the movement of a factor from one location to another.

More recent times have seen a large-scale movement of labour from the Mediterranean lands to the industrial nations in north-west Europe.

In spite of all this evidence of labour's mobility, we must bear in mind that most of these movements took place over fairly long periods of time, and in most cases there were severe political, economic, and social pressures stimulating the movements. There is plenty of evidence that labour is not very mobile geographically. Regions no more than 100 miles apart often record unemployment rates which are widely dissimilar. In the 1930s some areas of the UK experienced rates as high as 60 per cent while others had rates well below 10 per cent. If labour had been geographically mobile such divergencies would surely have been greatly reduced.

Occupationally, too, labour is relatively immobile. The evidence here lies in the large differentials in salaries and wages as between different occupations. A high degree of occupational mobility would certainly lead to a much narrower range of differentials.

The entrepreneur

The most mobile of the factors of production is probably the entrepreneur. While labour tends to be trained for some special task appropriate to some particular industry, the basic functions of the entrepreneur are common to all industries. Whatever the type of economic activity there will be a need to raise capital, to take risks and make the fundamental decisions on where, what, and how to produce. The creation of an efficient unit of production is a task of human relations the basic features of which are common to all industries. It requires qualities of initiative, leadership, organisation, and control. The relatively few people of first-class ability who possess such qualities are able to operate effectively in almost any industry.

7 Combining the factors of production

Varying the proportions

It is the task of management in providing a supply of goods and services to organise land, labour, and capital so that any given output can be produced at the lowest possible cost. In this chapter we shall be concerned mainly with the relationship between output and monetary costs. In order to understand the economics of production, however, we have to start by examining the purely physical aspects; that is, the relationship between the units of capital, land, and labour employed and the resultant physical units of output.

This relationship between the output of a good and the inputs (factors of production) used to produce it is known as the production function. For instance it may take two hairdressers, four bottles of shampoo, eight hairdryers, four combs, two pairs of scissors, amongst other equipment to cut, shampoo and style eighty customers' hair in one week. However in making a product, a firm does not have to combine the inputs in fixed proportions. Many farm crops can be grown by using relatively little labour and relatively large amounts of capital (machinery, fertilisers, etc.) or by combining relatively large amounts of labour with very little capital. In most cases a firm has some opportunity to vary the 'input mix'.

The effects of varying the proportions between the factors of production is a subject of great importance because nearly all short-run changes in production involve some changes in these proportions. When a firm wishes to increase (or decrease) its output, it cannot, in the short run, change its fixed factors of production, but it can produce more (or less) by changing the amounts of the variable factors (labour, materials, etc.). When farmers wish to increase their output they are usually obliged to do so by using more labour, more seed, more fertiliser (i.e. variable factors) on some fixed supply of land (the fixed factor).

Manufacturers are in a similar position. In the short run they cannot extend their factories or install more machinery but they can adjust their output by varying the quantities of labour, raw materials, fuel, and power. The short run is defined as the period of time in which at least one factor of production is fixed.

Diminishing returns

Many years ago economists pondered over the implications of varying the proportions in which the factors were combined and came up with a principle which has become famous as the Law of Diminishing Returns.

They applied this law to agriculture (and we shall use agriculture in our illustration), but it can hold true for all kinds of production. The operation of the law is best explained by means of a simple arithmetical example.

Let us assume that some particular crop is to be grown on a fixed area of land, say 20 acres. We shall also assume that the amount of capital to be used is also fixed in supply. Labour will be the variable factor. Table 7.1 sets out some hypothetical results obtained by varying the amount of labour employed and illustrates some important relationships, but before we examine them we must state the assumptions on which the table is based.

Table 7.1 Non-proportional returns

(1) Number of workers	(2) Total product (tonnes)	(3) Average product (tonnes)	(4) Marginal product (tonnes)
1	8	8	8
2	24	12	16
3	54	18	30
4	82	20.5	28
5	95	19	13
6	100	16.7	5
7	100	14.3	0
8	96	12	–4

- Labour is the only variable factor.
- All units of the variable factor are equally efficient.
- There are no changes in the techniques of production.

On the basis of these assumptions we can conclude that any changes in productivity arising from variations in the number of people employed are due entirely to the changes in the proportions in which labour is combined with the other factors.

Table 7.1 illustrates the Law of Diminishing Returns (or the Law of Variable Proportions) which states that, '*As we add successive units of one factor to fixed amounts of other factors the increments in total output will at first rise and then decline.*'

The details in Table 7.1 can be used to illustrate this law. Columns 1 and 2 are self-explanatory – they show the total products at different levels of employment. *Average product* (or output per worker) is shown in Column 3 and is obtained quite simply by using the formula

$$\frac{\text{Total product}}{\text{Number of workers}} = \text{Average product}$$

Marginal product, shown in Column 4, describes the changes in total output brought about by varying employment by one person. The addition of a third person adds 30 tonnes to total output, while the employment of a fourth person increases total output by 28 tonnes.

Returns to the variable factor

Since labour is the only variable factor, changes in output are related directly to changes in employment so that we speak of changes in the productivity of labour or changes in *the returns to labour*. As the number of people increases from 1 to 6, total output continues to increase, but this is not true of the average product (AP) and the marginal product (MP). As more people are employed, both the AP and the MP begin to rise, reach a maximum and start to fall. These movements are clearly seen in Fig. 7.1 which is based on Table 7.1. As the number of people increases from 1 to 3 the *marginal product* of labour is increasing. Up to this point the fixed factors are being underutilised – the people are 'too thin on the ground'. When the number of people employed exceeds 3 the marginal product of labour begins to fall – an indication that the proportions between the fixed and variable factors are becoming less favourable. Marginal product begins to fall before average product and we get the maximum average product of labour when 4 people are employed. If we now wished to increase output *and* maintain the same

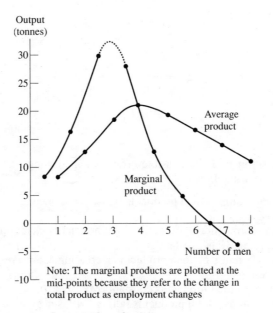

Fig. 7.1   Average and marginal productivity

productivity of labour it is obvious that an increase in the fixed factors must accompany the increase in the variable factors. This would be a change of *scale* and is discussed later in this chapter and in Chapter 9.

It is this feature of *increasing production* and *falling productivity* which is highlighted by the Law of Diminishing Returns. In Table 7.1 we see that diminishing marginal returns set in after the employment of the third person and diminishing average returns after the employment of the fourth person. Note that the marginal productivity of the seventh person is zero – his employment does not change total output. This may not be so unrealistic as it first appears. In some underdeveloped lands where peasant families are confined to their individual plots, it is quite conceivable that the marginal productivity of very large families is zero.

Figure 7.2 makes use of the total product curve and provides another view of the relationships between employment and output where some of the factors are fixed in supply.

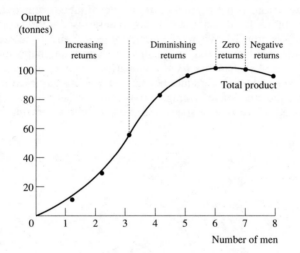

Fig. 7.2

We can summarise the possible effects of increasing the quantity of variable factors as follows:

- Increasing returns – total product increases at an increasing rate (MP is increasing).
- Constant returns (not illustrated) – total product is increasing at a constant rate (MP is constant).
- Diminishing returns – total product is increasing at a decreasing rate (MP is falling).
- Zero returns – total product is constant (MP is zero).
- Negative returns – total product is falling (MP is negative).

Application of the law of diminishing returns

It is important to note that although the illustrations used above have concentrated on labour as the variable factor, the law of variable proportions (or diminishing returns) is equally applicable to land and capital and, no doubt, to entrepreneurship. The marginal and average productivity of capital will, at some point, start to decline as more and more capital is applied to a fixed supply of land and labour. The same will apply to the productivity of land as more and more land is combined with a fixed amount of labour and capital.

Although the figures we have used in our example are hypothetical, a good many actual experiments have verified the pattern shown here. Experiments in which increased amounts of feed were given to a fixed number of dairy cows, and others where increased amounts of fertiliser were applied to a given area of land have clearly demonstrated the applicability of non-proportional returns. Increments in the yields at first increased more than proportionally but eventually there came a point where the law of diminishing returns asserted itself.

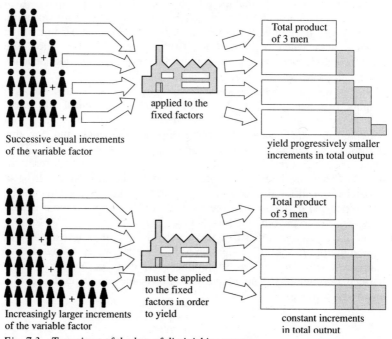

Fig. 7.3   Two views of the law of diminishing returns

Assumptions of the law of diminishing returns

The law of diminishing returns applies only when 'other things remain equal'. The efficiency of the other factors and the techniques of production are assumed to be constant. Now we know that these other things do not remain constant and improvements in technical knowledge have tended to offset the effects of the law of diminishing returns. Improved methods of production increase the productivity of the factors of production and move the AP and MP curves upwards. But this does not mean that the law no longer applies. It is still true that in the short period (when other things can change very little) increments in the variable factors will at some point yield increments in output which are less than proportionate. In some less developed regions where there is little or no technical change and population is increasing we can, unfortunately, see the law of diminishing returns operating only too clearly.

The least-cost combination

The preceding explanation of the law of diminishing returns should not be taken as an indication that the ratio of labour to land and capital which gives the maximum output per worker is the ratio which the firm should adopt. All we have done is to show the tendency of output per unit of the variable factor when the proportions between the factors are varied. The most profitable way of combining the factors of production depends upon their prices as well as their productivity.

So far we have been concerned with physical inputs and physical outputs. In other words, we have been discussing technical efficiency. Our measurement has been the *physical productivity* of labour. But entrepreneurs are concerned with economic efficiency and for this purpose they will measure output and input in monetary terms. Their inputs they measure as costs and their output is measured in terms of revenue. They are interested in making profits and their aim will be to maximise the difference between costs and revenue. They will not be very interested in maximising the productivity of labour if labour is very cheap relative to the other factors.

We have already noted that there will be several different ways of combining the factors of production to produce any given output. Let us suppose that a firm wishes to produce 100 units per week of some particular commodity. This output we will assume can be produced with any of the following combinations.

	Land	Labour	Capital
Method 1	20	10	4
Method 2	20	7	7
Method 3	15	9	9

The question now arises, 'Which is the *best* method?'. Given our assumption that entrepreneurs will always try to maximise their profits, it follows that the firm will adopt that method which minimises costs. Let us assume that the prices of the factors of production are as follows:

Land is £20 per unit; Labour is £10 per unit; and Capital is £15 per unit. Now,

Method 1 will cost £560
Method 2 will cost £575
Method 3 will cost £525

The entrepreneur will choose Method 3.

The reader should now check the effects of varying factor prices. It will be observed that any significant changes in the *relative* prices of the factors of production will lead to a substitution of the relatively cheaper for the relatively dearer factor.

Returns to scale

The law of diminishing returns deals with what are essentially short-run situations. It is assumed that some of the resources used in production are fixed in supply. In the long run, however, it is possible for a firm to vary the amounts of all the factors of production employed; more land can be acquired, more buildings erected and more machinery installed. What we are saying is that, in the long run, it is possible for a firm to change the *scale* of its activities. Strictly speaking a change of scale takes place when the quantities of all the factors are changed by the same percentage so that the proportions in which they are combined are not changed.

Table 7.2 Returns to scale

Units of labour	Units of land (acres)	Total output (tonnes)	Increase in size of firm	Increase in total output
4	20	100		
			100%	150%
8	40	250		
			50%	68%
12	60	420		
			$33\frac{1}{3}\%$	$33\frac{1}{3}\%$
16	80	560		
			25%	20%
20	100	672		
			20%	16%
24	120	780		

It is a feature of production that when the scale of production is changed, output changes are not usually proportionate. When a firm doubles its size, output will tend to change by more than 100% or less than 100%. The relationships between changes in scale and changes in output are described as *returns to scale*. In Table 7.3 some hypothetical figures are used in order to illustrate this important concept.

Table 7.2 shows the increases in total output as the scale of production increases. The firm increases its size but the proportion between the factors remains unchanged (e.g., 1 unit of labour per 5 acres of land). Using columns 4 and 5 we can compare the proportionate changes in total output with the proportionate changes in the size of the firm. As the firm increases its size from 4 people and 20 acres of land to 12 people and 60 acres of land, it experiences *increasing returns to scale* (output increases more than proportionately). A change of scale from 12 people and 60 acres to 16 people and 80 acres yields *constant returns to scale* (size and output change by the same percentage). Any further growth in the size of the firm yields *decreasing returns to scale* because output increases less than proportionately.

The relationships between returns to scale and economies of scale

Increasing returns to scale are usually associated with falling average (unit) costs which can also be referred to as economies of scale. This is because, in the absence of changes in the costs of inputs, if output increases by a greater percentage than input, each unit will become cheaper to produce.

In the same way decreasing returns to scale are usually matched by diseconomies of scale, with average costs rising as output increases more slowly than the change in the scale of operation. Constant returns to

Table 7.3

Total inputs	Total cost	Total output	Increase in inputs	Increase in output	Average cost
10	200	200			£1
			100%	150%	
20	400	500			80p
			50%	60%	
30	600	800			75p
			$33\frac{1}{3}\%$	$33\frac{1}{3}\%$	
40	800	1067			75p
			25%	20%	
50	1000	1280			97p

scale will result in constant costs i.e., unchanged average costs if, again, the cost of inputs remains unchanged.

Table 7.3 shows both the change in total output and the change in total cost as a firm increases its scale of output. It is assumed that the proportion of inputs remains unchanged and that the cost of each input is constant at £20.

When inputs increase from 10 to 30, output increases by a greater percentage (increasing returns to scale) and average costs fall (economies of scale). Output rises by the same percentage when inputs rise from 30 to 40 (constant returns to scale) and average costs remain unchanged. Finally as inputs rise from 40 to 50, output rises by a smaller percentage (decreasing returns to scale) and average costs rise (diseconomies of scale).

Economies of scale and diseconomies of scale are discussed in more detail in Chapter 9.

PART THREE

8 Costs of production

Opportunity cost

Costs as we all know are usually measured in monetary terms and include such items as wages, rent, rates, interest, and the amounts paid for raw material, fuel, power, transport, and so on. These are the costs measured and recorded by the accountant and they are an important part of the subject matter of economics. Before proceeding to analyse these costs, however, it is necessary to remind ourselves that economists also look at costs from a different viewpoint. They see the 'true' or 'real' costs of committing resources to a particular use as the output they might have produced had they been put to another use. This is the idea of opportunity cost explained in Chapter 1.

In devoting resources to the production of, say, roads, we have to forgo the houses which might have been built with the same resources. In wartime, the opportunity cost of the tanks, guns, and military aircraft is the 'lost' output of motor cars, washing machines, railway equipment, and so on.

This way of looking at cost is important because 'money' or 'paid out' costs may not provide a true measure of the sacrifices incurred in producing a commodity. If the production of a good leads to pollution of the atmosphere or water supplies, the opportunity costs of production would include the clean air or clean water forgone by society as well as the costs of the factors employed in production. The idea of opportunity cost has an important bearing on the economist's view of profits. The difference between the traditional 'bookkeeping' costs and total revenue may not provide an accurate indication of the true profits. An obvious example is the case in which a businessman uses his own savings in order to establish an enterprise. Part of the true cost of running his firm is the interest forgone on his money capital. In using his savings for the purchase of stock and equipment he incurs a 'cost' in the form of the interest he might otherwise have received on his savings.

Output and costs

In dealing with the relationships between output and costs there are two situations to consider. First, short-run changes which cover periods when it is only possible to adjust the amount of the variable factors being used and when there is at least one fixed factor. Secondly, long-run changes which apply to periods of time which are sufficiently long for all the factors to be varied.

We shall be mainly concerned with the short-run changes and our analysis of increasing and decreasing returns should give us a clue as to the behaviour of costs in the short period.

Increasing returns means that the ratio Output: Variable Input is increasing and this should mean that average cost is falling.

Similarly, diminishing returns means that the ratio Output : Variable Input is declining and we should expect average cost to be rising.

This may be clearer if we refer back to Table 7.1 (or Fig. 7.1) and see how many extra people are required in order to raise output by some given quantity, say, 18 tonnes. When 2 people are employed only $\frac{3}{5}$ extra people (1 person working part-time) will be needed to produce an extra 18 tonnes. When 4 people are employed, however, an additional 18 tonnes of output would require the employment of 2 more people. The cost per unit of output will be increasing under conditions of diminishing returns; it is falling when increasing returns are being experienced. These statements are based on the assumption that the prices of the factors do not change as more or less of them are employed. Changes in costs, then, arise directly from changes in productivity.

In the short run just as some inputs are fixed and others variable, so some costs are fixed and others variable.

Fixed costs

These are costs which do not vary as output varies. They are obviously the costs associated with the fixed factors of production, and include such items as rent, rates, insurance, interest on loans, and depreciation.

A major element in fixed costs, especially in capital-intensive industries, is the item known as *depreciation*. It may seem rather illogical to classify depreciation charges as a fixed cost for many people will think that the rate of depreciation of a capital asset is directly related to the extent to which it is used (i.e. to output). In fact the life of capital assets tends to be measured in economic rather than technical terms. Machinery depreciates even when not in use and, even more important, it becomes obsolete. It is normal practice, therefore, to fix an annual depreciation charge which will write off the cost of equipment over some *estimated* working lifetime. There are many ways of doing this, but the simplest is to make an annual charge equal to a fixed proportion of the total value. If a machine costs £20 000 and has an expected life of 5 years, then £4000 per annum will be added to costs and placed in a depreciation fund to cover the expenses of renewal.

Fixed costs (sometimes described as *overhead* or *indirect* costs) are not influenced by changes in output. Whether a firm is working at full capacity or half capacity the items of costs mentioned above will be unaffected. Indeed, fixed costs are the costs which have to be paid even when output is zero. Thus, when a super-tanker is lying empty in port, or a Jumbo-jet is standing in the hangar, a building society is closed over the Christmas holidays, or your new car is locked away in the garage, costs are still being incurred.

Variable costs

These are the costs which are related directly to output. The most obvious items of variable costs are the wages of labour, the costs of raw materials, and fuel and power. Variable costs are often described as *direct* or *prime* costs. Variable costs are not incurred when output is zero.

Total costs

Short-run total costs represent the sum of fixed and variable costs. When output is zero, total costs will be equal to fixed costs since variable costs will be zero. When production commences, total costs will begin to rise as variable costs increase. Total costs will continue to rise as production increases, because there must be some increase in variable costs as output expands. What is important, however, is the *rate* at which total costs increase; if they are rising at a slower rate than output, average costs must be falling. Figure 8.1 shows how total cost is composed of both fixed and variable costs.

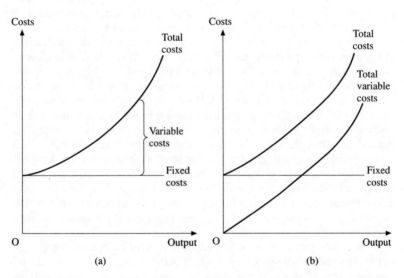

Fig. 8.1

Average cost

Average cost (or cost per unit) is equal to Total Costs/Output. When output is small, average cost will be high because fixed costs will be spread over a small number of units of output. As output increases, average cost will tend to fall as each unit is 'carrying' a smaller element of fixed cost. Average cost will also fall because, for a time, there will be increasing returns to the variable factors as more of them are employed and more specialised methods adopted. There will come a point, however, when diminishing returns are encountered and average cost begins to rise. If we drop our assumption of homogeneous factors and fixed factor prices there are other reasons why average cost may increase at higher outputs. Management problems will tend to increase; less efficient stand-by equipment may be pressed into use; less efficient labour may have to be recruited; it may be necessary to work overtime at higher wage rates and increasing demand may cause the prices of materials to rise.

Economic theory, therefore, assumes that, for the individual firm with a fixed capacity, average cost will at first decline, but as output increases there will come a point where it will rise. In other words, the average cost curve will be U-shaped. When the firm is producing at its minimum average cost we say that it has reached its *optimum* output. Figure 8.2 shows the short-run average cost curve.

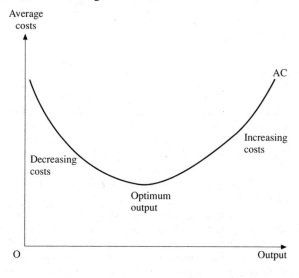

Fig. 8.2

Average variable cost

Average variable cost is total variable cost/output. The average variable cost curve is U-shaped.

Average fixed cost

Average fixed cost is total fixed cost/output. As total fixed cost is constant the average fixed cost falls with output. The fixed cost is spread over a greater and greater output. Figure 8.3 shows the three average cost curves.

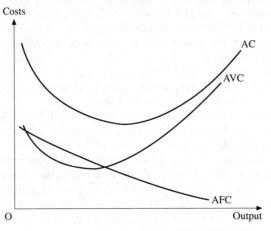

Note: AFC = distance between AC and AVC

Fig. 8.3

Marginal cost

The economist is interested in marginal quantities because most economic decisions involve changes in some existing situation. Marginal cost tells us what happens to total costs when we vary output by some small amount. More precisely, marginal cost is the extent to which total costs change when output is changed by one unit.

Marginal cost = Total cost of n units – Total cost of $(n-1)$ units

Since marginal cost is a measurement of *changes in* total cost it is obviously influenced by variable costs but not by fixed costs so marginal fixed cost is zero and marginal cost equals marginal variable cost (i.e., the change in total variable cost when output is changed by one unit).

On the basis of our assumption that a firm expanding its output with a fixed capacity will, to begin with, experience increasing returns to its variable factors and, later, diminishing returns, it follows that the marginal cost curve will be U-shaped. We have already demonstrated that, under increasing returns, the cost of producing an extra unit will be falling and, under diminishing returns it will be rising.

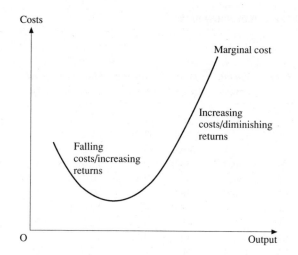

Fig. 8.4

Summary

1 Total costs = Fixed costs + Variable costs

2 Average cost = $\dfrac{\text{Total costs}}{\text{Total output}}$

3 Average variable cost = $\dfrac{\text{Total variable costs}}{\text{Total output}}$

4 Average fixed cost = $\dfrac{\text{Total fixed costs}}{\text{Total output}}$

5 Marginal cost = Change in total cost when output is varied by one unit

Short-run cost schedules and cost curves

Table 8.1 is designed to illustrate the relationship between the different categories of short-run costs.

The derivation of the details in the different columns is quite straightforward. Column 4 showing total costs at different levels of output is obtained by adding together the figures in columns 2 and 3. Average cost in column 5 is the result of dividing the figures in column 4 by those in column 1. Average fixed cost in column 7 is total fixed costs in column 2 divided by output. Average variable cost in column 8 is found by dividing total variable costs in column 3 by output in column 1. Marginal cost in column 6 is obtained from column 4 by the simple process of obtaining the *increments* in total costs for each unit increase in output.

Notice that, as output increases, the marginal, average costs and average variable costs begin to fall, reach a minimum and then begin to rise. The

Table 8.1 Costs of production (£)

(1) Units of output	(2) Fixed costs	(3) Variable costs	(4) Total costs	(5) Average costs	(6) Marginal costs	(7) Average fixed cost	(8) Average variable cost
0	18	0	18	Infinity	—	—	—
1	18	15.2	33.2	33.2	15.2	18	15.2
2	18	28.4	46.4	23.2	13.2	9	14.2
3	18	40.0	58.0	19.3	11.6	6	13.3
4	18	50.4	68.4	17.1	10.4	4.5	12.6
5	18	60.0	78.0	15.6	9.6	3.6	12
6	18	70.0	88.0	14.7	10.0	3	11.7
7	18	81.2	99.2	14.2	11.2	2.6	11.6
8	18	94.8	112.8	14.1	13.6	2.3	11.9
9	18	112.4	130.4	14.5	17.6	2	12.5
10	18	134.4	152.4	15.2	22.0	1.8	13.4

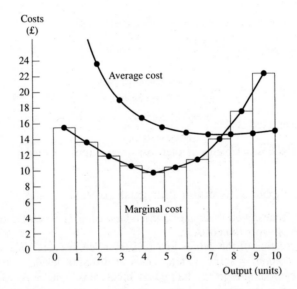

Fig. 8.5

relationship between average and marginal costs is an important one and it is clearly brought out in Fig. 8.5 which is a graphical representation of the details in Table 8.1. The marginal costs have been plotted on the mid-points of the ordinates for reasons explained in Fig. 7.1. Both the AC and MC curves are U-shaped and the main point to note is that when MC is below AC, AC is falling; when MC is above AC, AC is rising. Marginal cost is equal to average cost when average cost is at its minimum value.

The relationships between costs

The relationship between marginal and average cost can be proved mathematically, but they can also be easily understood on a common-sense basis.

Consider a cricketer's batting average. If, in his next innings, his score (i.e. his marginal score) is less than his existing average, then his average must fall. If, in his next innings, he scores more than his existing average, his average score must increase. Very simply, then, if the marginal quantity < the average quantity, the average must be falling; if the marginal quantity > the average quantity, average must be rising. Figure 8.6 presents another view of the cost relationships. It shows how the different kinds of costs can be derived from the total cost curve.

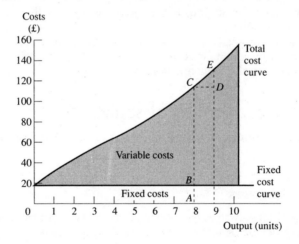

Fig. 8.6

When output is *OA* (i.e. 8 units), total costs = *AC*, and this is made up of fixed costs = *AB* and variable costs = *BC*. At this output, average cost = *AC/OA*, and marginal cost = *ED*.

9 The scale of production

We have already indicated that when an increase in the scale of production yields a more than proportionate increase in output, the enterprise is said to be experiencing *economies of scale*. These economies might be defined as those aspects of increasing size which lead to falling long-run average costs. Economies of scale are conveniently classified as internal and external economies.

Internal economies of scale are those which arise from the growth of the firm independently of what is happening to other firms. They are not due to any increase in monopoly power or to any technological innovation; they arise quite simply from an increase in the scale of production *in the firm itself*. A firm may grow as a result of increasing the size of its workplaces or increasing their number.

External economies of scale are those advantages in the form of lower average costs which a firm gains from the growth of *the industry*. These economies accrue to all firms in the industry independently of changes in the scales of individual outputs.

Economies of scale are worthy of our attention because they are associated with important economic policies, and they help to explain important features of economic structure.

Internal economies of scale

These can be divided into plant economies of scale and firm economies of scale.

Plant economies

These arise not only from the growth of individual workplaces, including individual factories and offices but also technical economies.

Increased specialisation

The larger the establishment the greater the opportunities for the specialisation of men and machines. In the larger firm the process can be broken down into many more separate operations, workers can be employed on more specialised tasks, and the continuous use of highly specialised equipment becomes possible. For example a large supermarket can employ electronic fund transfer at point of sale (EFTPOS).

Indivisibility

Some types of capital equipment can only be employed efficiently in units of a minimum size, and this minimum may well be too large for the small firm. There is a lower limit to the size of a blast furnace, a nuclear power station, a car assembly line, and a power press. This lower limit may be a technical limit; a smaller version of the equipment is impracticable. More generally the lower limit is an economic one; smaller versions of the equipment could be made but their usefulness would not justify their cost. Such indivisibility of plant means that firms with small outputs cannot take advantage of some highly specialised equipment. In a small firm this type of capital equipment would be standing idle for a large part of the time, the heavy fixed costs would be spread over small outputs, and average cost would be disproportionately high.

Increased dimensions

If one doubles the length, breadth, and height of a cube, the surface area is four times as great, and the volume eight times as great as the original. This simple arithmetical principle accounts for the remarkable increase in the dimensions of much capital equipment in recent years.

A modern oil tanker of 240 000 tonnes is only twice the size of a 30 000 tonne tanker in terms of length, width, and height, and only four times as large in terms of surface area. It will require very few, if any, more people to operate her and she will certainly not require eight times the power to propel her through the water. In recent years the super-tankers have been bringing oil to Europe from the Persian Gulf by way of the Cape of Good Hope, at a lower cost per tonne than the smaller tankers managed on the very much shorter route through Suez.

Likewise the economies of the Jumbo-jet compared with the previous and much smaller generation of jets are most impressive. Economies of increased dimensions account for the tendency in industries which make use of tanks, vats, furnaces, and transport equipment to operate larger and larger units. In the domestic scene we can see the principle at work in trends towards larger packs and larger tubes of many packaged foods, toothpastes, and other household articles.

The principle of multiples

Most industries make use of a variety of machines, each machine carrying out a different operation. Each of these different machines is likely to have a different capacity. The machine which moulds the blocks of chocolate will operate at a much slower speed than the machine which wraps the blocks in silver paper.

Assume that a particular process requires a team of four machines, A, B, C, and D, the productive capacities of which are 50, 60, 20, and 30 units per hour. If the team comprises only one machine of each type, the maximum output per hour will be 20 units and machines A, B, and D will be working below capacity. This would be the kind of problem facing the small firm producing a small output. For small outputs it is not possible to obtain a balanced team of machines such that each machine is being fully utilised.

The lowest common multiple of 50, 60, 20, and 30 is 300. This is the smallest output per hour which will enable a sequence of machines of this type to work at full capacity. Such a balanced team of machines would be:

Machine A	Machine B	Machine C	Machine D
6	5	15	10

This assembly of machines would provide an output of 300 units per hour and all machines would be working at full capacity. If output is to be increased it will only be possible to maintain 100 per cent utilisation if production is increased by multiples of 300 units (i.e. 600, 900, 1200, etc.). The reader can test this statement by trying to work out the most economic way of producing intermediate outputs of say 450 or 700 units.

By-product economies

A large plant may be able to sell or convert its by-products. For instance, a large stable may be able to sell the manure from its horses on a commercial basis. A large petroleum refinery plant may process chemicals extracted from oil and sell them. One of the most famous by-products is Tupperware which has become a very profitable concern.

Economies of linked processes

A large plant may enable more than one product to be produced. For instance, iron and steel may be produced together in a large factory. A large bank branch, in addition to carrying out standard banking services, may also operate an estate agency department.

Stock economies

A large plant can operate with smaller stocks *in proportion to sales* than the smaller firm. This is because variations in orders from individual customers and unexpected changes in customers' demands will tend to offset each other when total sales are very large.

Firm economies

There are a number of advantages which can be gained if a business unit such as a building society grows in size. This could be achieved by the building society opening more branches; the individual branches do not have to be larger.

Marketing economies

A large firm is able to buy its material requirements in large quantities. Bulk buying enables the large enterprise to obtain preferential terms. It will be able to obtain goods at lower prices and be able to dictate its requirements with regard to quality and delivery much more effectively than the smaller firm. By placing large orders for particular lines bulk buyers enable suppliers to take advantage of 'long runs' – a much more economical proposition than trying to meet a large number of small orders from small firms each requiring a different colour, or quality, or design.

The large firm will be able to employ specialist buyers, whereas in the small firm, buying will be a function of an employee who will have several other responsibilities. Expert buyers have the knowledge and skill which enables them to buy 'the right materials, at the right time, at the right price'. Expert buying can be a great economy; unwise buying can be very costly.

The selling costs of the larger firm will be much greater than those of the small firm, but the selling costs *per unit* will generally be much lower. The selling costs of a large business might be £100 000 per annum while those of a small firm might be as low as £5000 per annum. But if the large firm is selling 1 000 000 units while the small firm sells 20 000 per annum, the selling cost per unit in the large firm (10p) is very much less than that of the small firm (25p). In selling, as in buying, the larger firm can afford to employ experts whose specialised skills can give it great economic advantages.

Packaging costs per unit will be lower. A package containing 100 articles is much easier to pack than 10 separate packages each containing 10 articles. The clerical and administrative costs of dealing with an order for 1000 articles involves no more work than that involved in an order for 100, and, as we have just seen, transport costs do not increase proportionately with volume. Although many large firms spend huge sums on advertising, their advertising costs per unit sold may well be less than those of the small firm.

Financial economies

The large firm has several financial advantages. The fact that it is large and well known makes it a more credit-worthy borrower. Its greater selling potential and larger assets provide the lenders with greater security and make it possible for them to provide loans at lower rates of interest than would be charged to the smaller firm.

The larger firm has access to far more sources of finance. In addition to borrowing from the banks, it may approach a wide variety of other financial institutions as well as taking advantage of the highly developed market in the issuing of new shares and debentures. Most of the larger financial institutions and the new issue market are not structured to meet the needs of the smaller firm.

The terms on which funds can be borrowed are more favourable to the large-scale borrower because the lending of money in large amounts, like the bulk supply of materials, yields economies of scale.

Research and development economies

A research department must be of a certain size in order to work effect-ively. To the small firm this minimum effective size may represent a level of expenditure too large to justify any possible returns. To the large firm, however, the expenditure may be *relatively* small because the cost is spread over a large output.

Managerial economies

Large firms can employ specialist accountants, lawyers, personnel officers, etc. In large firms they could be fully utilised, but it is doubtful if the smaller firm could find enough specialised work to keep them fully occupied. Small firms, however, can overcome this problem to some extent by 'buying out' such expertise as they require from specialised agencies of accountants, surveyors, lawyers, management consultants, and so on.

Risk-bearing economies

Large firms are usually better equipped than small firms to cope with the risks of trading. They can benefit from the law of averages or the law of large numbers. It is often possible to predict what will happen *on the average* when we have no idea what will happen in any individual case (insurance is based on this principle). Total demand will be more stable and more predictable than will be the case with small firms where variations in individual orders will tend to have a relatively large impact on the total business.

This economy may be seen fairly clearly in the operation of a national grid to which many generating stations are connected. If each electricity-generating station supplied only its own locality, every station would have to maintain enough capacity to meet any possible exceptional demands. With a national grid, however, many of these exceptional vari-ations in demand will be 'balanced' by occurring at different times or in different places so that the total capacity required to meet the national demand will be much less than would be the case with many separate generating stations each supplying its own area.

Many large firms are able to reduce the risks of trading by means of a policy of *diversification*. They manufacture either a variety of models of a particular product, or, more likely nowadays, a variety of products. All their eggs are not in one basket. A fall in the demand for any one of its products may not mean serious trouble for the firm; it may well be cancelled out by a rise in the demand for one or more of the other products. A small firm, on the other hand, is likely to be specialising in one product, any fall in the demand for which may have serious con-sequences. The larger firm is also likely to have a diversified market structure. In the national market, demand fluctuations between regions may offset one another; a fall in the demand in the home market might be balanced by a rise in the demand overseas. A small firm with a restricted market is much more vulnerable to changes in market conditions.

Plant specialisation economies

A firm may be large enough for its individual plants to specialise. For instance, a large motor vehicle company may have plants producing buses, plants producing cars and plants producing lorries.

Staff facilities economies

A large firm may be able to offer, among other things, staff canteens, sports grounds and medical care. With a large number of staff the cost of providing these facilities per member of staff may be relatively low. The large retailer Marks and Spencer provides a range of facilities for its staff.

The main internal economies of scale are shown in Figure 9.1. It is interesting to note that whilst many of the plant economies may benefit society, some of the firm economies, like marketing and finance, benefit the firm often at the expense of other companies.

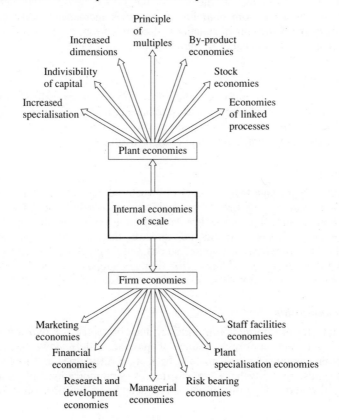

Fig. 9.1

Diseconomies of scale

Increasing size brings many advantages, but it can also bring disadvantages.

For each particular industry there will be some optimum size of firm in which average cost reaches a minimum. This optimum size will vary over time as technical progress changes the techniques of production. As firms grow beyond this optimum size, efficiency declines and average costs begin to increase.

There seems to be no good reason why such diseconomies of scale should arise from purely technical causes. Increased specialisation, increased dimensions, the principle of multiples, indivisibilities and so on should continue to offer potential reductions in average cost as the scale of production increases. Economists have usually attributed the major cause of diseconomies to management difficulties.

Management problems

There is no doubt that as the size of the firm increases, management problems become more complex. It becomes increasingly difficult to carry out the management functions of coordination, control, communication and the maintenance of morale in the labour force.

Coordination

Large organisations must be subdivided into many specialised departments (production planning, sales, purchasing, personnel, accounts etc.). As these departments multiply and grow in size, the task of coordinating their activities becomes more and more difficult.

Control

Essentially, management consists of two basic activities; the taking of decisions and seeing that these decisions are carried out. This latter function is that of control. The large firm usually has an impressive hierarchy of authority (managing director, director, head of division, head of department, foreman, and so on), but, in practice, the problem of seeing that 'everyone is doing what they are supposed to be doing, and doing it well', is a very difficult task.

Communication

The transfer of information in industry and commerce is a two-way process. It is not simply a matter of passing orders down the line; subordinates must be able to feed back their difficulties and problems. There must not only be a vertical line of communication, information must also move laterally, because one section of the firm must know what the other sections are doing. Keeping everyone informed of what is required of them and on what is happening elsewhere in the firm is a very severe test of management's abilities.

Morale

Probably the most difficult problem for organisations with large numbers of employees is the maintenance of morale. The attitude of workers to management is of critical importance to the efficient operation of the enterprise, and the cultivation of a spirit of willing cooperation appears to become more and more difficult as the firm becomes larger. It is not easy to make any individual worker in a labour force of thousands feel that they are an important part of the firm and people low down the pyramid of control often lack an identification of interest with the firm and regard it with apathy and sometimes with hostility. Indeed, industrial relations tend to be worse in large plants than in small plants.

Prices of inputs

A further possible reason why growth in the size of the firm may lead to rising average costs may be increases in the prices of the factors of production. As the scale of production increases, the firm will increase its demands for materials, labour, energy, transport and so on. It may, however, be difficult to obtain increased supplies of some of these factors, for example, skilled labour, or minerals from mines which are already working at full capacity. In such cases a firm attempting to increase the scale of its production may find itself bidding up the prices of some of its inputs.

Cost curves in the short run and the long run

The cost curves illustrated in Chapter 8 are short-run cost curves. They describe the behaviour of costs in a firm with a fixed amount of land and capital. In the long run, however, there are no fixed factors; a firm can increase or reduce the amounts of all the factors it uses. It may expand by acquiring new plant and equipment or it may reduce its scale of operations by not replacing plant and equipment as they wear out, or it may dispose of such assets by selling them.

Figure 9.2 helps to explain the changing cost structure of a firm as it changes its scale of production. If we assume that it begins operations as a small business, its original short-run average cost curve is represented by SAC(1). If this firm is successful and increases its size, a new short-run cost curve becomes effective for each particular scale of production. These short-run average cost curves are represented by SAC(2), SAC(3), SAC(4), and SAC(5). Each of these curves represents a different stock of capital and other fixed factors.

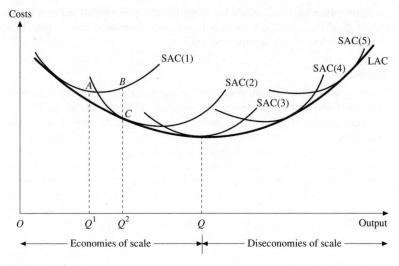

Fig. 9.2

Assuming that a firm will always choose the size of plant and equipment which minimises the cost of producing any given output, we can see why it will tend to increase its scale of production as the demand for its product increases. Assume that initially it is operating on cost curve SAC(1) producing an output of OQ^1 at an average cost of AQ^1. Now in order to meet an increased demand, its output increases to OQ^2. With its existing size of plant this change in output would raise average cost to BQ^2. But by increasing the size of the firm and moving to cost curve SAC(2), an output of OQ^2 can be produced at an average cost of CQ^2. This same reasoning can be applied to explain movements to cost curves SAC(3), SAC(4) and SAC(5). Instead of moving up an existing cost curve, lower costs of production can be obtained by moving on to a cost curve of a plant with greater capacity.

The long-run average cost curve, therefore consists of a series of points on the different short-run cost curves. These points represent the lowest costs attainable for the production of any given output. If we assume that there are many such short-run curves, the long-run average cost curve will assume a shape similar to LAC in Figure 9.2. The LAC curve is described as an 'envelope curve' to the series of SAC curves.

In Figure 9.2 it is assumed that as the firm expands its capacity, it will experience economies of scale until it achieves output OQ on SAC(3). This is the *optimum size* of the firm since any further increase in the scale of production leads to rising average cost (i.e. diseconomies of scale). In fact empirical evidence seems to indicate that, in many manufacturing industries, the LAC falls as the scale of production increases and then levels out; constant returns seem to apply over very large ranges of output.

Different shape long-run average cost curves

The conventional average cost curve is U-shaped. This is illustrated above in Fig. 9.2. However, this is not thought to be the most common shape. The practical experience of firms in such industries as aircraft production, motor cars, chemicals, oil, and the manufacture of televison tubes appears to contradict the idea that increasing size leads to diseconomies. It may be that the optimum size of the firm in such industries is very large indeed because the technical economies are so great that they more than offset any managerial and administrative diseconomies. In this case the long-run average cost curve will slope down from left to right.

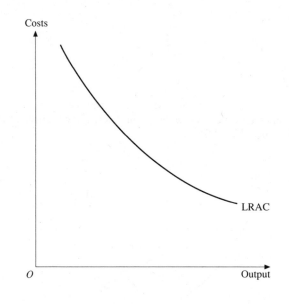

Fig. 9.3

In other industries the long-run average cost curve may fall as the scale of production increases and then level out. Constant returns may apply over very large ranges of output. In this case the curve will be L-shaped as shown in Fig. 9.4.

Q represents the minimum efficient scale. This is the lowest level of output at which a firm can produce and, by gaining all available economies of scale, minimise average costs.

Long-run marginal costs

The conventional long-run marginal cost curve, as with the short-run marginal cost curve is U-shaped. This time, however, it will fall because

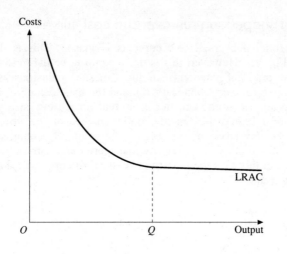

Fig. 9.4

of economies of scale and rise due to diseconomies of scale. The long-run marginal cost curve cuts the long-run average cost curve at its lowest point as shown in Fig. 9.5.

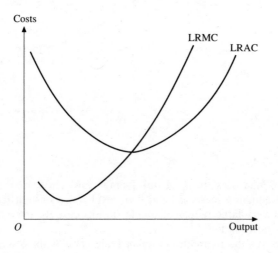

Fig. 9.5

The long-run marginal cost curve initially pushes down the long-run average cost curve as output increases and then pulls up the long-run average cost curve.

External economies of scale

External economies are the advantages which accrue to a firm from the growth in the size of *the industry*. These advantages may be gained by firms of any size. Indeed, a collection of relatively small independent firms can specialise on quite a large scale so that *collectively* they can achieve many of the economies of scale outlined earlier. External economies are especially significant when that industry is heavily localised. In this particular case they are often referred to *as economies of concentration*.

The cost advantages which a firm may obtain from the fact that a number of firms carrying out similar activities are situated in close proximity to one another are particularly relevant to policies on industrial location. We shall see later that these external economies of scale pose difficult problems for governments when they try to relocate industries in new areas.

Labour

The concentration of similar firms in any one area leads to the creation of a local labour force skilled in the various techniques used in the industry. Local colleges develop special courses of training geared to the particular needs of the industry. The further-education colleges in Cornwall and Devon have important travel and tourism departments and the further-education college in Witney has a stud and stable course attracting students from throughout the UK and abroad.

Ancillary services

In areas where there is a high degree of industrial concentration, subsidiary industries catering for the special needs of the major industry establish themselves. Thus we find many participants of the horse racing industry being based in Newmarket. Here too we find firms specialising in the provision of horse feed, vets specialising in the treatment of horses and blacksmiths to shoe horses.

Even when an industry is dispersed, if it is large enough ancillary industries will develop. For example, the fertilizer industry supplies farmers throughout the country.

Disintegration

Where an industry is heavily localised there is a tendency for individual firms to specialise in a single process or in the manufacture of a single component. The classic example is to be found in Lancashire, where the production of cotton cloth is broken down into many processes each carried out by a specialist firm (spinning, weaving, dyeing, finishing, etc.). A glance through the Trades' Telephone Directory for centres such as Bradford, Coventry, Stoke-on-Trent, or Leicester will provide a very good picture of the extent to which industries in these areas have 'disintegrated' into many specialist activities. This development produces among the firms the same sort of advantages which result from the economies of scale in the single large firm. It means, for example, that each individual firm may obtain its components and other requirements at relatively low cost because they are being mass produced *for the industry*.

Cooperation

Regional specialisation encourages cooperation among the firms. A good example is provided by the research centres established as joint ventures by the firms in heavily localised industries. The pottery firms in Stoke-on-Trent, the footwear firms in the East Midlands, and the cotton firms in Lancashire have all set up research centres for their particular industries. The opportunities for formal and informal contacts between members of the firms are much greater where the firms themselves are all in one locality. The formation of trade societies, the publication of a trade journal and other such cooperative ventures are more easily stimulated in localised industry.

Commercial facilities

External economies also arise from the fact that the service industries in the area develop a special knowledge of the needs of the industry and this often leads to the provision of specialised facilities. Banking and insurance firms become acquainted with the particular requirements of the industry and find it worthwhile to provide special facilities. Transport firms may find it economical to develop special equipment (e.g. containers and vehicles) to deal with *the industry's* requirements. Improved infrastructure in the form of better roads and airports may be provided. Again, each firm is a beneficiary, not because the firm itself is large, but because the industry as a whole provides a large demand for these services.

Specialised markets

When an industry is large enough specialised places and facilities to bring buyers and sellers into contact may be developed. An example is Lloyds of London.

External diseconomies

A firm may also experience external diseconomies of scale as the industry to which it belongs becomes larger. A shortage of labour with the appropriate skills may develop so that firms in this industry may find themselves bidding up wages as they try to attract more labour (or hold on to their existing supplies). Increasing demands for raw materials may also bid up prices and cause costs to rise. If the industry is heavily localised, land for expansion will become increasingly scarce and hence more expensive both to purchase and to rent. Transport costs may also rise because of increased congestion.

Shifts in the long-run average cost curve

Whilst a change in output will cause a movement along the long-run average cost curve, there are a number of factors which can cause it to change its position. One significant influence is external economies of scale, described above. If external economies of scale are being experienced the long-run average cost will shift down – since any level of output will now be cheaper to produce. Whereas if external diseconomies are encountered the long-run average cost curve will move up. Improved technology would lower the long-run average cost curve.

10 Growth of firms

Motives and methods

The motives which lead to growth in the size of the business unit are many and complex, but there are at least three which can be clearly distinguished: the desire to achieve economies of scale; the monopoly motive, or the desire to obtain a greater share of the market and hence greater market power; the wish to achieve greater security by extending the range of products and markets.

There are two methods by which such growth may be achieved. The first of these is by *internal growth* where the firm increases its size by making more of its existing product or by extending the range of its products. It grows within the framework of its existing management and control structure. Hoover is an example of a company which grew to a very large size on the basis of its original product (vacuum cleaners) and by using the same kind of technology to extend its range of products.

The second and much more common method nowadays is by *amalgamation, merger,* or *takeover*. A firm may amalgamate with one or more existing firms to form an entirely new enterprise, or a firm may take over another firm, the firm taken over losing its identity completely. Sometimes the amalgamation is carried out by forming an entirely new company for the sole purpose of acquiring the assets of a number of separate companies. Such a company is known as a *holding company*. The companies acquired in this way may retain their original identities but their trading policies are directed by the holding company. Hanson Trust controls companies producing bricks, typewriters, tobacco, batteries, engineering products and frozen food.

Growth by merger or amalgamation is usually referred to as integration which, in turn, may be vertical, horizontal, or conglomerate, although this is by no means a watertight classification.

Vertical integration

When a merger takes place between firms engaged in different stages of the productive process we speak of vertical integration. It is 'vertical' in the sense that the combination is a movement up or down the productive process which runs from extraction to distribution. Thus, a large manufacturer of tea may take over tea plantations.

Backward integration

When the movement is towards the source of supplies we speak of vertical integration backwards. The example quoted above is of this type.

It is often carried out so that a firm may exercise a much greater control over the quantity and quality of its supplies and be in a position of greater security with regard to their delivery. It may also have the aim of restricting the availability of such supplies to a competitor. An additional motive might be the absorption of the intermediate profit margins.

Forward integration

Where the movement is towards the market outlets the process is described as vertical integration forwards. The large oil companies now control most of the petrol stations.

Important motives for this type of combination are the desire to secure an adequate number of market outlets and the wish to raise the standard of those outlets. Since manufacturers carry the main burden of advertising costs it is only natural that they should be concerned that their products reach the public in a form and in an environment which lives up to the image created by their advertising. Firms may be forced to take over some market outlets when a major competitor has already made a move in this direction – they must react or face the prospect of being squeezed out of the market.

Other motives behind vertical integration

Quite apart from providing greater security and control of supplies or markets, vertical integration may give rise to economies in production. This is most noticeable when a series of production processes are brought together in one large plant. In iron and steel making, for example, the hot pig iron from blast furnaces can be converted into steel with minimum loss of heat and by-product gases from the coke ovens can be used to heat furnaces in the finishing department. Some industries have remained integrated from an early stage in their development because it was the only way in which balanced growth at the different stages of production process could have been achieved. The companies which found crude oil were obliged to build the necessary oil refineries and to develop the means of transporting oil from oilfields to distant markets.

Vertical integration is sometimes adopted as a means of accelerating the development of new discoveries. The production and adoption of a new fibre or new plastic may be speeded up if the producer of the new material takes over facilities for fabricating it into marketable products.

Problems

There are some possible disadvantages. A manufacturer moving back-wards to acquire the source of his raw materials may find himself with a rapidly depreciating asset if technology develops a superior substitute material. A rubber plantation may quickly lose its value if synthetic rubber proves a superior product in the manufacture of tyres. During a world recession raw material prices fall very sharply. The independent manufacturer will obtain very low-priced supplies – the burden of losses being borne by the supplier. The integrated firm, however, cannot avoid the losses due to the slump in raw material prices.

The optimum size of plants at different stages of production may be very different. The integration of firms with very different capacities will create the problem of finding enough 'outside work' to keep the plant with the larger capacity fully operational.

Horizontal integration

When firms engaged in producing the same kind of good or service are brought under unified control the procedure is described as horizontal integration. If several building societies or television companies amalgamate it would be a union of firms all engaged in *the same stage of production* and hence, in this sense, horizontal. Some of our largest companies have emerged as a result of a long process of horizontal integration. General Electric (electrical engineering), Burtons (retailing) and Smith Kline Beecham (pharmaceutical products) are good examples.

Motives behind horizontal integration

Market domination is undoubtedly one of the motives leading to horizontal integration. When a number of firms producing the same or similar products form a single combine there is clearly a reduction in competition and the unified group will be able to exert more market power by virtue of the fact that a much greater proportion of the total market supply is now under its control.

Firms may be led to integrate horizontally by a desire to carry out some rationalisation of the industry's capacity, particularly when demand is falling. If there are, say, three firms making similar commodities and each firm is only working at two-thirds capacity, a merger will enable the new organisation to close down the least efficient plant and work the two remaining at full capacity.

Horizontal integration also enables the joint capacity of the amalgamated firms to be operated with a greater degree of specialisation. Suppose there are three independent firms each making a vacuum cleaner, a washing machine, and an electric heater. A merger, in this case, would enable the group to concentrate the production of each product in one factory with the obvious gains from larger-scale production.

In many cases the horizontal combination is carried out with a view to obtaining economies of scale. The larger unit, as indicated above, will be able to achieve greater specialisation; it will also be in a position to take advantage of many of the other economies described earlier. By increasing the range of products (or models) horizontal integration provides greater security in the form of risk-bearing economies. Ford's wide range of vehicles provides it with a more stable pattern of demand than would be the case if it were highly dependent upon the demand for one type of vehicle.

Problems

The major criticism of the horizontal linking of firms is based upon the obvious tendency towards monopoly as the number of firms in an industry is reduced. This is one of the reasons why recent legislation in the UK has set up machinery for 'vetting' proposed mergers. (see Chapter 27.)

There is also the possibility of management diseconomies as the size of the firm increases. Integration may present particularly difficult management problems where a number of firms with different markets or using different technologies are brought together, or where firms are geographically dispersed. Problems also arise where it becomes necessary to bring together managers from firms with different histories, traditions and outlooks to form one management team.

Conglomerates

Conglomerates have been defined as those mergers or amalgamations which are neither substantially vertical nor substantially horizontal. They are generally understood to be those combinations of firms which produce goods or services that are not directly related to one another. For example, a firm producing cigarettes may take over a firm producing potato crisps, or a firm producing fertilisers may merge with a manufacturer of paint. BAT Industries has a range of interests including tobacco production and retailing.

Motives behind conglomerate integration

The major aim of the conglomerate is clearly to obtain a diversification of output so as to reduce the risks of trading. Conglomerate mergers may also arise where a firm believes that there is little scope for any further growth in the markets for its existing products. It may then satisfy a desire for further growth by taking over, or merging with, a firm in a different industry.

Although the output of a large conglomerate may appear to comprise a range of very different products, the diversification of output is rarely completely random. We often find that the products are linked by the use of common raw materials, a common technology, or common markets.

Nevertheless there are several conglomerates where the only common links seem to be those of managerial and financial services. The justification for such mergers appears to lie in the promised injection of better management techniques and a more efficient use of the available resources. A conglomerate which consists of an amalgam of several sub-optimum firms operating in many different industries may not achieve any worthwhile economies of scale.

Multinational companies

A multinational company is a company which produces goods and/or services outside its home country. UK multinational companies include British Petroleum, BAT industries, ICI, British Telecom, British gas and British Aerospace. Foreign multinational companies with branches in the UK include ESSO, Ford, Nestlé, IBM, Mitsubishi and Nissan.

Most multinational enterprises (often abbreviated to MNEs) come from advanced countries, particularly the USA. They are very significant with the combined output of the largest two hundred multinational companies being equivalent to approximately one third of the output of the world. Indeed the output of General Motors exceeds the output of many countries, including Denmark, Norway and Poland.

Advantages of operating abroad

Producing and selling in a major market abroad will reduce a company's transport costs, will enable it to keep in close contact with the market and may enable it to overcome any resistance to buying products made outside the host country. Companies also set up abroad to avoid import restrictions, take advantage of regional assistance or to obtain new materials. In some cases MNEs set up in countries where wages are lower and health and safety and other employment legislation is more lax than in the home country.

In the early 1990s a number of overseas companies, particularly US and Japanese companies, set up subsidiary companies in the UK. These companies have been attracted by gaining entry into the European Union. The UK also has the specific advantages for MNEs of having opted out of the Social Chapter of The Maastricht Treaty (and hence not having the restrictions on working hours which other members have), of providing government assistance if the firms set up in development areas and of speaking English (a language learned by many Japanese).

The effects of MNEs on their host countries

Multinational enterprises can bring a number of benefits to their host countries. They may provide employment although some of the top management jobs may be given to people from the MNEs' countries. They may bring in new methods of technology and a new approach to management. The production and management techniques in Japanese companies in the UK have been copied by a number of UK firms. They also contribute to growth and exports. For example, in 1992 Nissan exported 90 per cent of its Sunderland output. They are likely to assist regional policy since they are often more willing to set up in development areas than host firms. In 1994 Samsung, the leading Korean Conglomerate, announced its decision to open a factory near Stockton. It will receive £58 million in government grants.

Consumers in the host countries may benefit from the increased competition that MNEs bring in the form of more choice, higher quality and lower prices. However, not all the effects of MNEs are beneficial. They may eliminate domestic producers so that consumers will not receive the advantages of increased competition. They may exhaust natural resources at a rapid rate and may not follow as high health and safety standards as in their own home countries. They may engage in transfer pricing; this is essentially shifting profit from high-tax countries to low-tax countries, and this will cause high-tax countries to lose revenues. As we have seen MNEs may be larger producers than their host countries. Many also have the potential to shift production around the world. This gives them considerable bargaining power in wage negotiations and in discussions with governments. They may even use the threat of closing down plants in order to win concessions on health and safety standards.

The survival of small firms

The preceding discussion would seem to indicate that there are substantial net advantages to be obtained from increasing the size of the business unit. There is, indeed, evidence to show that the number of large firms is increasing and that these are getting larger. Nevertheless, the fact remains that about one-half of the manufacturing output of the Western world issues from factories employing fewer than 500 workers and about 80 per cent of UK factories employ between 1 and 50 workers.

There are hundreds of thousands of successful small firms in the UK (and in other developed countries) operating in all kinds of industries. In view of the many advantages of large-scale operation already discussed it is pertinent to ask why these small firms continue to survive and why industry and commerce is not dominated by a few giants.

Market limitations on mass production

The ability to profit from large-scale production is limited by the extent of the market. Where the market is small it is not possible to obtain significant economies of scale, most of which are dependent upon the existence of a large market for a standardised product. The size of the market may be restricted by a number of factors.

A demand for variety

Some industries are faced with the problem that consumers demand a wide variety of styles, patterns, and designs. The market for any one style or model may be very small indeed. Obvious examples are provided by the clothing, millinery, furniture, footwear, and jewellery trades. Firms in industries catering for such variety are confronted with the problem of 'short runs' and 'one-off' types of production – they cannot set up their capital and labour for specialised production. Such firms are invariably quite small.

Geographical limitations

If the commodity has great bulk in relation to value, transport costs will be high relative to production costs. In such cases the market for the product is likely to be local rather than national. Bread, bricks, and coal may be cited as examples of commodities where markets have been confined to fairly small regions, although improvements in transport have tended to weaken this particular restriction on the size of the firm. Transport costs, however, still provide the village or suburban shop with some protection against the out-of-town superstore.

Personal services

Industries which provide services rather than commodities are usually characterised by a large number of small firms. Where the element of personal attention required by the purchaser is an important part of the service, then it is not possible to introduce standardisation and mass-production methods. Thus, we find small firms in professions such as law, accountancy, architecture, and medicine where personal attention to individual problems is required. For similar reasons most firms specialising in repair work are relatively small. Hairdressing, the beauty parlour, and bespoke tailoring provide other examples of the demand for personal attention seriously limiting the size of the firm.

It is this same demand for personal service which accounts for the very large number of small firms in the retail trade although, in recent years, there have been major changes in the structure of this sector of the economy. New techniques in packaging, in food preparation, in the use of computers for stock control, and in shopping habits (e.g. the use of the motor car), have enabled the larger store to achieve great economies of scale. The supermarket and the discount store have successfully demon-strated that the public, for many of their requirements, prefer the lower-priced, standardised article presented on a 'serve-yourself' basis.

Luxury items

The market may be limited by income and wealth. Expensive sports cars, large limousines, luxury yachts, high-quality jewellery and fur coats are examples of goods produced by small firms for very restricted prestige markets.

Disintegration

We have already referred to the tendency for mass production industries to disintegrate into a large number of specialist firms each supplying some standardised part to a large assembly plant. This has been a structural change which has operated very much to the benefit of the small firm. It is possible for the industry's total requirements of some particular component to be supplied by one relatively small firm.

Joint ventures

Cooperation between smaller firms may lead to the setting up of jointly owned enterprises which enable them to enjoy many of the economies of scale obtained by larger firms. The smaller grocery shops have been successful in establishing links with wholesale groups (e.g. Spar) for the marketing of standardised and branded goods on a large scale. Farmers have, for a long time, operated similar schemes (farmers' cooperatives) in order to obtain the benefits of bulk buying in feedstuffs, seeds, fertilisers, and so on. The collective ownership of large units of capital (e.g. combine harvesters) makes such resources available to small farmers on an economic basis. Small manufacturing firms in some industries (e.g. footwear and pottery) operate jointly owned research establishments.

Entrepreneurs

Part of the explanation for the prevalence of small firms lies in the fact that there seems to be no shortage of would-be entrepreneurs – there is always a large number of people eager to start their own business. Small firms are born in large numbers ever day. Some will survive and grow, others will die, but the ranks will be quickly filled by new entrants.

Many firms remain small because of the reluctance of the proprietor to accept the increased risks associated with growth – he or she may prefer a reasonable income and a 'quiet life'.

Finance

Some firms remain small because they encounter difficulties in raising, on reasonable terms, the necessary finance for further expansion. Whereas large and medium-sized firms have a wide variety of sources of external finance available to them, internally generated funds and bank overdrafts tend to be the principal sources of finance for small firms. For some time there has been a widely held view that smaller firms are at a disadvantage compared with larger firms when seeking finance from external sources. These disadvantages have been identified as

- some facilities are available only to the larger firm, for example, the new issue market (some financial institutions do not deal with small loans);
- small firms have to pay more for their money than large firms due to the greater element of risk and the fact that administrative costs of small loans are proportionately greater than those for large loans;
- the unwillingness of some family-owned firms to share control of the business.

Management problems

Management problems may be a barrier to growth. Competent management is fairly easily obtained for a small-scale operation, but the ability to manage larger enterprises is probably a rather scarce commodity. The small firm is a more flexible unit than the larger firm; it is able to adjust quite quickly to changes in demand especially in those industries where fashions and tastes are subject to frequent changes.

11 UK industry – size and structure

Definitions

An industry

It is not easy to define an industry because economic activities can be grouped in a variety of ways. They may be classified according to the nature of the markets they serve, and this is how most people would define an industry, i.e., a group of firms making the same or very similar products. But economic units may also be grouped according to the process carried out, or on the basis of the kinds of factors of production they use, or the kind of technology they use.

The most common definition of an industry is that used in official statistics which group firms into industries according to the physical and technical properties of their principal products. This classification is often self-evident as in the cases of footwear, furniture, or pottery where the nature of the product clearly defines the industry. Sometimes it is not so easy – is the extraction of chemicals from petroleum a part of the oil industry or the chemical industry?

It is often necessary to use the nature of the process as the distinguishing feature. It would be misleading, for example, to define the hosiery industry as comprising those firms which make stockings and socks since this industry produces a very wide range of garments. It is, in fact, defined as the collection of firms in which knitting is the principal activity.

Statistics of industrial production must be used with some caution because there are so many multi-product firms and the whole of such a firm's output might, under certain circumstances, be classified under the industry of its major product.

An enterprise

An enterprise is defined as the unit of ownership and control. In the great majority of cases it corresponds to what most people understand by *the firm*, but where there is a parent company with several subsidiary firms the whole group is classified as an enterprise. When we use the term 'firm' in this section it will have the same meaning as 'enterprise'.

A plant

A plant is a workplace, for instance a factory, farm, or shop. A firm (enterprise), of course may own several plants.

Size

Further problems of definition concern the methods used to measure the size of an industry, a firm, or a factory. Again there is no 'right' method. Size may be assessed on the basis of the capital employed, the value of output, or on the number of employees. The use of different methods will often produce different answers to questions about size. An industry which is being increasingly mechanised may be employing less labour but increasing its output. This is true of agriculture.

The number of employees is probably the most frequently used criterion, but it must be used with care. The chemical industry, for example, employs about 6 per cent of the manufacturing labour force, but it uses about 12 per cent of the total fixed capital in manufacturing industry.

The size of plants

Most plants are very small. This might appear to indicate that economies of scale are either not important or are not being exploited. But the greater part of the total output is being produced by larger firms and it is likely that these firms are exploiting most of the potential of economies of scale. There have been several investigations into the extent of plant-level scale economies in different industries. These studies have attempted to estimate 'the minimum efficient plant size' (MEPS) for different industries. The MEPS may be defined as the point on the long-run cost curve at which average costs cease to fall. The MEPS is relatively large for such products as sugar, ethylene, cigarettes, detergents, TV tubes, motor cars, and domestic electrical appliances. These studies seem to indicate that the size structure of plants in British industry is such that, for the most part, they are able to take advantage of such scale economies as are available. Nevertheless it is unlikely in industries subject to rapid technical progress that many existing plants will be of optimum size.

Over the longer period there has been a steady trend towards larger establishments.

The size of firms

The UK had approximately 3 million businesses of all sizes in 1991, but around 95 per cent employed fewer than 20 people and these accounted for approximately 34 per cent of non-government employment. In contrast, less than one-tenth of 1 per cent of all firms employed more than 500 people. However, large firms account for not only a high proportion of total employment but also a high proportion of total output.

Industrial concentration

Recent trends towards larger and larger business units have led to an active debate on the possible dangers of the control of economic activity in certain industries passing into fewer and fewer hands. Some of these dangers are discussed later in the chapter on Monopoly, but it should be clear that when a firm becomes so large that it controls a preponderant share of the market, it may be tempted to use its market power to obtain excessive profits.

Definition and measurement

Economists have attempted to ascertain to what extent markets are becoming increasingly dominated by fewer and bigger firms. They have, therefore, devised a means of measuring the degree of *concentration* in an industry, that is, the extent to which an industry is dominated in terms of sales, employment or capital employed by the largest firms in the industry. The most commonly used concentration ratios measure the dominance of the three, five, or seven largest firms. For example, if we are using employment as the measuring rod and the number employed by the three largest firms in the industry is 1 million, while the total employment in the industry is 4 million, the *three-firm employment concentration ratio* is 25 per cent.

Most recent studies of UK industry have tended to use the market share criterion and the most generally used measure is the *five-firm sales concentration ratio*. This gives the percentage share of the total sales of any product (or group of products) accounted for by the five largest firms.

Concentration ratios are important indicators of market situations, but they can be misleading. The relative sizes of the top five firms may make a considerable difference to the degree of competition. A 75 per cent ratio may mean that the top five firms each supply 15 per cent of the total market or it may mean that one firm supplies 55 per cent and the other four each supply 5 per cent.

One must also take account of the number of firms in the industry and their average size. The five largest firms for example might account for 60 per cent of the market; the remaining 40 per cent may be shared by 50 firms or by only five firms. Concentration ratios unless supported by other data, do not clearly reveal the extent to which the largest firms exercise economic power. Another fact to be borne in mind is that some of these ratios only apply to domestic output. A high concentration ratio would not imply excessive market power if there is strong competition from imported goods.

Aggregate concentration

Whilst market concentration is the degree to which the markets for particular groups of products are dominated by a few large firms, aggregate concentration measures the percentage of manufacturing or total output accounted for by the larger firms. This aggregate measure is important when considering the extent to which the control of industry generally is concentrated. Aggregate concentration in the UK is usually measured by the share of total output accounted for by the 100 largest firms; this has increased substantially during the present century.

Causes of the increase in industrial concentration

It is noteworthy that little of the increase in concentration in manufacturing has been due to increases in the size of the plant. The main explanation of increasing concentration lies in the increase in the average number of plants owned by the larger firms. This indicates that technical economies of scale justify only a relatively small part of the growth in concentration. Much of the increase in the extent of concentration has been brought about by mergers and the main motives for this activity appear to have been the achievement of financial, marketing and administrative economies, the desire to achieve a diversified output; the elimination of excess capacity and the rationalisation of production; the acquisition of larger resources to finance research and development in capital-intensive industries where the costs of such development are relatively large (e.g. motor cars, aircraft, chemicals).

Consequences of the increase in industrial concentration

Increased concentration can yield benefits in the form of economies of scale, improved efficiency and a faster rate of technical progress. It can also yield disadvantages in the form of reduced competition; this aspect of market concentration is discussed in the chapter on Monopoly.

In recent years governments in the UK have paid increasing attention to the role of small businesses in the economy and, to some extent, this has been due to the increasing attention being paid to the disadvantages of the growing concentration in industry. In particular, measures have been taken (i) to make it easier for small firms to acquire finance either to start up in business or to expand, (ii) to reduce the overall weight of taxation on small businesses, and (iii) to reduce the administrative burdens on small firms. The small firm is seen to have certain advantages in the fields of *job creation*. Small firms tend to be labour-intensive and net job-creators.

Small firms were the main contributors to employment growth in the 1980s, with 1 million additional jobs created by small business between 1985 and 1989. A study of American industry showed that small firms produce more innovations per dollar spent on research than large firms. Small firms tend to have better labour relations than large firms and lose fewer days in strikes. The more independent firms there are in an industry, the greater the competition. Against these points, however, have to be set the massive technical economies of scale attainable by modern capital-intensive industries.

Types of business organisation

We have discussed some of the factors which affect the size of the firm as a unit of production. We now briefly look at the ways in which firms are organised and financed. The different types of business organisation to be found in the UK and most other countries may be classified under five headings: the sole proprietor, the partnership, the joint stock company, the cooperative society, and the public corporation.

The sole proprietor

This is the simplest and oldest form of business enterprise and is often referred to as the one-person business. A single person provides the capital, takes the decisions, and assumes the risks. He or she is solely responsible for the success or failure of the business and has, therefore, the sole rights to such profits as may be made, or, alternatively, bears the sole responsibility for such losses as may accrue. The one-person business is still far more numerous than any other type of business organisation, but in terms of total employment, value of capital employed, or value of total output, it is relatively unimportant compared with the joint stock company.

The strength of this type of firm lies in the direct personal interest of the proprietor in the efficiency of his enterprise. Ownership and control are vested in one person who enjoys all the fruits of success and hence has a great incentive to run the firm efficiently. Since the proprietor is the sole decision-taker and has no need to consult colleagues when changes of policy are required we should expect this type of organisation to be extremely flexible and capable of quick and easy adjustment to changes in market conditions.

The great disadvantage of the sole proprietor form of enterprise lies in the fact that the owner is personally liable for the debts incurred by his firm and this liability is unlimited. All his personal possessions are at risk and may be seized to meet creditors' demands in the event of the business becoming insolvent. Another disadvantage of this type of firm is the strict limitation on its ability to acquire capital for expansion. Finance is restricted to the amounts which the entrepreneur is able to provide from his own resources and whatever sums he can borrow on his own security.

We find the one-person business prevalent in farming, retailing, building, repair and maintenance work, and personal services such as hairdressing.

The partnership

Partnerships are voluntary combinations of from 2 to 20 persons[1] formed for the purpose of carrying on business with a view to profit. This type of

NOTE 1. Unlimited membership is allowed in the case of certain professional partnerships (e.g. solicitors, accountants).

organisation represents a logical development from the one-person business since the obvious method by which such as firm may acquire further capital is to form a partnership. The motive, however, may not be financial and partnerships are often formed in order to bring new ability and enterprise into the business.

The partners usually share in the task of running the business, but a partner need not play an active role. A person who joins a partnership, supplying capital and sharing in the profits, but taking no part in the management is known as a dormant or sleeping partner. Partnerships are a common form of business organisation in such professions as law, accountancy, surveying, and medicine.

The advantages of this type of firm are similar to those of the one-person business. It is a flexible organisation that allows a greater degree of specialisation than the one-person business. Partners usually specialise in one or more aspects of the business; one may be responsible for buying, one for selling, one for production, and so on. Since it has greater access to capital, it can achieve greater size than the sole proprietor.

The great disadvantage, like that of the one-person business, is the fact that the liability of the partners is unlimited and they are all fully liable for the acts of the other partners. There are, however, some limited partnerships which have to be registered with the Registrar of Companies. In such firms some partners (e.g. dormant partners) may have their liability limited to some specified sum, but at least one of the partners must have unlimited liability.

The survival of a partnership depends upon the continued harmonious relationship between a number of people in situations which often give much cause for disagreement. Thus, where trading risks are very great, the partnership is not a very stable type of organisation.

The joint stock company

The most important form of business organisation in the UK is the joint stock company. Basically, it consists of an association of people who contribute towards a joint stock of capital for the purpose of carrying on business with a view to profit. A company may be defined as a legal person created to engage in business, capable of owning productive assets, of entering into contracts, and of employing labour in the same way as an individual.

Public and private companies

There are two kinds of joint stock company, the private company and the public company. The public companies are much larger units and account for about two-thirds of all the capital employed by companies.

In general, private companies are small firms, often consisting of the members of one family. Both public and private companies must have at least two members. A public company must have a minimum allotted share capital of £50 000 of which at least one-quarter has been paid up. A private company must include the word 'limited' in its name while a public company must have the words 'public limited company' at the end of its name although this can be abbreviated to *plc*.

The basic distinction between a private and a public company is that a public company can offer its shares and debentures for sale to the general public. In the case of a private company it would be a criminal offence to ask the public to subscribe to its share. All companies must file annually, with the Registrar of Companies, details of their turnover, profits, assets, liabilities and other relevant financial information about their structures and activities.

Important features of the joint stock company

The first characteristic is the principle of *limited liability*. The company itself is fully liable for its debts in the same way as any other person, but the liability of the shareholders is limited to the amount they have agreed to subscribe to the capital of the company. When they have fully paid for their shares they cannot be called upon to meet any debts the company may incur. The introduction of the principle of limited liability was essential if people were to be persuaded to provide capital on the scale needed by modern industry. In the absence of limited liability the contribution of funds to business enterprise becomes an extremely risky undertaking – a very modest 'investment' would put all one's personal resources at risk.

A second feature of the joint stock principle is the prospect of *continuity* which it offers. Sole proprietorships and partnerships cannot continue in existence independently of the persons who own them. The death or bankruptcy of a sole proprietor or partner, or a mere unwillingness to continue, will bring an unincorporated business to an end. Modern industrial processes require resources to be committed for long periods of time and unless there is a real prospect of the continuing existence of the organisation such long-term investment will not be undertaken. A joint stock company offers just such a prospect, for its existence is independent of the lives and fortunes of its shareholders. If a shareholder dies his shares become the property of his heirs; if he does not like the way the company is being run he can sell his shares – the company is in no way affected.

Another very important feature of the joint stock company is the *transferability of shares*. In order to perform its function a company must have permanent use of its capital, but very few, if any, investors are prepared to lend money on a permanent basis. Life is uncertain and no one is prepared to put himself in a position where, in a possible emergency, he could not convert his wealth into cash. This dilemma is solved by making shares transferable. The company has the use of the capital subscribed by the original shareholders who, if they wish, may sell their shares at any time on the open market. The market value of shares changes from day to day so that although a shareholder may convert his holdings into cash, he cannot be certain of the amount he will receive for them.

Finally, the joint stock principle enables those who cannot, or do not want to take an active part in management to contribute towards economic activity by providing capital. There are people that have technical and commercial expertise but do not possess the necessary resources to make effective use of their skills. The joint stock principle makes it possible for the resources owned by one group to be utilised by another group. This has raised interesting problems, regarding the *divorce between ownership and management* which is a feature of modern capitalism.

Ownership and control

The owners of a joint stock company are clearly the shareholders who provide the money for the business, but the growth in the size of many public companies has meant that the shareholders are far too numerous and dispersed to be able to exercise the functions of management. Management is in the hands of directors who are elected by the shareholders. Shareholder control, therefore, often amounts to no more than the ability to vote against the recommendations of the directors at the annual general meeting and ultimately if necessary, to replace the directors.

But shareholders in the large companies are very numerous and may be widely dispersed throughout the country (many shares may be held overseas). Generally speaking only a very small percentage bother to attend the general meetings. Shareholders usually lack the knowledge and expertise to exercise effective control over the directors, and unless things are going badly wrong the directors will be fairly certain to have their policies endorsed.

Where the owners are not completely in control of the policy of the company a divergence of interests may arise. Economic theory has tended to assume that the maximisation of profits is the principal aim to private enterprise. Where, however, the executive directors (those who actually run the business) have only very limited shareholdings (and this is often the case) they may pursue objectives other than profit maximisation. As long as some satisfactory rate of return for the ordinary shareholders is achieved, directors may attempt to maximise sales rather than aim for even higher rates of return on capital employed. The status and salaries of executives may be more closely related to the size of the firm than the rate of return on the capital employed.

One feature of capitalism which has an important bearing on the question of ownership has been the growth in *institutional investment*. The major providers of funds for the larger companies are institutions such as insurance companies, pension funds, investment trusts, unit trusts, and other types of trust funds. Such institutions often control a significant proportion of the voting shares in the large companies and they could, if they wished, exercise a real influence on the policy decisions of these companies. Normally, however, providing the company is reasonably profitable, the institutions prefer not to interfere in its management. Institutional investment means that share ownership is more widely dispersed than would appear from the lists of shareholders. The shares held by insurance companies and pension funds, for example, are purchased, indirectly, by the many thousands of contributors to such funds.

Cooperatives

Cooperative organisations are owned by people with a common objective who share the risks and the profits. There are two main types. The less known in the UK is the producer, or worker cooperative. This is owned by the people who work in the firm. Whilst this type of organisation is quite common in some European countries, particularly Spain, it is not very common in the UK.

Better known in the UK is the second type which is the consumer or retail cooperative. Cooperative enterprise in the retail trade began in Rochdale in 1844, when a group of low-paid weavers opened their own very small retail shop. From these humble beginnings the movement has grown to become one of the largest retail organisations in the UK. A consumer cooperative is owned by the customers who purchase shares. The profits go to the owners in the form of a fixed dividend on shares and to the customers in the form of stamps and/or lower prices.

The public corporation

A public corporation, or nationalised industry, has a separate legal identity like a company but there are no private shareholders. The government owns the capital and appoints the members of the controlling Board who have functions very similar to directors except that they are answerable to the government and not to shareholders. In general, the policy to be pursued by a public corporation is determined by the government and a Minister of the Crown is usually given the responsibility for seeing that the corporation is acting within the broad policy requirements laid down by Parliament.

In contrasting the joint stock company and the public corporation the following features should be noted.

- *Control*. The joint stock company is controlled by a board of directors elected by the shareholders, whereas the public corporation is controlled by a board appointed by the state.
- *Ownership*. A joint stock company is owned by the shareholders, but there are no shareholders in the public corporation which is owned by the state.

- *Finance*. A joint stock company raises its capital by the issue of shares to the general public, but at the present time, the public corporations obtain most of their capital requirements direct from the Exchequer.
- *Motives*. While the joint stock company exists primarily for the purpose of making profits, the aim of the public corporation is to act in the public interest and to cover its costs.

The policy of privatisation, conducted in the 1980s and 1990s has considerably reduced the number of nationalised industries (see Chapter 28).

12 The finance of industry

In this chapter we discuss the ways in which firms raise the money required to finance their operations. The sources of funds for industry may be *external* or *internal*, that is, firms may borrow from different types of lender, or they may generate funds for investment purposes by allocating some of their profits for use within the firm.

It is also useful to distinguish between funds required for working or circulating capital, and funds required for longer-term investment in fixed assets. Some institutions tend to specialise in the provision of short-term loans for working capital while others provide funds on a long-term basis.

Internal finance

By far the most important sources of company finance are internal. More than 60 per cent of capital finance is obtained from retained profits. These are profits which are kept back to invest in the business rather than distributed to shareholders in the form of dividends. The significance of retained profits is not surprising. Firms are likely to want to buy new equipment and to expand when prospects are good and profit levels are high.

External finance

Firms can obtain funds from outside by issuing new shares, by borrowing, by obtaining grants or by using other forms of finance.

Shares

Shareholders are owners of companies and receive a share of profits called dividends. The principal type of share is known as an ordinary share.

The dividend on ordinary shares (equities) is not fixed and depends entirely on the profitability of the company and the policy of the directors with regard to the amount of profit to be retained in the company. The dividend may be very high or it may be zero. The ordinary shareholder is entitled to the residue of profits after all other claims have been met. Ordinary shares, therefore, are the riskiest type of investment and dividends on them may fluctuate from year to year. Since they bear the major risks, ordinary shareholders have the greatest say in the management and control of the enterprise, and most ordinary shares carry voting rights.

Borrowing

Firms can borrow in a number of different ways and from a number of different sources.

Debentures

Debentures are loans and the purchasers of debentures are creditors of the company and not owners. A debenture is a kind of IOU. The rate of interest on debentures is fixed and debenture holders rank before all classes of shares for payments out of profits. The holders of these securities are normally given special rights which add to the security of their loans. The company may give a pledge that certain of its assets will be attached to the debentures so that, in the event of default by the company, the debenture holders may seize and sell these assets to secure repayment of their loans. Debenture holders also have the right to sell their debentures to third parties.

Bank loans and overdrafts

By tradition British banks are providers of relatively short-term loans. For most firms they are the main source of short-term external finance. A typical bank loan is often described as a 'self-liquidating' loan, because it finances the purchase of raw materials which are transformed into saleable products in a matter of weeks or months. In other words, the means of repaying the loan is generated in a fairly short period of time. Apart from the provision of this type of working capital, banks also provide 'bridging' finance. Although over the long period a firm's income may exceed its expenditure this is not likely to be always the case over relatively short periods of time; income and outgoings do not balance week by week. Temporary deficits will arise during periods when expenditures exceed receipts and these are usually covered by 'bridging' loans from the banks. Medium- and long-term loans are also given for longer-term projects although UK banks have been criticised for not lending enough to UK industry.

Whilst bank loans are usually for a specific purpose, bank overdrafts are used, in the main, to meet short-term unexpected cash problems.

Other ways of financing investment

Leasing. Instead of using a medium-term loan to buy new assets, a firm may lease them. Under a leasing arrangement, the leasing company will purchase the plant, equipment or vehicles to the firm's requirements and then lease them to the firm for an agreed period at an agreed rental. The leasing company sometimes provides servicing and maintenance. The assets being leased remain the property of the leasing company.

Trade credit. Trade credit is an important source of finance for the smaller firm. When a company supplies goods on credit terms which allow the purchaser 3 or 6 months in which to make payment, it is, in effect, providing the buyer with a short-term loan. Trade credit, like leasing and hire purchase is an important source of working capital.

Hire purchase.   Hire purchase in industry and commerce works in much the same way as in the retail trade. After making an initial down-payment, and paying regular fixed amounts over an agreed period (covering interest and the balance of the capital cost), a business acquires ownership of the goods. When a firm buys goods on hire purchase it is, in effect, obtaining a loan from the finance company which supplies the funds to support the hire purchase scheme.

Factoring.   This involves a company selling its debts, usually to a finance company. This enables it to receive immediate payment less a charge for the service. It also saves the company time in vetting customers and passes the risk of bad debts on to the finance company. The service is used mainly by small and medium companies.

Loan capital and risk capital

Capital for industrial and commercial enterprises may be classified as either *loan capital* or *risk capital*. Loan capital consists of those funds advanced (by creditors) at fixed or variable rates of interest which may or may not be secured by some kind of mortgage on the assets of the company.

The interest payments on loan capital are regarded as part of the fixed costs of the business and, hence, may be deducted from profits before any assessment is made for tax purposes. Risk capital is that part of the capital stock which is raised by the sale of shares. The interest and dividends payable on these shares do not rank as costs of production for taxation purposes and they must be paid out of profits after taxation demands have been met. On the other hand, the interest charges on loan capital must be paid each year whereas dividends and interest on risk capital need not be paid in those years when the company has not prospered. Companies which operate in industries where the market for the product is subject to continuous fluctuation would not take the risk of having a high proportion of loan capital. Loan capital is more appropriate to firms operating in stable markets and which have a large part of their assets in the form of land and buildings which are good subjects for mortgages (e.g. brewery companies). Another feature of loan capital is that borrowing money in this form does not affect the pattern of ownership of the business. An issue of ordinary shares, of course, will cause the ownership of the business to be more widely dispersed.

Gearing

The ratio of loan capital to risk capital is of some significance since it has considerable influence on the variability of the returns from investment.

The ratio of a company's ordinary share capital to that part of the capital which carries a fixed rate of interest (preference shares and debentures) is known as *the gearing* of the capital structure. The greater the proportion of ordinary to other capital, the lower the gearing of the capital structure. Thus, if profits are rising, the dividends on the ordinary shares will rise very much faster in those companies with high gearing than in those with low gearing. The opposite will apply when profits are falling. If the profits are unchanged but the proportions between the ordinary shares and the fixed-interest securities are varied it will be found that the dividends on ordinary shares are much more variable when the gearing is greater.

Government and international assistance

State aid to industry takes several forms and has a variety of objectives.

A large part of it, in the form of grants, loans and the direct provision of factories, is directed towards the task of changing the location of industry. This is an important component of the government's regional policy and is described in Chapter 13.

The UK government is less involved in promoting industrial investment than most other European countries. In the 1970s UK governments gave financial assistance to large-scale prestigious projects such as Concorde and to help firms in serious finance difficulty, including British Leyland, now known as Rover. Since the 1980s there has been a change. The government has cut state funding and now concentrates selective support on promoting technology, research and development, and assisting small firms.

Most government spending on research and development involves schemes linking government departments and the private sector. Small firms, in addition to being exempt from paying VAT and paying lower corporation tax, can get a variety of state grants for, for example, training staff and developing new technologies. The Enterprise Investment Scheme helps small firms find investment funds and the Government has underwritten a number of loans (i.e. acted as a guarantor) made to small firms by commercial banks. The Enterprise Allowance Scheme helps the establishment of new firms by giving a weekly allowance and some training to the unemployed in the first year of running a new business. Financial assistance is also given to UK firms by the European Union. Loans and grants are provided by a variety of organisations, the European Regional Development Fund, The European Investment Bank, The European Social Fund, The European Agricultural Fund, and the European Coal and Steel Community.

The Stock Exchange

As we have seen, some firms can raise investment finance by issuing shares. People and institutions are encouraged to buy these shares in the knowledge that there is a well-established market where they can sell these shares on. This is the Stock Exchange. It is a market in existing securities, that is, shares and debentures issued by companies, and securities issued by the government.

The Stock Exchange and the capital market

In order to finance long-term projects, both limited companies and the government need to borrow money for long periods of time. Company shares represent permanent loans – there is no right to repayment. Many government securities and company debentures are not redeemable for many years after the date of issue. The largest single market in the Stock Exchange is the gilt-edged market. Gilt-edged securities are issued by the government and carry a fixed rate of interest.

In the absence of some kind of stock exchange, securities such as these would be very illiquid assets. It would be difficult to find buyers for them. The existence of a stock exchange solves this problem because it provides a market where holders of shares and long-term securities can always sell them. This means that companies and the government can have the use of funds for long periods, but the providers of these funds can, at any time, convert their securities back into cash. Since the prices of shares and government securities change from day to day, a seller might receive more or less than he or she paid for them.

A company which has obtained permission to have its shares traded on the Stock Exchange will find it much easier to raise new capital by making an issue of shares. The Stock Exchange, therefore, is an essential part of the capital market, for long-term loans.

The investors

Broadly speaking there are two classes of 'Investors', those who buy shares because they are seeking income in the form of dividends and those who buy shares because they hope to make a capital gain from the resale of the shares. This latter group are known as *speculators* and they are usually described as *bulls* and *bears*. Speculators who buy in the expectation that share prices are about to rise are known as bulls. The bear sells shares that he does not possess because he expects prices to fall before the account is settled. If he anticipates correctly he will be able to buy the shares at a lower price than that at which he contracts to supply them. Nowadays the terms 'bullish' and 'bearish' are more generally applied to describe markets where share prices are tending to rise or fall.

Pension funds and insurance companies have become the major providers of funds for industry. The large-scale transfer of ownership of industry from the public sector to the private sector (*privatisation*) has led to an important increase in the individual ownership of shares.

Share prices

Since the Stock Exchange is a relatively free market, share prices are subject to fluctuations as market conditions change. The Stock Exchange publishes its own *Daily List* showing the prices at which transactions have taken place. Prices are determined by supply and demand and the willingness to buy and sell is subject to many influences. The following is a brief list of some of these influences.

- The recent profit record of the company and especially the recent rates of dividend paid to shareholders.
- The growth prospects of the industry in which the company operates.
- The economic policy of the government. Changes (or proposed changes) in the system of taxation, in government spending, in monetary policy (e.g. changes in interest rates) and in industrial policy (e.g. privatisation) can have important effects on people's willingness to buy or sell shares.
- Rumours, and announcements, of mergers and takeover bids. Since takeover bids usually offer generous terms to the shareholders of the company being approached, the shares in that company tend to rise in price.
- The state of management–labour relations. Industrial unrest accompanied by frequent strikes can tend to lower share prices.
- Foreign political developments are another important influence, especially where an economy is heavily dependent on world trade.
- Changes in the rate of interest on government securities will often affect share prices. A rise in the market rate of interest might cause some 'switching' from shares to government securities.
- The news of such things as a major oil strike tends to have a dramatic effect on the shares of the companies concerned.
- The views of experts are an increasingly important influence. Articles by well-known financial writers can persuade people to buy or sell certain classes of share.

The role of the Stock Exchange in the economy

People will be prepared to purchase shares and bonds much more readily when an institution such as the Stock Exchange provides a market where they can, if they wish, sell their securities. Thus, the raising of capital by private industry and governments is greatly facilitated.

It provides a daily 'barometer' of industrial and commercial efficiency to the extent that movements in share prices reflect commercial success. Stock Exchange price movements, therefore, tend to direct funds to those industries where share prices are rising. The assumption is, of course, that rising share prices indicate that the relevant companies are using capital more profitably than other companies. We must bear in mind, however, that irrational speculative pressures can also move share prices.

Stock Exchange prices provide a means of valuing wealth held in the form of securities. This is important for the assessment of taxes on capital and wealth. The market prices of shares are also used for the assessment of compensation payments when firms are nationalised.

The Stock Exchange is primarily a market for existing securities, although some new shares are privately placed with Stock Exchange firms.

13 Influences on the location of industry

One of the fundamental decisions to be taken by entrepreneurs concerns the geographical location of their enterprises. They have not only to decide 'How to produce' and 'What to produce' but 'Where to produce'. We must now consider the various influences which bear upon this decision.

From the entrepreneur's viewpoint the major determinant of location will be the private costs associated with different locations. In practice most UK firms are footloose. This means the costs of being based in a number of different locations will be very similar. They are not restricted to one or two locations and moving will not cause serious problems.

In deciding exactly which location to select a firm will take into account a number of factors, which are discussed below. The final decision will rest upon some calculation of the maximum net advantages of alternative sites.

Availability of raw materials and power

In the early days of industrialisation the great localising factors were the proximities to raw materials and power. The first factories were dependent upon water power and were sited on the banks of fast-flowing streams. Arkwright built his mill on the banks of such a stream at Cromford. The introduction of steam power moved industrial activity to the coalfields. Coal became the prime source of energy and since, in these early years, transport facilities were primitive and costly, any locations other than coalfield sites were hopelessly uneconomic. All the basic industries in Britain – cotton, wool, iron, and steel – became established on or near coalfields.

Iron and coal were found in close proximity in many areas, as were clay and coal. Hence, the iron and steel industry, the pottery industry, and brick-making all came to be established on coalfields. Industries highly dependent upon imported raw materials tended to be located on coastal sites, especially where coal was also available (e.g. South Wales, North West England, and North East England).

The sources of raw materials and power no longer exert such a strong geographical pull on industry. The electricity grid and the gas and oil pipelines have made the newer sources of power available in all parts of the country. In addition great improvements in transport have cheapened the movement of raw materials and finished products. Nevertheless the location of raw materials where they happen to be particularly bulky still has some influence on industrial location. Where the industrial process is *bulk reducing* (weight losing), there is a strong incentive to carry out the processing at the source of the basic material. The iron and steel industry built plants on the Lincolnshire and Northamptonshire ore deposits. This was because British ore has a very low iron content and technical progress, in this industry, has led to great economies in the fuels used for heating purposes. The sugar beet processing plants are located on or near the beet fields, since the yield of sugar is very low in relation to the weight and volume of the beet. Chemical plants are located on the salt beds of Cheshire and South Lancashire for similar reasons.

Markets

When the process is *bulk increasing* (weight gaining), the pull of the market will be very strong since transport costs will be much less for locations near to the market. Thus, we find much of the furniture industry and the manufacture of domestic appliances such as refrigerators and washing machines located near to the great centres of population in the South East and the Midlands.

Brewers and bakers produce commodities which are of low value in relation to their bulk so that these activities tend to be carried out fairly close to their markets. Proximity to the market may also be an important consideration where the product is durable and requires an efficient after-sales service.

The significance of these arguments depends upon the ratio of transport costs to total costs. Generally speaking, this ratio has tended to decline in the UK. The industrial structure has been changing and a much greater proportion of total output is now made up of lighter, easily transportable products, while the role of the heavy industries where transport costs are relatively high has been declining. Added to this we have the fact that the UK is a small country and there have been major improvements in transport. For many industries it seems that transport costs may no longer be an important determinant of location.

Labour

The availability of labour is an essential requirement for economic activity, and when an industry is dependent upon particular labour skills, local supplies of such skills will exert a great influence upon the location decision. More important though is the general availability of labour since, for many modern industries, the bulk of the labour force can be quickly trained. Where there is a high national level of employment but significant variations as between regions, those areas with surplus labour will tend to attract firms which are unable to expand in areas where there are labour shortages.

Since we are concerned with the relative costs of operating in different locations any regional variations in labour costs will also influence location decisions. In industries and occupations where there are national wage negotiations one would not expect to find any very great differences in regional wage rates, but, in areas of labour shortage, firms may be obliged to pay well above the agreed minimum wage rates.

The 1990s have seen a decline in national wage agreements and a rise in local pay settlements.

Physical features and accessibility

For some industries the physical features of the site are of prime importance in deciding location. Industries producing steel, rayon, paper, and chemicals require very large quantities of water and tend to be found near rivers. The atomic power stations are all located on estuaries because of the vast quantities of water required for cooling purposes. Certain industries have serious problems of waste disposal, especially the chemical-based industries, and, again, they are usually located on river-bank sites. The problem of dust control has made it necessary to site cement works in fairly remote situations.

The accessibility of the site is an important factor. Before the development of efficient road transport, proximity to the railway network was an essential requirement for any large-scale enterprise. This is no longer the case since the overwhelming proportion of passenger and freight traffic now uses the road network and proximity to the new motorways has become an important localising factor.

Acquired advantages

Once an industry has become localised the economic advantages of the situation in relation to other areas tend to increase. It is these acquired advantages of existing centres of industry which tend to exert the greatest influence on location decisions. These economies of concentration, as they are sometimes called, gradually develop and persist long after the initial localising factors have disappeared from the scene. The availability of local clays and coal was a major factor in the establishment of a pottery industry in Stoke-on-Trent, but this industry has for a long time been completely dependent on clay transported from Cornwall and the industrial heating is now supplied by gas and electricity. The industry, however, remains very heavily concentrated in the same area, because of the very important *external economies* of scale available to pottery firms. We discussed these external economies at some length in Chapter 9. Some industries have remained in areas long after the initial locational advantages have disappeared. This unwillingness to move is referred to as industrial inertia.

Personal preferences

A general survey of the causes which have influenced location in the past gives the impression that their operation was frequently unknown or imperfectly understood by the original producers. In fact, many decisions on location seem to be haphazard or based purely on personal consider- ations. An important factor has been the local ties of the entrepreneur. He has tended to set up business where he is known and has useful local contacts and where he is more likely to raise finance from associates and local banks. Lord Nuffield established a motor car industry in his native Oxford. The Pilkington's glassworks at St Helens is another example of a large industrial development in the home town of its founder.

Government and European intervention

Firms' locational decisions can be influenced by the government's regional policies and by financial assistance from the European Union. These are discussed below.

Regional policies

Regional policies seek to reduce regional disparities. These disparities can be measured in terms of income per head, growth of income per head, migration into and out of the area, the quality of jobs, lifespan, doctors per head, cars per head. The most frequently used measure is the unemployment percentage. Table 13.1 shows the unemployment per- centages in the government-classified regions of the UK.

Table 13.1 Regional unemployment

Region	January 1979	January 1994
UK (average)	4.2	9.9
South-East	2.9	9.8
East Anglia	3.5	7.8
South West	4.5	9.0
East Midlands	3.5	9.2
West Midlands	3.8	10.3
Yorks & Humberside	4.1	10.0
North West	5.3	10.3
North	6.2	11.8
Scotland	5.8	9.5
Wales	5.6	10.1
Northern Ireland	7.9	13.3

Source: *Economic Trends and Employment Gazette* (July 1994)

These regional differences have led to debates about a North–South divide in the UK, with the South East, East Anglia, South West and East Midlands being regarded as the South and the remaining regions grouped together as the North. The South does have lower unemployment, higher income per head, a greater percentage of management and high-tech jobs, more consumer durables per head and more doctors per head. However the 1990s have witnessed some narrowing of the gap between the North and the South.

In the UK the problem of regional unemployment arises from the localisation of the major industries which provided the basis for industrial development in the nineteenth century. Since the First World War several of these basic industries have experienced a serious decline in their home and overseas markets. Thus coal, cotton, and shipbuilding declined because overseas buyers developed their own industries, or major new competitors appeared in foreign markets (e.g. Japan), or because technological progress produced new and superior substitutes (e.g. oil for coal), or new techniques that led to a massive replacement of labour by capital (e.g. coal and steel). These industries happen to be heavily concentrated in areas such as Lancashire, South Wales, Clydeside, North East, and North West England.

We live in a world of change so that at any time there will always be some industries in decline, while others will be growing. A declining industry, therefore, would present no serious economic problems if labour and capital were extremely mobile; resources could move from declining to expanding industries. Unfortunately, the newer industries that have developed during the twentieth century (e.g. motor vehicles, electrical appliances, radio and television, and food processing) have tended to prefer locations away from the traditional industrial centres. The attraction for these mainly consumer goods industries has been the large markets in the Midlands, London, and the South East.

Why regional differences matter

Regional differences result in a number of problems.

The unemployment in the less prosperous areas represents a serious waste of economic resources and national income is lower than it might otherwise be.

The drift of population to the more prosperous areas leads to housing shortages and general overcrowding in these areas and there will be added social costs incurred in trying to overcome the problems of the over-crowded areas. In other regions community life might be damaged by the loss of population and the distortion of the age composition (since younger persons are the ones most likely to move). In addition there may be social costs in the form of underutilised social capital.

When the total demand for goods and services is running at a high level, there is excess demand for labour (and other factors) in the prosperous areas giving rise to upward pressures on incomes and other prices. Inflationary pressures are generated while manpower resources are underutilised elsewhere.

Regional policy approaches

There are basically two approaches to regional disparities.

Removing market imperfections. Supply-side economists (see Chapters 34 and 63) believe that if market forces are allowed to operate unimpeded, regional differences will be eliminated. They envisage the unemployed moving to the more prosperous areas and firms moving to where land and labour are cheaper. The resulting fall in labour supply in the depressed areas and increase in supply in the prosperous areas will cause wages to equal out.

The main market imperfections which they believe prevent this process occurring are the immobility of labour, lack of information, nationwide wage bargaining and inappropriate government intervention.

Among the policies they advocate to remove these impediments to free market forces are removing rent controls to reduce the shortage of rented accommodation in prosperous areas, advocating locally negotiated wage agreements, reducing unemployment benefit, increasing information about job and investment opportunities and reducing government restrictions on private-sector investment.

Intervening to off-set market imperfections which are always likely to exist. These economists believe that regional differences will not be self-correcting without government action. They think that firms will tend to gravitate towards prosperous regions whilst the unemployed will experience difficulty in moving out of depressed regions. Those who do move out of depressed regions may, rather than helping these regions, further depress them by reducing demand for goods and services in those regions.

Most interventionist economists advocate policies to move firms rather than the unemployed workers. This is because most firms are footloose whereas the unemployed are not. Entrepreneurs, as we have seen, may, in the absence of government intervention, base their locational decisions purely on personal preferences. They may do equally well in another region. The locations which entrepreneurs do choose may increase congestion and lead to increased public expenditure on roads, houses, schools, etc. as people move to take up the jobs which have been created. It may be the case that similar social capital is being underutilised in other areas.

In practice the unemployed may find it difficult to move to prosperous areas because of high cost or lack of availability of housing, family ties including their partners having jobs in depressed regions, lack of suitable vacancies and attachment to their home areas.

The policies which interventionist economists advocate are of four broad types:

- development of the infrastructure of the depressed areas by improving roads, railways, and airports, increasing the availability of fuel and power, and providing the necessary social capital and amenities;
- training to improve the occupational and geographical mobility of labour so that workers can move more readily to the new jobs provided by firms moving into areas with surplus labour;
- measures to stimulate industrial expansion;
- restrictions on expansion in more prosperous or overcrowded regions.

Regional policy in the UK

Regional policy in the UK really started in 1934 with the Special Areas Act. However, the measures had little or no effect mainly because the *national* rate of unemployment was high throughout the inter-war period. During the Second World War the problem disappeared, but the return to peace-time conditions saw the reappearance of the regional imbalance in unemployment rates and the problem has persisted with varying degrees of severity.

From 1945 until 1982, regional policy was designed to attract new investment in manufacturing industry from areas where unemployment was low to areas where unemployment was high. The principal measures used for this purpose were subsidies to manufacturing firms which located their new plants in areas with high rates of unemployment, and strict controls on the location of new plants in the more prosperous areas − it was very difficult to get planning permission for new factories in these areas. In 1982 the restrictions on new investment in the more prosperous areas were removed.

In the 1980s the government started to reduce regional assistance and made it more selective. Regional Development Grants, which were given automatically to firms in development areas creating jobs, were ended in March 1988.

Assisted areas

Certain regions of the UK have been designated as qualifying for special government aid. Although the level of unemployment is the main determinant of an area's status as an assisted area, regional variations in income per head, in the state of the infrastructure, and in the general economic and social environment are also taken into account.

Regional Selective Assistance (RSA)

This form of aid is available in assisted areas. Both manufacturing and service industries qualify for selective assistance. The amount of aid is calculated as the minimum assistance needed to persuade a firm to undertake a project which will either create new jobs or preserve existing jobs. Financial aid will be provided only if it can be demonstrated that the project would not go ahead without government assistance. Two types of grant are available under this scheme, project grants, which are based on the capital costs of the project or on the number of jobs created and training grants, which are based on the costs of the additional training required as a result of the new investment.

Regional Enterprise Grants (REGs)

These have been available since 1988 to help small businesses in assisted areas. Firms employing fewer than 25 people can receive grants towards capital expenditure and firms employing fewer than 50 people can receive grants towards product development.

Enterprise zones

In 1980 the government announced plans for dealing with the serious problems of decline and decay in the centres of several large industrial cities. Demolition of slums and older industrial and commercial properties had not been followed up by redevelopment and the centres of many large cities were becoming less and less attractive to new enterprises. The government decided to create 'enterprise zones' in a number of cities with a view to attracting firms to set up in inner-city areas. Firms located within an enterprise zone do not have to pay rates, planning controls are less rigid so that factories can be built more quickly, and such firms can obtain very favourable tax treatment of their capital expenditures.

Simplified Planning Zones

These were first established in 1990 to help deprived inner city areas. They have fewer planning restrictions but, unlike enterprise zones, do not provide financial aid to firms.

Urban Development Corporations

These bodies are appointed and wholly financed by the government. They have been given powers to buy and manage land, and to provide buildings, roads and services, and they can also be given planning and building powers. Their main purpose is to encourage private-sector investment in the inner cities. The London Docklands Development Corporation is probably the best-known example. It is claimed that this particular development has encouraged private-sector investment equal to six times the amount of public money devoted to the project.

European Union Assistance

Since 1985 the European Regional Development Fund provides grants of up to 50 per cent for job-creating and infrastructure projects. In the UK this assistance is available to firms in assisted areas and in Northern

Ireland. However, the Department of Trade and Industry deducts the amount of any ERDF grant from the selective assistance that it gives. Assistance from the ERDF is becoming increasingly important.

One form of European Union assistance which firms in the UK have not yet benefited from is the cohesion fund. This was introduced in 1993. Its aim is to reduce regional differences in regional income throughout the Union by helping the low-income countries. Assistance is available to countries with income which is less than 90 per cent of the European average.

Effectiveness of regional policy

It is extremely difficult to measure the effectiveness of regional policy. This is because it is difficult to work out what would have happened in the absence of the policy. Nevertheless, it can be argued that the differences in regional unemployment rates would have been much greater if there had been no regional policy.

Interventionist economists criticise current regional policy expenditure as being inadequate whilst supply-side supporters would like to see more attention being devoted to remaining market imperfections. As this debate continues structural factors still appear to favour the South East and East Anglia. For example, much of the investment in new industries involving micro-electronics is taking place within 50 miles of London. The gradual process of de-industrialisation is moving capital and labour away from older industries to the services sector, especially financial services, technical services and tourism. Many of the assisted areas are unattractive locations for enterprises in these industries.

14 Demand

Markets

Prices arise in exchange transactions and this implies some kind of market. This need not, necessarily, be a fixed location – a building, or a market place. We are all familiar with the open and covered markets in the centres of our towns, but in the modern world the word 'market' has a much wider meaning. Any effective arrangement for bringing buyers and sellers into contact with one another is defined as a market. The small-ad. columns of the local newspaper provide a very efficient market for second-hand cars. Face-to-face contact between buyers and sellers is not a requirement for a market to be able to operate efficiently. In the foreign exchange market, buyers and sellers are separated by thousands of miles, but the knowledge of what is happening in the market is just as complete, and the ease of dealing is just as effective as if the participants were in the same room.

For some commodities, notably fresh fruit and vegetables, the traditional market is still the normal arrangement, but for most goods the market is a national one. Most consumer goods, in developed countries, are bought and sold on a countrywide basis. For other commodities the market is worldwide. This is particularly true of the more important primary products such as rubber, tin, copper, and oil, and of the basic foodstuffs such as meat, wheat, sugar, tea, and coffee. Most of the products of advanced technology also have world markets; for example, computers, aeroplanes, ships, and motor cars.

In the absence of government intervention price is determined by the forces of supply and demand. There is some kind of market arrangement where buyers and sellers are in contact with one another, and the forces of supply acting through the sellers and the forces of demand acting through the buyers, determine the market price.

Demand

The first thing to understand is that demand is not the same thing as desire, or need, or want. We are looking for the forces which determine price, and the strength of the desire for something will not, in itself, have any influence on the price. Only when desire is supported by the ability and willingness to pay the price does it become an effective demand and have an influence in the market. Demand, in economics, means effective demand, and may be defined as *'the quantity of the commodity which will be demanded at any given price over some given period of time'*.

Individual and market demand

For the great majority of goods and services, experience shows that the quantity demanded will increase as the price falls. Economists have found this out by studying markets. First they look at the relationship between the quantity demanded of a product by a single individual and the price of that product. Then by adding the quantities demanded by each individual buyer at each price they obtain the market demand.

Demand schedules and curves

Individual and market demand information can be expressed in the form of demand schedules and demand curves. A demand schedule is a table giving the quantities demanded at a range of prices. A demand curve plots this information on a graph with price on the vertical axis and quantity demanded on the horizontal axis. A market demand curve is the horizontal summation of all the individual demand curves. A demand schedule and the corresponding demand curve is shown in Fig. 14.1.

The demand curve

The demand curve tells us what quantities would be demanded at any given price, *if other things do not change*. These other things are discussed later in the chapter, but it is most important to realise, right at the beginning, that the demand curve tells us what happens to quantity demanded *when price changes* and there is *no change* in any of the other factors influencing demand (e.g. incomes, taste, fashion, and so on).

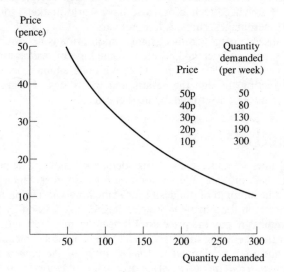

Price	Quantity demanded (per week)
50p	50
40p	80
30p	130
20p	190
10p	300

Fig. 14.1

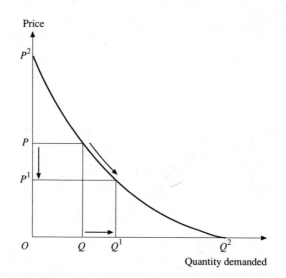

Fig. 14.2   Typical demand curve

Figure 14.2 shows a typical demand curve and we can see that at a price of *OP* the quantity demanded would be *OQ*. If price fell to *OP*¹ quantity demanded would increase to *OQ*¹. Alternatively we can use the demand curve to tell us the maximum price consumers are willing to pay for a given quantity. In this case the demand curve also shows us that at a price of P^2 none of the good would be demanded and if the good were to be provided free OQ^2 quantity would be demanded.

The areas of the rectangles under the demand curve represent the Total Revenues forthcoming at different prices, since they are equal to Price × Quantity.

Extensions and contractions in demand

Movements along a demand curve can be referred to as extensions and contractions in demand or changes in quantity demanded. Fig. 14.2 shows an extension in demand from *OQ* to *OQ*¹, as a result of a rise in price from *OP* to *OP*¹. This can also be referred to as an increase in the quantity demanded.

Figure 14.3 shows a contraction in demand (decrease in quantity demanded) from *OQ* to *OQ*¹ caused by a rise in price from *OP* to *OP*¹. It is very misleading to speak of this as a *change in demand* since this term is usually applied to movements of the whole demand curve. (discussed below).

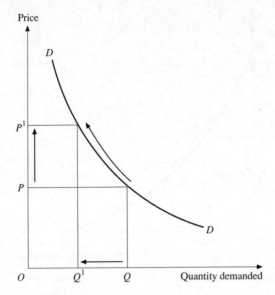

Fig. 14.3   Contraction in demand

The common relationship between demand and price

For most products the quantity demanded increases (extends) as price falls. This means that in most cases the demand curve slopes down from left to right.

We examine below two explanations of why there is usually an inverse relationship between price and quantity.

Income and substitution effects

Price changes have both income and substitution effects. Other things being equal, when the price of a good changes, the real income of the consumer changes. The purchasing power of his money income will be greater when the price of the good falls, it will be less when the price rises. When the price of a good falls, therefore, we would expect consumers to buy more because they can afford to buy more (the income effect). Existing buyers will probably increase their purchases and new buyers, who did not purchase at the higher price, will tend to enter the market.

A fall in the price of a commodity also makes it *relatively* cheaper when compared with competing goods. There will probably be some 'switching' of purchases away from the now relatively dearer substitutes towards the commodity which has fallen in price. This is the substitution effect.

Both the income and substitution effects cause consumers to buy more of a product when it becomes cheaper. Consumers become more able and more willing to buy the product. The opposite effects will apply when the price of a good rises. Consumers' purchasing power will fall, reducing their ability to buy the product and they are likely to switch to substitute products which have become relatively cheaper.

Diminishing marginal utility

The shape of the typical demand curve may also be explained by the action of diminishing marginal utility. Utility is defined as the satisfaction which is derived from the consumption of some good or service. A person buys a commodity because it yields utility or satisfaction. As more is bought of any good the total utility derived increases, but the increase in total utility is not proportionate to the increase in consumption.

The additional utility derived from the last unit purchased is defined as the *marginal utility* of the commodity and it is generally accepted that marginal utility diminishes as consumption increases. After a strenuous session of work, the first cup of tea provides us with great satisfaction; the marginal utility of the first cup is very high. A second cup of tea might also be very welcome, but it will not yield as much utility as the first, while a third cup will provide an even lower level of satisfaction. If we continue to consume cups of tea we should eventually reach a stage where it became positively distasteful and marginal utility would become negative.

Table 14.1 shows that total utility rises until six cups of tea are drunk. Then disutility occurs as marginal utility becomes negative and total utility falls. In this case it would not make sense for us to drink a seventh cup of tea even if it was free. The information in Table 14.1 can also be plotted on graphs, see Fig. 14.4.

Table 14.1 Diminishing marginal utility

No. of cups of tea	Total utility	Marginal utility
1	80	80
2	150	70
3	210	60
4	250	40
5	275	25
6	280	5
7	278	−2

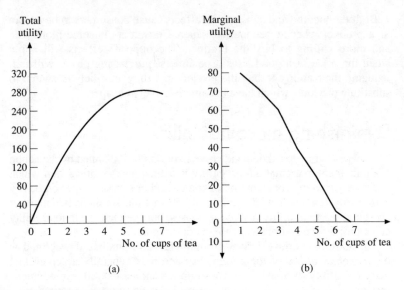

Note: The scales on the vertical axes differ

Fig. 14.4 (a) Total utility; (b) marginal utility

As logical consumers would not consume the product when marginal utility falls to zero, the marginal utility curve in practice would be as shown in Fig. 14.5. This curve may look familiar. It is the basis of the demand curve, indeed, people's demand curve for a product is the same as their marginal utility curve for that product, measured in money terms. Whilst utility is a subjective matter and so is difficult to measure, it can be estimated. One way of doing this is to look at what a person is prepared to sacrifice in order to obtain a commodity. Price measures sacrifice in the sense that it indicates what other things might have been obtained with the money. Since marginal utility diminishes, consumers will be tempted to buy more of a good only if its price is lowered.

By assuming that the sacrifices a person is prepared to make in order to obtain something gives us an indication of the utility derived from that good, we obtain the demand curve. Individuals will derive different satisfaction and so will have different individual demand curves. As we mentioned earlier the market demand curve is found by adding together the amount each person will demand at the different prices. Fig. 14.6 shows how the market demand curve is calculated in a simplified market which consists of only three consumers.

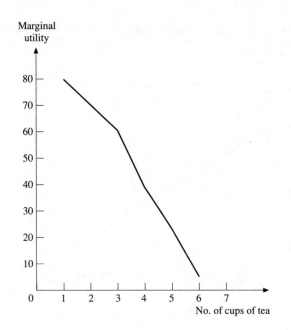

Fig. 14.5

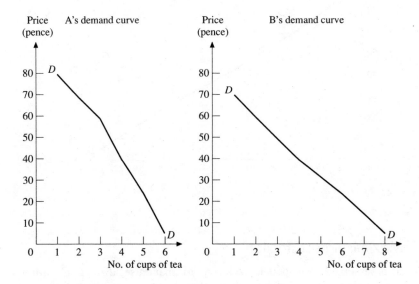

Fig. 14.6   Demand curves

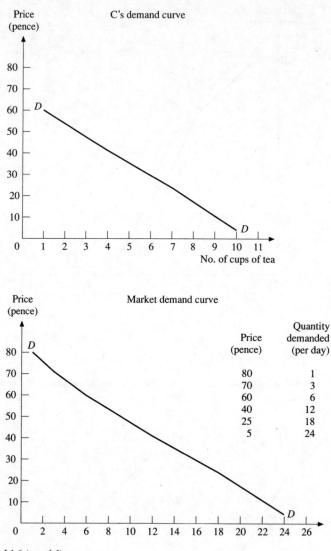

Fig. 14.6 (cont'd)

Maximising satisfaction

It is assumed that people will try to maximise their total utility (satisfaction). This is achieved when they equate the marginal utility per penny they spend on the goods they buy:

$$\frac{\text{marginal utility of good A}}{\text{price of good A}} = \frac{\text{marginal utility of good B}}{\text{price of good B}} = \frac{\text{marginal utility of good C}}{\text{price of good C}}$$

This is logical since if one could obtain more satisfaction per penny spent from good A than from good B one would buy more of good A and less of good B. Think of an example. If at the moment you are deriving more satisfaction from the last apple than from the last bar of chocolate per penny you spend, you should buy more apples and less chocolate. As you do so the marginal utility you obtain from apples will fall whilst the marginal utility you obtain from chocolate will rise. You will continue to alter your purchases until the marginal utilities per penny spent are equal.

Marginal utility and changes in price

Marginal utility explains why a change in price will cause a change in a person's spending pattern. Presume originally that a person divides her expenditure between steak and trout and that she buys six steaks and four trout. Further presume that steaks cost £3 each and trout £2 each and that she gains six units of marginal utility from steak and four units from trout so that

$$\frac{\text{marginal utility of steak}}{\text{price of steak}} = \frac{6}{3} \quad \frac{\text{marginal utility of trout}}{\text{price of trout}} = \frac{4}{2}$$

Now if the price of steak rises to £6 each, the marginal utility per £1 spent on steak will fall and will be less than the marginal utility per £ spent on trout. The consumer will then buy more steak and less trout. As she does so the marginal utility derived from steak will rise (as she has less she will appreciate each unit more) and the marginal utility from trout will fall until

$$\frac{\text{marginal utility of steak}}{\text{price of steak}} = \frac{9}{6} = \frac{\text{marginal utility of trout}}{\text{price of trout}} = \frac{3}{2}$$

Consumer surplus

Consumer surplus occurs when people pay less for a product than they were willing to pay (i.e. less than the value they place on the product based on their marginal utilities). Fig. 14.7 shows an individual's demand curve for wine.

The person would have been prepared to pay £6 for the first bottle, £5 for the second bottle, £3.50 for the third bottle, £2 for the fourth. If the actual price charged is £3.50, the person will buy three bottles receiving a benefit of £2.50 on the first bottle, £1.50 on the second and no consumer surplus on the third bottle. So the total consumer surplus received is £4. The area of consumer surplus is the area under the demand curve and above the price line.

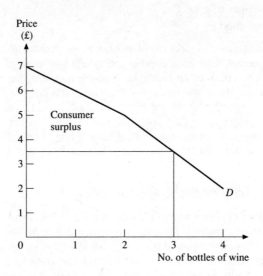

Fig. 14.7   *Consumer surplus*

Exceptional demand curves

As we have seen most demand curves slope downwards from left to right and hence obey the general law that more will be demanded at lower prices than at higher prices. There are, however, some unusual demand

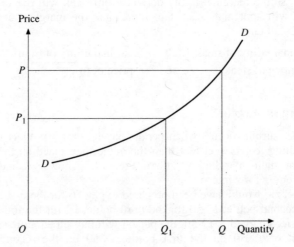

Fig. 14.8   *Exceptional demand curve*

curves which do not obey this 'law' and which represent conditions where 'more will be demanded at a higher price'. This relationship is shown in Fig. 14.8 where a fall in price from OP to OP_1 causes a contraction in demand from OQ to OQ_1.

Examples of exceptional demand curves are sometimes provided by goods which have a 'snob' appeal. These goods can be referred to as Veblen or ostentatious goods. Some people buy expensive things because they are expensive; the ownership of such goods puts them in a rather exclusive class. Where goods are bought for ostentatious reasons a fall in price might cause them to lose some of their appeal and the quantities demanded might fall. They will not be so effective as a means of displaying wealth.

Another exception to the general law of demand is provided by the demands for the staple foodstuffs such as potatoes, bread, rice, and corn in countries where living standards are very low. In these countries expenditure on basic foodstuffs comprises the greater part of the income of most families. In circumstances like these, an increase in the price of the staple food could well lead to *an increase* in the quantity demanded. If consumers' income and the prices of other goods remain unchanged, people will be obliged to buy at least the same quantity of potatoes, or rice, as before and they would have less to spend on other things. The amount of money remaining for the purchase of those 'extras' to the staple diet may now buy such negligibly small amounts of them that consumers may well decide that they would get much better value by using the remaining income to buy more of the staple foods. A fall in the prices of basic foodstuffs, under the conditions outlined, would tend to have the opposite effects. These are examples of Giffen goods (see Chapter 15).

Changes in demand

A change in demand means that one or more of the factors which determine demand (other than the price of the product) have changed. It means that the whole demand curve will move.

An increase in demand means that more is now demanded at each and every price.

A fall in demand means that less is now demanded at each and every price.

These changes are illustrated in Figs. 14.9 and 14.10 which may be used to illustrate either an increase or a decrease in demand. An increase in demand would mean that the curve D^1D^1 has replaced curve DD. We can see that the result of the movement is that an increased quantity is now demanded at any given price. At the price OP the quantity demanded has increased from OQ to OQ^1; at the price OP^1 the quantity demanded has increased from OQ^2 to OQ^3.

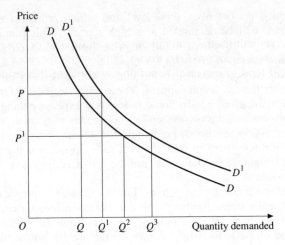

Fig. 14.9   Increase in demand

A fall in demand would mean that the demand curve would have moved from DD to D^1D^1, a shift to the left, and less would be demanded at any given price. In the modern world there are many possible causes of changes in demand. The following are some of the more important of these causes.

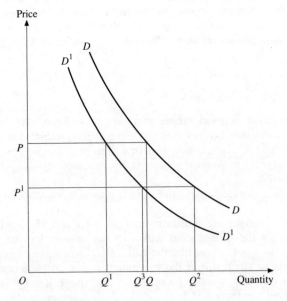

Fig. 14.10   Decrease in demand

Changes in disposable real income

For most commodities the really important determinant of demand is the level of incomes. If incomes are rising, the demand for most goods and services will tend to increase. A striking example of this tendency has been the remarkable increase in the demand for motor cars which has accompanied the general rise in incomes since the war.

Rising incomes, however, may cause the demands for some goods to fall. These items are described as *inferior goods* and comprise such things as the cheaper basic foodstuffs and cheaper clothing. An example is provided by the demand for bread which has been declining in Western Europe for several years.

In considering the relationship between changes in income and changes in demand we must note that it is disposable real income which is the relevant variable. *Disposable income*, as the name implies, refers to the amount of income which the individual has available for spending. It differs from the amount of income he is paid for services rendered by the amount of taxation he pays and/or the various state benefits he might receive in the form of social security benefits. Changes in demand, therefore, will be brought about by changes in government policy on taxation and on social expenditures.

Finally we should note that purchasing power is related to *real income* rather than to money income. If money incomes rise by 5 per cent, but over the same time period prices rise by 10 per cent, real income will have fallen, and this means that people's ability to buy things has fallen.

Changes in the distribution of income

If income becomes more unevenly distributed, demand for luxury goods will increase whilst demand for basic necessities like heating will decrease.

Changes in the prices of other goods

Many of the goods and services we buy have close *substitutes*, and, in making our purchases, we are influenced by the relative prices of competing goods. The demand for a commodity will be influenced by changes in the prices of substitutes. If the price of butter fell, the demand for margarine would probably fall. An increase in the fares on public transport might increase the demand for private transport. Thus a change in the price of a substitute will move the demand curves for competing goods.

The demands for some goods will be affected by changes in the prices of *complementary goods*. Goods are complementary when they are jointly demanded – the use of one requiring the use of the other. The demand for videos is linked to the demand for video recorders; the demand for petrol is associated directly with the demand for motor cars. Thus a sharp increase in the price of motor cars might cause the demand for petrol to fall.

Changes in taste and fashion

The demands for some goods and services are very susceptible to changes in taste and fashion. Particularly affected are the clothing trades, but industries producing furniture, processed foods, and beverages are also subject to movements in taste and fashion. Peer group pressure can influence demand for products. For example, many youngsters influenced by their friends, buy, or have bought for them mountain bikes rather than ordinary bikes.

Advertising

In advanced capitalist societies, advertising is a powerful instrument affecting demand in many markets. Its aim, quite clearly, is to move the demand curve to the right. In highly competitive markets, a successful advertising campaign will move the product's demand curve to the right and at the same time move the demand curves for competing goods to the left.

The availability of credit

In developed countries the demands for many durable consumer goods depend very much on the provision of credit facilities. Any changes in the terms on which this type of finance can be obtained will have a marked effect on the demands for such things as motor cars, electrical appliances, furniture, and other types of household equipment. A similar situation applies in the housing market since the overwhelming majority of houses are purchased with borrowed funds and a shortage of funds in the building societies can lead to a drastic fall in the demand for houses.

Changes in population

The influence of this factor is of a longer-term nature unless the change comes about by large-scale migration. Changes in the total population and changes in the age distribution will affect both the total demand for goods and services and the composition of that demand. For instance, a fall in the death rate will increase demand for residential homes, for greater health care, for holidays for the elderly, etc.

15 Elasticities of demand

Meaning of elasticity

Elasticity is concerned with the extent to which one variable, for example, demand, responds to a change in another variable, for example, price. The three types of elasticity of demand measure how the quantity demanded responds to changes in the key influences on demand; price, price of related products and income. With elasticity of demand we will be concerned not only with the direction of the change in demand but also the size of the change.

Price elasticity of demand

Price elasticity of demand refers to the responsiveness of quantity demanded to a change in price. Where quantity demanded is very responsive to price changes – a small change in price leading to a relatively large change in quantity demanded – we say that demand is elastic. Where quantity demanded is relatively unresponsive to price changes we say that demand in inelastic. To be more precise, *elasticity of demand is the relationship between the proportionate change in price and the proportionate change in quantity demanded.*

Measuring price elasticity of demand

The concept of elasticity is concerned with proportionate changes in price and quantity and not absolute changes. Price elasticity of demand can be given a numerical value by using the following formula:

$$\text{price elasticity of demand} = \frac{\text{percentage change in quantity demanded}}{\text{percentage change in price}}$$

$$PED = \frac{\%\Delta QD}{\%\Delta P}$$

For example, if the price of a product rises from £20 to £24 and demand falls from 400 to 300 the coefficient will be $\dfrac{-25\%}{+20\%} = -1.25$

Alternatively price elasticity of demand can be calculated by using the following formula:

$$PED = \frac{P \times \Delta QD}{QD \times \Delta P}$$

So that using the example above:

$$PED = \frac{20 \times -100}{400 \times 4} = -1.25$$

In practice, for most goods, price elasticity of demand will be negative and the negative sign is not always given. It is only in the case of goods with exceptional demand that price elasticity of demand is positive.

Degrees of price elasticity of demand

Demand for most products is either elastic or inelastic. Products with elastic demand have a coefficient greater than one and less than infinity. In this case a given percentage change in price will cause a greater percentage change in demand. Demand tends to be elastic for goods which take up a large portion of consumer's incomes and goods whose purchase can be postponed.

When a given change in price causes a smaller percentage change in demand, the product has inelastic demand and the coefficient is more than zero but less than one. Basic necessities, goods which take up a small portion of consumers' incomes, addictive goods, goods with no substitutes and goods which have a number of different uses have inelastic demand.

The other three degrees of price elasticity of demand are less common and may, with certain products, occur over a limited price range.

Unit price elasticity of demand occurs when a percentage change in price results in an equal percentage change in demand. In this case the coefficient will be 1.

Perfectly inelastic demand is when a change in price causes no change in the quantity demanded. For instance, a person with a serious illness might be prepared to buy the same quantity of a medicine when its price rises and may not find it beneficial to increase the quantity they take when its price falls. However, there are few products with perfectly inelastic demand just as there are few products with perfectly elastic demand.

When demand is perfectly elastic a change in price will cause an infinite change in the quantity demanded and the coefficient is infinity. For example if there are a number of people selling CDs of a pop group at one of their concerts, then if one lowered her price below those of her competitors she may capture all the customers at the concert.

The determinants of price elasticity of demand

We summarise here the main determinants of price elasticity of demand which we have touched on in the previous section.

• The major influence on elasticity on demand is the availability of close substitutes. When a close substitute is available in the relevant price range, demand will be elastic. If the supplier of such a commodity were to raise the price, many buyers would turn to the close substitute. If the supplier were to lower his price he would attract many customers away from the substitutes. For example, the demands for a particular brand of cigarettes or paint will be elastic, because there are several other brands which are close substitutes. The total demands for cigarettes and paint, however, will be inelastic because there are no close substitutes for these commodities.

- The more widely defined a good is the less elastic demand will be. This is because there will be fewer substitutes. Whereas the narrower the definition the more substitutes there are likely to be and hence the more elastic demand will tend to be. For instance the demand for meat will be less elastic than demand for beef which in turn will be less elastic than demand for rump steak.
- Some commodities are habit forming and the demands for such goods will obviously tend to be inelastic.
- If it is possible to postpone the purchase of a product, for example, a dishwasher, demand will tend to be elastic.

The time factor

Demand tends to be more elastic in the long run than in the short run. This is because it takes consumers time to adjust to price changes. For instance, if the price of electricity rises people may try to reduce their consumption by economising on heating in the short run. However, in the long run the consumption of electricity will fall by a greater extent as people replace electric cookers and heating systems with gas. Figure 15.1. Shows that the long-run demand curve for electricity is more elastic than the short-run demand curve.

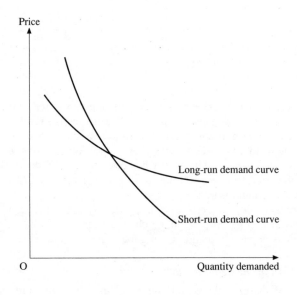

Fig. 15.1

Price elasticity of demand and total revenue (expenditure)

The degree of price elasticity of demand a product possesses can be judged by what happens to total revenue when price changes. When demand is elastic price and total revenue will move in the opposite direction. So that a rise in price will cause a fall in total revenue, and a fall in price will cause a rise in total revenue.

Figure 15.2 shows a product with elastic demand over the given price range. When price is £4 total revenue is £120 (£4 × 30). A fall in price to £3 causes a larger percentage rise in quantity demanded and total revenue to rise to £180 (£3 × 60). Elasticity of demand is 2.

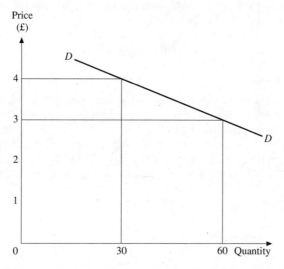

Fig. 15.2   Elastic demand

When demand is inelastic price and total revenue will move in the same direction so that a rise in price will cause a rise in total revenue, and a fall in price will cause a fall in total revenue. Figure 15.3 shows inelastic demand over the given price range. When price is £4 total revenue is £80 (£4 × 20). This time when price falls to £3, demand changes by a smaller percentage to 24 and total revenue falls to £72 (£3 × 24). Elasticity of demand is 0.8.

Total revenue does not change when price elasticity of demand is unity. This is because a given percentage change in price will cause an equal percentage change in demand, leaving total revenue unchanged.

The gradient of the demand curve

Elasticity of demand is *not* measured by the slope or gradient of the demand curve. Normally, on any demand curve, elasticity will be different

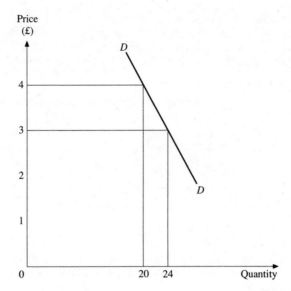

Fig. 15.3   Inelastic demand

at different prices (the exceptions are explained below). In order to avoid any confusion between elasticity and the gradient of the demand curve we can demonstrate that a downward sloping *straight line* demand curve does *not* have constant elasticity.

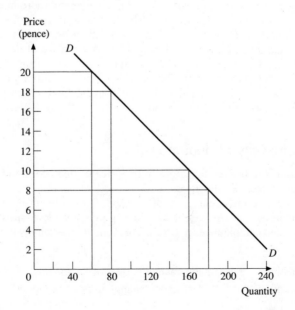

Fig. 15.4

Let us examine the elasticities of demand in the price ranges illustrated in Fig. 15.4. In each case there has been a price change of 2p and, since the demand curve is a straight line, the resulting quantity changes are also equal (i.e. 20 units), but the elasticities of demand are certainly not equal.

When price changes from 20p to 18p,

$$\text{Elasticity of demand} = \frac{\text{Percentage change in quantity demanded}}{\text{Percentage change in price}}$$

$$= \frac{33\frac{1}{3}\%}{10\%} = 3.33$$

When price changes from 10p to 8p,

$$\text{Elasticity of demand} = \frac{\text{Percentage change in quantity demanded}}{\text{Percentage change in price}}$$

$$= \frac{12\frac{1}{2}\%}{20\%} = 0.625$$

This example brings out very clearly the fact that elasticity of demand is a relationship between proportionate and not absolute changes in price and quantity demanded.

The three exceptional cases where elasticity of demand is the same at all prices are illustrated in Fig. 15.5

Shifts in the demand curve

A shift in the demand curve will alter the elasticity of demand at any given price. An increase in demand will make demand more inelastic. At higher levels of demand people will be less sensitive to price changes. This is illustrated on Fig. 15.6. Initially a fall in price from £10 to £8 causes demand to extend from 100 to 160, so elasticity of demand is 3. When demand increases to D^1D^1, a change in price from £10 to £8 causes demand to extend from 200 to 260 giving an elasticity of demand of 1.5. A decrease in demand will make demand more elastic as people become more sensitive to price changes.

Cross elasticity of demand

The relationship between changes in the price of one commodity and the resulting changes in the quantity demanded of another commodity is described as the cross elasticity of demand. This concept is useful as a means of assessing the extent to which goods are close substitutes or closely related complementary goods. This form of elasticity is measured as follows,

$$\text{Cross elasticity of demand} = \frac{\text{Percentage change in quantity demanded of Good A}}{\text{Percentage change in price of Good B}}$$

$$CED = \frac{\%\Delta QD \text{ of good A}}{\%\Delta P \text{ of good B}}$$

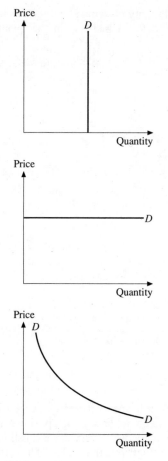

(a) A perfectly inelastic demand curve

Quantity demanded does not change as price changes

Elasticity of demand = 0

(b) A perfectly elastic demand curve

The amount demanded at the ruling price is infinite

Elasticity of demand = ∞

(c) A demand curve with unit elasticity

Quantity demanded always changes by exactly the same percentage as price

Elasticity of demand = 1

(The demand curve is a rectangular hyperbola)

Fig. 15.5

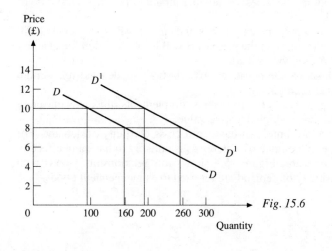

Fig. 15.6

In the case of substitute goods, cross elasticity of demand will be positive; an increase in the price of B will lead to an increase in the quantity demanded of A (and vice versa).

Figure 15.7 shows the relationships between a change in the price of apples and a change in the demand for pears.

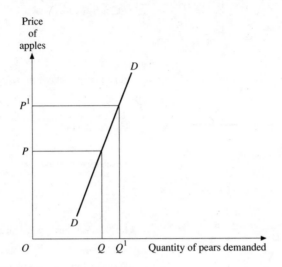

Fig. 15.7   Positive cross elasticity of demand

As the price of apples rises the demand for pears increases. Apples and pears are not very close substitutes and so do not have a high positive cross elasticity of demand. Whereas if the two goods are very close substitutes, cross elasticity of demand will have a high positive value. Thus, if an increase of 10 per cent in the price of one brand of petrol leads to a rise of 40 per cent in the sales of another brand, the cross elasticity of demand is + 4.

In the case of complementary goods, the cross elasticity of demand will be negative; an increase in the price of B will lead to a fall in the quantity demanded of A (and vice versa).

Figure 15.8 shows the negative cross elasticity of demand relationship which exists between gin and tonic.

When two goods are closely related complements, the cross elasticity of demand will have a high negative value.

Goods which are unrelated have zero cross elasticity of demand. For instance, a rise in the price of watercress is unlikely to have any effect on the demand for jeans. Figure 15.9 shows this relationship. Goods with zero cross elasticity of demand are referred to as independent goods.

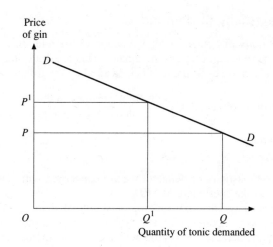

Fig. 15.8   *Negative cross elasticity of demand*

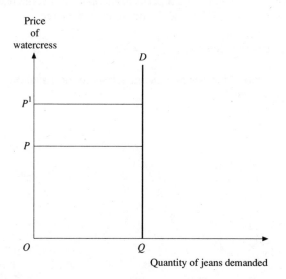

Fig. 15.9   *Zero cross elasticity of demand*

In practice, a change in the price of one product may affect demand for what appear to be unrelated products. This is because a change in the price of a product will affect a person's purchasing power. Obviously, the larger the price change and the greater the proportion of income spent on the product, the larger the effect will be.

Income elasticity of demand

Income elasticity of demand is concerned with the relationship between changes in income and changes in demand. This relationship is known as the *income elasticity* of demand. It is measured by the following formula:

$$\text{Income elasticity of demand} = \frac{\text{Percentage change in quantity demanded}}{\text{Percentage change in income}}$$

$$YED = \frac{\%\Delta QD}{\%\Delta Y}$$

As with cross elasticity of demand, we are concerned with both the sign and the size of the coefficient of *YED*.

Most goods have positive income elasticity of demand. This means that in most cases income and quantity demanded will move in the same direction – an increase in income will lead to an increase in quantity demanded and vice versa – so that the income elasticity of demand will be positive. For example, if a 5 per cent increase in income leads to a 10 per cent increase in the demand for motor cars, we have

$$\text{Income elasticity of demand} = \frac{10\%}{5\%} = +2$$

Figure 15.10 shows the positive income elasticity of demand which exists in the case of wine.

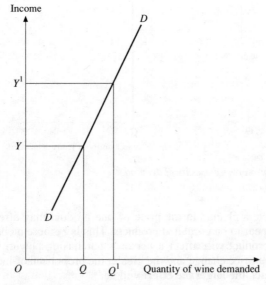

Fig. 15.10   Positive income elasticity of demand

Goods which have positive cross elasticity of demand are called normal goods. Those normal goods which have a positive income elasticity of demand greater than one are sometimes referred to as superior goods.

In the case of inferior goods, as explained on p. 125, increases in income will lead to decreases in the quantities demanded so that income elasticity of demand will be negative. Here income and quantity demanded move in opposite directions. Figure 15.11 shows negative income elasticity of demand.

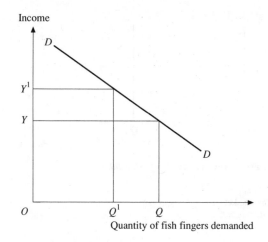

Fig. 15.11   Negative income elasticity of demand

When quantity demanded does not change as income changes, income elasticity of demand is zero. Fig. 15.12 illustrates zero income elasticity of demand.

For any particular commodity, income elasticity of demand depends very much on the current standard of living. In Western Europe, relatively expensive household goods, motor cars, and holidays abroad have a positive income elasticity of demand, while the demands for some staple foodstuffs (e.g. bread), poor-quality clothing, and public transport have negative income elasticities of demand. In developing countries, however, commodities such as clothing and footwear, which in Europe probably have zero income elasticities, will have large positive income elasticities of demand.

Income elasticity of demand can also vary over time. Figure 15.13 shows demand for blankets increasing as a country becomes richer, then demand remaining constant when a certain standard of living is reached, and then falling as people become richer and replace blankets with duvets.

Economists are concerned not only with the direction of the change in demand when income changes but also the extent to which demand changes. Products may have income elastic demand. This will mean that a given percentage change in income will cause a greater change in

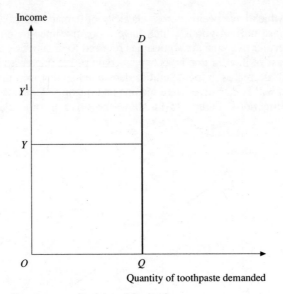

Fig. 15.12   *Zero income elasticity of demand*

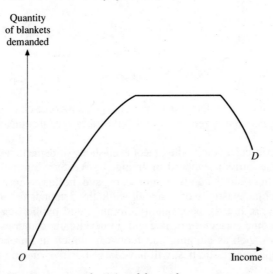

Fig. 15.13   *Varying income elasticity of demand*

demand. Foreign travel and double glazing are two examples of products with income elastic demand.

Products with both negative and positive income elasticity of demand can have income elastic demand. Figure 15.14 shows income elastic demand in the case of (a) an inferior good and (b) a normal good. Income inelastic demand means that a given change in income will cause a

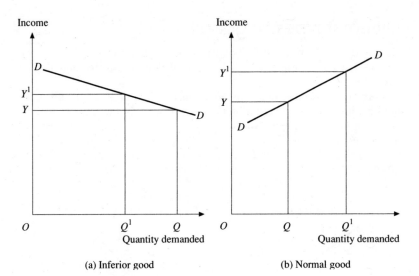

(a) Inferior good

(b) Normal good

Fig. 15.14   Income elastic demand

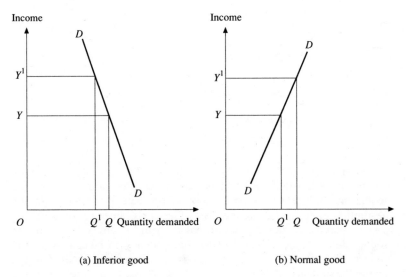

(a) Inferior good

(b) Normal good

Fig. 15.15   Income inelastic demand

smaller percentage change in demand. Potatoes, beer and postage stamps have income inelastic demand. Again, products with both negative and positive income elasticity of demand can have income inelastic demand. Figure 15.15 shows income inelastic demand in the case of (a) an inferior good and (b) a normal good.

Different types of goods

Having discussed price, cross, and income elasticity of demand we can now review the differences between normal, inferior, Giffen and Veblen goods.

Normal goods have negative price elasticity of demand. In this case both the income and substitution effects will work in the same directions and reinforce each other. Normal goods have positive income elasticity of demand.

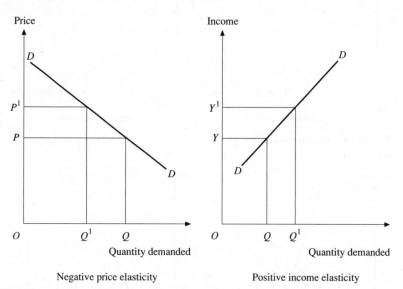

Negative price elasticity   Positive income elasticity

Fig. 15.16   Normal goods

Most inferior goods have negative income elasticity of demand and negative price elasticity of demand. In the case of inferior goods the income and substitution effects work in opposite directions with the substitution effect being stronger. So whilst a rise in price, by lowering people's purchasing power, may stimulate them to purchase more of the product this is more than offset by the tendency to switch to a rival product. Therefore with inferior goods a rise in price will cause a contraction in demand.

Giffen goods are a special type of inferior good. They have negative income elasticity of demand but positive price elasticity of demand. As with inferior goods the income and substitution effects work in opposite directions but this time the income effect will be stronger so that a rise in price will cause an extension in demand.

It is interesting to note that whilst all Giffen goods are inferior goods, not all inferior goods are Giffen goods. For instance bus travel is an

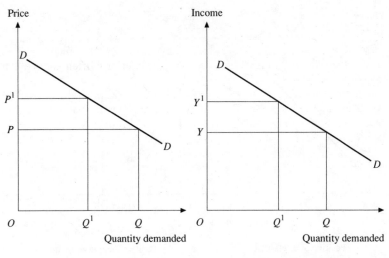

Fig. 15.17   *Inferior goods*

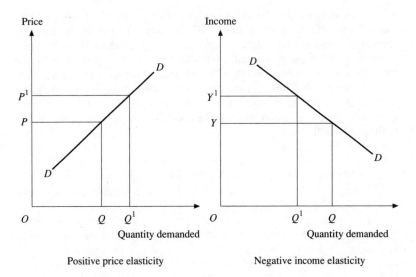

Fig. 15.18   *Giffen good*

inferior good but not a Giffen good. So that whilst a rise in income will be likely to lead to a fall in demand for bus travel, as people switch to alternative means of transport, a rise in price of bus travel is unlikely to cause people to make more journeys by bus.

Veblen goods have both positive price elasticity of demand and income elasticity of demand. People buy more of a Veblen good as its

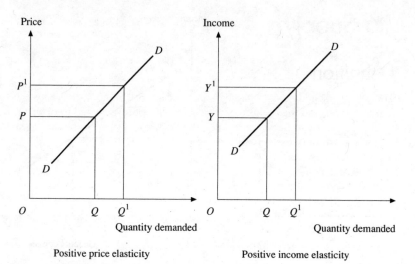

Fig. 15.19   Veblen good

price rises because they associate quality with price. So in this case the income and substitution effects work in opposite directions but the 'perverse' substitution effect is stronger. As a product rises in price peoples' purchasing power falls but this time as the product becomes more expensive, people switch to it and away from cheaper substitutes. Veblen goods also have increasing rather than diminishing marginal utility. As people have more of a Veblen good, their satisfaction from extra units increases often because they are able to impress other people with their wealth.

16 Supply

Definition

The supply schedule and supply curve show the relationship between market prices and the quantities which suppliers are prepared to offer for sale. Supply is not the same thing as 'existing stock' or 'amount available'. We are only concerned here with the amounts actually brought to market and these amounts depend to a large extent on the ruling market price. A car producer, seeing the price of cars falling, may choose to keep more cars in store at the factories. These are part of the existing stock but do not become part of the supply until they are delivered to the car showrooms and put on sale.

The supply curve

The basic law of supply says 'More will be supplied at a higher price than at a lower price'. Supply curves, therefore, will slope upwards from left to right as in Fig. 16.1 which is derived from the accompanying supply schedule. To supply larger quantities firms need higher prices in order to cover their higher costs.

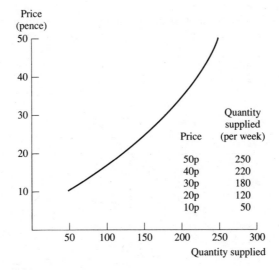

Price	Quantity supplied (per week)
50p	250
40p	220
30p	180
20p	120
10p	50

Fig. 16.1   Supply curve

Movements along a supply curve

Movements along the supply curve are referred to as extensions and contractions or as changes in the quantity supplied. Figure 16.2 shows an extension in supply. A rise in price from OP to OP^1 causes an increase in the quantity supplied from OQ to OQ^1.

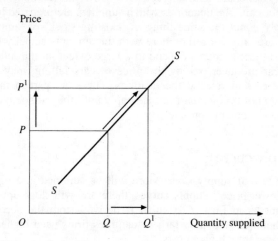

Fig. 16.2   Extension in supply

Figure 16.3 shows a contraction in supply. A fall in price from OP to OP^1 causes a decrease in the quantity supplied from OQ to Q^1.

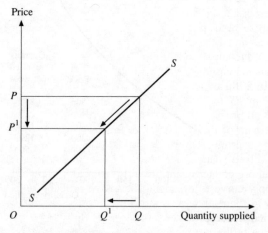

Fig. 16.3   Contraction in supply

Changes in supply

An increase in supply means that more is supplied at each and every price. A decrease in supply means that less is supplied at each and every price.

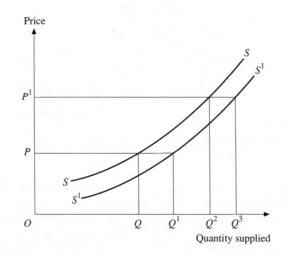

Fig. 16.4   An increase in supply

Figure 16.4 illustrates an increase in supply. It shows the supply curve shifting from SS to S^1S^1. This leads to an increase in the quantity supplied at any given price.

For example, at the price OP suppliers are now prepared to offer quantity OQ^1 whereas under the original supply conditions, at this price, they were only prepared to supply quantity OQ. Similarly at price OP^1 the quantity supplied has increased from OQ^2 to OQ^3.

Figure 16.5 illustrates a decrease in supply. The supply curve shifts to the left from SS to S^1S^1. The effect will be to reduce the quantities supplied at all prices.

A movement of the supply curve indicates some basic change in the conditions governing supply. The most obvious cause of such a movement would be a change in the costs of production. If producers are prepared to supply greater quantities at given prices, shown by a movement of the supply curve to the right, they have probably experienced some reductions in their labour costs, material costs, or capital costs (or they have decided to accept lower profit levels). Similarly a movement of the supply curve to the left means that suppliers now require a higher price before they supply any given quantity, indicating that they have experienced an increase in their costs of production. Some possible causes of changes in the conditions of supply are set out below.

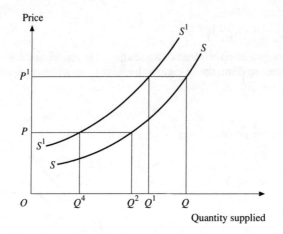

Fig. 16.5   A decrease in supply

Weather

The supply of agricultural products is seriously affected by variations in weather conditions. Output in this industry is subject to variations from year to year which are independent of the acreage planted, and hence independent to a large extent of the costs incurred in preparation and planting. An unfavourable season which results in a poor harvest may be seen as an increase in the average cost of production since a given outlay on fertilisers, ploughing, seeds, and planting yields a smaller return than it would have done in a good season. A bad harvest means that the supply curve moves to the left; a bumper harvest is represented by a movement of the supply curve to the right.

Technical progress

Technical progress is a term which covers improvements in the performances of machines and labour, in the quality of raw materials, in organisation and management, in factory layouts, in communications, in techniques of production, and so on. It is the main source of improvements in productivity and these increases in output-per-person-hour will move the supply curve to the right, because, if other things remain unchanged, average costs of production will fall.

Changes in the prices of the factors of production

An important determinant of changes in the conditions governing supply, especially in recent years, is changes in the prices of the factors of production. Movements in wages, the prices of raw materials, fuel and power, rates of interest, rents, and other factor prices will clearly affect the costs of production. It must be pointed out, however, that movements in factor prices may be offset by changes in the productivity of the factors so that factor cost may not change very much, if at all. For example, if wage rates rise by 10 per cent, but labour productivity also increases by 10 per cent, then labour costs per unit have not changed. In fact, in recent years factor prices have risen quite sharply, far more than movements in productivity, so that the supply curves for most products have been moving to the left. If factor prices fall, of course, the supply curve moves to the right.

Changes in the prices of other commodities

Changes in the prices of other goods may affect the supply of a commodity whose price does not change. If, because of increases in demand, the prices of other goods increase, the production of these goods will become more profitable, and resources would tend to move towards the industries making these higher-priced commodities. The production of goods, with prices unchanged, would now be less attractive to suppliers.

In the case of products which are substitutes in supply, a rise in the price of one good will cause the supply of that good to extend and the other good/goods to decrease. However some products are in joint supply, for instance, petrol and paraffin. So if there is a rise in the price of petrol this will cause the supply of petrol to extend and the supply of paraffin to increase.

Taxation and subsidies

The imposition of indirect taxes will bring about changes in supply. A tax on a commodity may be regarded as an increase in the costs of supplying that commodity and the supply curve will move to the left. Subsidies will have exactly the opposite effect. They lower the costs of bringing the goods to the market and increase the supply.

Changes in the number of producers

Supply will increase if new firms enter the market. For instance, in the 1980s and early 1990s the number and range of magazines increased with the rise in the number of producers, many using desk-top publishing.

Unexpected events

The Gulf War (1990–91) decreased the supply of oil. Natural disasters, diseases in crops and animals and terrorist bombs can all affect supply.

Elasticity of supply

Elasticity of supply is a relationship between the proportionate changes in price and the associated proportionate changes in quantity supplied. The formula used to measure elasticity of supply is similar to that used for the elasticity of demand.

$$\text{Elasticity of Supply} = \frac{\text{Percentage change in quantity supplied}}{\text{Percentage change in price}}$$

$$PES = \frac{\%\ \Delta QS}{\%\ \Delta P}$$

Most products have either elastic or inelastic supply. Elastic supply is when a given percentage change in price causes a greater percentage change in supply. Whereas inelastic supply is when a given percentage change in price causes a smaller percentage change in supply.

Figure 16.6 illustrates these two degrees of elasticity of supply plus the three less common cases.

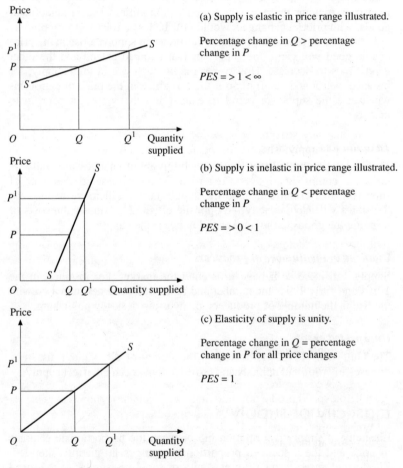

(a) Supply is elastic in price range illustrated.

Percentage change in Q > percentage change in P

$PES = > 1 < \infty$

(b) Supply is inelastic in price range illustrated.

Percentage change in Q < percentage change in P

$PES = > 0 < 1$

(c) Elasticity of supply is unity.

Percentage change in Q = percentage change in P for all price changes

$PES = 1$

Fig. 16.6   Degrees of elasticity of supply

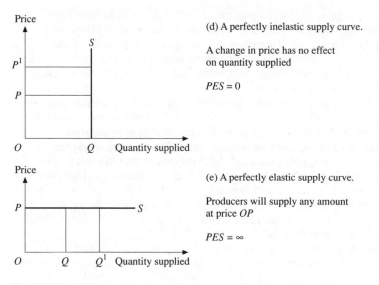

(d) A perfectly inelastic supply curve.

A change in price has no effect on quantity supplied

$PES = 0$

(e) A perfectly elastic supply curve.

Producers will supply any amount at price OP

$PES = \infty$

Fig. 16.6 (cont'd)

Note that any straight line passing through the origin will have unit elasticity of supply. The proportionate changes in quantity supplied will be equal to the proportionate changes in price at any point on the line.

The determinants of elasticity of supply

The extent to which supply is elastic depends upon the flexibility or mobility of the factors of production. If production can be expanded very easily and quickly in response to an increase in demand, supply will be elastic; if not, supply will be inelastic. Similarly, when demand falls, supply will be elastic if it can be cut back very quickly to match the lower demand. To make this more realistic we should discuss some possible supply conditions in the real world.

Possible supply conditions

- Where an industry is operating below capacity and there are unemployed resources, supply will be elastic. The industry will be able to expand production fairly easily by engaging more variable factors and bringing into use its idle fixed factors.
- Where suppliers are holding large stocks, supply will be elastic. In this case an increase in demand can be met by running down stocks, and while these last, supply will be elastic. Once the stocks are depleted, however, it may be difficult to increase output and supply will then be inelastic.

- In a situation of full employment, the supply of most goods and services will be inelastic. Supply may be increased by improved productivity, but in the short run no significant increases in output will be possible. Supply in the home market may still be elastic if it is possible to obtain supplies from abroad, but this may lead to balance of payments difficulties.
- In the case of agricultural products, supply in the short run must be fairly inelastic because the quantity supplied in any one year is governed by the acreage planted in the sowing season. Some commodities such as natural rubber, coffee, and cocoa will be inelastic in supply over fairly long periods of time since it takes several years for newly planted trees to reach maturity. Thus, in the short run, an increase in demand will lead to a sharp increase in price. The supplies of products such as beef and milk will also be inelastic because it takes a considerable time to increase the sizes of the herds of beef and dairy cattle.
- In some industries the expansion of capacity takes a long time. Once such industries are operating at full capacity, therefore, supply will be inelastic (as far as expansion is concerned) for several years. This is true of mining industries because the sinking of new mines and the extension of existing ones is a lengthy procedure. Thus, the supply of most minerals tends to be inelastic.

An increase in the demands for primary products (such as those mentioned above) cannot call forth an immediate increase in supply. Inevitably the short-run effect is an increase in price.

Elasticity of supply over time

Generally speaking while changes in demand can take place in the very short period, especially in markets subject to changes in fashion or where advertising is very effective, changes in supply, because of technical problems and the immobilities of the factors of production, take much longer. It is usual to distinguish three time periods in supply and demand analysis.

The momentary period

This is defined as the period of time during which supply is restricted to the quantities actually available in the market. Supply is fixed (i.e. perfectly inelastic) in the momentary period, and the supply curve will be a straight line parallel to the price axis. Normally, this period will be a very short one. In the case of perishable goods such as fish, fruit, and vegetables, the supply for the day, in local markets, is limited to the quantities delivered in the morning.

The short period

The short period is the interval which must elapse before more can be supplied with the existing capacity. More fish can be supplied by trawlermen fishing longer hours or further afield. More fruit can be supplied by speeding up the harvesting, or by using up existing stocks more quickly. More shoes can be produced by taking on more labour or by working overtime. The short period in some industries (e.g. manufacturing) may be only a matter of a few days, but in others (e.g. housebuilding) it may be many months. The short period, then, is the period of time which allows for changes to take place in the quantities of the variable factors employed. Changes in supply in this period are shown as movements along the normal supply curve. The supply curves used in most of our supply and demand analysis are short period supply curves.

The long period

This is the time interval which is long enough for fundamental changes to take place in the scale of the industry. In other words, in the long period, the quantities of both fixed and variable factors of production may be changed. Existing firms may expand (or contract) their capacity; they may extend their factories, install more machines, adopt new methods and so on. New firms may enter (or existing firms leave) the industry. The fishing industry may expand by bringing new boats into use; the supply of fruit may be increased by planting more trees; and the output of the steel industry may be increased by building new plants.

The long period may be a matter of months in the case of some manufacturing industries, or several years in the case of mining, steel production, electricity generating, or fruit growing. The long-period changes in supply represent changes in the basic conditions of supply (the capacity of the industry has changed) and these changes involve a series of shifts in the short-period supply curves. Each short-term supply curve describes the supply situation *for a given capacity*.

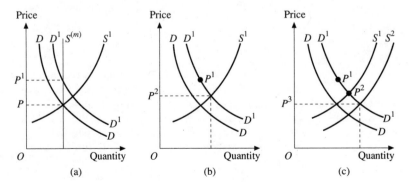

Fig. 16.7

The relationships described above are illustrated in Fig. 16.7, which shows the effects of an increase in demand, in the momentary period, the short period, and the long period. $S^{(m)}$ is the momentary period supply curve and S^1 the original short-period supply curve.

In Fig. 16.7 (a) we see the situation following an increase in demand in the momentary period. Supply is perfectly inelastic and price rises from OP to OP^1, that is, by the full extent of the change in demand.

Fig. 16.7 (b) shows the situation after sufficient time has elapsed for the industry to react to the increase in demand. The higher price has stimulated an increase in output and this is represented by a movement along the existing short-period supply curve. Quantity supplied has increased and price has fallen from OP^1 to OP^2. This higher (short period) price, if sustained, will lead to changes in the productive capacity of the industry. Existing firms will be encouraged to expand and new firms will enter the industry.

In Fig. 16.7 (c) we see the effects of this increase in the scale of production. The new supply situation is represented by an entirely new short-term supply curve S^2. The increase in supply has caused the price to fall from OP^2 to OP^3 and the quantity demanded has increased. The price OP^3 may be higher or lower than the original price OP depending upon the extent to which the expansion of the industry has yielded economies of scale.

17 Market price

Equilibrium price

In the previous chapters we looked at the two market forces which determine price. For each economic good there is a supply schedule and a demand schedule. If the two are brought together we find that the quantity demanded and the quantity supplied will be equal at one and only one market price. This is *the equilibrium price*. The equilibrium price may be determined from the supply and demand schedules, or, as is more usually the case, from the point at which the demand and supply curves intersect. In Fig. 17.1 for example, the equilibrium price is 30p, for only at this price is the quantity brought to the market by willing sellers equal to the amount taken off the market by willing buyers.

At prices higher than the market price (e.g. 40p) the quantity supplied will be greater than the quantity demanded and the excess supply would oblige sellers to lower their prices in order to dispose of their output. This situation is sometimes described as a buyers' market.

At prices lower than the market price (e.g. 20p) the quantity demanded will exceed the quantity supplied, giving rise to a shortage. Competition between buyers will force up the price giving rise to a condition known as a sellers' market.

The equilibrium or market price is 30p, because at any other price there are market forces at work which tend to change the price.

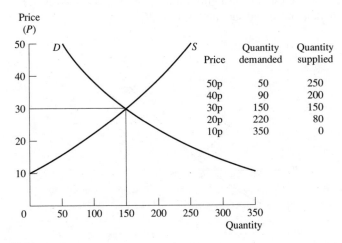

Price	Quantity demanded	Quantity supplied
50p	50	250
40p	90	200
30p	150	150
20p	220	80
10p	350	0

Fig. 17.1

Changes in equilibrium

Market prices are determined by the interaction of demand and supply and in competitive markets changes in market prices must be due to changes in demand or supply, or both. Price does not move independently of the demand and supply situations.

The effects of shifts in demand

The effects of changes in demand may be stated in terms of economic 'laws'.

- In the short run, other things being equal, an increase in demand will raise the price and increase the quantity supplied (extension in supply).
- In the short run, other things being equal, a decrease in demand will lower the price and reduce the quantity supplied (contraction in supply).

These statements are generalisations based upon observations of human behaviour, and since they indicate what happens in the great majority of cases they are decribed as laws. Figure 17.2 shows the effects of a change in demand.

We can use Fig. 17.2 to explain the effects of an increase in demand by assuming that DD is the original demand curve so that the equilibrium price is OP and the quantity OQ is demanded and supplied. Assume that demand now increases from DD to D^1D^1. The immediate effect is to cause a shortage (shown by dotted line) at the ruling price OP. This shortage will cause the price to be bid upwards and quantity supplied will increase until a new equilibrium price is established at OP^1. The quantity demanded and supplied is now OQ^1.

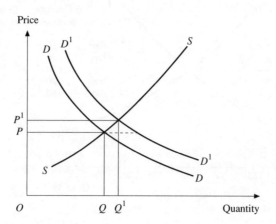

Fig. 17.2   Demand increases – price rises – supply extends

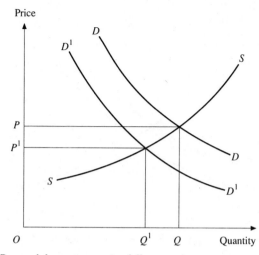

Fig. 17.3   Demand decreases – price falls – supply contracts

Figure 17.3 shows a decrease in demand. The demand curve shifts to the left (D^1D^1). There is a surplus at price OP (equal to the horizontal distance between the demand curves). Suppliers will be obliged to lower prices in order to clear their stocks. This fall in price will tend to reduce the quantity supplied and increase the quantity demanded until a new and lower equilibrium price is established at OP^1.

The effects of shifts in supply

The effects of changes in supply may also be summarised in the form of two economic 'laws'.

- In the short run, other things being equal, an increase in supply will lower the price and increase the quantity demanded (extension in demand).
- In the short run, other things being equal, a decrease in supply will raise the price and reduce the quantity demanded (contraction in demand).

Figure 17.4 demonstrates the effects of an increase in supply. The supply curve moves from SS to S^1S^1. The immediate effect is a surplus (shown by dotted line) at the ruling price OP. This surplus will force the price downwards, quantity demanded will increase and eventually a new equilibrium price OP^1 will be established. The quantity demanded and supplied will be OQ^1.

Figure 17.5 shows a decrease in supply. When supply falls from SS to S^1S^1 there will be excess demand at price OP (equal to the horizontal distance between the supply curves). This excess demand will cause the

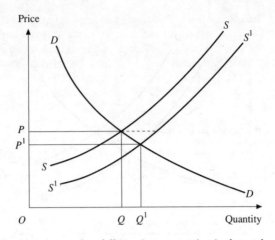

Fig. 17.4   Increase in supply – fall in price – extension in demand

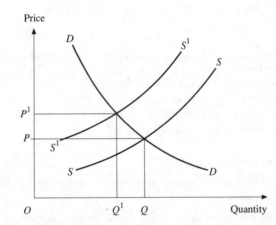

Fig. 17.5   Decrease in supply – rise in price – contraction in demand

price to rise: quantity demanded will fall and quantity supplied will increase until a new equilibrium price is established at OP^1.

A common confusion between the causes and effects of price changes

This is an aspect of economics that students beginning their studies often find rather puzzling. Having learned the first law of supply and demand (i.e. 'more is demanded at lower prices'), many students then automatically associate an increase in price with a fall in the quantity demanded and vice versa. This is not necessarily the case. One cannot draw any conclusions about the *effects* of a price change unless one knows the *cause* of the price change. For example, Fig. 17.2 can be used to illustrate the case where an *increase in price* is associated with an *increase in the quantity sold* (the cause of the change is an increase in demand). On the other hand, Fig. 17.5 may be used to show how an *increase in price* is associated with a *decrease in the quantity sold* (the cause of the change is a fall in supply). By reversing the movements just described one can see that a fall in price may be associated with an increase or a decrease in quantity demanded – it all depends upon what caused the price change.

Price elasticities of demand and supply

We have noted that changes in demand and supply will lead to changes in market prices and in the quantities demanded and supplied. We know the direction of such changes, but it is also important to know the extent of such changes. Elasticity of demand and elasticity of supply will enable us to calculate the extent to which changes in demand affect prices and quantities supplied and the extent to which changes in supply affect prices and quantity demanded.

For example, if demand is elastic, an increase in supply will cause a relatively small fall in price and a greater percentage change in quantity demanded. In this case total revenue will rise. Figure 17.6 shows the effect of an increase in supply when demand is elastic.

If demand is inelastic an increase in supply will cause a relatively large fall in price and a smaller percentage change in quantity demanded.

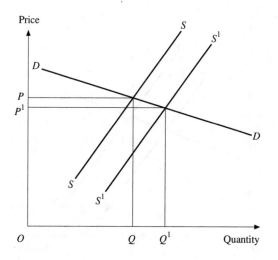

Fig. 17.6

In this case total revenue will fall. Figure 17.7 shows the effect of an increase in supply in a market where demand is inelastic.

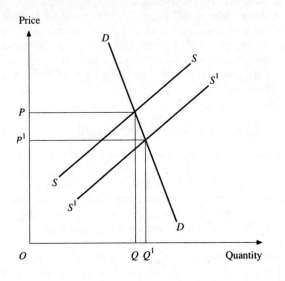

Fig. 17.7

If supply is elastic an increase in demand will cause a relatively small rise in price and a greater percentage change in quantity supplied as shown in Fig. 17.8.

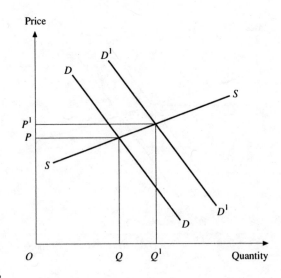

Fig. 17.8

On the other hand if supply is inelastic an increase in demand will cause a relatively large rise in price and a smaller percentage change in the quantity supplied. This is shown in Fig. 17.9.

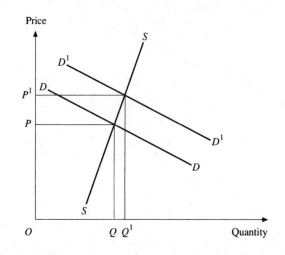

Fig. 17.9

In markets where both demand and supply are inelastic, as occurs in the markets for many agricultural products, a shift in demand and/or supply will have a significant effect on price. This is illustrated in Fig. 17.10 which shows the effect of a decrease in supply.

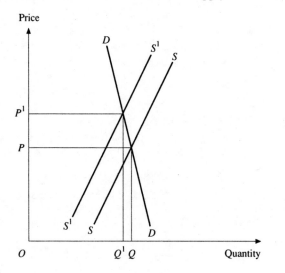

Fig. 17.10

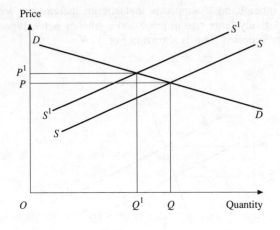

Fig. 17.11

In markets where both demand and supply are elastic, a change in demand and/or supply will have a significant impact on the quantity bought and sold but only a small impact on the equilibrium price. Figure 17.11 shows the effect of a decrease in supply in such a market.

18 Relationships between markets

Relative prices

The price we pay for a product is its nominal or absolute price. However, economies are concerned mainly with relative prices. This is because when people consider what to buy they look at the price of a product in comparison to the price of other products.

In the previous chapters in this part of the book it is relative prices that we have been considering. This means that when we have discussed the effects of, for example, a rise in the price of electricity we have assumed that other prices have remained constant. If this is true electricity will have become relatively more expensive.

However, if all prices are changing at the same time (as occurs when there is inflation), it becomes more difficult to work out changes in relative prices. In this case electricity will experience a rise in its relative price, if its price rises faster than the average of all other prices.

Demand relationships

Joint demand

Some goods are jointly demanded; they are *complementary* in the sense that the use of one implies the use of the other. The demand for petrol is associated with the demand for motor cars; the demand for tennis balls is linked to the demand for tennis racquets. Where goods are complementary a change in the price of one of them will cause a change in the demand for the other. For example, technological progress might lead to a drastic reduction in the costs of producing cameras and make them available at much lower prices. Such a development would almost certainly increase the demand for films (the complementary good). Figure 18.1 provides a diagrammatic explanation of the movements just described.

This relationship can also be shown on a cross elasticity of demand curve as Fig. 18.2 illustrates. As we have seen in Chapter 15, complements have negative cross elasticity of demand.

Competitive demand

Goods which are close substitutes for one another are said to be in competitive demand. Other things being equal, the demand for a commodity will tend to vary directly as the price of its substitute. If the price of butter falls we should expect the demand for margarine to fall. Figure 18.3 explains this relationship between goods in competitive demand. In Fig. 18.3(a) we note that a fall in the supply of beef has raised the price

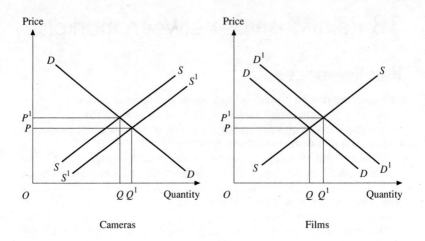

Fig. 18.1

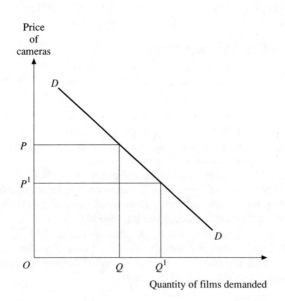

Fig. 18.2

and reduced the quantity demanded. This has caused an increase in the demand for pork, an increase in its price, and an increase in the quantity supplied, as shown in Fig. 18.3(b).

The information can also be shown on a cross elasticity of demand curve. This time, as Fig. 18.4 illustrates, it is one showing positive cross elasticity of demand.

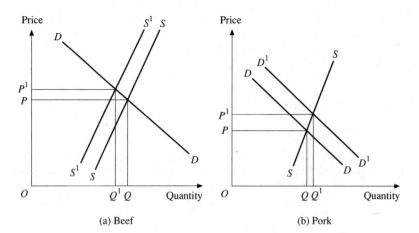

(a) Beef   (b) Pork

Fig. 18.3

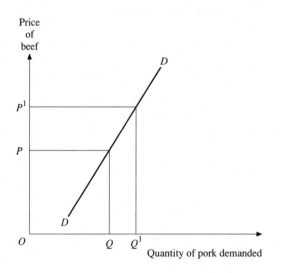

Fig. 18.4

Composite demand

A good is said to be in composite demand when it is demanded for several
different uses. The demands for such goods are the aggregates of the
demands of the various users. Wool will be demanded by the textile
industry, carpet manufacturers, blanket manufacturers, the hosiery industry,
and many others. An increase in the demand for wool by any one industry
will raise the price and affect the prices of all the other commodities
made from wool. Copper, nylon, and rubber provide good examples of

basic commodities widely used in many different industries. Thus, we might have a situation where a large increase in the demand for central heating (copper pipes) might increase prices in the electrical components industries (printed circuits and cables).

Supply relationships

Joint supply

An interesting relationship, and one which gives rise to a number of difficult economic problems, is that of joint supply, where the production of one good automatically leads to an output of another. Lead and zinc are found in the same ore so that the extraction of one leads to the extraction of the other. We cannot produce beef unless we produce hides and the production of mutton leads to a supply of wool. An oil refinery produces many different fuels from crude oil and, in the short period, an increased output of any one product, say petrol, will automatically increase the output of the others (benzine, fuel oil, etc.).

One very important, but not so obvious, example of this relationship is to be found in the transport industry. Haulage contractors, bus companies, and the railways cannot, normally, supply an outward journey without supplying an inward journey. This gives rise to the very costly problems of 'empty running'.

Where commodities are in joint supply an increase in the demand for one of them will cause a fall in the price of the other. This is demonstrated in Fig. 18.5. We have two commodities, A and B, which are

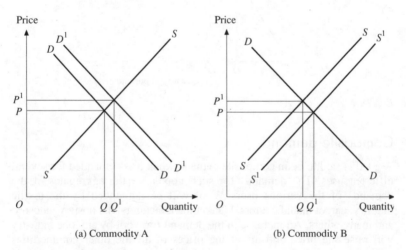

(a) Commodity A   (b) Commodity B

Fig. 18.5

jointly supplied. In Fig. 18.5(a) the demand for A increases, causing the price to rise from OP to OP^1 and the quantity supplied to increase from OQ to OQ^1. But this increase in the quantity supplied of A means an increase in the supply of B. The effect of this is shown in Fig. 18.5(b).

Competitive supply

Most products are in competitive supply. As we saw in Chapter 2, if a country producing on its production possibility frontier decides to produce more of one type of product, it will have to reduce its output of the other type of product.

Similarly, if a firm wishes to expand its output of one product it produces, perhaps because of a rise in its profitability, it may have to shift resources away from making other products, thereby reducing their supply. Figure 18.6(a) shows that an increase in demand for Flintstone toys causes their price to rise and their supply to extend whilst the supply of Trolls made by the same firm decreases.

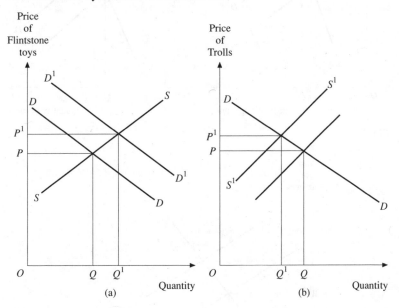

Fig. 18.6

Relationships between product and factor markets

A change in demand and/or supply of a product will affect not only the market for that product but also the factor markets involved (the markets for the inputs that produce the product). Similarly changes in the factor markets will have repercussions in the product markets.

We can examine these inter-relationships by looking at two examples. If in a country there is a move away from eating meat towards vegetarianism, the price of vegetables will increase and the price of meat will fall. Figure 18.7 shows how an increase in demand for vegetables

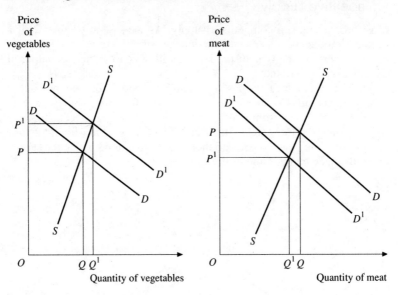

Fig. 18.7

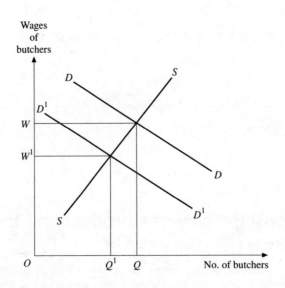

Fig. 18.8

causes their price to rise and supply to extend, whilst the decrease in demand for meat causes its price to fall and its supply to contract.

If the rise in the price of vegetables leads to an increase in the profitability of vegetables, demand for greenhouses, for workers in the vegetable industry, for vegetable-processing equipment, for vegetarian restaurants, etc., will increase. Whilst if the profitability of meat falls the demand for land to graze cattle or for lorries to transport animals, for hot-dog stalls, for abattoirs, etc., will decrease. Figure 18.8 shows the likely effects on the market for butchers.

Changes in factor markets affect product markets. For example, if actors at the Royal Shakespeare Company, based in Stratford, receive a rise in real pay, then the cost of producing plays will rise. This will be likely to raise the price of theatre tickets.

19 Perfect competition

In this part we look at the various market conditions under which prices are determined. We start by looking at the highest degree of competition possible.

Definition

The economist's model of perfect competition is highly theoretical, but it does provide a useful tool of economic analysis and helps us to make some sense of real world conditions. The real world is much too complicated to understand all at once; it is necessary to examine one feature at a time. Economists are able to use their model of a perfect market as a means of assessing the degree of competition in real world markets. They set out the conditions necessary for a perfect market and then contrast these with the situations found in the markets for goods and services. The degree of competition in these real markets is based upon the extent to which they approximate to the model of perfect competition. It is necessary to point out that the competition referred to here is *price competition*. Firms are assumed to be engaged in a rivalry for sales which takes the form of underselling competitors.

In a market operating under the conditions of perfect competition, there will be one, and only one, market price, and this price will be beyond the influence of any one buyer or any one seller.

Characteristics

A perfectly competitive market has a number of key characteristics.

- All units of the commodity are homogeneous (i.e. one unit is exactly like another). If this condition exists, buyers will have no preference for the goods of any particular seller.
- There must be many buyers and many sellers so that the behaviour of any one buyer, or any one seller, has no influence on the market price. Each individual buyer comprises such a small part of total demand and each seller is responsible for such a small part of total supply that any change in their plans will have no influence on the market price.
- Buyers are assumed to have perfect knowledge of market conditions; they know what prices are being asked for the commodity in every

part of the market. Equally sellers are fully aware of the activities of buyers and other sellers.

- There must be no barriers to the movement of buyers from one seller to another. Since all units of the commodity are identical, buyers will always approach the seller quoting the lowest price.
- Finally, it is assumed that there are no restrictions on the entry of firms into the market or on their exit from it.

We can now see why, in a perfect market, there will be one and only one market price which is beyond the control of any one buyer or any one seller. Firms cannot charge different prices because they are selling identical products, each of them is responsible for a tiny part of the total supply, and buyers are fully aware of what is happening in the market.

The individual firm under perfect competition

Under conditions of perfect competition the firm is powerless to exert any influence on price. It sees the market price as 'given', that is, established by forces beyond its control. For example, in most countries, the individual farmer has no influence on the prices at which he sells his wheat, or beef, or milk, or vegetables. Any changes in the amounts of these things which he brings to market will have negligible effects on their prices. The firm, under perfect competition, is a 'price-taker'.

The demand curve for the output of the single firm, therefore, must be a horizontal line at the ruling price; in other words, a perfectly elastic demand curve. No matter how many units the firms sells it cannot change the price. It can sell its entire output at the ruling market price. If it tries to sell at higher prices its demand will drop to zero, and there is obviously no incentive to sell at lower prices. Again, we must guard against a common misunderstanding. The demand curve for the product of *the firm* will be perfectly elastic, but the *market demand curve* for the output of *the industry* will be of the normal shape (i.e. sloping downwards from left to right). Market price will be determined by the total demand and supply curves. Figure 19.1 should make this clear.

Figure 19.1 (*a*) shows the determination of the market price (*OP*) by the forces of market demand and supply. D^1D^1 is the demand curve facing the industry and *SS* is the total supply provided by all the firms in that industry. In Fig. 19.1 (*b*) we have the situation facing the individual firm. Market price (*OP*) is externally determined and the firm sees the demand for its product as being perfectly elastic. In the two diagrams, the scales on the price axes will be the same, but the scales on the quantity axes will be very different, because the firm supplies a negligibly small part of the total output of the product.

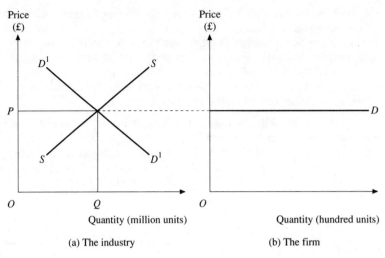

Fig. 19.1

Average and marginal revenues

When a firm faces a perfectly elastic demand curve, how does it deter-mine its output? In theory it could sell an infinite amount at the existing market price, because no matter what quantity it sells, it has no influence on the price. The answer to the question is to be found in the shape of the firm's average and marginal cost curves. As explained earlier these curves are assumed to be U-shaped and, if increasing output eventually leads to rising unit costs, there must come a point where the cost of pro-ducing a unit of output will exceed its price. It should be apparent that a firm will continue to expand its output as long as the revenue it receives from additional output exceeds the cost of producing that additional out-put. This leads us to consider how a firm's revenue changes as its output changes. There are three ways of looking at a firm's revenues.

- *Total revenue (TR)* is quite simply the money value of the total amount sold.
- *Average revenue (AR)* is another name for price because it is equal to revenue per unit sold.

$$\text{i.e. } AR = \frac{\text{Total revenue}}{\text{Number of units sold}}$$

In economic theory, the demand curve or price line is often referred to as the average revenue curve.

- *Marginal revenue (MR)* is the additional revenue obtained when sales are increased by one unit, or, more precisely, it is the change in total revenue when the quantity sold is varied by one unit. For example,

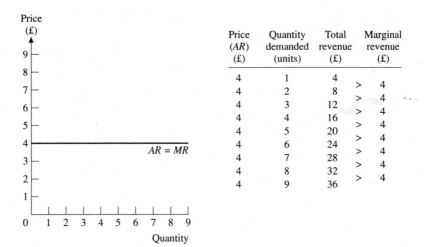

Fig. 19.2   Perfectly elastic demand curve

Price (AR) (£)	Quantity demanded (units)	Total revenue (£)	Marginal revenue (£)
4	1	4	
			> 4
4	2	8	
			> 4
4	3	12	
			> 4
4	4	16	
			> 4
4	5	20	
			> 4
4	6	24	
			> 4
4	7	28	
			> 4
4	8	32	
			> 4
4	9	36	

$$\text{The marginal revenue of the 10th unit} = \text{Total revenue from sale of 10 units} \ minus \ \text{Total revenue from sale of 9 units}$$

Figure 19.2 shows a perfectly elastic demand curve of the type faced by the firm operating under perfect competition. In this case *MR* must always be equal to *AR*. As the quantity sold increases, the price remains unchanged so that each additional unit sold increases total revenue by an amount equal to its price.

The total revenue curve of a firm operating under conditions of perfect competition is a straight upward sloping curve as illustrated in Fig. 19.3.

The output of the firm under perfect competition

We assume that the firm is in business to make profits and that it will aim to maximise profits. As long as the price (*AR*) it receives for each unit exceeds the average cost of production, the firm will be making profits. Thus, in Fig. 19.4 when price = *OP*, the firm will be making profits in the range of output *OQ* to OQ^3, because at all outputs in this range, *AR* is greater than *AC*.

We have to determine which output between *OQ* and OQ^3 yields the maximum profit. It should be apparent that output OQ^1 will yield the maximum profit *per unit*, but firms seek to maximise total profit not profit per unit. We notice first that as output increases from *OQ* to OQ^2, the firm's total profit will be increasing because for each additional unit

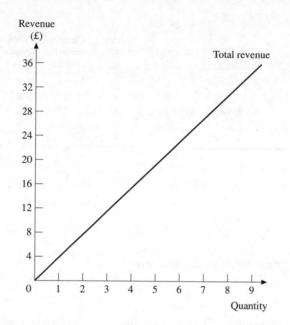

Fig. 19.3

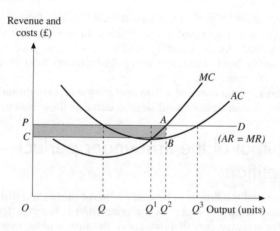

Fig. 19.4

produced, the increase in total revenue (i.e. *MR*) is greater than the increase in total cost (i.e. *MC*). Remember that in this particular case, *MR* = *AR*.

As output is expanded beyond OQ^2, total profit will be decreasing, because, for each additional unit produced, the increase in total revenue (i.e. *MR*) is less than the increase in total cost (i.e. *MC*).

Therefore since total profit is increasing up to OQ^2 and falling beyond OQ^2, profits must be maximised when output is at OQ^2, that is, when Marginal Revenue = Marginal Cost. It is important that the explanation above is fully understood, because the relationship which has been derived, i.e. *profits are maximised when output is at the point where MR = MC*, applies to all firms, whatever market structure they are operating in.

In the case of the perfectly competitive firm illustrated in Fig. 19.4 demand is perfectly elastic so that $AR = MR$. Thus, *in this particular case*, we can say that maximum profits will be earned where $AR = MR = MC$.

Normal and abnormal (supernormal) profit

The economist takes the view that some level of profit, described as *normal profit*, should be regarded as a cost of production. Normal profit is the minimum level of profit which will persuade an entrepreneur to stay in business. It will vary from industry to industry depending upon the degree of risk involved. Since production will not continue unless this minimum level of profit is forthcoming, normal profit may be legitimately regarded as a cost of production. Normal profits, therefore, are included in the calculations which produce the AC curve. Therefore, when price exceeds average cost, the firm is said to be earning *abnormal profits* (or supernormal profits). Supernormal profit is illustrated by the shaded area in Fig. 19.4. When output is at OQ^2, the cost per unit is equal to BQ^2, but the price is equal to AQ^2. Supernormal profit per unit, therefore, is AB. Total supernormal profit is equal to the area $AB \times OQ^2$ (i.e., the shaded area). Supernormal profits arise when either costs fall or demand increases.

The elimination of supernormal profits

Although the firm in Fig. 19.4 is in equilibrium, the industry is not in equilibrium. There will be forces at work tending to change the size of the industry. One of the assumptions of perfect competition is freedom of entry. The situation depicted in Fig. 19.4 will not persist in the long run, because the supernormal profits being earned by the existing firms will attract other firms into this industry. As new firms come in, total supply will increase, market price will fall, and the process will continue until the supernormal profits have been 'competed away.' Figure 19.5 shows that the entry of new firms moves the industry's supply curve to the right and lowers price. This will cause firms to move into a position of long-run equilibrium.

Long-run equilibrium

The long-run equilibrium of the firm is shown in Fig. 19.6. The market price has fallen to OP^1 and the most profitable output is now OQ^1, where $AR = MR = MC$. Note that price, or average revenue, is now equal to average cost so that the firm is making only normal profits. There is no

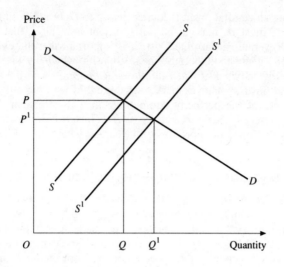

Fig. 19.5

incentive for firms to enter or leave the industry so that both the firm and the industry are in equilibrium. The long-run equilibrium of the firm, therefore, is to be found where,

$$AR = MR = MC = AC$$

In theory, the system of perfect competition produces a long-run equilibrium where all firms earn only normal profits *and* produce at minimum cost.

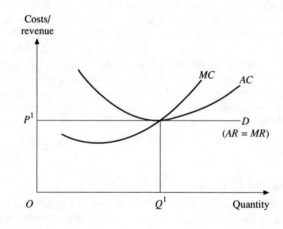

Fig. 19.6

Subnormal profits

In the short run firms may experience subnormal profits (i.e. losses). This will mean that firms will be producing where average cost exceeds average revenue. Subnormal profits occur if either costs rise or demand falls. Figure 19.7 shows subnormal profit arising due to a decrease in demand.

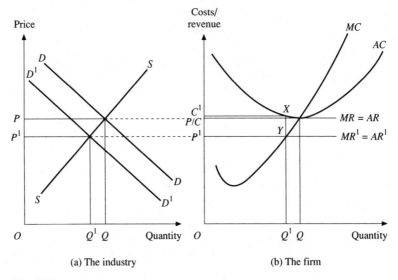

(a) The industry   (b) The firm

Fig. 19.7

The area $C^1 \times YP^1$ represents the area of loss that the firm is making. It is costing the firm C^1 per unit to produce the good but the firm is receiving a price of only P^1 so it is not covering all of its costs.

In this situation some firms will leave the industry but some will remain. Those that stay in the industry will be those that believe that they will be able to return to earning normal profits and that currently can cover their variable costs. If the price a firm is receiving is covering its average variable costs it will be covering the direct cost of production and may be making some contribution to average fixed costs. Whereas if the firm shut down it would not be able to cover any of the fixed costs that it would still have to meet. Figure 19.8 shows two firms making subnormal profits. Firm (a) is covering its average variable cost and will stay in the industry, at least in the short run, whilst firm (b) is not and will leave the industry.

Firms in perfect competition are usually assumed to have identical cost curves. However, this is not a very realistic assumption. This is because even if all units of land, labour, and capital were equally efficient and available to all firms on identical terms, it is most unlikely that all entrepreneurs will have the same outlook, the same ability, and the same

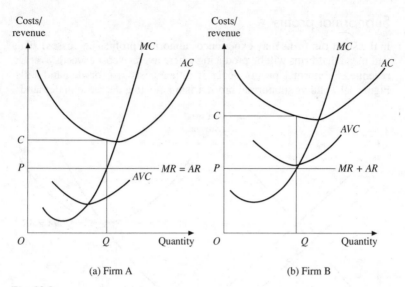

(a) Firm A   (b) Firm B

Fig. 19.8

energy. It is the marginal firms (i.e. those with the highest costs) which
will be the first to leave the industry when subnormal profits are being
made and the last to enter when supernormal profits are experienced.

Long run adjustment to subnormal profits

As we discussed above the existence of subnormal profits will cause some
firms to leave the industry. This will move the industry's supply curve to
the left, raise price and return profits to the normal profit level. Figure
19.9 shows the industry and a firm returning to long-run equilibrium
where there is no incentive for firms to enter or leave the industry and
where firms are earning normal profit.

The firm's supply curve under conditions of perfect competition

The previous explanation of how a firm under perfect competition determines its output may be used to explain the shape of the individual firm's
supply curve and the general shape of the total supply curve for the
industry. It has been shown that firms attempt to set their outputs at the
point where $MR = MC$. For the firm in perfect competition, MR is always
equal to AR (i.e. price) so that the individual firm will try to adjust its
output so as to equate price and marginal cost.

In the conditions shown in Fig. 19.10 when the market price is OP the
firm will produce output OQ. If the market price falls to OP^1, the firm, in

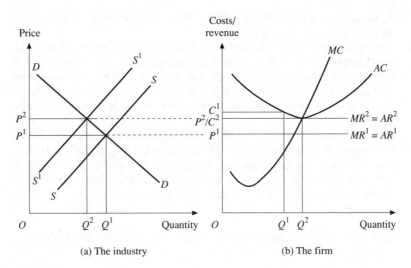

(a) The industry   (b) The firm

Fig. 19.9

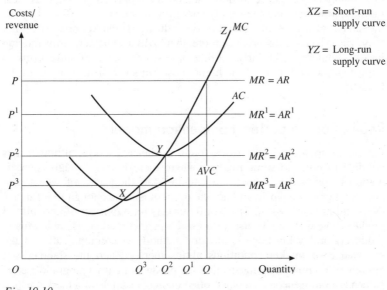

Fig. 19.10

trying to maximise profit, will reduce output to OQ^1. The MC curve, therefore, is acting as the firm's supply curve, because it is determining the quantity supplied at any given price. If the market price falls to OP^2, the firm will adjust its output to OQ^2 (where price equals marginal cost).

At this point, however, Price = $MC = AC$ so that the firm will be making no more than normal profits.

If market price falls below OP^2, the firm will be making losses because, at all outputs, price will be less than average cost. Thus when price is OP^3 the firm will be making losses, but at this price, OQ^3 still represents the 'most profitable' output in the sense that it represents the output at which losses are minimised. In the short-run, the firm may still produce even when price is less than average total cost provided it is above average variable cost. So the short-run supply curve is that part of the MC curve which lies above the AVC curve. In the long run all costs have to be covered so the long-run supply curve is that part of the MC curve which lies above the AC curve. It slopes upwards from left to right because increasing output gives rise to increasing marginal cost.

The industry's supply curve under conditions of perfect competition

The total or market supply curve for a commodity is obtained by adding together the supply curves of all the firms producing that commodity. This total supply curve is described as the industry supply curve. We must bear in mind, however, that the supply curve for an industry is affected by the movement of firms into and out of the industry. If market price rises, not only will existing firms produce more, there will also be new firms moving into the industry. Similarly, falling prices will cause existing firms to reduce output and some of the higher cost firms will be driven out of the industry.

Realism of the perfect competition model

Perfect competition is not to be found in the real world, although it is possible to point to some markets where there is some rough approximation to this 'ideal'. There are hundreds of thousands of wheat producers all over the world and no one of them is large enough to influence the world price of wheat. The world markets for a number of agricultural products contain many of the features of a perfect market. There are many producers and many buyers; modern methods of communication make knowledge of market conditions almost perfect, and the standardised grading of commodities means that the products in any one grade are regarded as homogeneous. Another, often quoted, example of a market which bears some resemblance to a perfect market is the Stock Exchange, the market in stocks and shares.

20 Monopolistic competition

Definition

Monopolistic competition is a market structure in which there are a large number of firms making similar products. It derives its name from the fact that it contains elements of both perfect competition and monopoly (see Chapter 22). This form of market structure is common in the service sector, for example, public houses, car repair firms and restaurants.

Characteristics

There are a number of characteristics of monopolistic competition. We have already mentioned that there will be a large number of firms. We have also stated that the products are similar. They are, but nevertheless each firm's product is unique and each firm's products are differentiated from those of the other firms in the industry. For instance, one public house may have a games room, one may specialise in vegetarian food, and one may participate in a pub quiz competition. This means that there can be consumer loyalty to a particular seller (in this case to a particular landlord/landlady).

There are no or very low barriers to entry. The firms do not require large-scale capital investment and use equipment which can be sold on (there are few sunk costs). Indeed the firms tend to operate on a relatively small scale.

It is assumed that the firms are profit maximisers and so produce where $MC = MR$.

Average and marginal revenue

Although there are many firms producing under monopolistic competition, as each one is selling a differentiated product, its output will influence price. Hence firms are price makers.

To sell more a firm will have to lower its price. This is shown in the table under Fig. 20.1. For example, in order to increase sales from 3 units to 4 units, price must be reduced from £7 to £6. The extra unit will be sold for £6, but TR will only increase by £3. The net gain in revenue (MR) of £3 is equal to the additional £6 from the sale of the 4th unit minus the revenue forgone (£3) resulting from the £1 reduction in the price of the first 3 units. If the demand curve slopes downward, therefore, MR will always be less than AR (i.e. price).

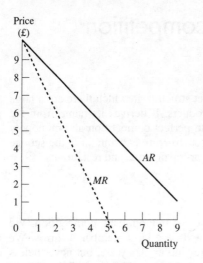

Price (£)	Quantity demanded (units)	Total revenue (£)	Marginal revenue (£)
9	1	9	
8	2	16	7
7	3	21	5
6	4	24	3
5	5	25	1
4	6	24	−1
3	7	21	−3
2	8	16	−5
1	9	9	−7

Fig. 20.1   Downward-sloping demand curve

Total revenue

The firm's total revenue curve will rise at first when marginal revenue is positive and demand is elastic, reach a peak when marginal revenue is zero and elasticity of demand is unity, and fall when marginal revenue is negative and demand is inelastic.

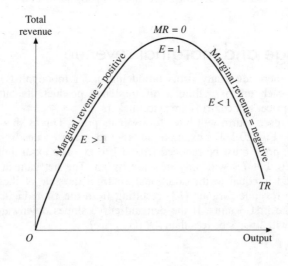

Fig. 20.2

Short-run output and profit levels

In the short run, firms may experience supernormal, normal or subnormal profits.

As with perfect competition, supernormal profits will arise if there is a fall in costs or an increase in demand. Figure 20.3 shows a firm making supernormal profits. It is producing where $MC = MR$ and where AR exceeds AC. Subnormal profits (losses) arise when costs rise or demand decreases. Figure 20.4 shows this position with AC exceeding AR.

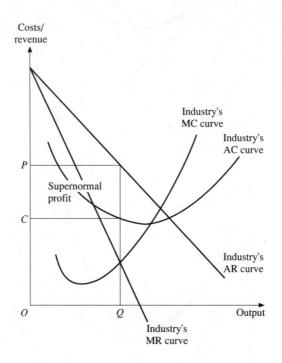

Fig. 20.3

The long run equilibrium position

As there are no or very low barriers to entry, i.e., nothing or virtually nothing to stop firms entering or leaving the industry, normal profits will be earned in the long run. If supernormal profits are experienced, new firms will be attracted into the industry; causing supply to increase, price to fall and profits to return to the normal profit level. Figure 20.5 shows the long run equilibrium position where $MC = MR$, $AC = AR$ and $AC = AR > MC = MR$.

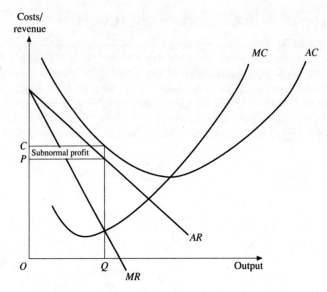

Fig. 20.4

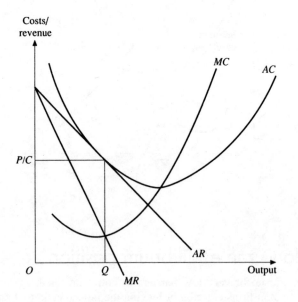

Fig. 20.5

Monopolistic and perfect competition compared

Monopolistic competition is similar to perfect competition in a number of ways. Both market structures contain many buyers and sellers, although the number is less in monopolistic competition than in perfect competition.

In both cases the firms are profit maximisers and because of the absence of barriers to entry and exit, will earn normal profits in the long run. However, there are a number of key differences. As we have seen, firms in monopolistic competition are price makers with their output affecting price whereas firms in perfect competition are price takers.

Firms in monopolistic competition have elastic demand whereas firms in perfect competition have perfectly elastic demand. In a monopolistic competition market the products are differentiated and not homogeneous. Consumers can prefer the goods or services of one producer in monopolistic competition and there can be an attachment between consumers and producers. There may even be advertising, albeit on a small scale, in monopolistic competition.

Whereas firms operating under conditions of perfect competition produce at the bottom of the average cost curve in the long run, firms operating under conditions of monopolistic competition produce where average costs are falling and there is spare capacity. (See Chapter 23 for more comparisons.)

21 Oligopoly

Definition

In many industries, especially the science-based, and technologically advanced industries, we find a market situation known as oligopoly. As the name implies, this is where the market is dominated 'by the few'. In other words, a small number of very large firms account for practically the whole output of the industry. Good examples of oligopoly are to be found in the industries producing oil, detergents, tyres, motor cars, synthetic fibres, and cigarettes.

Where there are important technical economies of scale to be gained, the processes of merger and amalgamation have drastically reduced the number of firms in an industry and brought into being some very large business units. In several industries in the UK more than 90 per cent of the market is supplied by no more than three or four firms.

Characteristics

As we noted above, this market structure is characterised by a high degree of industrial concentration. The good or service produced may be very similar, for example, cement, sugar (perfect oligopoly) or differentiated (e.g. cars, newspapers).

There are barriers to entry. One of the more significant barriers is the large scale on which the dominant firms are producing and the resulting economies of scale which they are able to enjoy. Indeed the industry is likely to be a high-technology industry with significant indivisible costs and with the long-run average cost curve falling over a large range of output.

The firms in this market structure are capable of earning supernormal profits in the long run. However, in practice, the profits may not always be as high as possible.

Prices are likely to be sticky in the sense that, in theory at least, they are unlikely to change very often, even sometimes when demand and costs change.

Although the industry may contain hundreds of firms, as we have stated it will be dominated by a few large firms. These firms will be interdependent. They will know a considerable amount about each other and will be influenced by expectations about how the other firms will react. Indeed, firms may engage in open or tacit collusion.

Economists have found it difficult to predict the behaviour of firms in oligopolistic markets. What is reasonably certain is that there will be a considerable amount of non-price competition.

Non-price competition

Firms may use non-price competition either because they have agreed not to compete by means of price (collusion) or because they are afraid they will lose out in a price war.

Non-price competition can take many forms. These include the use of brand names, distinctive packaging, free gifts, special features to the products and competitions. In perfect oligopoly competition based on research and development, free delivery, after-scales services and guarantees are common. The most important form of non-price competition is advertising.

Collusion

Firms may engage in open collusion in order to maximise their joint profits and to reduce uncertainty. Collusion may take the form of agreeing on the price to charge, the market share the firms are going to have and/or the advertising expenditure each firm is going to undertake.

Firms are more likely to agree not to compete on price where the product is fairly standardised. The agreed price is normally well above the average costs of the more efficient firms since, in order to persuade enough firms to join the scheme to make it operational, the price must be high enough to provide profits for the less efficient. In order to make the price effective, a price agreement is usually supported by a complementary agreement to limit output (e.g. firms agree to accept output quotas).

One form of open collusion is the cartel. This includes firms producing separately but acting as one firm in determining output and price. Figure 21.1 shows the position of the industry in which firms are operating as a cartel.

Tacit collusion

Firms may also reduce price competition and thereby increase price stability by:

- following a dominant firm's price lead, i.e., moving their prices in line with that firm's prices.
- following a barometric firm's price lead. A barometric firm is a firm which seems to be sensitive to changing market conditions.
- using average cost pricing. This involves mark-up pricing, i.e., estimating long-run average costs and then adding a percentage for profits to find price. Firms producing under conditions of oligopoly may set this price fairly low in order to ensure that they can sell a large output and thereby spread their indivisible costs over a high number of units.

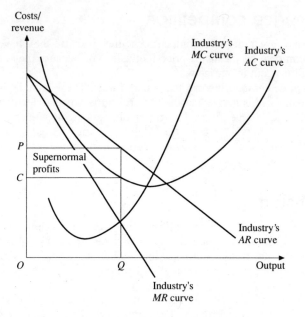

Fig. 21.1

Factors favouring collusion

There are a number of circumstances which would make collusion more likely to be successful. These include the market being stable with firms having similar production methods, costs and objectives. Firms should know a lot about each other, be able to estimate their costs and revenue reasonably accurately and be willing to share information. The number of dominant firms should be small, for instance four rather than nine, and there should be significant barriers to entry, so that firms would not be afraid that their arrangements would be disrupted by the entry of new firms.

Reasons for collusion breaking down

In practice, in most cases, collusion does not last. There are a number of reasons for this. Firms are likely to have different costs and so a set price is likely to be more beneficial to some than others. Overtime market conditions will change and so any agreement will have to be renegotiated, which may not prove to be easy. Collusion agreements are also difficult to monitor and, if known, are likely to be unpopular with the general public. Collusion may be illegal and, if it is, the firms will risk investigation and possible penalties. However, the most common reason for collusion breaking down is that some firms try to capture a larger share of the market by breaking the agreement.

Non-collusive behaviour

Firms which do not collude will have to consider carefully other firms' reactions before changing their price, product range or advertising. They may be reluctant to change their price, in particular, for fear of how rival firms will react. The kinked demand curve, as shown in Fig. 21.2 seeks to explain this.

The price is *OP* and output is *OQ*. The demand curve is kinked at *G*. At prices higher than *OP*, demand is very elastic. The explanation is that the oligopolist fears that if his prices are raised competitors will not follow suit and a large part of his market will be lost. At prices lower than *OP*, demand is more inelastic because the oligopolist believes that if he cuts his price his rivals will follow suit and he will gain relatively little in the way of additional sales.

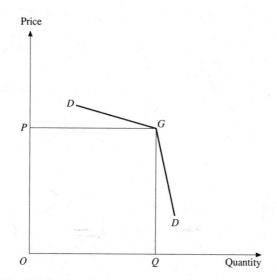

Fig. 21.2   The kinked demand curve

It is widely thought that oligopolists are not very keen to indulge in severe price competition. They know that any move on the part of one firm to reduce its price will provoke similar action from the other firms. The final result is likely to be that all the firms will finish up selling at lower prices while their market shares remain much the same as before the price war.

The price war which broke out in the newspaper industry in the UK in 1993–4 proved an exception with *The Times* and the *Sun* increasing their market shares markedly by lowering their prices.

Games theory

In seeking to explain the behaviour of oligopolist firms' behaviour economists often make use of games theory. This suggests that firms, concerned about how rivals will react, often opt for the second-best strategy. This is frequently illustrated by the 'Prisoner's Dilemma'. Two people are arrested for robbery and held separately. Each is told that if he confesses and implicates his partner he will receive a sentence of three years. However, if the prisoner does not confess but is found guilty on the evidence of his partner he will receive a sentence of ten years. The best outcome for each prisoner is for neither to confess and both to be released. However, each is likely to be afraid to take the risk that the other one will not confess, so the second-best option of confessing is likely to be taken.

22 Monopoly

Definition

There are two definitions of monopoly. A pure monopoly exists when there is a sole supplier. In this case the firm will be the industry. An example is the Bank of England which is the only supplier of banknotes in England and Wales.

The government definition is a firm which has a minimum 25 per cent share of the market. For example, Thomson, in 1993, had a 34% share of the tour operators' market and the *Sun* had a 29 per cent share of the national daily papers market.

However, market share is not always a good guide to monopoly power. A firm with one quarter of the total market may have great market power (where the rest of the market is shared by numerous small firms), or it may face very keen competition (where the rest of the market is supplied by four or five firms of almost equal size).

Reference is also often made to natural monopolies. A natural monopoly occurs when there is room for only one firm in the industry producing at minimum efficient scale. This situation arises when there is just one source of supply of a raw material or more commonly when economies of scale are significant and permit one firm to supply the entire market at a lower price than any other number of firms.

Monopoly power

A monopolist has the power to determine either

- the price at which he will sell his product;
- the quantity he wishes to sell.

He cannot determine both price and quantity, because he cannot control demand. If he decides on the price at which he is prepared to sell, the demand curve will determine the quantity he can dispose of at the chosen price. If he wishes to market a given quantity per month, then the demand curve will determine the price at which this quantity may be disposed of. The monopolist's power to influence price depends upon two factors: the availability of close substitutes and the power to restrict the entry of new firms. These two features are closely related because the latter has some influence on the former.

If there are a number of substitutes available, the prices of which compare favourably with the price of the monopolist's product, his market power will be very limited.

Monopoly power has been defined as the ability to earn long-run supernormal profits. We know from our analysis of perfect competition that this will only be possible if there are some effective barriers to the entry of new firms. The more effective the restrictions on the emergence of new firms, the greater will be the power of the monopolist to exploit the consumer by charging prices well above his average cost.

Barriers to entry

Monopoly power depends upon the effectiveness of the barriers which prevent potential competitors from entering that particular industry. These restrictions on entry can arise in a number of ways.

Concentration of raw materials

The geographical distribution of natural resources is very uneven and the known or workable deposits of some materials are concentrated into very small regions (although new discoveries are continually changing the situation). At one time most of world's nickel was obtained from a certain area in the Rockies; a large proportion of the total world supply of gold and diamonds comes from South Africa; and, until the development of artificial fertilisers, Chile had a virtual monopoly of the world supply of nitrates. Peculiarities of soil and climatic conditions can also provide certain regions with monopoly powers. Until quite recently parts of the southern USA had a monopoly in the supply of soyabeans. This particular feature is most strikingly illustrated in the supply of wines where we have such products as Champagne, Burgundy, and Moselle clearly associated with the areas where they are produced.

Technical barriers

In modern capitalist states there are a number of industries which are dominated by a few giant firms. Where the existing firms are already operating on a vast scale, making use of expensive indivisible units of capital, and enjoying extensive technical economies of scale, the barriers to the entry of new firms are quite formidable. There is very little prospect of a new entrant starting in a small way and growing larger by increasing his share of the market. The smaller producer could not compete with the existing firms because his average cost of production would be so much greater. Only by commencing operations on a scale comparable to that employed by existing firms would a new entrant be able to compete effectively. Even this would be very risky unless the market had a very large growth potential, because the large increase in supply would seriously depress market prices. Existing firms in such industries are in a protected position and this is an inducement to form a monopoly.

Advertising and branding

Where a market is dominated by a pure monopoly or by firms with 25% or more share of the market, each of which is marketing a number of heavily advertised brands, it is extremely difficult for a new firm to break into the market. The initial advertising costs of establishing a new brand in such a market is a formidable deterrent. For example, if there are 3 existing firms each selling 4 brands, a new producer faces the prospect of very costly advertising in order to establish his product. But, even if he succeeds in taking a proportionate share of this market, he will only have one-thirteenth of it – he is competing with 12 brands rather than 3 firms.

Legal barriers

Probably the most formidable restrictions against the entry of new firms are legal barriers where the law of the land operates to prevent the emergence of competing firms. This particular form of restriction has a long history. The great overseas trading companies formed in the fifteenth and sixteenth centuries were granted monopoly rights in specified geographical areas. These rights were granted by the Crown in the form of Royal Charters. The Hudson's Bay Company and the East India Company are two of the more famous of these trading companies which were granted the sole right to trade in certain regions. Much later, public utility companies formed by Act of Parliament to provide water, gas, and electricity were granted local monopoly powers, but were subject to some degree of public regulation (they were privately owned). More recently we have the examples of the nationalised industries where the controlling boards have been granted monopoly powers.

The granting of patent rights is a further important example of competition being limited by law. The firm holding the patent is protected from the threat of competition from new firms (or existing firms) making identical products, at least for the period of time which is the life of the patent, usually 16 years.

Transport costs and tariffs

Although two or more firms may be making identical products and operating at similar costs, it is possible for such firms to enjoy local monopoly positions. Firm A will be able to sell more cheaply in its own locality than Firm B since Firm B's additional transport costs will increase its selling prices in Firm A's local market. Thus Firm A will be able to raise its prices, in the local market, above its production costs by an amount which does not exceed Firm B's transport costs. We know that shops in villages or suburbs are sometimes able to charge a little more than the larger stores in city centres because they have some degree of protection in the form of transport costs (e.g. bus fares).

Tariffs operate to protect a home market against competition from foreign producers. They have the same economic effect as transport costs, for they raise the price in the home market above the foreign producer's costs of production. Tariffs may encourage the formation of monopolies among domestic producers since, as a monopoly, they could raise market price by the extent of any differential between their own costs and the artificially high price of the foreign commodity.

Restrictive practices

Although in most countries they are now subject to legal control and many of them have been made illegal, agreements between firms to restrict competition in an industry have been an important means of establishing monopoly situations. There are many ways in which the existing firms in an industry can combine to prevent the entry of new firms. For example, they might act collectively to withhold supplies from any wholesaler or retailer who stocks the goods of any new producer. They may also, as with oligopolists, engage in price and output agreements.

There are also barriers to exit with, for example, a high degree of capital expenditure making firms reluctant to leave the industry.

Cost and revenue curves

Since a pure monopolist is a sole supplier of a commodity, the demand curve for his product is the total or market demand curve. The AR and MR curves for the monopolist, therefore will be similar to those illustrated in Chapter 20 (Fig. 20.1). If we combine these AR and MR curves with the conventional cost curves, as in Fig. 22.1 we can determine the most profitable output. It has already been demonstrated that this output occurs where $MR = MC$.

Figure 22.1 is an important diagram and may be interpreted as follows.

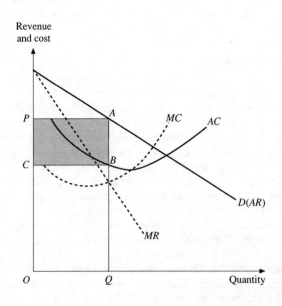

Fig. 22.1

- Maximum profits are attained when output is at OQ where MR = MC. The reasoning should now be familiar. At lower outputs each unit produced adds more to revenue than to costs. When output is greater than OQ each additional unit adds more to costs than to revenue.
- The price at which output OQ can be sold is determined by the demand curve. Thus, output OQ will be marketed at price OP.
- At the output level OQ, average cost equals QB and supernormal profit per unit is AB.
- Total supernormal profit, therefore, is equal to $AB \times OQ$ and is represented by the shaded area.

Possible output positions

Monopolists may pursue a number of objectives. These are described under the following headings.

Profit maximisation

Private-sector firms may seek to maximise profits and so will produce where $MC = MR$ as illustrated in Fig. 22.1 above. Monopolists can earn supernormal profits in the long run because of the barriers to entry. This means that new firms will not be able to enter the market to compete away the supernormal profits.

Sales maximisation

Monopolists may seek to maximise sales revenue. This is achieved where MR is zero (remember that where $MR = 0$, total revenue is at its peak). Figure 22.2 illustrates the sales maximisation output.

The directors of a firm may seek to maximise sales in order to increase their salaries and to make it more difficult for another firm to take over the company.

Normal profit

State monopolists may be instructed to break even (i.e. earn normal profits). This is achieved where average cost equals average revenue and is illustrated in Fig. 22.3.

Optimum output

Again, a state-owned monopoly may be told to produce not at the maximum profit output but at the minimum average cost output, where marginal cost equals average cost. Figure 22.4 shows a monopolist achieving productive efficiency (producing at the optimum output).

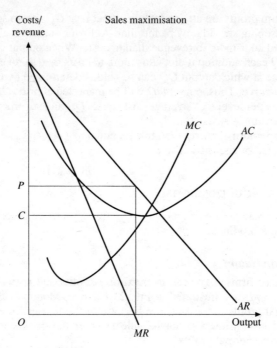

Fig. 22.2   *Sales maximisation*

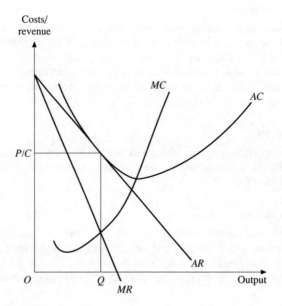

Fig. 22.3   *Normal profit output*

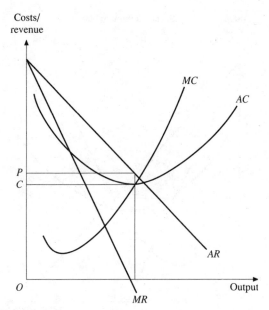

Fig. 22.4   Optimum output

Socially optimum output

This can also be referred to as the allocatively efficient output (and with productive efficiency is discussed in more detail in the next chapter). It is achieved where price (average revenue) is equal to marginal cost and is shown in Fig. 22.5.

Predatory pricing output

Predatory pricing involves a firm setting its price with the objective of drawing a competitor out of the market or discouraging potential rivals from entering the market.

Figure 22.6 shows a firm setting the price above the normal profit level but below the maximum profit level.

Price discrimination

Where there is some degree of monopoly power, firms may engage in price discrimination. This includes charging different prices in different markets for the same commodity for reasons other than costs.

In order to charge different prices the seller must be able to control the supply otherwise competitors would undersell him in the dearer market. A monopolist has the power to determine the price (or prices) at which he sells his commodity. The markets must be clearly separated so that those paying lower prices cannot resell to those paying higher prices and

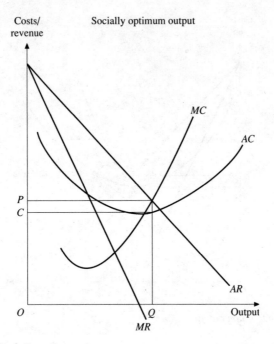

Fig. 22.5   Socially optimum output

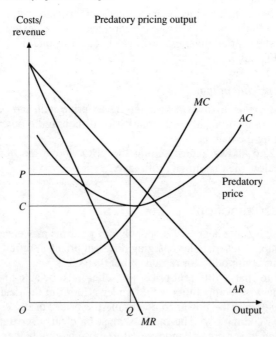

Fig. 22.6   Predatory pricing output

the demand conditions in the separate markets must be different so that total profits may be increased by charging different prices. It is really a matter of separating a group of consumers willing to pay higher prices from those who are only able or willing to pay lower prices.

The higher prices will be charged in the market/s with the less elastic demand. The firm will be likely to produce where the *MR*s in the individual markets are equal to the *MC* of producing the output. This is shown in Fig. 22.7.

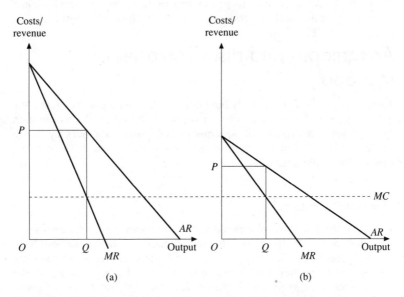

Fig. 22.7   (a) Market with inelastic demand; (b) market with elastic demand

Separation of markets

There are a number of ways in which markets can be separated. One is by a time barrier. Most passenger transport undertakings charge cheaper rates for off-peak journeys.

Markets may be separated by transport costs and tariffs. Firms often sell their goods more cheaply in export markets than in the home market. The price differential, of course, cannot exceed the cost of transporting the good back to the home market plus any tariff on imports.

A third type of price discrimination is found where it is possible to separate buyers into clearly defined groups. Before the National Health Service was established doctors commonly charged lower fees to poorer patients than to their wealthier clients. Milk is sold more cheaply to industrial users than to householders. Electricity charges also vary according to the type of consumer.

Effects of price discrimination

Price discrimination means that some groups are charged higher prices than others and although this may be regarded as an 'unfair' practice it is possible for price discrimination to be beneficial. Where it leads to a great expansion of sales and output and a significant fall in average costs of production, even those in the higher priced market may be obtaining goods at lower prices than they would be charged in a single market. For example, a large export market (gained by selling at prices lower than the home price) may lead to economies of scale which benefit home consumers even though the home price is higher than the export price.

Advantages and disadvantages of monopoly

There appears to be a generally held opinion that monopoly is against the public interest. The case against monopoly is based on the assumption that it results in higher prices, supernormal profits, inefficiency and a slower rate of technical progress. So monopoly is usually held to be against the public interest.

The public interest

The great problem with this approach to monopoly is that it requires some indicators of what is meant by 'the public interest'. The people who have to administer the policy have to come to some decision on whether the trading practices they find in the business world are operating in the public interest or against it. Unfortunately the legislation has not given any very clear guidelines. The 1948 Monopolies and Restrictive Practices Act laid down that in judging whether a monopoly was operating contrary to the public interest the investigators should consider

all matters which appear in the particular circumstances relevant ... and among other things ... the need to achieve the production, treatment and distribution by the most efficient and economical means of goods of such types and in such quantities as will best meet the requirements of home and overseas markets.

The 'other things' to be taken into account included

the organisation of industry and trade in such a way that their efficiency is progressively increased and new enterprise encouraged; the fullest use and best distribution of men, materials, and industrial capacity in the UK; the development of technical improvements, and the expansion of existing markets and the opening up of new markets.

These guide lines have been described by one former member of the Monopolies Commission as a string of platitudes, much too wide and general to be of any great assistance to those who had to reach some conclusion on a particular case. One problem of course is that some of these objectives might, in particular circumstances, be incompatible. For example, a measure which leads to greater efficiency may lead to greatly increased local unemployment. It is interesting to note that the 1948 Act did not specifically mention 'competition' among the public interest criteria. The 1973 Fair Trading Act provides more guidance in the form of a new definition of the public interest. This includes such phrases as 'the desirability of maintaining and promoting effective competition', the need for 'promoting through competition the reduction of costs and the development of new techniques and new products, and ... facilitating the entry of new competitors into existing markets'. The emphasis is now much more on competition as a means of stimulating efficiency, but the 1973 Act clearly lays down that 'all matters which appear relevant' must be considered, and it makes particular mention of the need to maintain a balanced distribution of industry and employment in the UK. The aim of promoting competition, therefore, will not be the overriding consideration. An increase in monopoly power (e.g. by merger) which, it is believed, would improve employment prospects in, say, a development area would most probably be judged to be in the public interest.

Advantages of monopoly

In the case of a natural monopoly where large-scale capital is required, average and marginal costs can fall significantly if the output is produced by one firm. Even in the case of monopolies, which are not natural monopolies, significant advantage may still be taken of economies of scale. The lower average costs may result in prices being lower than under other forms of market structure. Monopolists may spend significant sums on research and development as they are likely to have the finance to do so and the ability to protect the gains derived from any ideas/projects developed.

Some economists argue that innovations are more likely to occur under conditions of monopoly. This is because existing firms may bring new techniques and products into use to strengthen their barriers to entry and because firms outside the industry will try to innovate to get round the barriers to entry.

In addition monopoly in the home market might be necessary in order to obtain important economies of scale which, in turn, would lead to lower-priced exports. Firms which operate agreements to restrict competition between themselves might, as a consequence, collaborate in cost-reducing research and development. An agreement to restrict competition might be necessary in order to ensure a domestic source of supply. For example, an efficient plant designed to produce some synthetic fibre might have to be very large and require an enormous outlay on capital equipment. A firm may hesitate to embark on such an investment unless it can be guaranteed the whole of the home market. If a competitor were allowed to operate in the market, it would probably mean two large plants each working well below capacity with much higher costs per unit, lower profitability, and reduced prospects in export markets.

Another argument in favour of monopoly is that it provides greater stability of output and prices. In a competitive market producers respond to market signals (i.e. price changes) in the expected manner. If an increase in demand leads to higher prices, producers will react by revising their production plans upwards. But the aggregate effect of a very large number of individual decisions to raise output is likely to be excess supply in the next marketing period. This will lead to a sharp fall in prices and producers will revise their output plans downwards. Again, the total effect is likely to be an over-adjustment and a severe shortage in the next marketing period with a corresponding rise in prices. A highly competitive market, especially where there is a substantial time lag between the decision to produce and the availability of supplies, is likely to be characterised by fairly extensive price swings.

A monopolist, on the other hand, is likely to react to demand changes in a more effective manner. He supplies the total market and should be capable of estimating the true extent of market trends much more accurately than a small firm supplying a tiny part of the market. His adjustments of output, therefore, are likely to bring about an equilibrium situation fairly quickly.

Disadvantages of monopoly

Let us return to the disadvantages of monopoly to examine them in more detail. Economic theory indicates that, under monopoly, output will be lower and price will be higher than would be the case under perfect competition. We have seen that firms in a perfect market produce where price equals marginal cost, and competition between these firms forces price downwards until it is equal to minimum average cost (see Chapter 19).

A monopolist, however, has the power to restrict market supply and he will adjust his output until marginal revenue equals marginal cost. At this output, as Fig. 22.1 shows, price is greater than marginal cost, and greater than average cost.

Under perfect competition, $PRICE = MC = AC$
Under monopoly $PRICE > MC$ and $PRICE > AC$

This is probably the major argument against monopoly. Critics point to the power to exploit consumers by charging prices well above average cost and they assume that the desire for profits will lead to the abuse of this market power. Allied to this argument is the charge that monopolists can indulge in price discrimination and oblige one group of consumers to subsidise another group. The argument here is not against the principle of subsidisation, but against the system which allows the monopolist to decide which group should benefit and which group lose.

In contrast to those who believe monopolists will be innovative, some argue that a monopolist has little incentive to innovate. Market control guarantees profits, with or without innovation. Monopolies are also accused of retarding technical progress by restricting the entry of new firms. It is important that entrepreneurs with progressive ideas should be free to put them to the test in the open market. When an industry is monopolised, this source of new ideas may be lost to the community.

In addition, under conditions of monopoly, whilst there may be a range of products on offer there will be a lack of choice of producers. The producers will be in a stronger position than consumers with consumer sovereignty likely to be low. Consumer surplus is likely to be less under monopoly than under other market conditions and there may be a deadweight loss under monopoly. (These last two points will be discussed in more detail in the next chapter.)

23 Comparisons of market structure

In this chapter we compare the different market structures in which firms operate. This involves consideration of the number of firms in the market, how they compete, the size of the firms and how easy or difficult it is for firms to enter or leave the industry.

We also contrast the influence individual firms have over the price of their products, how much information consumers and producers have, how efficient the firms are and what their objectives are. We start with this last aspect.

Do firms maximise profits?

In the real world of imperfect competition, firms have some degree of discretion in determining the prices of their products. In the previous chapters it has been largely assumed that private-sector firms will always adjust prices or outputs so as to maximise profits. There is much argument as to whether this is a realistic assumption about the behaviour of firms in modern industrialised societies. The validity of the assumption of profit maximisation has been questioned on several grounds.

It has been pointed out that many businesspeople are not aware of the concepts of marginal revenue and marginal cost and, of those who do have knowledge of these ideas, many would find it extremely difficult to obtain any precise measurements of MC and MR. It is sometimes said, therefore, that firms do not maximise profits because they lack the knowledge necessary for them to do so. But even if the foregoing assertions are true, they do not destroy the profit-maximisation theory. If businesspeople try to increase profits by trial and error adjustments of their prices, they will be tending towards the output where $MR = MC$, even if they are unaware of these concepts.

If firms tried to maintain output at the point where $MR = MC$, it is likely that prices would be very unstable because firms would have to adjust price and output levels following every change in cost and demand conditions. Many firms are reluctant to carry out frequent changes in price because such changes impose administrative costs and they lead to a loss of goodwill on the part of their customers. Instead of making frequent changes in price so as to equate MR and MC and maximise profits in the short run, firms may be more concerned with the longer-run effects of their pricing policies, that is, they will take into account the effects of today's prices on tomorrow's sales. It has been suggested that this type of behaviour does not conflict with the idea that firms try to maximise profits since they are attempting to maximise long-run rather than short-run profits.

Some studies of businesspeople's activities have led to the view that, rather than trying to maximise profits, some firms tend to opt for a 'quiet life'. They seem content with some acceptable level of profit which might be less than they could earn if they adopted more fiercely competitive policies. Managements may be reluctant to accept the increased risks and pressures which go with more aggressive and ambitious practices. While this option may be available to a firm with some degree of monopoly power, firms in very competitive markets, where no firm has any significant market power, must attempt to maximise profits in order to survive.

The fact that larger firms are not directly controlled by shareholders (the people most likely to be interested in profit-maximisation), but by professional managers provides another basis for criticising the theory of profit-maximisation. The status, prestige, and remuneration of managers is closely linked to the size of the firm and it is likely, therefore, that such people will be more interested in maximising sales rather than maximising profits. They cannot be indifferent to the profit and loss account of the firm, but, having achieved a level of profit which they believe will satisfy shareholders, managers are more inclined to make sales-maximisation their major objective.

Several investigations into business practices have revealed the fact that a large number of firms fix their prices on what is described as a *full-cost* basis. Estimates are prepared of the firm's average total cost. There is evidence that this may be constant over a wide range of output. To this average cost figure management adds some conventional profit margin (described as the 'mark-up') and this determines the price at which the product is marketed. Sales are determined by what the market will absorb at this price (i.e. by demand). Under this system the critical decision is the extent of the mark-up. It seems that the mark-up is periodically adjusted in the light of changes in demand conditions and the extent of competition from other firms. If this is so, full-cost pricing may be the industrialist's way of moving towards the price/output combination which yields maximum profits.

Firms' objectives

As indicated above, it is in market structures with some degree of mono- poly power, in particular monopolies and oligopolies, that objectives other than profit maximisation may be pursued. Firms which operate in these markets may have several goals, for example, profits, stability, maximum sales, protecting their share of the market, management status, and so on.

At any one time one goal may be paramount. Whether this is the case and which goal it is will depend on the relative strengths of the different groups who influence a firm's objectives. These groups include not only managers and shareholders but also workers, consumers, the govern- ment, the local authority and environmental groups. The power, objectives and activity of these groups can change over time. For instance the power of trade unions declined in the 1980s. At any one time groups may follow similar or conflicting aims. For instance managers and workers may be interested in growth, whilst shareholders may favour profit maximisation as the main objective and environmental groups see pollution reduction as a key aim.

Firms' behaviour is significantly influenced by the behaviour of their rivals. In August 1994 pressure from animal-welfare groups, including the RSPCA, persuaded Brittany Ferries to stop transporting live animals. This was followed by an announcement by P & O to follow suit.

Barriers to entry and exit

There are no barriers to entry and exit in perfect competition and no, or in practice low, barriers to entry and exit in monopolistic competition. In these two market structures capital expenditure is low and firms new to the industry can set up easily. These firms may have previously been producing another product or may be newly established firms. Entrepreneurs will be encouraged to enter the industry by the knowledge that there are no barriers to exit in the form of, for example, heavy advertising expenditure, and other sunk costs.

In contrast there are barriers to entry and exit in both oligopoly and monopoly. As we saw in Chapter 22 the main barrier is the high cost of capital expenditure required to compete with the dominant firms who will be operating on a large scale. There may also be barriers to exit. For instance, government regulation requires the Post Office to deliver to remote rural areas and the sunk costs involved in coal-mining may make it difficult for a private-sector firm to leave the industry.

Profit levels

The existence of barriers to entry means that firms producing under conditions of oligopoly and monopoly can earn supernormal profits in the long run. Figure 23.1 shows a firm producing where $MC = MR$ and $AR > AC$.

The absence of barriers to entry, in contrast, means that firms producing under conditions of perfect competition and monopolistic competition, can earn supernormal profits only in the short run. The existence of supernormal profits will, in both cases, encourage new firms to enter the industry. The increase in supply will compete away the supernormal profits and return the industry to the long-run position of normal profits.

Figure 23.2 (a) shows the long-run position of a firm operating under conditions of perfect competition and (b) a firm operating under conditions of monopolistic competition.

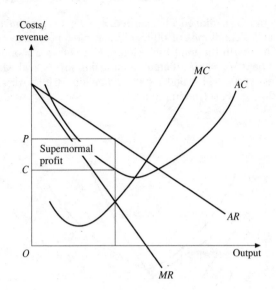

Fig. 23.1

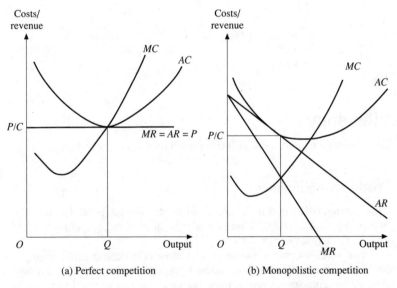

(a) Perfect competition   (b) Monopolistic competition

Fig. 23.2

There are no barriers to exit under conditions of perfect competition and monopolistic competition so subnormal profits will exist only in the short run. Firms will leave the industry, causing supply to decrease, price to rise and normal profits to be earned again.

It is not often mentioned that barriers to exit may mean that firms producing under conditions of oligopoly and monopoly may experience subnormal profits in the long run. Figure 23.3 shows a monopoly firm producing where $MC = MR$, thereby minimising losses, and where $AC > AR$. For some years, whilst under state ownership, British Airways made substantial losses but stayed in production.

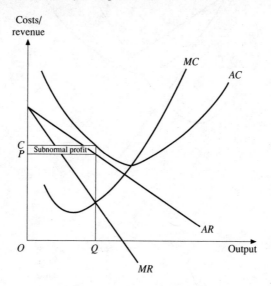

Fig. 23.3

Efficiency

Economists are concerned with three main measures of efficiency.

Productive efficiency

This occurs when output is produced at the lowest possible cost and occurs where $MC = AC$. This is achieved in perfect competition in the long run as shown in Fig. 23.4.

Private-sector firms producing under monopolistic competition, oligopoly and monopoly do not produce at the bottom of the average cost curve and so do not achieve productive efficiency. Indeed, one of the main criticisms of monopolistic competition is that firms produce with spare capacity. A higher output would lower their costs. Most state-sector monopolies are also unlikely to achieve productive efficiency unless specifically instructed to produce at minimum average cost.

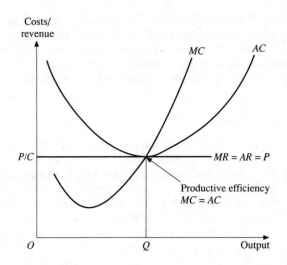

Fig. 23.4

X efficiency

This is achieved when average and marginal costs are as low as possible. It is usually thought that this will occur under conditions of perfect competition where the force of competition will drive down costs. It is expected that X inefficiency will occur under conditions of oligopoly and monopoly. This means that average cost and marginal cost curves are higher than they could be. X inefficiency occurs, in part, from complacency. Lack of competition may mean that production methods

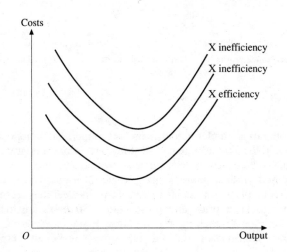

Fig. 23.5

become slack. There may be overstaffing, failure to develop new products and use of out-of-date machinery and methods. All these features will push up the *AC* curve. However remember some economists argue that monopolists and oligopolists are more likely to innovate and it is not only the position of the *AC* curve which matters but also its shape.

Allocative efficiency

Productive and X efficiencies are concerned with how products are produced, whilst allocative efficiency is concerned with the quantity produced. It is achieved where price $(AR) = MC$. At this point the cost of producing the extra unit (MC) matches the value that people place on the good. The resources devoted to the production of the good will be sufficient to meet the demand of consumers at a price which matches the marginal utility they receive from the good. Perfectly competitive firms always produce at the allocatively efficient output, irrespective of what type of profits they are earning. Figure 23.6 shows the firm producing where $P = MC$ when making (a) supernormal, (b) normal and (c) subnormal profits.

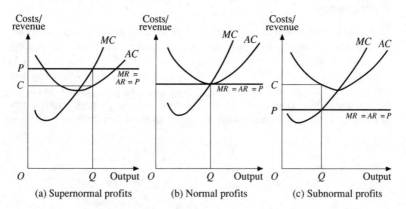

(a) Supernormal profits   (b) Normal profits   (c) Subnormal profits

Fig. 23.6

Firms operating under conditions of imperfect competition do not achieve allocative efficiency. If they are profit maximisers they will produce where $MC = MR$ but also where $P > MC$. This means that they could produce more of the product at a cost below the value that consumers place on it. However, firms deliberately restrict output in order to keep price and profits high. So there are insufficient resources devoted to making the product. Figure 23.7 compares the profit maximising output and the allocatively efficient output of a monopolist.

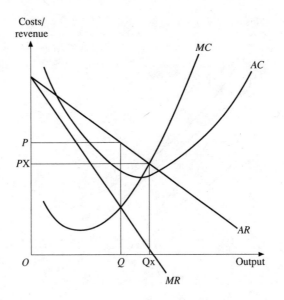

OP = Profit maximising price
OQ = Profit maximising output
OPX = Allocatively efficient price
OQX = Allocatively efficient output

Fig. 23.7

There is one exception to the above discussion. A state-run monopoly may be instructed to produce at the allocatively efficient output. This is sometimes referred to as marginal cost pricing. One problem with marginal cost pricing is that firms which have large-scale economies of scale may experience subnormal profits. This is because if average costs fall over a large range, the firm is likely to be producing where *AC* is above *MC* and so price will be below average cost. This is illustrated in Fig. 23.8.

Innovation

As mentioned above and in Chapter 22, there is debate about which form of market structure is most likely to promote efficiency. The monopolist, it is argued, has little incentive to innovate, that is, to develop new products and new techniques of production. If he does not innovate, his control of the market means that he can still make profits. The competitive firm, however, may fear that if it does not innovate it will lose its market to its competitors who *will* take advantage of new developments.

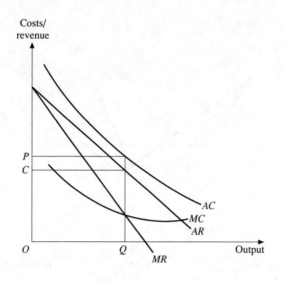

Fig. 23.8

On the other hand there is much support for the view that monopoly organisation encourages technical progress. A unified monopoly is more likely to have the resources required for research and development than a small firm in a competitive market. In addition the monopolist has more incentive to innovate since his secure market ensures that he obtains all the gains from any successful new technique or product. He can, more-over, retain these gains over the long run. Under competition any innovation will soon be copied and the gains to the innovator will be short-lived (although the patent laws provide some protection).

Consumer surplus

A comparison often made is between the consumer surplus which is earned under conditions of monopoly/oligopoly and perfect competition. In the discussion on allocative efficiency we saw that monopolists deliberately restrict output. Consumers lose out by having less of the product and paying more for it than under conditions of perfect compe-tition. A simplified diagram is often used to highlight this. Figure 23.9 presumes a constant *MC* curve and shows monopoly and perfect com-petition on the same graph.

According to this diagram if an industry moves from perfect com-petition to monopoly, price would rise, output would fall and consumer surplus would decline by *PPMBC*. Of this decline in consumer surplus, *PPMBD* converts to the monopolist and becomes producer surplus (a payment above what producers are willing to accept to supply the good). *BDC* is lost to consumers and producers and is referred to as a deadweight loss. However, if a monopolist's costs are lower than those

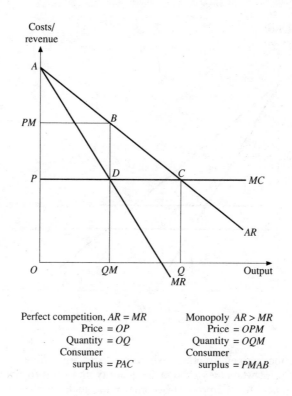

Perfect competition, $AR = MR$
Price $= OP$
Quantity $= OQ$
Consumer
surplus $= PAC$

Monopoly $AR > MR$
Price $= OPM$
Quantity $= OQM$
Consumer
surplus $= PMAB$

Fig. 23.9

of firms operating under conditions of perfect competition, due to economies of scale, price and output may be lower and may offset the deadweight welfare loss.

In Fig. 23.10 the cost savings of *PXYZ* exceed the deadweight loss of *SXT*.

Other comparisons

Whilst under conditions of perfect competition the product is homogeneous, it is differentiated under conditions of monopolistic competition, oligopoly and monopoly (taking the government definition). In a pure monopoly there will be an exclusive product.

Firms in imperfect competition will use a variety of forms of non-price competition whilst in perfect competition the high level of price competition will reduce prices down to their lowest variable level (i.e. where $AR = AC$ in the long run).

Firms in perfect competition are price takers ($AR = MR$) whilst firms in all other market structures are price makers ($AR > MR$). So the output of firms in perfect competition is too insignificant to influence price,

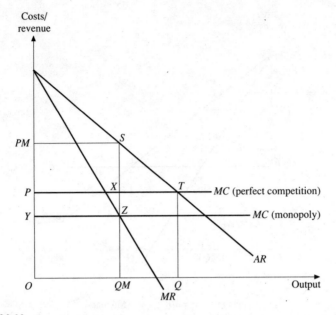

Fig. 23.10

whilst in the market structures where products are differentiated, firms influence price when they change the quantity they offer for sale.

The demand for the product becomes more inelastic the more market power a producer has. Demand for the product of a perfectly competitive firm will be perfectly elastic since the consumer will be willing and able to switch to rival producers should the price rise. Whilst a monopolist, especially a pure monopolist, will be able to raise the price of the product and retain a high proportion of consumers.

The number of firms is large under perfect competition. However, apart from pure monopoly, it is possible that there may be a significant number of firms producing under the other market structures. What differentiates the others is the number of dominant firms in the market (i.e. the degree of industrial concentration). In monopolistic competition the firms are of a similar size whilst under conditions of oligopoly approximately four to eight firms are likely to dominate the market and under monopoly even fewer.

In perfect competition consumers are assumed to be fully informed and have considerable power (consumer sovereignty). If they want more of a product, producers will respond and, as we have seen allocate a sufficient quantity of resources to be output of the product. The fewer the number of dominant firms in the market the less power and influence consumers have and the more power and influence the producer will have.

Contestable markets

Recently some economists and politicians have adopted a new approach to market structures. They argue that what is important in determining how firms behave is not the degree of actual competition but the degree of potential competition.

A market is contestable when there are no significant barriers to entry, new entrants would face similar costs to existing firms and exit costs are zero. Entry costs will either be low or will be recoverable on exit. In this case the capital which is used will be specific, it will be capable of being transferred to other uses and there will be no sunk costs. For example, a coach company may be willing to operate on a particular route if it knows that if it proves to be unprofitable it can use its coaches on alternative routes.

In the knowledge that new firms would be encouraged and would be able to enter the market if supernormal profits are earned, it is argued that costs and prices will be kept low in contestable markets so the threat of competition has a similar effect to actual competition.

In theory, monopolists and oligopolists operating in contestable markets may benefit consumers more than firms operating under conditions of perfect competition. This is because not only may the firms be able to achieve low costs through economies of scale, but also the potential competition will ensure that the firms act in a competitive way, keeping profits and prices low.

24 Costs and benefits

Market failure arises when the free market forces of demand and supply
fail to produce the quantities of goods and services people want at prices
which reflect their marginal utilities. The market fails when there is
allocative inefficiency. This occurs, in part, because private costs and
benefits differ from social costs and benefits.

Private costs

Private costs (which can also be called internal costs) are the costs
incurred by those who buy products and by those who produce products.
For example if a person buys a bottle of whisky the cost (in the form of
the price charged) may be £15, and if a firm produces a car the cost (in
terms of wages, parts, overheads etc.) may be £4000.

Private benefits

Private benefits (which can also be called internal benefits) are the
benefits received by those who buy products and by those who produce
products. So continuing the examples given above the private benefit
from buying a bottle of whisky is the enjoyment received from drinking
the whisky as reflected in the marginal utility gained. The private benefit
to the car company of selling the car is the revenue it receives.

Externalities

Private costs and benefits go through the market mechanism and they
have a price attached to them. Whereas externalities (which can be called
spill-over effects) do not go through the price mechanism and so do not
have a price attached to them. An externality is a cost or benefit to third
parties, i.e., to those not directly involved in the production or consumption
of the good. As we will see externalities are the differences between
social costs and benefits and private costs and benefits.

Negative externalities

Negative externalities (which can also be called external costs) are the
costs imposed on third parties of the economic activity of others. For

instance, if someone buys and drinks a bottle of whisky over a short time span, this may have a number of adverse effects on others. They could become drunk and cause a nuisance in a public place. They could also make mistakes or become ill, thereby placing a burden on the health service.

As well as consumption having the potential to impose costs on third parties so can production. The production of cars may, for instance, cause noise, air and visual pollution in the area where the factory is located.

Positive externalities

There can also be benefits to third parties (which can be called either positive externalities or external benefits) from the consumption and production of others. Drinking some whisky may actually make someone more sociable, and friends and colleagues can benefit from a more cheerful manner. If someone spends more time and money on their front garden, neighbours may take pleasure in this without paying anything for the enjoyment they derive. Similarly, if a firm spends money on training staff who leave on completion of the training, it is rival firms which gain the benefit and which are unlikely to compensate the firm which undertook the training.

Production can also lead to positive externalities. The production of cars in an area, through creating employment, will benefit the shops, places of entertainment, etc., in which the car workers spend their money. In addition to this benefit, the provision of rail services will reduce congestion, accidents and pollution on roads.

Social cost

Social cost is the total cost to society of an economic activity. It is the full opportunity cost, i.e., what the individual consumers and producers forgo (in terms of the price paid or expenditure on factors of production) plus what third parties forgo (e.g., clean air, safety). To summarise, social cost is private costs plus negative externalities (external costs).

It is often the case that the costs to society as a whole are greater than the costs to the individuals who buy and produce goods and services. Indeed, social cost will equal private costs only when there are no negative externalities.

An example often used to illustrate social costs is smoking. The social cost of people smoking consists of the price they pay for the cigarettes (private cost) plus the secondary smoking and the air pollution they cause and the burden they impose on the health service (negative externalities).

Figure 24.1 shows negative externalities (external costs) arising in (a) the production of a good and (b) the consumption of a good.

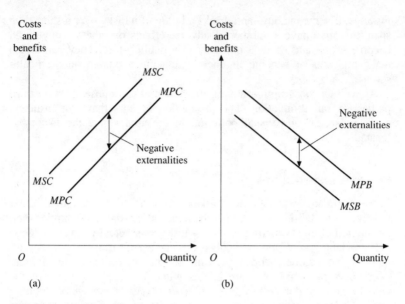

Fig. 24.1   (a) Production (b) consumption

Social benefit

Social benefit is the total benefits to society from an economic activity. It consists of private benefits plus positive externalities (external benefits). Social benefit will equal private benefits only if there are no positive externalities. However, where the benefit to society as a whole from the consumption or production of a good or service is greater than the benefits to the individual consumers or producers, there are positive externalities. This situation is illustrated in Fig. 24.2 showing positive externalities (external benefits) arising in (a) the production of a good and (b) the consumption of a good.

Education is often used to illustrate how social benefit can exceed private benefits. People undertaking education receive consumption and investment benefits. Most will enjoy the education and it may stimulate lifetime interests (consumption benefit) and will increase their future earning power (investment benefit). In addition to these private benefits, third parties will gain from having a more educated, inventive workforce and a more informed population (positive externalities).

Socially efficient (optimum) output

Profit maximising firms will produce where marginal private cost (*MPC*) equals marginal private revenue (benefit) (*MPB*). However, the socially efficient (optimum) output is achieved where the marginal social cost (*MSC*) equals the marginal social benefit (*MSB*) as shown in Fig. 24.3.

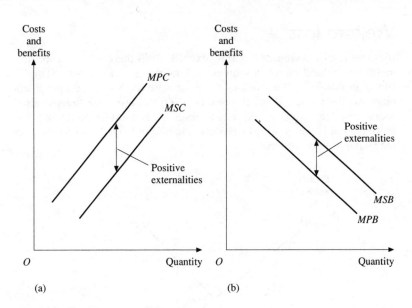

Fig. 24.2   *Positive externalities*

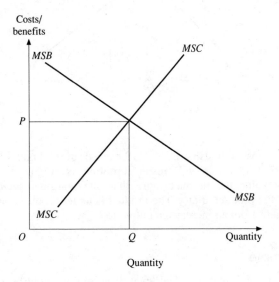

Fig. 24.3

Where marginal social cost equals marginal social benefit the value that consumers place on the last unit produced will be equal to the full cost of producing that last unit. Pareto optimality is achieved when *MSC* equals *MSB* in all industries. In this situation it is not possible to make one person better off without making someone else worse off.

Welfare loss

If output is undertaken where *MSC* exceeds *MSB* there will be a socially inefficient allocation of resources and hence a welfare loss. This is shown in Fig. 24.4. Welfare loss arises because the value that consumers place on the extra unit of the output at *OQ* is less than the marginal social cost (i.e., what society has to forgo as a result of producing that unit). Output is too high and a reduction in output to *OQX* would increase the welfare of consumers.

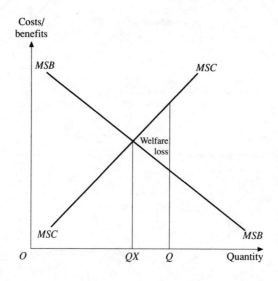

Fig. 24.4

A welfare loss will also arise if *MSB* exceeds *MSC*. Figure 24.5 shows the welfare loss which will result if output is at *OQ*. In this case consumers value the product more than the marginal social cost of producing the product at *OQ*. The product is under produced and society would benefit from an increase in output to *OQX*.

An example

People often think that the ideal level of pollution would be zero. What they are failing to take into account is the cost of achieving that Utopian state. The socially efficient level of pollution is actually where the marginal cost of pollution reduction equals the marginal social benefit of pollution reduction. Figure 24.6 shows that the optimum level of pollution is *OQ*.

The welfare of the community would be reduced by lowering pollution to *OQ1*. This is because the benefit people would receive would be

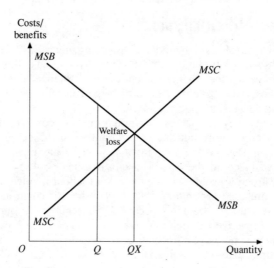

Fig. 24.5

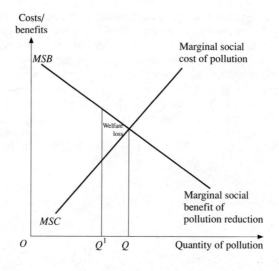

Fig. 24.6

less than the cost of achieving that benefit. People would receive more benefit if the resources were used in alternative occupations. For instance, to remove all litter from a town centre might require the employment of one hundred workers. The alternative goods and services that these workers could produce may be valued more highly than the removal of all crisp packets, etc.

Cost benefit analysis

Cost benefit analysis is a method of assessing investment projects by considering social costs and benefits. It is usually applied to those projects where it is expected there will be a significant difference between private and social costs and benefits. The project will usually go ahead if the social benefits exceed the social costs.

Cost benefit analysis ensures that policy makers consider the effects on the wider community but there are a number of difficulties involved in the process. The private costs involved can be identified reasonably easily. For instance, in the case of a city overhead railway the private costs of construction would include the cost of labour involved, materials used, land purchased for stations, etc. Private benefit could also be calculated as it will be the fares received. External costs and benefits (negative and positive externalities) are not so easy to measure since by definition they do not have a price attached to them.

The possible external costs arising from an overhead railway may include visual pollution, congestion near the stations and some noise pollution. The external benefits are likely to be greater and may include less air pollution, less overall road congestion, fewer road accidents (thereby reducing the burden on police, health services, etc.), and savings in travel time. Economists often use 'shadow prices' to estimate these. Shadow prices are imputed prices based on opportunity cost. For example, to estimate the value to passengers of the time they save it would be necessary to measure the national average hourly wage rates. An additional problem is that the costs and particularly the benefits occur over a period of time. This means that the costs and benefits have to be discounted to present values. For instance, £100 earned in three years is worth less than £100 earned now since £100 received now can be saved. So the £100 to be received in three years time will have to be adjusted downwards.

25 Causes of market failure

As we have seen, a market system would achieve allocative efficiency if it were to produce the products people want, in the quantities they desire and at prices which reflect their marginal utilities.

In a market system the price mechanism is used to transmit information from consumers to producers. If consumers demand more of a product, the price will rise and in the short run supply will extend. In the long run supply will increase as new firms, seeing higher profits being made from producing the product, move into the industry. In theory resources should move towards making those products which are increasing in demand.

For this to occur a number of conditions have to be met. Producers must be willing and able to respond to changes in demand, there must be no barriers to entry and exit, perfect mobility of factors of production and costs and prices must reflect social costs and benefits.

Externalities

As we saw in Chapter 24 market failure will occur when marginal social cost and marginal social benefit are not equal. As externalities in production and consumption often exist and output is usually based on private costs and benefits, this is a significant cause of market failure.

David Pearce, professor of environmental economics at University College London, published in January 1994 a study comparing the revenue raised from road and fuel taxes (£14.7 bn.) and the cost of road use by cars (£25.7 bn.). This highlighted the negative externalities arising from car driving including air and noise pollution, accidents, congestion and damage to the road network.

Public goods

Public (also called collective) goods are characterised by two important features, (a) non-rivalry in consumption and (b) non-excludability.

The first feature simply means that consumption by Mrs Brown does not in any way reduce the consumption of Mrs Green or any other individual. The second feature (non-excludability) refers to the fact that consumption of a public good cannot be confined to those who have paid for it so there can be free riders. People can enjoy the good without paying for it.

Non-rivalry and non-excludability are the two key characteristics of public goods although there are a few other characteristics which most public goods share. They often have large external benefits relative to private benefits. The marginal cost of providing the good or service to one more individual is often zero. They may also be non-rejectable. This means that individuals may not be able to abstain from consuming them even if they want to.

Examples of public goods include national defence, law and order, lighthouses, flood-control schemes, street lighting, pavements and public drainage. Public goods and services will not be provided by the price mechanism because producers cannot withhold the goods and services for non-payment and, since there is no way of measuring how much a person consumes, there is no basis for establishing a market price.

As a result the state must finance the provision of public goods by means of taxation (and sometimes borrowing). Some public goods are provided directly by the state, for example, defence by central government and street lighting by local authorities. Whereas some, such as flood control, are provided by giving contracts to private-sector firms.

Most goods are private goods. They have rivalry in consumption and excludability. This means that if one person consumes a piece of cake it prevents someone else consuming it, and that enjoyment of the good can be made dependent on direct payment to the producer.

Some economists now identify a third category, mixed goods. These lie in between public and private goods, having some of the characteristics of both types; the most widely quoted example is roads. Some economists claim that many miles of road are non rival. However with advances in technology, it is becoming increasingly possible to exclude non payers.

Merit goods

The state is concerned to increase or maximise the consumption of certain goods which it considers to be highly desirable for the welfare of the citizens. Such goods are described as *merit goods* and the best known examples are the public health and education services.

Other examples include training, insurance, innoculation and seat belts. In a pure market system private spending on merit goods and services would be determined by the private benefits derived from them. Merit goods usually have positive externalities so that the social benefits derived from consuming them exceed the private benefits.

Most economists argue that state intervention is necessary in the case of merit goods to ensure a greater provision of these goods and services than would be supplied under the operation of the price mechanism in free markets.

To increase the provision of merit goods a number of measures can be used. They can be provided free by the state as occurs in the UK with state education and the NHS. Training can be subsidised to consumers by giving education vouchers and contracts for services like refuse collection can be given to private-sector firms. The state can also encourage the consumption of merit goods by providing information, for example, about the benefits of innoculation and passing legislation requiring cars to take and pass MOT tests.

A few economists claim that merit goods do not exist because individuals are the best judges of what to consume and that the government is taking an over-paternalistic approach in promoting the consumption of these goods.

Demerit goods

Demerit goods include cigarettes, and certain forms of drugs. These are over provided by the market mechanism as individuals are unaware of the true cost of consuming them which includes negative externalities. In this case the government can ban their consumption or reduce it by taxation and by providing information about their harmful effects.

Imperfect competition

In practice power often lies to a greater extent with producers than with consumers. Most firms operate under conditions of imperfect competition and, as we have seen, monopolists and oligopolists can restrict output, raise prices and produce where price exceeds marginal costs. They can also prevent new firms from entering the industry thereby preventing a full adjustment to changes in consumer demand occurring.

Advertising can be used to provide information to consumers but it can also be employed to promote producer sovereignty. Firms can encourage people to buy the products they want to sell by persuasive advertising. Firms will also delay the introduction of improved products and new products if it is in their financial interest to do so. For instance, firms had the technology to produce long-life light bulbs for some time before they went on the market and it is debatable whether a cure to the common cold would find its way onto the market easily.

Lack of information

For consumers to maximise their utility they need to have full information about the products they may wish to buy. They obviously do not have this and so may buy less of a product than they should to maximise their welfare. They may also be operating on the basis of incorrect information, believing for instance, that a cream cures acne. This mistake may arise from a misunderstanding or from incorrect information provided by the producer.

Workers may also be unaware of job opportunities outside their current employment and may not fully appreciate all the advantages and disadvantages, including the health risks of their jobs.

Entrepreneurs may also lack information about the costs, availability and productivity of factors of production and may be operating on the basis of incorrect information about the reliability and life span of machines.

Immobility of factors of production

Factors of production, particularly labour, can experience difficulty in moving occupationally and geographically to meet changes in consumer demand. This means that supply may adjust slowly and may fail to adjust to an adequate extent. During periods of high demand UK firms often experience problems in increasing their output because they cannot attract sufficient skilled workers. There may be unskilled workers available but these may not be able, willing, or have the time to gain the necessary skills. With greater technological change there is an increasing need for workers to be flexible, willing to update their skills throughout their working life, change employers, occupations and work patterns.

Short termism

Private-sector entrepreneurs often have short-term objectives at the expense of long-term planning. In April 1994 a Gallup Survey of 501 medium-size firms found that 79 per cent of entrepreneurs blamed short termism by the city for the UK's industrial decline and 69 per cent also blamed short termism by management.

Short termism can result in the over production of consumer goods, the under production of capital goods, and the failure to develop new methods of production and new products.

Imperfect distribution of income and wealth

The market economy provides opportunities for people to earn an income and to acquire wealth. But the opportunities for earning an income are not equally distributed. People do not have equal opportunities in education. Some are also limited in their capacity to learn or they may have acquired a skill only to find the demand for that skill is declining. Discrimination distorts earnings and frequently results in women, people from ethnic minorities and the disabled earning less for the same work as able-bodied, white male employees. In addition people are subject to illness and incapacity and people also grow old. The market system does not guarantee that everyone will have the same opportunity to accumulate wealth and once an inequality in the distribution of wealth arises it tends to be self-perpetuating because wealth can be inherited.

26 Government response to market failure

A government can seek to correct market failure by operating a number of different types of policies. One group of policies uses the price mechanism and it is these we examine in this chapter. We first look at the effects on demand and supply of these measures and then how they can offset market failure.

Indirect taxes

Taxes placed on goods and services are known as indirect taxes (or expenditure or outlay taxes) as opposed to direct taxes which are placed on income and wealth. When a tax such as a purchase tax, a value-added tax, or an excise duty is levied on a commodity it has the same economic effects as an increase in the costs of production. The costs of bringing the good to market are now increased by the amount of the tax. In terms of supply and demand analysis, therefore, the imposition of a tax may be seen as a fall in supply. This will be clear from the data in Table 26.1.

Table 26.1 The effects of imposing a tax of 2p per unit

Market price	Quantity supplied (before tax)	Quantity supplied (after tax)	Quantity demanded
(p)			
10	1100	900	100
9	1000	800	200
8	900	700	300
7	800	600	400
6	700	500	500
5	600	400	600
4	500	300	700
3	400	—	800
2	300	—	900

The second column in Table 26.1 shows the quantities supplied at different prices before the tax is imposed, and the first two columns of the table are represented by the supply curve SS in Fig. 26.1. The third column in Table 26.1 shows the quantities supplied at different prices

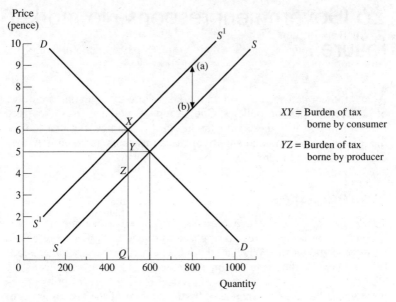

Fig. 26.1

after the tax has been imposed. It is derived fairly easily from columns one and two. In the new situation, a *market price* of 10p represents a *supply price* of 8p. Producers do not receive the full market price; 2p per unit is now taken by the government. It is, however, the supply price which determines how much suppliers are prepared to offer to the market. Thus when the market price is 10p, the market supply will now be 900 units. Similarly a market price of 9p will only give rise to a market supply of 800 units and so on.

What has happened in fact is that supply has fallen; less is now supplied at each and every market price. Columns one and three make up the new supply schedule which is represented by the supply curve S^1S^1 in Fig. 26.1.

All the data in Table 26.1 is contained in Fig. 26.1. The supply curve has shifted upwards by the amount of the tax (i.e. ab = 2p). At the original equilibrium price (5p), 600 units were demanded and supplied. The imposition of the tax reduces supply, price rises to 6p, and the quantity demanded falls to 500 units.

Note that the price has not risen by the full amount of the tax. The burden of the tax has been shared by producers and consumers. The amount of the tax per unit is equal to XZ. Of this, XY is borne by the consumers in the form of higher prices. YZ, however, is the part of the tax borne by suppliers since they now receive ZQ per unit whereas before the tax they were receiving YQ per unit.

In terms of the hypothetical figures used in the example,

Original equilibrium price	= 5p
New equilibrium price	= 6p (consumers pay 1p per unit more)
New supply price	= 4p (suppliers receive 1p per unit less)
Total revenue	= 3000p (i.e. 500 × 6p)
Tax yield	= 1000p (i.e. 500 × 2p)
Suppliers receive	= 2000p (i.e. 500 × 4p)

Specific and *ad valorem* taxes

The example we used above is a specific tax. A specific tax is a fixed-sum tax, in our case 2p per unit. The tax does not change with the price of the product. An example of a specific tax is the excise duty on whisky and other spirits. A specific tax causes a parallel shift to the right of the supply curve.

The second type of indirect tax is an *ad valorem* tax. This is a percentage tax, such as VAT. As it is a percentage tax the amount of tax paid in £s will rise as price rises. An *ad valorem* tax causes a non-parallel shift of the supply curve to the left as shown in Fig. 26.2.

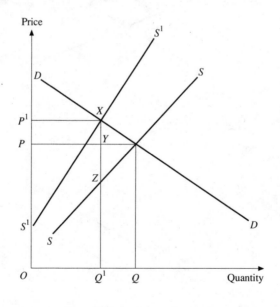

Fig. 26.2

The incidence of the tax burden. In the first graph, Fig. 26.1 (Table 26.1) the burden of taxation was shared equally between buyers and sellers, but this is a particular case. The incidence of an indirect tax depends upon the particular supply and demand conditions in the market.

Whether the tax is borne largely by producers or whether they can pass the greater part of it on to consumers in the form of a higher price depends largely on the elasticities of demand and supply. Fig. 26.3 shows the effect of a tax under differing demand conditions.

In Fig. 26.3(a) the demand is elastic and suppliers experience a fall in supply price greater than the increase in market price experienced by the buyers ($YZ > XY$).

In Fig. 26.3(b) demand is perfectly elastic; if suppliers raise the price demand falls to zero. In this case suppliers must bear the whole burden of the tax and the supply price falls by the amount YZ. Market price does not change but there is a substantial fall in quantity demanded.

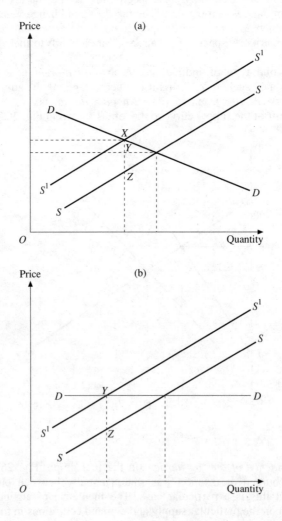

Fig. 26.3

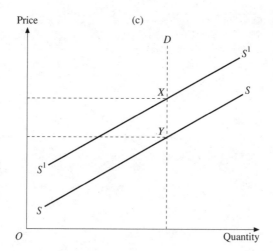

Fig. 26.3 (cont'd)

In Fig. 26.3(c) demand is perfectly inelastic so that suppliers can pass on the full amount of the tax in the form of a price increase. The consumers bear the whole burden of the tax.

But the elasticity of supply is also relevant. It would be an instructive exercise if the reader now used supply and demand diagrams to show that the more inelastic the supply curve, the greater is the proportion of the tax borne by the producers. In general, if elasticity of demand is greater than elasticity of supply, the producers bear the greater share of the tax burden; if elasticity of demand is less than the elasticity of supply, the consumers bear the greater share.

Reasons for imposing indirect taxes

The two main reasons for a government placing a tax on a good or service is to raise revenue and/or to discourage consumption and output. If the Chancellor wishes to raise large sums of money from indirect taxation he must concentrate heavily on those commodities for which demand is inelastic (although this is not the only consideration).

If the prime objective is to reduce the output and consumption of the product, it is more advantageous if demand is elastic.

Indirect taxes and welfare

The market overproduces and undercharges for products with negative externalities. If the government is able to measure the negative externalities it can impose an indirect tax equivalent to the marginal external cost. This will internalise the cost and reduce output to the socially

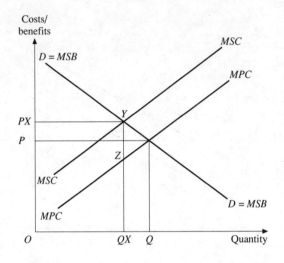

Fig. 26.4

optimum level. Fig. 26.4 shows the market for a good, the production of which causes pollution.

The market output is OQ and the price changed is OP. The socially optimum output is OQW and the price is OPX. So the tax per unit should be YZ.

Subsidies

Subsidies may be regarded as negative taxes. They normally take the form of payments by governments to producers and are particularly important in the case of agricultural products (wheat, milk, meat, etc.). The effect of a subsidy is to reduce the costs of supplying a commodity. In terms of our supply and demand analysis this means that the supply curve moves downwards by the amount of the subsidy – more is now supplied at any given *market price*. Price will fall and the quantity demanded will increase. This is demonstrated in Fig. 26.5. Initially the equilibrium price was OP and quantity OQ was demanded and supplied. A subsidy to producers has moved the supply curve from SS to S^1S^1, price has fallen to OP^1 and quantity demanded has increased to OQ^1.

The amount of the subsidy is XZ. Consumers have benefited by a price fall equal to YZ. They now consume more at a lower price. Producers have benefited from an increase in the *supply price* from YQ^1 to XQ^1. They now supply more and receive a higher supply price.

If the demand is elastic, the granting of a subsidy would lead to a relatively small reduction in price, but a relatively large increase in consumption. If demand were inelastic, the movement of the supply curve

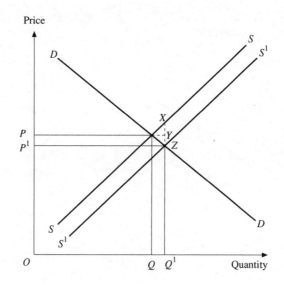

Fig. 26.5

would lead to a relatively large fall in price and a relatively small increase in the quantity demanded.

Specific and *ad valorem* subsidies

A subsidy can be either specific or *ad valorem*. A specific subsidy is a fixed sum payment. Figure 26.5 shows a specific subsidy. An *ad valorem* subsidy, in contrast, is a percentage payment. This causes a non-parallel shift in the supply curve as shown in Fig. 26.6.

Reasons for giving subsidies

A subsidy may be given to assist the poor, to help producers and/or to encourage the consumption and output of goods with positive externalities. Subsidies can be given to consumers as well as to producers. For instance, it is possible to get grants from local authorities to install inside toilet and bathroom facilities in old houses.

Where a subsidy is given to consumers it will be the demand curve which will shift to the right as shown in Fig. 26.7.

Subsidies and welfare

The market under produces products with positive externalities. In this case to promote welfare, the government may subsidise the product. Figure 26.8 shows the market for a product where the marginal social

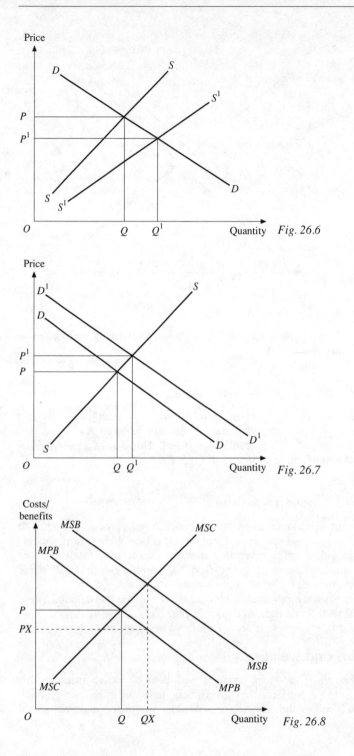

Fig. 26.6

Fig. 26.7

Fig. 26.8

benefit exceeds the marginal private benefit. The market will produce an output of *OQ*. The socially optimum output is at *OQX* since this is where *MSC* and *MSB* are equal. To persuade people to consume this quantity price will have to be lowered, via a subsidy to *OPX*.

Maximum price

A government or another body may set a maximum price. This will only affect the market price and quantity if the maximum price is set below the equilibrium price. A government may introduce a maximum price in order to promote equity and enable poorer members of the community to purchase necessities like food, housing and public transport. Figure 26.9 shows the effect of introducing a maximum price. The initial market equilibrium price is *OP* and the quantity bought and sold is *OQ*. When the maximum price is imposed at *OPX* the quantity demanded expands to *OQD* but the quantity supplied contracts to *OQS*. A shortage of *QD* – *QS* arises.

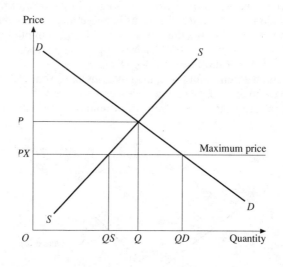

Fig. 26.9

This is the major problem with a maximum price. Some method will have to be used to allocate the good. For example, allocation could be on the basis of first come, first served (queuing) or there could be rationing. However, whichever system is used, a black market is likely to develop. For instance the demand for tickets for the last right of the Proms exceeds the supply. The tickets are allocated in a number of ways including a lottery and queuing before the performance. The excess demand, however, also results in tickets being sold outside the Royal Albert Hall by ticket touts.

Maximum prices increase the welfare of those who are able to purchase the product. They are able to pay less for it than under free market conditions, and hence increase their consumer surplus. However others, some of whom would have been willing to pay the market price, would be unable to buy the product and so would not be able to enjoy any consumer surplus.

The use of controls on the price of rented accommodation in the UK led to a reduction in its supply. With the gradual removal of the maximum price set it has become evident that some of the fall in supply has been permanent. A number of landlords have sold their property or changed its use. This has significantly reduced the size of the private rented sector in the UK.

Minimum price

A minimum price will only affect a market if it is set above the equilibrium price. A government or other body may impose a minimum price if it considers that the market price is too low. This may be because the government wishes to raise workers' wages, in the case of minimum wage legislation (see Chapter 36), or to increase and protect producers' incomes. Figure 26.10 shows the effect of introducing a minimum price.

Pushing the price up to OPM causes supply to extend, demand to contract and creates a surplus of $QS - QD$.

To maintain the minimum price, the government or some other official body will have to buy up the surplus. Measures to cope with the surpluses in agricultural products arising from the Common Agricultural Product

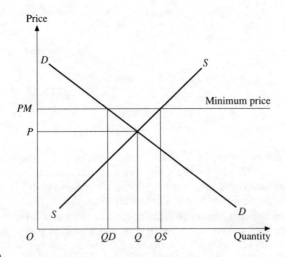

Fig. 26.10

(CAP) operated by the European Union have included storing the surpluses, destroying some products and selling some to East Europe and third-world countries at reduced prices. More recently quotas have been introduced on sugar and milk to reduce supply. The set aside scheme, introduced in 1988, seeks to reduce cereal production. It involves paying farmers a subsidy to convert arable land to an alternative use or to leave it fallow.

Buffer stocks

A buffer stock makes use of both minimum and maximum prices. It is a scheme operated by a central authority and its main aim is usually to stabilise prices and protect producers from sudden shifts in demand and supply. Figure 26.11 shows the effect of setting up a buffer stock for oil seed rape. If the market price is within the two boundaries set by the central authority no action is taken. However, if the market price starts to move outside, the buffer stock operators will intervene.

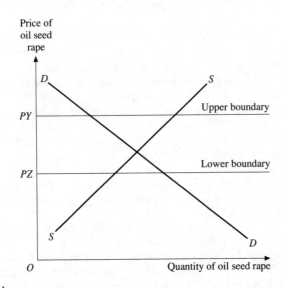

Fig. 26.11

Figure 26.12 shows the effect of a good harvest of oil seed rape. The supply curve shifts to the right. This puts downward pressure on the price and to prevent the price falling below the lower boundary the operators step in to increase demand.

The quantity purchased will be put into storage, ready to be sold if there is a threat that price will rise above the upper boundary.

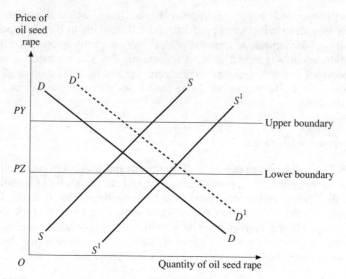

Fig. 26.12

A buffer stock can only be operated with products which can be stored. In practice this has often proved to be unsuccessful. This is because the upper and lower boundaries have often been set too high. This has resulted in the buffer stock operators having to buy more often and in larger quantities than they sell so storage and purchase costs have been high and the buffer stocks have sometimes run out of money.

One of the most spectacular collapses was the failure of the International Tin Council in 1985. This was operated by a number of member governments on the London Metal Exchange. Its aim was to stabilise tin prices above the market clearing price. However, when tin prices came under downward pressure from a combination of events, including a world recession, and a rise in tin production from non-members and from members circumventing their export quotas, the ITC ran out of funds and trading in tin had to be suspended.

A more recent, but less well publicised example, was the collapse of the International Coffee Organisation's market support scheme. This occurred in 1989 when again the available funds proved inadequate in the face of downward pressure on the price.

27 Other forms of government intervention

In addition to using indirect taxes, subsidies, maximum and minimum prices a government can seek to improve allocative efficiency by a number of methods.

Public provision of goods and services

The government may seek to overcome the problem of non-provision of public goods and the underprovision of merit goods by the private sector by producing the goods itself (e.g., the National Health Service) or by giving a contract to a private-sector company (e.g., for the building of a hospital).

In the case of public goods there is the problem of deciding on the quantity to produce since the price mechanism will not reveal consumers' demand. The socially optimum output will be, as with all goods, where marginal social cost equals marginal social benefit. To estimate benefits people can be asked the maximum amount they would be willing to pay for an additional unit of the good. Then to find the economy's marginal benefit curve, the marginal benefit that each individual gains at each quantity of provision is added up.

In practice, of course, the scale of provision of a good by the government is influenced by pressure groups, revenue constraints and the government's priorities of objectives.

In the case of state provision of education and health the government is seeking to make more use of market forces. For instance, GPs can buy the services of hospitals for their patients and local authority colleges now manage their own budgets.

Competition policy

Competition policy in the UK aims to promote efficiency and to protect the interests of the consumer. It is based on the assumption that the possession of market power by monopolies and oligopolies is not, in itself, against the public interest. What has to be considered is how market power is used and the behaviour of firms is considered on a case-by-case basis. Three main aspects of market power are targeted, and these are how existing monopolies and oligopolies behave, the growth of market power through mergers and oligopolistic collusion. This policy is operated by three government-created agencies which are the office of Fair Trading (OFT), the Monopolies and Mergers Commission (MMC) and the Restrictive Practices Court.

The Director-General of Fair Trading (DGFT)

This very important office was created by the Fair Trading Act of 1973. The Director-General is obliged to maintain a continuous survey of and collect information on all types of trading practices in relation to the supply of goods and services. He is, in fact, a kind of official watch-dog in the market place. The office of Fair Trading operates in three main areas.

- Competition policy: monopolies, restrictive trade practices, mergers.
- Consumer credit.
- Consumer affairs.

The Monopolies and Mergers Commission (MMC)

The functions of the MMC are to investigate monopolies and proposed mergers referred to them and to report on whether they consider the existing situation or the proposed changes to be in the public interest. They also make recommendations to the government on any actions they think are necessary to protect the public interest.

The MMC does not have the power to initiate investigations; it can take action only when a case is referred to it by the DGFT or by the President of the Board of Trade. It has no powers to enforce its recommendations, whether or not any action is taken on the findings of the MMC rests upon a decision by the President of the Board of Trade.

The number of investigations is limited by the resources of the MMC. Its maximum capacity is about 15 investigations of monopolies and mergers at any one time. In practice the MMC is able, on average, to produce about 6 monopoly reports and 6 merger reports each year.

The duties of the MMC are to conduct enquiries into:

- monopolies in the supply of goods and services;
- merger proposals;
- local (or geographical) monopolies;
- the general effects of specific monopolistic practices (e.g. price discrimination);
- the efficiency, costs, and quality of services provided by public enterprises;
- anti-competitive practices pursued by any individual firm whether or not it is a monopoly.

Monopolies

As mentioned earlier the MMC can only carry out an investigation where a company has a 25 per cent market share or where two or more companies together having a 25 per cent market share are acting together so as to restrict competition. The DGFT has the duty to keep the UK market under continuous review and to ascertain the existence of monopoly situations. He decides the priority for references to the MMC. The Commission looks into the supply of particular goods and services and not into the activities of large companies as such. This means that a large multi-product firm may be the subject of more than one MMC investigation.

The way in which the MMC works has been criticised for being a much too lengthy process; there is an average interval of about two years between the initial reference and the publication of the MMC's report. The reports have been wide ranging and have provided detailed authoritative accounts of the structure and performance of the firms investigated. They have greatly extended public knowledge of the way in which the business world conducts its affairs.

There has also been criticism because some of the reports and re-commendations of the MMC have not been followed by strong legal action by the government.

The President of the Board of Trade has the power to make orders giving legal effect to any recommendations of the MMC, but this power has rarely been used. Even so, the reports of the MMC have led to substantial changes in business practices. Adverse comments have usually led to voluntary agreements by the firms concerned (in negotiations with the President of the Board of Trade to modify or abandon the offending practice. The fear of investigation and unwelcome publicity may also have had some beneficial effects on business behaviour.

Over the years the MMC has made a variety of recommendations for the control or modification of firms' policies. These have included proposals for price reductions; government supervision of prices, costs and profits; the lowering of tariffs on competing imports; substantial reductions in advertising and other selling costs, and the prohibition of any further take-overs of competitors.

A recent MMC investigation into British Gas, published in 1993 recommended that the company's network should be open to other suppliers.

Mergers

A proposed merger may be referred to the MMC for investigation where it would involve the transfer of gross assets of at least £30 million or where the merger would lead to a monopoly situation (i.e. the control of at least 25 per cent of the market). The Director-General of Fair Trading has the responsibility of keeping himself informed of all merger situations qualifying for possible reference to the MMC. He carries out preliminary investigations and then advises the President of the Board of Trade on whether the proposed merger should be referred to the MMC; only the President of the Board of Trade can refer a proposal merger to the MMC. In fact only a small percentage (approximately 3%) have been referred to the MMC and of these about 60 per cent were either found to be against the public interest or were abandoned. The restraining effects of merger control are greater then the official statistics indicate because some merger proposals are dropped after informal consultations with the DGFT.

Decisions on merger references are taken on a case-by-case basis. The key considerations are whether there is a threat to competition and whether the merger is being undertaken openly and legally, what is, without insider dealing and fraud.

Obviously, the number of mergers which are investigated is, in part, a function of the number of mergers proposed. In the late 1980s there was a boom in merger activity, including Nestlés acquisition of Rowntree Mackintosh, GEC Siemens purchase of Plessey and Hanson's acquisition of Consolidated Gold Fields. However, between 1990 and 1993 merger activity declined and indeed de-mergers became more common with, for example, ICI dividing into two companies, ICI and Zeneca (1993). In 1994 merger activity began to increase again.

A number of economists have suggested that the government should take a more critical approach to mergers. This is because several recent studies of the effects of mergers have shown that a high proportion (at least 50 per cent) of them have proved unprofitable or much less successful than had been anticipated. One explanation for this may be the fact that the planned gains from mergers often depend upon substantial reorganisation of production facilities which may include the closure of some plants with inevitable redundancies. Such changes are likely to meet with strong resistance especially from organised labour and hence may take a long time to carry out. There is also concern that many mergers appear to have been motivated by a desire to increase market power (by reducing competition) rather than by a desire to increase efficiency.

The Restrictive Practices Court

The legal regulation of restrictive trade practices began with the Restrictive Trade Practices Act of 1956, the provisions of which have been extended and modified by several other Acts of Parliament. There is an obligation on the parties to certain types of restrictive agreement to place them on a public register which is maintained by the Director-General of Fair Trading. An agreement is registrable if the parties to it include two or more persons (whether individuals or companies) who are engaged in business in the UK in the manufacture or supply of goods or in the supply of services. Two or more parties to the agreement must accept restrictions (i.e. some limitation on their freedom to make their own decisions) on such matters as prices, conditions of sale, persons dealt with and areas or scale of production. Typical examples of the types of practice which are registrable are cartels, pooling of patents and collusive tendering.

It is the job of the DGFT to select practices on the register for reference to the Restrictive Practices Court which then has the task of deciding whether or not the practices are operating in the public interest. The RP Court has the status of a High Court and its judgments become the law of the land. All registered agreements are presumed to be against the public interest and the onus is on the parties to the agreements to prove to the satisfaction of the court that they are not harmful to the public interest.

The great majority of restrictive agreements on the register have been voluntarily abandoned or have been modified so that they do not qualify as registrable agreements.

The firms or trade associations which choose to defend their agreements must select a form of defence from a restricted list set out in the Restrictive Practices Act. There are eight approved grounds for defence, generally referred to as the eight 'gateways'.

The eight gateways

The respondents must show that the agreement confers benefits in one or more of the following ways:

1 by protecting the public against injury in connection with the installation, use or consumption of goods;
2 by making available other specific and substantial benefits;
3 by counteracting restrictive measures taken by any one person who is not party to the agreement;
4 by permitting negotiation of fair terms for the purchase or sale of goods or services with buyers or sellers who represent a preponderant part of the trade;
5 by preventing the occurrence of serious and persistent unemployment in an area heavily dependent upon the particular trade;
6 in maintaining the volume or earnings of the export trade in the commodity or service where this is substantial in relation to the export trade of the UK as a whole, or in relation to the whole business of the particular trade;
7 in maintaining some other restriction which the Court holds to be justified on its own merits;
8 the restriction does not directly or indirectly restrict or discourage competition.

The defendants must, in addition, show that any gain from the operation of the practice is not outweighed by any detrimental effects on persons not party to the agreement.

The number of cases considered by the court has not been very great, but by carefully selecting the agreements to be judged by the court it has been possible to make each reference a test case for a large number of similar agreements. If a particular case is lost then similar agreements are likely to be abandoned.

Resale price maintenance

One particular restrictive practice was the subject of its own legislation. The Resale Prices Act of 1964 prohibited resale price maintenance, but made provision for suppliers to claim exemption.

Resale price maintenance is the practice whereby the manufacturer fixes the price of his product at each stage of distribution. Although the goods are being distributed by independent wholesalers and retailers they are obliged to charge prices which are laid down by the manufacturers. It means, of course, that the profit margins at these subsequent stages are being fixed by the manufacturers. Resale price maintenance can be enforced by manufacturers either collectively or individually by the threat of withholding supplies if the distributor breaks the price agreement. One example of RPM, currently under investigation, is the Net Book Agreement. This permits publishers to set a minimum price for which a book may be sold.

European Union legislation

Mergers and restrictive practices are also subject to regulation by the European Commission. Articles 85 and 86 of the Treaty of Rome lay out the main provisions of European competition law. Article 85 relates to collusive behaviour and prohibits agreements and restrictive practices which reduce competition within the EU and which affects trade between member states. Article 86 bans the abuse of a dominant position within the EU. The European Commission can impose fines, up to 10 per cent of a firm's turnover, if the firm is found to have abused a dominant position or to have operated anti-competitive agreements. In 1990 a Merger Control Regulation was introduced. This gives the European Commission responsibility for the regulation of large mergers which occur within the EU. It can decide to prevent the merger, allow it to occur or permit it subject to various conditions.

Regulating firms

The UK government can also employ regulations and legislation to influence firms' behaviour in relation to how they produce, what they produce and their method of production. Although the current government favours reducing government intervention in the behaviour of firms a number of regulations are in force.

Environmental measures

The use of organochlorine pesticides such as DDT, dieldrin and aldrin by farmers is banned, and there are controls on firms discharging chemicals into inland rivers. The Environmental Protection Act (1990) places limits on emissions from factories, controls on the release of bacteria and viruses that have undergone genetic engineering and on waste disposal by firms. The imposition of VAT on fuel and increased petrol taxes are intended, in part, to encourage firms to save on energy and use more environmentally friendly sources of energy.

Health and safety standards

Under the Health and Safety at Work Act (1974) employers are required to do what is reasonably possible to look after their employees' health and safety. This includes providing a safe place of work, a safe system of work and adequate plant and equipment. If a firm employs five or more people it must give its staff details of its policy on health and safety. Firms also have to maintain minimum and maximum work temperatures.

Providing information

As we have seen, consumers, workers and producers sometimes fail to make optimal decisions because of lack of information. A consumer may pay a high price for a product in ignorance of cheaper substitutes, a worker may train in a skill which is no longer in demand and a producer may use inefficient production methods.

The government can seek to increase the quantity and quality of information available to economic agents in a variety of ways. The government can provide information directly. In the UK the government's Central Statistical Office publishes detailed information about the economy, and the government now provides a range of consumers of government services, (students, NHS patients) with details about the treatment they are entitled to. The government, by giving subsidies and grants to research institutions and universities, can promote the gathering and interpretation of information.

For example, a number of studies have established the link between smoking and lung cancer, making people more aware of the true costs of smoking.

The government can also increase people's access to information and the quality of information by passing legislation. Producers of processed food products and patent medicines have to list their contents and full-time employees have to be given written terms of employment.

The government also controls the information producers and retailers provide about their goods. For instance, the Trade Descriptions Act 1968 makes it an offence to give false descriptions about the size and fitness for purpose of manufactured goods and the Consumer Protection Act 1987 makes it an offence to give any consumer a misleading indication of the price of goods and services.

28 Ownership of industries

The 1980s and 1990s have witnessed a large-scale transfer of ownership from the public to the private sector. The number of nationalised industries and state ownership of shares in private-sector companies has declined significantly.

Nationalisation

Nationalisation is one possible solution to market failure. Under state ownership, industries can be run in the public interest and attempts can be made to avoid the creation of negative externalities, allocative inefficiency and lack of provision of basic necessities which may occur in the private sector.

Arguments for nationalisation

'Natural' monopolies

The technical conditions of production in some industries are such that competition would lead to a wasteful use of resources. Competition in the distribution of gas, electricity and water would lead to a costly duplication of the networks of mains, pipes, etc., which are required to supply these goods and services. It is also argued that the full potential economies of scale can only be obtained by one undertaking operating on a national basis. These are arguments for monopoly rather than for public ownership. The arguments for nationalisation are that these basic industries should be operated in the national interest and not with a view to private profit, and only public ownership can ensure that a powerful monopoly position will not be used to exploit consumers.

Adjustment to changing conditions

One of the main arguments used in presenting the case for public ownership when basic industries such as steel, coal and the railways were nationalised was that only the state could and would provide the very large injections of capital which were needed to restructure and modernise these capital-intensive industries, which had become badly run down during the Second World War.

Helping to manage the economy

A further argument for having a large sector of the economy directly under government control is that it can be used as a powerful lever to control the economy. During a recession, for example, the investment programmes of the nationalised industries can be increased and, via multiplier effects, will help to stimulate an increase in income and employment. In the past, governments have used their powers to restrict price increases by nationalised industries as a means of reducing the rate of inflation. This use of government power, however, makes it very difficult for the nationalised industries to carry out long-term planning.

Social costs and benefits

It was explained in Chapter 24 that social costs and benefits may be quite different from private costs and benefits, owing to externalities. Generally speaking, privately-owned firms will only undertake production if private benefits (revenues) are greater than private costs; they will not take account of externalities. Nationalised industries, charged with operating in the public interest, will be under strong political and social pressures to give much more attention to externalities. They may be obliged to operate some loss-making activities where social benefits are clearly greater than social costs – for example, rural postal and transport services. The government has recognised these social obligations and, in some cases, provides sub-sidies for such non-commercial operations.

Political arguments

The motives for nationalisation are political as well as economic. Many socialists believe that public ownership enables people to exercise full democratic control over the means whereby they earn their living and provides an effective means of redistributing wealth and income more equitably.

Ownership or control

It is possible that the purely economic objectives of state control may be achieved without resorting to complete public ownership (i.e. national-isation). There are various ways in which a government can control the policy and performance of privately owned enterprise.

- It may control the industry's prices, profits, and dividends.
- It may take up shares in public companies and place its representatives on the board of directors.
- It may exercise constant supervision of the costs and marketing policies of the firms in the industry.
- It may take over the wholesale stage and hence control the prices received by the producers and those charged to distributors.
- It may lay down technical specifications governing the quality and performance of the industry's products, or, through a system of licensing, control the nature of the services provided by the industry.

As for some of the other objectives, a redistribution of income may be achieved by subsidies on the prices of certain goods, or by a straight transfer of income to the poor, and social costs may be dealt with by taxing those who create the social burdens (e.g. 'taxing the polluters'). These alternatives would, of course, be unacceptable to those who are politically committed to public ownership.

Privatisation

The Conservative government elected in 1979 was committed to reducing the size of the public sector. It embarked upon a policy, described as *privatisation*, followed throughout the 1980s and 1990s of selling state-owned assets to the private sector. The major feature of this policy was denationalisation – selling off the nationalised industries. But the programme also included the sale of government-owned shares in public companies, the sale of council houses to sitting tenants, and the contracting out of certain services by government and local authority departments, for example, catering and laundry services in hospitals.

Among the major firms and industries which have been transferred to the private sector are those shown in Table 28.1.

Table 28.1 Examples of denationalised industries and industries in which the government has sold its share holdings

Associated British Ports	Cable and Wireless
British Airports Authority	Electricity distribution companies
British Aerospace	Electricity generators
British Airways	Jaguar
British Gas	Rolls-Royce
British Petroleum	Sealink
British Steel	Water Companies
British Telecom	Britoil

Arguments for privatisation

Raising revenue for the government

By 1994 privatisation had generated approximately £50 billion in revenue for the government. This revenue clearly makes it possible for the government to reduce its public-sector borrowing requirement and to make tax cuts without reducing its own spending. Extra government revenue may also arise in the form of higher corporation tax receipts if the privatised concerns become more profitable.

Increased competition

It is argued that the private sector has the spur of competition since inefficiency is punished with bankruptcy. The firm will go out of business and resources will be reallocated in line with consumer demand whereas state enterprises cannot go bankrupt because the government guarantees their borrowings.

A private sector firm may have to compete in financial markets for funds and has to persuade banks, and other financial institutions or its own shareholders that its plans are viable.

Greater competition may also be created in the product market if an industry, which was run as a monopoly under state ownership, is split into competing parts, for example, separate coal mines operating in competition with each other.

Increased efficiency

Managers of privatised firms will be freed from political control and interference – they will be able to charge the prices they regard as commercially sensible and to make the investments they think will pay.

The stock market may also put pressure on private-sector firms to be efficient. If they are not performing well their share prices will fall and they will risk being taken over by another firm.

Wider share ownerships

The broadening of share ownership is another aim of privatisation. The idea is to shift ownership away from the state and large institutions towards individuals. Privatisation has been largely responsible for the increase in the number of private shareholders from 2½ million in 1979 to more than 9¼ million in 1992. This has been accomplished because the sales of shares in privatised undertakings have been arranged so that small investors, and in many cases, workers in the industry, have been given preferential treatment. Shareholding is thought to have peaked at around 11 million in 1990 following the privatisation of the electricity companies.

Cost-push inflation may be reduced

Private-sector managers may be more reluctant to concede wage rises not matched by higher productivity and may be less willing to accept inefficient working practices.

Arguments against privatisation

Long-term loss of revenue

Whilst selling off profitable state assets raises revenue for the government, the state loses the future profits from these industries. Indeed privatisation has been likened to 'selling the family silver'. If the loss of profits is greater than any rise in corporation tax resulting from the privatisation, future public-sector borrowing requirements may be larger.

Competition in product markets may not be increased

If a public-sector monopoly is replaced by a private-sector monopoly, competition will not increase. In cases of natural monopoly it is difficult to provide competition.

Market forces may not ensure greater efficiency

Privatised firms, if they remain monopolies, are likely to be able to earn supernormal profits even if they are inefficient. Consumers will not be able to take their custom elsewhere. The stock market may also fail to put pressure on the firms to become efficient. Monopolies are likely to be able to rely exclusively on retained profits for their investment finance and their large size is likely to prevent other firms from being able to take them over.

Loss of potential revenue from privatisation

It is thought that some state concerns have been sold off too cheaply. Evidence for this is provided by the sharp rise in price which has occurred the day after shares in many former state concerns have just been sold. Whilst there has often been a speculative gain for the purchasers there has often been a corresponding sacrifice in revenue for the state. The increase in share ownership, in part, reflects the increase in the number of privatised shares. It has also failed to stop the trend towards an increasing percentage of shares being held by institutions.

Private-sector firms may not act in the public interest

As we have seen in our discussion of the arguments for nationalised industries private-sector firms do not take account of externalities. They are also unlikely to base their output and pricing decisions on fairness and social justice.

Regulation in government control over the economy

The government's ability to influence pay, prices and output decisions directly will be reduced.

Nationalised and privatised industries compared

In practice it is very difficult to compare the efficiency of industries operating under different ownership. Efficiency is a measure of success in achieving a given objective, but if the objective includes such non-measurable elements as 'operating in the best interest of the public', then any single measure of efficiency is misleading.

The research which has been undertaken into this question suggests that it is not private ownership which generates greater efficiency but competitive product markets and as we have seen privatisation is not always synonymous with increased competition.

Regulation of privatised industries

The Acts of privatisation have set down a number of constraints on the pricing and output decisions of privatised industries. For instance, British Telecom has to provide public telephones and has been obliged to allow its smaller rival Mercury to use its lines.

Regulatory agencies have been established including OFFER (Office of Electricity Regulation), OFGAS (Office of Gas Supply), OFTEL (Office of Telecommunications) and OFWAT (Office of Water Supplies). In August 1994 OFFER announced price curbs on the regional electricity companies.

There is also the possibility that the industries could be investigated by the Office of Fair Trading and referred; if appropriate, to the Monopolies and Mergers Commission or to the Restrictive Practices Court. The regulatory agencies can also refer companies directly to the MMC. In 1992–93 British gas was investigated by the Monopolies and Mergers Commission.

29 Marginal revenue product

Marginal revenue productivity theory seeks to explain the determinants of demand for factors of production. The demand for factors of production is a derived demand. The factors are not wanted for their own sake but for what they can produce. The more the factors can produce and the more that output can be sold for, the more they will be in demand.

Marginal product

Marginal product is the change in total output resulting from the employment of one more unit of a variable factor. As we saw in Chapter 7 the law of diminishing returns tells us that the average product (AP) and marginal product of a factor of production will, sooner or later begin to decline. This is shown in Fig. 29.1.

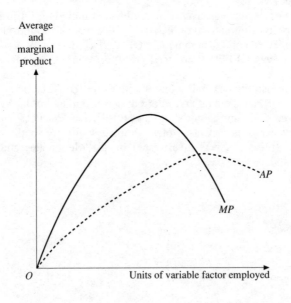

Fig. 29.1

Marginal product is often referred to as marginal physical product since it is measured in physical units; tonnes of wheat, number of cars, metres of silk.

Marginal revenue productivity

Although entrepreneurs are interested in the physical productivity of a factor of production, they are even more concerned with the revenue yielded by the input's efforts.

If we assume that the objective of entrepreneurs is to maximise profits their main concern will be the relationship between the cost of employing a factor of production and the revenue yielded by selling its output. We call the amount added to the firm's revenue resulting from employing one more unit of a variable factor of production, marginal revenue productivity.

$MPP \times MR = MRP$

If the firm is operating under conditions of perfect competition the price of the product does not change as the firm changes its output so that the *MRP* of a factor is clearly equal to its marginal physical product multiplied by the price of the product. This is shown in Table 29.1. where labour is the variable factor.

Table 29.1

No. of workers	Total output	MPP	Price of good (MR) (£)	MRP (MP × MR) (£)	Total revenue (£)	Wage rate (£)
1	40	40	20	800	800	800
2	90	50	20	1000	1800	800
3	150	60	20	1200	3000	800
4	200	50	20	1000	4000	800
5	240	40	20	800	4800	800
6	260	20	20	400	5200	800
7	275	15	20	300	5500	800
8	285	10	20	200	5900	800

It is assumed in Table 29.1 that the firm is one of a very large number of buyers of this type of labour and cannot influence the wage rate, (the supply of labour (to the firm) will be perfectly elastic at the ruling wage rate, in this case £800). It can obtain as many workers as it wishes at the market wage. How many workers will it employ?

The equilibrium condition is already familiar to us since it has been encountered when dealing with the output of the firm. The profit-maximising firm will employ additional workers as long as those workers are adding more to the firm's revenue than to the firm's costs. In other words, *labour will be employed up to the point where its marginal revenue product is equal to the wage rate.* Since the wage rate is constant, we can regard it as the marginal cost of labour, so that our equilibrium is nothing more than another application of the $MC = MR$ profit-maximising condition.

In our example five workers will be employed. At this level of employment the gap between total revenue and the total cost of the factor of production is greatest: £4800 – £4000 (5 × £800) = £800.

Marginal revenue productivity in imperfect product markets

Marginal revenue productivity will also fall after a certain point in an imperfect competitive product market. This is because not only will marginal product decline when diminishing returns set in but also because price and marginal revenue fall as output rises. Again, the quantity of a factor of production employed will be such that its marginal revenue product equals the cost of the factor of production. Table 29.2 shows a firm producing in an imperfect market but employing workers from a perfect market. The number of workers employed would be six since this is the number where MRP = wage rate.

Table 29.2

No. of workers	Total output	Marginal product	Marginal revenue (£)	MRP (£)	Wage rule (£)
1	30	30	10	300	200
2	100	70	9	630	200
3	180	80	8	640	200
4	250	70	7	490	200
5	300	50	6	300	200
6	340	40	5	200	200
7	370	30	4	120	200
8	390	20	3	60	200

The demand curve for a factor of production

In Fig. 29.2, when the wage rate is OW the firm will employ OM workers. At this wage, as employment increases up to OM, each additional worker is adding more to the firm's revenue than to the firm's costs. Beyond OM the employment of extra workers adds more to costs than to revenue. If the wage rate falls to OW^1, employment will rise to OM^1. It now becomes worthwhile to employ MM^1 extra workers since the marginal revenue products of these workers are higher than the new lower wage rate. The *MRP* curve then tells us how much labour will be demanded at any given price (i.e. wage). Since this is the function of a demand curve, *the MRP curve is the firm's demand curve for labour*. But note that it is only that part of the *MRP* curve which lies below the *ARP* curve which is relevant. The *ARP* curve represents the average monetary return per worker employed. When *OM* workers are employed, the *ARP* is equal to *MB* so that the firm is earning a surplus per worker equal to *AB*. The section of the *MRP* curve which lies above the *ARP* curve is not part of the demand curve because a firm will not employ labour when the wage is higher than the *ARP* of labour; it would be making a loss on each worker employed.

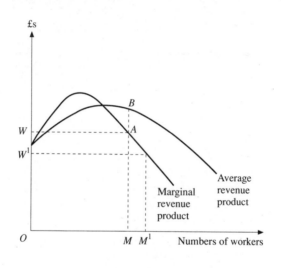

Fig. 29.2

Causes of changes in MRP

The marginal revenue productivity of a factor of production is determined by its physical productivity and by the price of the product produced (changes in price cause changes in marginal revenue in both perfect and imperfect competition). A change in either or both of these variables will change demand for the factor. For instance, an increase in the productivity of machinery (due perhaps to changes in technology) or an increase in the price of the product will shift the curve upwards. This means the demand curve for machines moves outward from the origin and more machines will now be demanded at any given price. This is shown in Fig. 29.3.

Similarly, a fall in productivity or a fall in the price of the product will reduce the amount of a factor of production demanded at any given price.

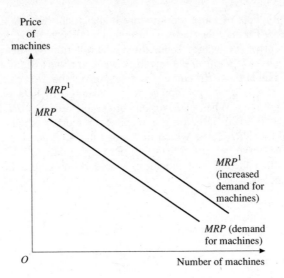

Fig. 29.3

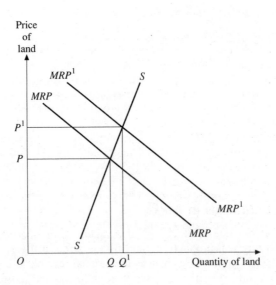

Fig. 29.4

The effects of changes in MRP

If the marginal revenue productivity of a factor of production increases, its price will rise and its supply extend. Figure 29.4 shows the effect of an increase in the *MRP* of land used for theme parks. A fall in marginal revenue productivity will have the opposite effect, lowering the price of the factor of production and reducing its supply.

30 Profit

Definition

Profit is usually defined as a reward for bearing the burden of uncertainty, or as a return to the function of risk-bearing.

The risks incurred in running a business are of many kinds. Some of these, such as the risk of loss due to flood, fire, or burglary, or injuries to employees, are insurable, because the laws of probability can be applied to such events, and insurance companies can calculate the degree of risk involved. But no statistician can calculate the numerical probability that a firm, or group of firms, will make profits or losses in the future. Economic conditions are changing all the time and the success or failure of a particular enterprise in the past is no good guide as to the likely success or failure of a similar enterprise in the future. Profits then are the reward for taking non-insurable risks.

The nature of profit

It is very difficult to isolate the return described as profit from other factor income – wages, interest and rent. This is especially true in the case of the one-person business.

A person owning and working in their own business may declare a £45 000 profit during the year. This figure probably represents the firm's gross profits and is obtained by deducting the 'paid out' costs from the total revenue. If the entrepreneur has contributed her own labour, capital and premises to the business, the opportunity cost of these contributions represents *implicit* wages, interest and rent. These must be deducted from the gross profits in order to arrive at the true, or pure profit. The deductions take the following forms: (*a*) an item for wages, equal to what the entrepreneur could earn as an employee of some other firm; (*b*) an item for interest, equal to the interest forgone on the savings which she has invested in the business and (*c*) an item for rent equal to the amount which could be obtained by letting the premises to a tenant.

A major problem is to distinguish between interest and profit because the terms are often used as though they were interchangeable. Both are payments made to the providers of capital. If the funds for investment are supplied by creditors of the company in the form of loans, the returns to capital are described as interest. When the money is provided by shareholders, who by purchasing shares become owners of the business, the returns to capital are described as profits. Strictly speaking, the opportunity cost principle described above should be applied to shareholders' profits. Shareholders have forgone the interest their funds might have earned if they had been used to buy virtually risk-free bonds. A deduction equal to this implicit interest should be made from their dividends in order to arrive at the true profit. In practice it is very difficult to isolate pure profit and the profit figures produced by the accountant will include elements of implicit wages, interest, and rent.

Features of profit

Profit differs from the other forms of income in three ways.

It may be negative

Capitalism is a *profit and loss system*. A firm may make losses, but wages, interest, and rent are most unlikely to be negative items.

It fluctuates far more than other forms of income

Rent, interest, and wages are normally fixed at some agreed rates for some given period of time (e.g. a wage of £350 per week, or interest at 10 per cent per annum). Profit cannot be agreed in advance because future revenue and costs are uncertain.

It is a residual item

Profit is what remains of the receipts after all expenses have been met. Wages, interest and rent are usually fixed in advance of the performance of the services for which they are payments.

Profits and innovation

Some economists emphasise the role of profit as a necessary incentive for innovation. All enterprises in a capitalist economy involve a degree of risk, but the introduction of a new product, or a new method of producing an existing product, or the attempt to open up a new market, are examples of innovations which carry a much higher degree of risk. It is this type of activity – trying something new – which is so vitally necessary for economic growth. Successful innovation provides a great stimulus to new investment and may well lead to the growth of large new industries. Innovators may well be encouraged by the prospects of large profits which may, and often do, accrue to the first in the field.

Types of profit

As we have seen in earlier chapters there are three types of profit.

Subnormal profit

This is experienced where average cost exceeds average revenue and hence a loss is made. In this case some entrepreneurs will leave the industry in search of positive profit levels elsewhere.

Normal profit

This is earned where average revenue equals average cost. It is also called the supply price of entrepreneurship as it is the minimum the entrepreneur has to receive to provide his services.

Supernormal profit

This is earned where average revenue exceeds average cost. This will encourage other entrepreneurs to seek to enter the industry. This will be possible under conditions of perfect competition and monopolistic competition. However under conditions of oligopoly and monopoly there are barriers to entry, which may be difficult to overcome.

Risk bearing and profits

Normal profits will vary from industry to industry according to the degree of risk involved. This is because entrepreneurs will require more reward for the greater skills needed and the higher level of stress involved. The minimum expected rate of profit required to persuade a firm to carry on prospecting for oil will obviously be much greater than that needed to keep a firm in the brewing industry.

The role of profit

We can now summarise the role of profit in a capitalist society.

- It is a reward for bearing the uncertainty associated with carrying on business.
- It is a stimulus to innovation. Profit is seen as the necessary inducement which encourages people to introduce new products and new techniques.
- It is a source of funds for investment. We saw in Chapter 12 that retained profits provide an important means of financing expansion and modernisation.
- It is an indicator for potential investors. Profit plays an important part in determining the allocation of resources. Industries earning high profits will attract more resources than those where profits are relatively lower.

31 Rent

Everyone is familiar with the procedure of renting something. It is a procedure which has undergone rapid development in recent years and it is now possible to rent land, houses, factories, machines, offices, cars, television sets and almost any durable good. Rent, in everyday speech, simply means the periodical payment which is made for the use of some particular asset. It is a contractual payment fixed in terms of money and normally arranged on an annual basis. The type of payment ordinarily known as rent, the rent payable for the use of a car for example, contains an element of wages (labour is employed in providing the service), an element of interest (money has been invested in the business), and an element of profit.

Economic rent

Economists have given a much more restricted meaning to the word rent. When the theory of rent was first propounded it was applied specifically to land. However it is now applied to all factors of production. To understand its meaning we also have to appreciate what supply (transfer earnings) means. The *supply price* of a factor may be defined as the minimum reward necessary to retain a factor in its present employment. Any payment to a factor of production which is greater than its supply price is a kind of surplus and it is this surplus which is known as economic rent. Thus,

Present Earnings – Supply Price = Economic Rent

How economic rent is created

Whenever a factor is earning more than its supply price, it is receiving a part of its income in the form of economic rent. This situation arises when demand increases and the supply cannot fully respond to the increased demand. Factors of production already employed will experience an increase in income so that they must be earning more than their supply prices. There are particular circumstances where labour, capital, and the entrepreneur may all be receiving part of their remuneration in the form of economic rent.

Economic rent and transfer earnings

The *transfer earnings* of a factor of production is the minimum payment required to prevent that factor transferring to another employer or another occupation. It is determined by what that factor could earn in its next best paid employment. Transfer earnings may be regarded as the *opportunity cost* of keeping a factor of production in its present use, or, as we said earlier, it may be regarded as the factor's *supply price* in its present occupation. For example, suppose the minimum weekly wage which would persuade someone to work as a lorry driver is £300, but he actually receives a wage (as a lorry driver) of £350 per week. We can say that his transfer earnings amount to £300 per week and he is receiving £50 per week in the form of economic rent.

Economic rent, therefore, may be defined as any payment made to a factor of production which is in excess of its transfer earnings.

Just how this concept may be applied to any factor of production may be seen in Fig. 31.1.

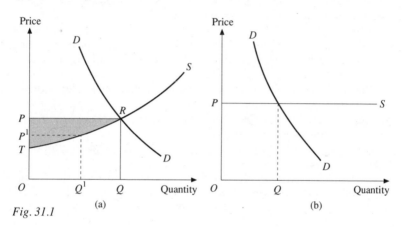

Fig. 31.1

In Fig. 31.1a we have the demand and supply curves for a factor of production. The equilibrium price is *OP* and *OQ* units of the factor are employed. Total earnings are equal to the area *OPRQ*, and all units of the factor receive the same reward, *OP* (it will be the wage rate if the factor is labour). But all units of this factor, except the last one taken into employment, were prepared to offer their services at prices less than *OP*. For example, OQ^1 units would be available to firms at a price of OP^1. Provided that the supply curve slopes upwards (i.e. it is less than perfectly elastic) an increase in demand will give rise to rent payments to those factors which were already employed at the original price. The shaded area *PRT* is the economic rent element in the total earnings. The area *OTRQ* represents the total transfer earnings. Only the last unit of the factor to be employed earns no rent, because the price *OP* is the supply price of this particular unit.

In Fig. 32.1b we have a situation where the supply of the factor is perfectly elastic, as it might be to the individual firm where there is perfect competition in the factor market. Thus, the firm can obtain any amount of the factor at the ruling price *OP*. At prices less than *OP* there will be no supplies available to the firm. The whole of the factor earnings represent transfer earnings, and, in this case, an increase in demand will not give rise to any economic rent. The price *OP* is the minimum payment which will prevent the factor leaving the firm.

Economic rent and labour

The amount of economic rent in the return to labour obviously depends upon the elasticity of supply and the level of demand. The greater the occupational mobility of labour, the smaller will be the element of economic rent. If labour is very mobile, quite small changes in the wage rate will cause large movements of labour, into the industry when wages rise, and out of the industry when wages fall.

Highly specialised labour is in very inelastic supply. This is true of specialists such as surgeons, highly qualified architects, physicists, and first class managers. The earnings of such persons probably contain a large amount of economic rent. Their relatively high rewards are due to the fact that they are in very scarce supply relative to the demands for their services. Their transfer earnings will be very much less than their current remuneration because their market values outside their own specialised professions are probably very low.

Figure 31.2 shows that when supply is inelastic, a high proportion of earnings consists of economic rent.

A most frequently quoted example of earnings which contain a large proportion of economic rent are those of 'star' entertainers, and particularly those of pop stars. Each one has, it seems, some unique characteristic

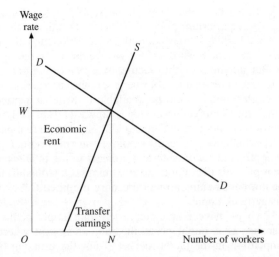

Fig. 31.2

and the supply of his or her particular talent is perfectly inelastic. The earnings of pop stars can reach amazing figures in a very short time period and there is no doubt that transfer earnings make up only a very small percentage of their incomes. In many cases the economic rent element in their earnings is, unfortunately, only too clearly revealed. The popularity of many individuals and groups is very short-lived and the weekly earnings collapse almost as quickly as they rose.

Economic rent and capital

Much of the nation's capital consists of very specialised equipment. It is designed for a particular purpose and cannot be transferred to another use. Once the equipment (e.g. a blast furnace) has been installed it could be said that any income greater than the variable costs is economic rent. No matter how low this net revenue falls, the equipment cannot be transferred to another use and any net return (i.e. greater than operating costs) is better than no return at all. It will only be beneficial to leave the equipment idle when the revenue falls below the running costs. This view is perfectly correct if we take the short-run view. Looking at the situation over the life of the existing equipment we can say that its transfer earnings are the current operating costs – if it does not cover these expenses it will leave the industry (i.e. go out of use). But if we take a longer-term view, there will come a time when the capital equipment will be worn out, and it will not be replaced if its earnings have not been sufficient to cover both variable costs and depreciation. If it does not earn this minimum return the supply of capital to this particular use will cease. Over the longer period, therefore, the transfer earnings of capital will be the variable costs plus the fixed costs.

Economic rent and land

In the case of land which has only one use (i.e. it is completely specific) the whole of its income is economic rent, as shown in Fig. 31.3. The land cannot transfer to another use and it will remain in that use indefinitely even when its earnings are zero. Most land, however, has alternative uses and whenever this is the case a particular piece of land will be earning economic rent only to the extent that its income in its present use exceeds what it could earn in its next most remunerative use.

Suppose some land is being used for growing wheat and farmers are paying a rent of £300 per acre for it. Its next most profitable use would be for growing barley, but farmers are only prepared to pay £250 per acre for barley-land. Payments for the land in its present use, therefore, contain an element of economic rent equal to £50 per acre. Now *any* price greater than £250 per acre will lead to land being transferred from barley to wheat – why pay £300 per acre? The explanation lies in the strength of demand relative to supply. If wheat is a very profitable crop,

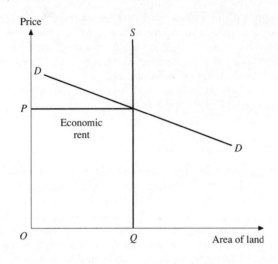

Fig. 31.3

farmers will bid against each other for suitable and available land and this could lead to prices rising well above the land's transfer earnings.

The land values which have attracted most attention in recent years have been those paid for urban land and especially for city-centre sites. The number of sites in the High Street is strictly limited – no matter what price is paid, there is no way of increasing the land available in this location for offices, shops, restaurants, cinemas, and so on. The high prices paid for such sites is explained by the inelasticity of supply and a rapidly increasing demand. Since these sites have many alternative uses the economic rent element in the price paid for any one use may be quite small, although the price itself may be very high. Figure 31.4 illustrates the situation. D^1, D^2, and D^3 represent different demands for a particular urban site. D^1 may be the demand from companies building cinemas, D^2 the demand from supermarket developers, and D^3 the demand from developers of office blocks. The highest bids come from people wishing to build office blocks and the market price is OP^3. Of the total revenue only the shaded area represents economic rent.

Taxing economic rent

Some economists argue that economic rent should be taxed as a surplus. Two main reasons are put forward. One is that such a tax, provided it does not take all the surplus, is unlikely to alter the allocation of resources. For example, if a Eurobond dealer is earning £3000 a week and could earn only £400 a week as an advertising agent in her next best paid job, taking, for example, 40 per cent of her economic rent in tax is unlikely to make her change her job.

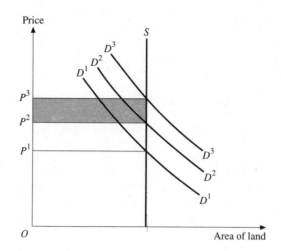

Fig. 31.4

Another argument is that at least part of the economic rent may have arisen because of government expenditure. Workers and entrepreneurs who receive high salaries may have benefited from state education (including university education), capital equipment may have been developed in part by government expenditure on research and development and part of the economic rent earned by land may have arisen from government expenditure on infrastructure.

However, in practice it is difficult to identify and measure economic rent. This is because it requires knowledge of what a factor could earn in its next best paid employment and this information may not be available.

Quasi-economic rent

We have noted that where the supply of a factor is less than perfectly elastic an increase in demand will lead to some units of that factor receiving economic rent. This rent may be of a temporary nature, however, because the higher price may lead to an increase in supply which will, in turn, lower the price. Increased earnings in an occupation may persuade more people to undertake the necessary training.

Also, as we have seen, the earnings above variable costs of machinery with a specific use can be regarded as economic rent in the short run, i.e. quasi-economic rent. As supernormal profits experienced by perfectly competitive firms will be competed away in the long run they are another example of quasi-economic rent. So quasi-economic rent is short run economic rent.

32 Interest

Definition

Interest is the earnings of capital, or the price which has to be paid for the services of capital. In a monetary economy it may be regarded as the price which has to be paid for the funds which are required to purchase capital equipment. Loans are demanded, however, for purposes other than the purchase of capital and it would be more realistic to describe interest as a payment for the use of money. In order to create a supply of loans, people with the necessary financial resources have to be persuaded to lend. In normal circumstances, loans can only be obtained when lenders are offered some reward for the sacrifices, risks, and trouble involved. This reward is the rate of interest and it contains several elements.

- A payment for the sacrifice of current spending power. The lender forgoes the opportunity to spend and consume *now*.
- A payment for the risks involved. The future is always uncertain and circumstances are always changing. All lenders run the risk that the borrower may default.
- A payment to compensate, if only partially, for any fall in the value of money. In recent years most countries have experienced some degree of inflation and lenders have come to expect some payment to make up for the loss in the purchasing power of the money loaned.

The rate of interest is generally seen as a reward to lenders, but it is also the 'price' which has to be paid when a purchaser of an asset uses his own savings. In this case the rate of interest is the opportunity cost of using one's own resources; it is the interest forgone when one decides to buy rather than lend.

If the rate of interest is a price, then, in a free market, it must be determined by the forces of supply and demand. We shall deal with two well-known theories which attempt to explain the rate of interest in terms of supply and demand.

The Loanable Funds Theory (sometimes known as the Classical Theory) explains the rate of interest in terms of the demand for capital (i.e., investment) and the supply of savings. The Keynesian (or Liquidity Preference) Theory holds that the rate of interest is the price which equates the demand for money (i.e., the desire to hold wealth in the form of money) and the supply of money.

Theories of interest rate determination

The Loanable Funds Theory

This is the older theory. According to this theory the rate of interest is determined by the interaction of the demand for loanable funds and the supply of these funds, as shown in Fig. 32.1.

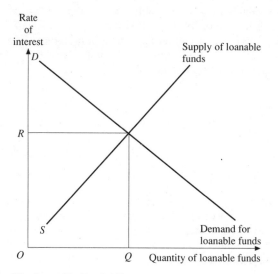

Fig. 32.1   The Loanable Funds Theory

The demand for loanable funds

In early versions of the theory, the demand for loanable funds was assumed to come entirely from firms seeking investment funds. Firms invest (i.e., create capital) because they expect to earn profits. They anticipate that the newly created capital will yield a series of returns during its lifetime which will exceed the costs incurred in its purchase and maintenance. The firm undertaking investment will estimate the net additional profits to be derived from the increased output and these expected net annual receipts can then be expressed in the form of a percentage annual return on the initial outlay. This percentage yield is the productivity of capital. We express the productivity of capital in this way because it is the only way in which we can compare the productivity of capital in different industries. If additional investment in the chemical industry is expected to yield a return of 20 per cent per annum while an addition to the stock of capital in the footwear industry is expected to earn 15 per cent per annum, capital will tend to flow to the chemical industry rather than to the footwear industry.

If we assume that the stock of capital is being increased relative to the stocks of the other factors of production, the returns to capital will be diminishing. Capital, like the other factors of production, is subject to the Law of Diminishing Marginal Productivity. The marginal product curve, then, will slope downwards from left to right.

In Fig. 32.2 the *DD* line represents the marginal productivity of capital. It shows us the expected net profitability of additions to the firm's stock of capital. The price of capital is taken to be the current rate of interest on the funds available to purchase capital equipment, and we assume that the individual firm cannot influence this market rate of interest. In Fig. 32.2 therefore, the price of capital appears as a horizontal line. The entrepreneur will employ capital up to the point where the value of its marginal product is just equal to its price.

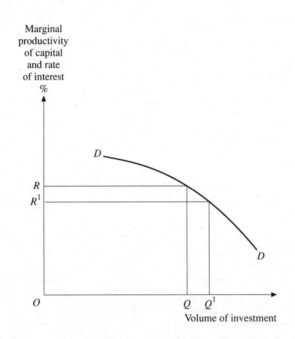

Fig. 32.2

When the rate of interest is *OR*, the firm will expand its capital stock to *OQ*. Any further additions to the capital stock would only reduce the firm's profits because the cost incurred in acquiring the capital (i.e. the interest charges) would exceed the expected annual returns from the extra units of capital. If the rate of interest falls to *OR*¹, the demand for capital increases to *OQ*¹. Investment projects (*QQ*¹) which appeared unprofitable at the higher interest rate will now offer the prospect of profitable employment. Similarly an increase in the rate of interest will reduce the demand for investment goods. This analysis applies whether the firm is borrowing money or using its own savings. The rate of interest is the opportunity cost of investment in both cases. When the firm uses its own savings to purchase capital it sacrifices the interest it could have earned on those savings.

The marginal productivity curve tells us what quantity of capital will be demanded at any given price and it is, therefore, the demand curve for capital. The equilibrium condition for the firm is the familiar one. It will employ additional units of capital up to the point where the last unit employed adds as much to revenue as it does to costs. More formally we say that profitability is maximised when,

The MP of Capital = The Rate of Interest

Influences on the marginal productivity of capital

The marginal productivity of capital has two components, (i) the physical productivity of the capital, and (ii) the price of the goods produced with that capital. Changes in either of these components will shift the *MP* curve which is, of course, the demand curve for capital. The demand curve will move outwards when the efficiency of capital increases (due to technical progress) or when the price of the product increases. A fall in the price of the product will move the demand curve inwards towards the origin.

An important point to remember is that the calculations of the marginal productivity of capital are based on little more than guesswork. In trying to assess the profitability of an addition to the capital stock, the business person must estimate his revenues and costs for several years into the future (the expected life of the capital). It is the *expected profitability* of capital which is the basis of the investment decision. All manner of political, economic, and technical developments can influence entrepreneurs' views regarding the future prospects for their enterprises and for this reason we must expect private investment to be a fairly unstable element in the economy.

Other sources of demand for loanable funds

Present-day supporters of the loanable funds theory include more than the firm sector when they consider the demand for loanable funds. Households also borrow. They borrow in order to purchase new houses and durable consumer goods and for these purposes make use of a variety of credit arrangements and loans. People also demand loans in order to buy existing assets both financial (e.g. securities) and real (e.g. second-hand houses). The government is also a large-scale borrower of loanable funds. Whilst the government's demand for loanable funds is likely to be less influenced by changes in the rate of interest, the demand from both households and firms will be expected to move in the opposite direction to changes in the rate of interest. This gives a downward sloping demand curve for loanable funds.

The supply of loanable funds

According to the loanable funds theory and the classical economists, the major determinant of the supply of funds for investment purposes is the current rate of saving. In return for a reward (i.e. interest) people will be prepared to forgo some current consumption in order to enjoy a higher level of consumption in the future. This reward is necessary because people have a *time preference*. They prefer present satisfactions to the promise of satisfactions in the future. The greater a person's time preference, the greater the inducement required to overcome it. If you are presented with the choice of having £100 now, or £110 in one year's time and you feel that £10 is just sufficient compensation for waiting, a rate of interest of at least 10 per cent is required to overcome your time preference. It would seem logical, therefore, to assume that a higher rate of interest will bring forth a greater supply of saving, since, as interest rates rise, people with a stronger time preference will be persuaded to start saving, and existing savers will increase their rate of saving. On this basis it is assumed that the supply curve of savings was of the normal shape sloping upwards from left to right. The rate of interest then is determined by the interaction of the demand for loanable funds (derived from the demand for capital), and the supply of these funds (derived from current saving). This is shown in Fig. 32.1. However, in practice a high proportion of saving by the personal sector is contractual, for example insurance policies, and this will not be sensitive to interest rate changes.

The supply of loanable funds is not dependent solely on the level of current saving, and the current level of saving is not the same thing as the supply of loanable funds. Saving makes lending possible, but it does not follow that what is saved is automatically loaned. The rate of interest is a reward for *lending* rather than saving. People may abstain from consumption, but they may be reluctant to lend. In addition to the supply of funds from current saving, the banks are able to create additional supplies of money which may be made available as loans. A further supply of loanable funds becomes available when people decide to reduce the amount of wealth they are holding in the form of money – this means that lending may increase even when there is no increase in the current rate of saving.

The Keynesian (liquidity preference) theory

Keynes stated that the demand for money was not related solely to the demand for new capital goods and the supply of funds was not dependent solely on the current level of saving. He pointed out that money was demanded not simply because it was a medium of exchange – it was also in demand as an *asset*. When he speaks of the 'demand for money', Keynes is referring to a demand for money *to hold*. In everyday speech the expression 'a demand for money' is usually taken to mean a demand for money to spend, but this is not a demand for money as such, but a demand for the things which money will buy. In monetary theory, 'the demand for money' must be interpreted literally; it refers to a desire to hold wealth in the form of money.

Liquidity

This preference for money over other kinds of assets is known as *liquidity preference*. Liquidity describes the readiness with which an asset can be converted into cash without any significant loss in value. Wealth held in the form of money provides us with the maximum freedom of action, because it is readily convertible into any other type of asset, and money, by definition, has a constant money value. If we exchange money for, say, a share in a company, the money value of our wealth is now uncertain, but we have an income-yielding asset. Money has the disadvantage that it does not earn an income. The great advantages of holding money are that it is the most liquid of all assets and its money value is certain. Note, however, that during inflation its exchange value falls.

Money, therefore, is one way in which an individual may choose to hold his or her wealth, but it is only one of many ways. Wealth may be held in the form of land, buildings, works of art, jewellery, bonds and shares, and so on. People hold wealth in all these forms and they adjust the proportions held in each form according to their means, desires, and the circumstances prevailing. We shall assume that decisions to change the amount of money they hold will cause people to hold more, or less, fixed-interest government securities (bonds).[1] A decision to hold less money will give rise to an increased demand for bonds, and a desire to hold more money will lead to a greater willingness to sell bonds. There are three motives for holding money.

The transactions motive

Most of us receive our incomes at regular intervals (per week or per month) and spend it fairly evenly over the intervals between pay days. We receive regular payments in the form of a cash balance and then run it down over the intervals between one pay day and the next. We may not, of course, spend it all – some of it may be transferred to a savings account, but in most cases the greater part of it will be held as a cash balance to finance day-to-day expenditures. There is no alternative to this procedure because it is not feasible to transfer our incomes into income-earning assets and then to sell, each day, enough shares or securities to provide our cash requirements for that day. The pattern of daily life, therefore, means that, nationally, a large stock of money is demanded for transactions purposes.

The amount of money held as transactions balances depends upon the level of income, the movements in prices, and the frequency with which income payments are made. If our income rises, we tend to buy more and

NOTE 1. The next most liquid asset.

better goods and services and so we will hold larger transactions balances. If prices rise, we would hold larger cash balances because the things we buy now cost more. The frequency with which income is paid also has an important influence on the size of the average transaction balance. If a person receives a weekly wage of £320 and spends the whole of it evenly during the week, the average balance over the week will be £160. If she is now paid at the same rate but receives her remuneration monthly (i.e., £1280 per month) and she maintains the same spending pattern, her average daily holding of money will be £640.

The precautionary motive

In addition to the cash balances needed to finance the regular day-to-day expenditures, most people hold additional money balances to deal with emergencies or to take advantage of some unexpected bargain. We may have to make an unplanned journey; unexpected visitors may involve us in unplanned spending on entertainment; something in a shop window catches our eye, or some domestic appliance requires urgent repair; such are the contingencies which encourage people to hold precautionary balances.

The transactions and precautionary motives are equally applicable to firms. A firm will hold a 'working balance' to meet payments during periods when the flow of income is less than the flow of expenditures. It will also need money balances to meet unexpected deviations in the pattern of trade (e.g. an unexpected rise in costs). The amount of money held for transactions and precautionary purposes is determined by factors which are not likely to change significantly in the short run.[2] The demand for these *active balances*, as they are called, will be fairly stable and will not be influenced by changes in the rate of interest.

The speculative motive

Any money which is held in excess of the requirements outlined above must be held for speculative purposes. People holding money in excess of the amounts needed for transactions and precautionary purposes must be convinced that, for the time being, it is more rewarding to hold money than financial, or real, income-earning assets. Why should people prefer to hold a sterile asset rather than one which brings them an income? In the case of government securites, the income is guaranteed – there is no risk of default. But there is a risk of making a capital loss. People will prefer to hold money rather than securities when they believe that the prices of securities are about to fall.

Example: An undated government security has a face value of £100 and carries a fixed rate of interest of $2\frac{1}{2}$ per cent. The holder of such a security will receive £2.50 per annum. Its current market price is £30. This means that purchasing 100 such securities will cost £3000 and bring

NOTE 2 An increasing rate of inflation would have short-run effects.

in an annual income of $100 \times £2.50 = £250$. This income represents a yield of $8\frac{1}{3}$ per cent on the outlay of £3000.

Now suppose a prospective purchaser believes that over the coming year security prices will fall and decides to hold on to his money. In the event he is proved correct and at the end of the year the price of this particular security has dropped to £15. £3000 will now purchase 200 such securities giving an annual return of £500 (i.e. $16\frac{2}{3}$ per cent).

By waiting for one year our investor has sacrificed £250 in the form of income forgone, but he will enjoy a net gain of £250 per annum as long as he holds these securities.

When people expect the prices of securities to fall, there will be a strong preference for holding money rather than securities. When security prices are expected to rise, there will be a much weaker liquidity preference: people will be anxious to buy securities before the expected price increase.

The prices of securities and the rate of interest

When the prices of fixed interest securities change, the rate of interest changes. The market rate of interest is quite simply the current yield on undated government securities. This is often described as the 'basic' rate of interest because the government is able to borrow at lower rates than any other borrower. Government securities are described as 'gilt-edged' because there is no risk of default. A simple example should make the relationship between security prices and the rate of interest quite clear.

a   An undated 5 per cent security, nominal value £100 (i.e. owner receives £5 per annum), stands at £80.

$$\text{Yield} = \frac{5}{80} \times \frac{100}{1} = 6\frac{1}{4} \text{ per cent} = \text{current rate of interest}$$

b   The price of the security now falls to £60

$$\text{Yield} = \frac{5}{60} \times \frac{100}{1} = 8\frac{1}{3} \text{ per cent} = \text{current rate of interest}$$

c   The price of the security rises to £120

$$\text{Yield} = \frac{5}{120} \times \frac{100}{1} = 4\frac{1}{6} \text{ per cent} = \text{current rate of interest}$$

Thus, the rate of interest varies inversely as the market prices of fixed interest securities.

Liquidity preference and the rate of interest

The reasons for holding money form the basis of the Keynesian (liquidity preference) Theory. For purposes of analysis the transactions and precautionary demands are usually added together and described as *active balances.* We have already noted that the demand for such balances will not be influenced by changes in the rate of interest and so it appears as the vertical straight line L^a in Fig. 32.3 (a). Before proceeding further it is necessary to emphasise the relationship between changes in the prices of fixed interest securities (or bonds) and changes in the rate of interest. A statement about one of these changes implies a statement about the other. Thus, if we read that interest rates are falling we know that the market price of securities must be rising (see examples above). If we read that the market prices of fixed interest securities are falling we know that interest rates are rising.

The speculative demand for money *is* influenced by changes in the rate of interest (i.e. in security prices), or, to be more accurate, by *expected changes* in the rate of interest. We saw this fairly clearly in the arithmetical example on p. 271. When security prices are expected to fall, speculators will be anxious to sell securities and hold money balances in order to avoid capital losses and also because they can increase their income by buying the securities at a later date when security prices are lower (as did the person in our earlier example). Now expectations of falling prices will be very strong when security prices are high – the next movement is likely to be downwards. Putting it another way, we are saying that *when interest rates are low, liquidity preference will be high*. There is the further point that the opportunity cost of holding cash balances will be low when interest rates are low (the amount of interest forgone is relatively small).

When security prices are low (i.e. interest rates are high), speculators will expect the next movement in prices to be upwards. They will want to buy securities now, before prices rise, either in anticipation of re-selling at the expected higher price, or to secure the higher yield which the low-priced securities now offer (i.e. before rising prices reduce this yield). Speculators will, therefore, be anxious to exchange their money balances

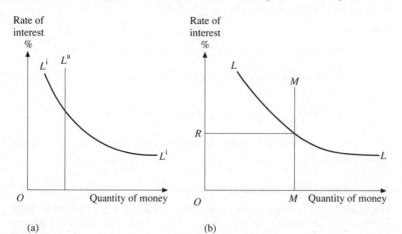

Fig. 32.3

for securities. Thus, *when interest rates are high, liquidity preference will be relatively low.*

This analysis indicates that when the quantity of money demanded is related to the rate of interest we shall obtain a demand curve of the normal shape. At high rates of interest very little money is demanded for speculative purposes; at low rates of interest, large amounts of money are demanded. The speculative demand for money is represented by the curve L^i in Fig. 32.3 (a). Note that the curve becomes horizontal at a positive rate of interest. This is because it is believed that some minimum reward (about 2 per cent?) is required to persuade people to forgo the advantages of holding money.

If the demand for active balances (L^a) is added to the demand for speculative balances (L^i) we obtain the total demand curve for money (LL) and this is shown in Fig. 32.3 (b). This curve is the liquidity preference schedule which tells us how the quantity of money demanded varies as the rate of interest varies. Speculative balances are often referred to as *idle balances*.

The rate of interest determined

If the supply of money is determined by the monetary authorities (The Treasury and the Bank of England) it can be taken as fixed in the short run. It is identified as the vertical line (MM) in Fig. 32.3 (b). The rate of interest is now determined by the intersection of the demand curve for money (LL) and the supply curve (MM). It is equal to OR.

Let us now examine the effects of changes in the demand for money and the supply of money. For this purpose we make use of Fig. 32.4.

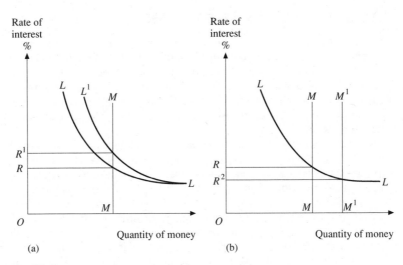

Fig. 32.4

An increase in liquidity preference (i.e. a stronger desire to hold money) brought about by an increase in income, or an increase in prices, or a widely held conviction that prices in general are about to fall, will raise the liquidity preference curve from LL to L^1L as in Fig. 32.4 (a). This causes the rate of interest to rise from OR to OR^1. What happens is that the increased preference for money balances leads to an increased desire to sell securities and the increased supply of securities in the market depresses their prices. In other words, the rate of interest rises. A fall in liquidity preference, other things being equal, will lower the rate of interest as the demand for securities increases.

The effect of a change in the supply of money is illustrated in Fig. 32.4 (b). When the supply of money increases from MM to M^1M^1, the rate of interest falls from OR to OR^2. This comes about because an increase in the supply of money must leave some groups holding excess money balances (assuming no change in liquidity preference). They will be holding a greater proportion of their wealth in the form of money than they wish to hold at current rates of interest. In trying to adjust the distribution of their wealth among the different types of asset these people will try to buy more bonds. The increased demand for bonds increases their prices and the rate of interest falls. A fall in the supply of money will leave the community with less money than it wishes to hold at current interest rates. People will try to increase their money balances by selling securities and in doing so they will raise the rate of interest. Note that an increase in the supply of money when the LL curve is horizontal will have no effect on the rate of interest. This horizontal part of the LL curve is known as the 'liquidity trap' because any increase in the supply of money in this range will be held in *idle balances*.

The structure of interest rates

Throughout this chapter we have been discussing the rate of interest as though there were one and only one rate of interest. In fact, the slightest of contacts with the real world reveals not one but very many rates of interest. The National Savings Bank may offer us, say, 7 per cent on deposits, the building societies may tempt us with offers to pay 8 per cent on our savings, we are asked to pay, perhaps, 11 per cent for a mortgage and so on.

The rate of interest referred to in the foregoing analysis is the rate of interest on undated government securities which, as explained earlier, represents the lowest rate at which funds can be borrowed. Rates of interest paid by other borrowers will differ from this basic rate by margins which depend upon the factors discussed a little later in this section. The existence at any given moment of time of different rates of interest does not invalidate the preceding analysis of the forces which determine the rate of interest. There is a particular structure of interest rates and while one individual rate may change relative to another, the whole structure will be affected by changes in the demand for and supply of money. The general level of interest rates will tend to move with the basic rate of interest. The major reasons for so many different rates of interest existing at the same time are as follows.

The duration of the loan

The longer the period for which the money is borrowed, the greater the risk of default by the borrower. The future is uncertain and the longer the period of the loan, the greater is the uncertainty. Short-term loans, therefore, will normally carry lower rates of interest than long-term loans. Lenders will accept lower prices because they feel more capable of estimating the course of events over the next few weeks than over the next few years, and, of course, they are postponing the ability to consume for a much shorter period.

Note that a current account in a bank usually carries no interest because these funds are subject to immediate withdrawal, whereas a deposit account earns interest because the money is loaned for at least seven days.

The credit-worthiness of the borrower

Lending is a risky business and the degree of risk varies according to the evidence of the borrower's ability to repay. The risk of default by the government is negligible because it has the power to tax the whole of the nation's wealth in order to meet its liabilities. Borrowers with a credit standing almost as high as governments are the great industrial and commercial companies. Lenders will demand relatively low rates of interest from borrowers such as these. Individuals and firms with low credit ratings (probably because they are unknown quantities) will be charged much higher rates of interest. Much depends upon the nature of the security which the borrower can pledge against his loan. Borrowers who are able to offer claims on land and property as securities for loans will be able to borrow at relatively low rates.

The marketability of the IOU

Loans are made to governments when lenders purchase financial claims on the government in the form of Treasury Bills or longer-term securities. Loans are made to companies by purchasing shares or debentures. These certificates (or IOUs) may or may not be easily marketable. Most government securities are marketable and may be bought and sold on the Stock Exchange (or in the Money Market). The same is true of the shares in most public limited companies. Where the ownership of the claim can be transferred very easily, the lender has a liquid asset. He can, if he wishes, 'change his mind' about lending his money and recover his cash. If he does decide to sell his security he cannot be sure of recovering the full amount of his loan, because the market prices of securities are always changing; he may get more than he loaned, he may get less. Where the acknowledgement of the loan is in the form of a marketable security, the loan will attract lower rates of interest, because the loan is a liquid asset.

33 Labour markets

Different labour markets

When economists discuss the labour market they are often looking at total (aggregate) demand for labour and total (aggregate) supply of labour. They also, however, study individual labour markets.

Labour markets can be classified according to the demand and supply of labour in a particular industry, in a particular firm, in a particular occupation and in a particular region.

Demand for labour

The demand for labour is a derived demand. Labour is required not for itself, but for what it will produce. The demand for labour derives directly from the demand for the product of labour. The greater the demand for the product, the greater the demand for labour. No matter how skilful the worker, no matter how long his period of training, if what he produces is no longer in demand, his services will no longer be required.

The aggregate demand for labour is influenced by the level of economic activity. If the economy is expanding more labour will be demanded either in terms of more hours from existing workers (overtime) or in terms of more workers.

The demand for labour in individual labour markets will be determined by the marginal revenue productivity of labour. Demand will increase if either there is an increase in demand for the final product, a rise in the productivity of labour, a rise in the price of a substitute factor of production or a fall in the price of a complementary factor of production. In the 1990s the increased interest in gardening has resulted in a rise in the number of people employed in garden centres whilst the increased application of technology in banking has reduced demand for bank tellers.

Elasticity of demand for labour

Demand for labour will be elastic if a given percentage change in wages causes a greater percentage change in demand. Figure 33.1 shows that the rise in the hourly wage rate from £10 to £12 results in a greater percentage fall in demand for workers from 400 to 300.

It will be inelastic if demand changes by a smaller percentage than the change in wage rate. There are four main influences on the elasticity of demand for labour in an industry.

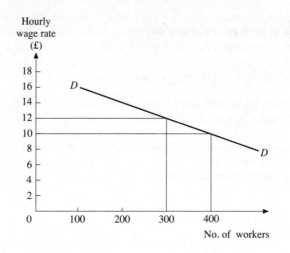

Fig. 33.1

The elasticity of demand for the product

If labour is producing a commodity which has a very inelastic demand, an increase in wages will have a relatively small effect on the demand for labour. Even if the whole of the increase in wages is passed on in the form of higher prices, the fall in the quantity demanded of the product will be relatively small, and there will be a correspondingly small reduction in the demand for labour. If, however, the demand for the product of labour is very elastic, a small increase in price will lead to a relatively large reduction in the quantity demanded. Under these circumstances an increase in wages which is passed on in the form of higher prices will cause a relatively large reduction in the demand for labour.

The proportion of total costs accounted for by labour costs

Where wages account for only a small proportion of total costs, the demand for labour will tend to be inelastic. Some industries such as house-building, are labour intensive and labour costs make up a large part of the total costs of the product. Other industries are capital intensive (e.g. chemicals and oil refining) and in these industries the cost of labour accounts for a relatively small part of the cost of the product.

Let us assume that wages increase generally by 10 per cent while productivity remains unchanged. In a labour-intensive industry, labour costs might account for, say, 60 per cent of average total cost and the effect of the increase in wages will raise unit cost by 6 per cent. In a capital-intensive industry where labour costs are, say, 20 per cent of average total cost, the increase in wages will raise unit cost by only 2 per cent. If these increased costs are passed on in the form of higher prices, the effects on the demand for labour are likely to be much greater in the former example than in the latter.

The degree to which labour can be substituted by other factors of production

Other things being equal, an increase in wage rates will increase the cost of labour relative to the costs of the other factors. Where possible, therefore, entrepreneurs will tend to substitute other factors for the now relatively dearer labour. As wages increase, the substitution of labour-saving machinery becomes more and more attractive. In low-wage countries like India we find that methods of production are labour intensive and it is countries with relatively high wage rates such as the USA which make the most use of labour-saving machinery. Where it is fairly easy to substitute capital for labour, the demand for labour will become more and more elastic as wage rates rise relative to other factor prices.

The period of time

Demand for labour will be more elastic in the long run. This is because it will take time for firms to change their methods of production and replace some workers by machines. Labour may also have fixed contracts and periods of notice may have to be given.

The aggregate (total) supply of labour

The supply of labour available to an economy is not the same thing as the number of people in that community. The labour supply is a measure of the number of hours of work which is offered at given wage rates over some given period of time. It is determined, therefore, by the number of workers and the average number of hours each worker is prepared to offer. Both of these features are subject to change and, at any moment of time, they will depend upon a number of things.

The size of the total population

This is obviously very important because the size of the total population sets an upper limit to the supply of labour.

The age composition of the population

The age composition of a population takes account of the proportions in the different age groups. Two countries might have the same total populations, but very different age compositions and hence very different numbers in the working age groups.

The working population

In many countries the minimum age at which a person may engage in full-time employment is legally controlled. In the UK this is now 16 years and the normal age for retirement is 65 years. The age range 16 to 65 covers the working age groups, but this does not mean that the total working population embraces all the people in these age groups. Many people now continue in full-time education well beyond the age of 16. Another large group which must be excluded consists of people who do not engage in paid employment outside the home. A number of people also retire early.

The working population may be defined as the number of people who are eligible for work and offer themselves for employment. As a proportion of the total population it will differ widely from country to country, especially where the levels of economic development are substantially different. In the UK the working population is rather less than one half the total population; about 26 million out of a total of 57 million.

The working week and holidays

The number of people who work (or are available for work) is an important determinant of the supply of labour, but so is the average number of hours each person works. The supply of labour provided by 20 people working for 40 hours is the same as that provided by 40 people working for 20 hours. The recognised working week in most developed countries has been progressively reduced and the 40-hour week has become a general pattern. Other things being equal, the shorter the working week, the smaller the supply of labour.

The gradual reduction in the working week has been accompanied by an extension of the annual holiday period. Again this amounts to a reduction in the supply of labour.

It must not be assumed, however, that a fall in the supply of labour implies a reduction in the output of goods and services. In spite of the decline in the average number of hours worked by each person, output per worker has continued to rise because of improved technology.

Remuneration

Generally speaking, when wage rates are relatively low, increases in wages will tend to lead to an increase in the supply of labour, but there comes a point when higher incomes make leisure more attractive. When incomes are relatively high, therefore, higher wage rates may reduce the amount of labour offered by the individual worker.

Social attitudes

In countries where it is considered unacceptable for married women or the disabled to work, the size of the workforce will be correspondingly lower.

The supply of labour to a given occupation/industry

The main influences on supply are the wage rate offered, the non-monetary aspects of the job, the qualifications and skills demanded and the extent of unemployment. The higher the wage rate offered the more workers will be attracted. However, workers will also take into account more than financial reward. They also consider working conditions, promotion chances, job security, number of days holidays, working hours, etc. The more attractive these are the more inclined people will be to work in the occupation. For instance, most actors do not earn high wages but the possibility of high earnings and the fame and glamour attached to the job cause many people to train as actors. The general level of education and training in a country will influence the relative supply of skilled and unskilled labour. If education and training standards are low, a high-skill industry such as the chemical industry will find it difficult to recruit staff. Supply of potential workers to a particular industry, in contrast, will be high if there is sufficient unemployment among suitably qualified people.

The individual's supply of labour

In many occupations individual workers cannot freely choose the number of hours they are prepared to work. Most jobs have some agreed and contractual working week. It is true that most self-employed persons such as taxi-drivers, shop-keepers, and small-scale builders can vary the number of hours they work, and many employed persons can exercise some choice on the amount of overtime they are prepared to work, but for the vast majority of the working population the length of the working week is settled by negotiation between trade unions or professional bodies and employers but the choice between work and leisure is, indirectly, available to individual workers by virtue of the part they can play in deciding the policy approach of their union or professional organisation.

The supply curve of labour for the individual worker will be of the normal shape for only part of its length. A higher price (i.e. wage rate) will call forth a greater supply up to a point. Beyond this point a higher price will probably lead to a reduced amount of labour being supplied. As income rises so does the demand for more leisure. As real income increases people can buy a much wider range of goods and services and they will demand more leisure in order to enjoy the consumption of these commodities. One has only to think of such activities as motoring, sailing, golf, and foreign travel to appreciate the increasing preference given to leisure as income rises. As the hourly wage rate rises, there will come a point at which the individual's supply curve of labour will bend backwards. This is illustrated in Fig. 33.2.

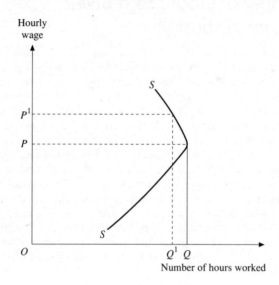

Fig. 33.2

As the hourly wage rate increases up to the level *OP*, the worker is tempted to work longer hours – the higher price calls forth a greater supply. As the wage rate rises above *OP*, the worker reduces the number of hours he is prepared to work. At the wage rate *OP¹* he offers *OQ¹* hours of work per week. This does not mean of course that he is reducing his weekly income. For example, he might be prepared to work a 40-hour week when the wage rate is £8.00 per hour, giving him a wage of £320. If the hourly wage rate increases to £10.00 he might offer 36 hours of work each week giving him a wage of £360 per week.

What we are saying is that, up to the rate *OP*, the substitution effect is more powerful than the income effect. Leisure is becoming more costly in terms of income forgone and the individual chooses more work and less leisure. At wage rates higher than *OP*, however, the income effect predominates. Alternatively, in terms of utility analysis, we can say that at wage rates higher than *OP* the marginal utility of leisure exceeds the marginal utility of income. This is true of the labour supplied by an individual; it will not be true of the supply of labour to an industry. The supply curve of labour to an industry will be of the normal shape because higher wages will attract *more workers* to that industry.

The elasticity of the supply of labour

The supply of labour is elastic when a given percentage change in the wage rate causes a greater percentage change in the supply of labour. The supply of labour is inelastic when a percentage change in the wage rate causes a smaller percentage change in the supply of labour. This is shown in Fig. 33.3.

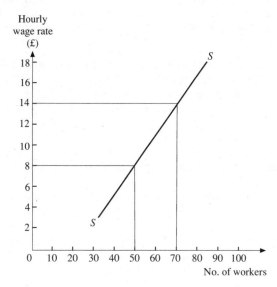

Fig. 33.3

The main determinants of the elasticity of supply in an industry are:

1 *The level of employment.* If there is high unemployment the supply of labour will be relatively elastic. A small rise in the wage rate is likely to attract a high number of job applicants.
2 *The mobility of labour.* The more occupationally and geographically mobile labour is, the more elastic the supply of labour will be.
3 *The length of training.* The longer it takes to train a worker, the more inelastic supply will tend to be. For instance, it takes approximately seven years to train a surgeon. So a rise in wages of surgeons will take some time before it is reflected in a rise in the number of surgeons.
4 *The qualifications and skills required.* The higher the level of qualifications and skills needed, the fewer potential workers there will be to draw on and hence the more inelastic supply will be. So surgeons are in inelastic supply not only because they have to undergo a longer period of training but also because they have to possess high academic qualifications before they start their medical training.

Changes in the nature of the labour force

The last few years have seen significant changes in the nature of the labour force. These include:

1 *A rise in part-time employment.* Part-time employment has risen by more than 25 per cent in the last decade. A number of firms have switched full-time into part-time jobs, including Burton and Sock Shop and other firms now have a majority of part-time staff including Marks and Spencer where 80 per cent of the workforce are on part-time contracts.

Women constitute four-fifths of the part-time workforce and part-time working in the service sector accounts for 35 per cent of the workforce whereas it accounts for 8 per cent in the manufacturing sector. However, it is manufacturing that has seen the sharpest proportional rises in part-time work and the rise in male part timers is exceeding that of female part timers.

Employers are attracted to the increased flexibility part-time working offers them and to what they perceive to be the lower non-wage employment costs, Employees working fewer than 15 hours a week do not have to be covered for National Insurance and those working fewer than 16 hours a week do not qualify for employment protection or for any statutory benefits such as redundancy pay and maternity benefit. However, some employers may be underestimating the costs of part-time employment. There is a management cost included in manoeuvring work rotas, training part-timers and keeping part-timers informed and involved.

2 *A rise in temporary employment.* More workers are being offered temporary contracts. This enables employers to adjust their workforces more cheaply and quickly but it also creates uncertainty among workers about job security.

3 *A rise in the participation of women in the workforce.* In 1944 68 per cent of the working population was male and there were 14.9 million men in work and 7.1 million women in work. Now 54 per cent of the workforce are male and hence 46 per cent are female. Also whilst the number of women in work has increased to 11.6 million the number of men in work has fallen to 13.7 million. There are a number of reasons why more women are working. These include the increase in part-time employment, changing social attitudes to women working, the invention of labour-saving household appliances, higher educational standards, achieved by women and the expansion of the tertiary sector where a high proportion of married women are employed.

4 *A change in the pattern of employment.* Figure 33.4 and Tables 33.1 and 33.2 give projected employment change by industry and by occupation.

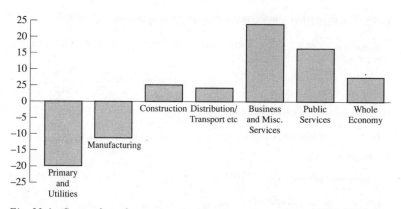

Fig. 33.4   Sectoral employment projections, percentage change 1991–2000

Table 33.1 Projected employment change by industry group 1991–2000

Industry	% Change 1991–2000
Agriculture	−15
Mining, etc.	−35
Utilities	−26
Metal, minerals, etc.	−17
Chemicals	−18
Engineering	−6
of which: mechanical engineering	−14
electrical engineering	−8
Motor vehicles	−3
Food, drink and tobacco	−25
Textiles and clothing	−23
Other manufacturing	−10
Construction	+5
Distribution, etc.	+6
of which: distribution	+3
hotels and catering	+17
Transport and communication	−5
Banking, insurance and business	+13
Miscellaneous services	+31
Health and education	+21
Public administration	+5
Whole economy	+7

Source: Labour market trends & skills 1993–94 Dept of Employment

Table 33.2 Projected employment change by occupation 1991–2000

Occupation	Percentage Change
Corporate managers and administrators	+31
Managers/proprietors in agriculture and services	+17
Science and engineering professions	+31
Health professions	+24
Teaching professions	+22
Other professional occupations	+40
Science and engineering associated professions	+20
Health associate professions	+13
Other associate professional occupations	+28
Clerical occupations	+2
Secretarial occupations	+4
Skilled construction trades	+7
Skilled engineering trades	−8
Other skilled trades	−17
Protective service occupations	+16
Personal service occupations	+16
Buyers, brokers and sales representatives	+6
Other sales occupations	+10
Industrial plant and machine operatives	−21
Drivers and mobile machine operatives	−5
Other occupations in agriculture	−18
Other elementary occupations	−5
All occupations	+7

Source: Labour markets & skills trends, 1993–94 Dept of Employment

34 Wage determination

Wages are the price of labour, and like any price in a free market would be determined by demand and supply. We will discuss wage differentials first and then consider the influences of demand and supply and the other factors which in the real world influence wages.

Wage differentials

We are all aware of the fact that there are very great differences in wage rates as between different occupations and the commonsense explanation for this would be that labour is not a homogeneous factor. There are very great differences in the skills and abilities of, and in the demands for, different types of worker giving rise to not one labour market, but many different markets each with its own supply and demand conditions. The variations in the conditions of supply and demand as between these markets will give rise to different prices, hence the existence of wage differentials.

This is all very true, but we have to explain why these wage differentials persist. Why is there no large-scale movement of workers from the lower-paid jobs to those more highly paid? Such a movement would tend to equalise wages, for the movements out of the lower-paid jobs would reduce the supply of this type of labour and raise its price, while the movements into the more highly paid jobs would increase the supply and tend to lower the price. Adam Smith asked the question, 'If labour were perfectly mobile would wages in all occupations then be equal?' In fact, they would not, because some jobs are more attractive than others. If wages were equal in all occupations, the dirty and disagreeable jobs would attract little labour, most people would seek the jobs with pleasant and congenial conditions. Smith pointed out that under such circumstances it would be the *net advantages* of occupations which would tend to equality. There would be differences in money wages and these differentials would measure, in money terms, the values which people placed on other aspects of their work such as the degree of security, the element of danger, and the satisfaction of the work. If we turn to the real world again, we find that dirty and disagreeable work is often less well paid than the more pleasant and attractive jobs. It is apparent that existing wage differences do not equalise the attractiveness of different occupations. To explain why one job pays £x per week while another pays £y per week, we must examine the supply and demand conditions to find out what makes them equate at different price levels in the different markets.

Demand and supply influences

In a particular occupation the wage rate will be determined by the demand and supply conditions in the market. The demand for labour depends on the physical productivity of labour and the price of the product. These two facts determine the marginal revenue productivity of labour and hence the shape of the demand curve. As we saw in Chapter 33 the elasticity of demand for labour in any occupation depends on the elasticity of demand for the product, the extent to which labour can be substituted by other factors of production and the proportion of labour costs in total costs. The supply of labour to a particular occupation will be influenced by the skills required, the ability of trade unions and professional associations to influence recruitment, relative pay and the non-monetary advantages of the job.

It is fairly obvious that these different influences on supply and demand will apply to very different degrees in the different labour markets and hence give rise to different wage rates. In each labour market the wage rate will be determined by the interaction of the relevant demand and supply curves.

Figure 34.1 shows the effects of an increase (or decrease) in demand in two such markets. In one of the markets the supply of labour is elastic; in the other it is inelastic. There is not a separate market for each and every occupation, but rather separate markets for groups of occupations. Within these groups it is possible for labour to move from one occupation

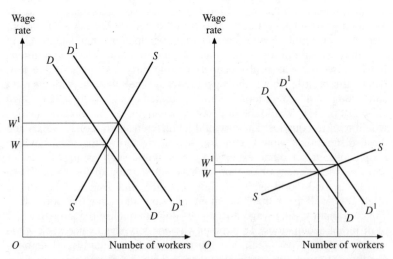

Fig. 34.1   (a) *Supply inelastic – labour highly skilled – long training period required*
(b) *Supply elastic – no barriers to entry – labour unskilled – little or no training required*

to another (e.g. a bus driver may become a lorry driver). Nevertheless for the highly skilled professions and those which require long periods of training each occupation does represent a separate labour market.

It should now be possible for the reader to discuss, analytically, questions on wage differentials. If asked to explain, for example, why solicitors earn more than their clerks, it is necessary to seek out those factors which give rise to different supply and demand conditions for these professions.

Figure 34.2 shows the average weekly earnings of the main occupational groups, including clerical and related workers.

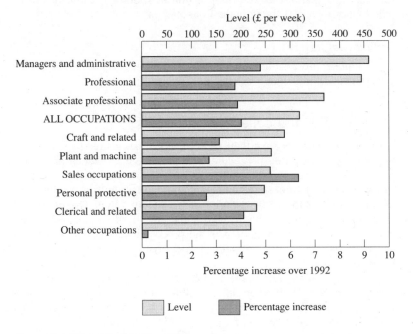

Source: *Employment Gazette*, Nov. 1993

Fig. 34.2   Average gross weekly earnings by occupational major group, April 1993

Within an occupation

Quite apart from the differences in wage rates between occupations we also find wage differences *within* an occupation. These arise for many reasons. In many occupations, particularly those of a clerical, administrative, or professional nature, there are scales of pay which allow for annual increments over a period of years, presumably because it is believed that labour's productivity varies directly with experience as well as education and training. The more senior workers, therefore, will be receiving higher wages than those who have recently joined the profession. There are various methods of remuneration which apply the payment-by-results principle (e.g. piece-work and bonus schemes) and in these cases wages will vary according to the individual worker's output. There may also be regional discrepancies in the wages paid to the same occupation. Workers with a particular skill may be in short supply in one area but not in another, but union negotiations, conducted on a national basis, tend to eliminate such regional differences in wage rates. Regional differences in the cost of living also play a part and the national scales for many occupations make provision for an additional allowance to be paid to those workers living in the London area.

Institutional factors

Trade unions, professional organisations, employer organisations and the government all influence wages.

Trade unions and collective bargaining

A number of workers have their wages and salaries settled by some kind of collective bargaining procedure. The individual worker is in a weak bargaining position and the main purpose of a trade union is to remove this weakness by forcing the employer to negotiate with representatives of the whole, or the great majority of his labour force. The growth of trade unions has been accompanied by the growth of employers' associations and collective bargaining is the process whereby representatives of the employers in any one industry negotiate with representatives of the workers in that industry.

In the UK trade union memberships was 7.3 million in 1993 in comparison with 1979 when union membership peaked at 13.3 million, half of the working population. Figure 34.3 shows this significant decline, on a year-by-year basis.

Government estimates suggest that 35 per cent of employees are now in trade unions. The proportion in private industry is 23 per cent but in the public sector it remains high at 63 per cent. The sharpest decline has been in membership of the National Union of Mineworkers which in 1979 had 372 122 members and in 1993 approximately 7000. Figure 34.4 shows the changes in membership and leadership of the UK's largest unions.

Union membership has fallen because of the rise in unemployment, the weakening of trade unions as a result of government legislation and changing social attitudes.

Trade unions are autonomous bodies; that is, they have complete freedom to act in their own interests. Most unions, however, are affiliated to the Trades Union Congress (TUC), which speaks for the movement as a whole and has an important role in bringing trade union points of view to bear on government decisions.

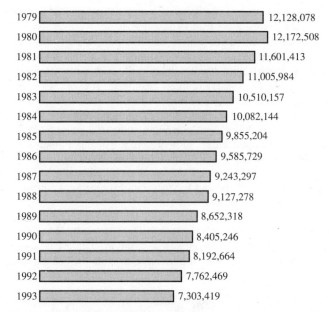

1979	12,128,078
1980	12,172,508
1981	11,601,413
1982	11,005,984
1983	10,510,157
1984	10,082,144
1985	9,855,204
1986	9,585,729
1987	9,243,297
1988	9,127,278
1989	8,652,318
1990	8,405,246
1991	8,192,664
1992	7,762,469
1993	7,303,419

Fig. 34.3   Decline in union membership

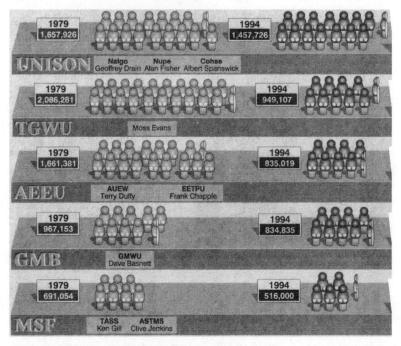

Fig. 34.4   Unions: the members and their leaders

Source: *The Times* 5 Sept. 1994

Although large numbers of workers are not members of trade unions, in many cases it would be true to say that their pay and working conditions are settled by trade union negotiations. Such settlements are widely applied and are not normally confined to trade union members.

With so many different unions in the UK, it is almost impossible to classify them into any clearly defined groupings. It is possible, however, to distinguish four basic types of trade union.

Craft unions represent workers with particular skills (e.g. the National Union of Tailors and Garment workers), industrial unions represent all the workers in a particular industry (e.g. the National Union of Mineworkers), general unions represent anyone wishing to join (e.g. the Transport and General Workers' Union and 'White-collar' Unions (e.g. the Manufacturing, Science and Finance Union) represent administrative, clerical and other non-manual workers.

Recent years have witnessed an increase in mergers between unions, the most significant being the merger in 1993 between NALGO, NUPE and COHSE, to form Unison, the largest union. There has also been a rise in the significant of white-collar unions with MSF even recruiting vicars.

Trade unions and wages

Trade unions have two major functions, first, to bargain on behalf of their members for better pay and working conditions, and to persuade the government to pass legislation in favour of the working class. Quite early in their history unions realised that many of their aims could only be achieved by political action. Trade unions played a leading part in the development of the Labour Party and they remain a major source of its funds.

Wages and collective bargaining

How great is the power of unions to influence wages? At one time it was thought that the unions' powers depended very much on the conditions in the labour market. In a situation of full or near-full employment when their membership would be high and their funds in a healthy state unions would be very strong. On the other hand, it was thought that unions would be in a weak bargaining position when large numbers of workers were unemployed. Events in the 1970s and 1980s cast serious doubts on this theory because unions demonstrated their ability to push up wages even when unemployment was *relatively* high.

Whether unions can exert a significant influence on *real wages* is a more difficult question to answer. Real wages depend upon the movements in money wages relative to the movements in prices. Increases in money wages unaccompanied by any increases in the output of goods and services are almost certain to lead to increased prices. Real wages then are determined very much by the movements in productivity.

To the extent that unions cooperate in schemes to increase efficiency they may play an important part in raising real wages although their very real fears of redundancy may lead them to resist the introduction of new techniques of production. They may also believe that, given the monopolistic structure of many industries, an increase in productivity may result in higher profits rather than higher wages. Even when there has been no increase in productivity it is still possible for trade unions to increase real wages if they can increase labour's share of the national income at the expense of profits, interest, and rent. It is also possible for one union to increase the real wages of its own members at the expense of other income groups including other wage earners. Each union tends to direct its efforts at increasing the welfare of its own members; this, after all, is the main reason for its existence. The more powerful unions, if they make full use of their bargaining strength, could succeed in getting proportionately larger and/or more frequent wage increases than the weaker groups. If the share of income going to labour remains the same, this will mean a redistribution of income within the wage-earning groups from those with weaker bargaining powers to those with stronger positions.

Since the 1970s there has been an increasing tendency for bargaining on pay and working conditions to move away from industry-wide negotiations to company or plant-level bargaining. The government has encouraged this move in a bid to promote labour flexibility.

The bases of wage claims

Trade union demands for higher wages are normally based on one or more of four grounds:

- A rise in the cost of living has reduced the real income of their members.
- Workers in comparable occupations have received a wage increase.
- The increased profits in the industry justify a higher return to labour.
- Productivity has increased.

The cost of living argument. If the rise in the cost of living is due to a rise in costs of production brought about by a previous wage increase then it seems difficult to justify the wage claim on purely economic grounds. If productivity has not increased and the share of income going to profits, rent, and interest does not change, an increase in wages can only lead to a further increase in prices. This is the familiar pattern of the wage-price spiral. If the cost of living has increased because of a rise in import prices, then, once again, if other things do not change, any wage increase must lead to a further rise in prices. If the rise in the general price level is due to an increase in monopoly profits, labour would seem to be quite justified in claiming a compensating wage increase, although the community as a whole would benefit from more competition, lower prices, and the elimination of the excess profits. The cost of living argument is one which attracts powerful social and political support and, in recent years, its acceptance has led to the widespread use of measures which link wages to the retail price index (a process generally described as 'indexation').

The differential argument. This argument rests on the widely held conviction that it is 'fair' that workers doing similar jobs should get similar rewards. One of the problems here is the meaning given to the term 'comparable occupation'. In many cases it is difficult to establish strict comparability; is there a job which is strictly comparable to, say, that of a policeman or an engine-driver? But the differential argument is also applied in a way which often leads to a situation where a wage settlement in one sector of the economy causes a chain reaction of wage claims in other sectors of the economy. If one occupation is granted a wage rise it means that the existing pattern of wage differentials has been upset. This will invariably provoke demands in other occupations for wage increases to restore the previous differentials. There is a strongly held conviction that wage differentials which have existed for a number of years are 'fair'. One often hears complaints from workers in different industries that they 'have lost out in recent wage settlements'.

The economic case against the differential argument is based on the necessity for a high degree of mobility in the labour force. If differentials are frozen, how do we get workers to move from declining or less 'essential' industries to the expanding industries? The only practical way in which such a movement may be brought about in a free society is by using wage differentials. If the growth industries offer higher rates of pay they will attract workers from other industries. But if these higher rates of pay lead immediately to compensating awards in other industries, the differentials remain unchanged, and there will be no monetary incentive for labour to move.

The profitability argument. The individual union in pursuing the interests of its own members feels completely justified in pressing for an increase in wages whenever the profits in the industry are increasing. In view of the imperfections in the product markets and the labour markets, it is difficult to say that the union claims are unjustified. Yet it appears from the point of view of the community as a whole that certain privileged groups (the shareholders and workers in these industries) are gaining at the expense of the general public. If the degree of competition were not restricted and the markets were more perfect, more labour and capital would move into these more profitable industries, more would be produced, prices would be lower, and excess profits would be eliminated.

The productivity argument. Improvements in labour productivity are widely accepted as justifiable reasons for increases in wages and most official incomes policies seem to accept this argument. There are, however, some serious problems involved. Most increases in productivity arise from improvements in the quality and performance of the capital equipment on which the labour is employed. Many would regard it as unfair that workers who happen to be employed in those industries where there is a rapid rate of technical progress should obtain all the benefits from the resulting increases in productivity. A large number of workers are employed in occupations where it is difficult or impossible to measure productivity, or where, due to circumstances beyond their control, it cannot be increased (e.g. increased traffic congestion *decreases* the productivity of the bus driver).

It can also be argued that gains from technical progress should accrue to the whole community in the form of lower prices. Where increases in productivity result from the workers' acceptance of new methods of production which impose greater strain, or responsibility, or call for retraining, claims for higher rewards are fully merited since the MRP of labour will have increased. A good example of this sort of change would be where labour agrees to drop some traditional restrictive practice.

Whatever the cause of increased productivity, where competition is ineffective, workers might reasonably argue that if they did not take the gains from the higher productivity in the form of higher wages, they would go to the owners of capital in the form of increased monopoly profits.

Trade unions and economic theory

It is often said that the determination of wages is a matter for unions and employers to settle by negotiation and the theory of supply and demand has little relevance in fixing wages. But market forces do have a part to play and they are, as it were, 'present at the bargaining table'. Employers and unions must take some account of the various supply and demand considerations discussed earlier. They will be aware of the extent to which labour can be substituted by capital and they will be conscious of the extent to which changes in labour costs affect total costs. They will also have some idea of the elasticity of demand for the product. Whether labour is in short supply or excess supply will also have some influence on the attitudes of the two sides. These matters will tend to set some limits to the range in which bargaining can take place.

The power of the unions rests ultimately on their ability to call an effective strike and employers must consider the effects of such a strike on their costs and future sales. The unions' bargaining power also depends upon their ability to control the supply of labour to the industry. In cases where the union has established a *closed shop*, only union members may be employed and the union can effectively control the supply of labour. Trade unions can also influence recruitment in other ways such as by enforcing apprenticeship regulations and restricting employment to those who possess qualifications acceptable to the union. These latter restrictions are particularly important in such professions as law and medicine.

Employer organisations

Employer organisations, the most famous of which is the Confederation of British Industry (CBI) can influence wages directly in their bargaining with labour and indirectly in the influence they can seek to exert on government policy.

Government policy

The government is the largest employer in the UK so the government's approach to the pay of its own workers has a significant impact on wage determination. In recent years the government has imposed cash limits on public-sector pay, thereby depressing it which in turn tends to reduce the growth of private-sector pay.

The government can also influence pay in both the private and public sectors by passing legislation such as the Equal Pay Act, and by introducing incomes policies, which may themselves have statutory power.

Government measures on trade union reform will affect the bargaining position of workers and thereby influence wage rates. Similarly government policy on education, training, housing and unemployment-related benefits will affect the mobility and supply of labour. Changes in, for example, government spending, taxation, the rate of interest and the exchange rate will alter the level of aggregate demand and thereby the demand for labour.

35 Labour market failure

The nature of labour market failure

In a perfect labour market all employers and all employees would be price takers, there would be perfect mobility of labour, no discrimination, perfect knowledge about vacancies, wage rates and working conditions. Wage rates would adjust quickly and smoothly and the market would clear ensuring full employment. These conditions clearly do not hold and in this chapter we examine the reasons why and their consequences.

Causes of labour market failure

Barriers to mobility

There are a number of factors which may prevent labour from moving from low-paid jobs and regions to high-paid jobs and regions.

Geographical

Monetary cost. Moving a family together with all its possessions can be an expensive operation. In addition to removal costs it might well entail the numerous expenses involved in buying and selling a house. This latter aspect of mobility can be a deterrent to movements into areas where house prices are well above the national average (e.g. the London area).

Housing. A number of features of the UK housing market make it difficult for people, particularly the low paid, to move from one area to another. There is a shortage of rental accommodation in both the private and public sectors. The price and availability of owner-occupied houses varies from region to region and the costs of moving are high.

Social ties. Many people are very reluctant to 'tear up their roots'. They do not wish to leave behind their friends and relatives and face the prospect of establishing new social relationships in a strange town. This is probably not such an important barrier for many professional groups where promotion often depends upon a movement to another town.

Education. Many families will tend to be immobile at certain stages of their children's education. They would regard it as inadvisable to move at some critical period in their child's schooling. This could also be a barrier if different parts of the country are operating different systems of education.

Occupational

Natural ability. People differ in natural ability and some occupations require a high level of intelligence, or particular natural aptitudes which are only possessed by a certain proportion of the population. For this reason surgeons, physicists, mathematicians, designers, and entertainers form a relatively small proportion of the population.

Training. Many professions demand a very long period of education and training (e.g. doctors, architects). In spite of the government aid in the form of training grants, such extended periods still require considerable financial sacrifice by the student and his family. The length of the training period itself may prove a deterrent to some people.

Capital. A certain amount of capital is required in order to enter some occupations. In order to establish oneself as an entrepreneur in the retail trade or some other form of one-person business (e.g. jobbing builder, or hairdresser), capital is needed to purchase the necessary stock and equipment. The purchase of a practice or partnership may be necessary if one wishes to become established as a solicitor, accountant, or estate agent. These requirements will constitute a financial barrier to many prospective entrants.

Class. It is held by many people that the existing class structure is responsible for some restrictions on the occupational mobility of labour. A particular type of social background with an education at one of the more famous public schools provide, it is believed, definite advantages in certain fields of employment.

Lack of information

Workers and employers may lack information about the labour markets in which they operate. Most workers are unaware of all the available vacancies. They are unlikely to know about the promotion chances, wage rates and wage conditions in all the jobs that they are capable of undertaking. This means that they may stay in less well paid jobs. Employers may also be unaware of the wage rates being paid by rival firms and the number of people willing and able to undertake jobs in their companies.

Workers seeking jobs and employers seeking workers will incur search costs. Workers have to spend time, money and effort applying for jobs and employers may have to advertise jobs, produce shortlists and interview applicants. In seeking to cut down on these search costs workers may not find the jobs to which they are most suited and employers may not find the most skilled employees.

Discrimination

Discrimination in labour markets occurs when a group of workers receive a different wage and/or are given different chances of employment and promotion from the other workers performing the same jobs. Discrimination may be on the basis of gender, colour, age, social background and a number of other grounds such as height.

The effects of discrimination can be shown on a diagram. Figure 35.1 shows that demand for women is lower than their marginal revenue product. This results in their wate rate (*OW*) and the number being employed (*OQ*) being lower than in a perfect market (*OWX* and *OQX*).

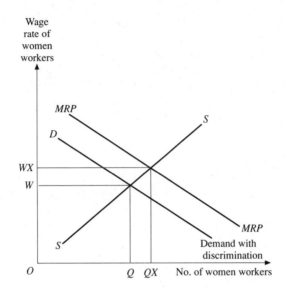

Fig. 35.1

Discrimination in one labour market will have a knock-on effect on other labour markets. If women are discriminated against in one industry, their supply in industries which do not discriminate will increase. The effect of this higher supply will be to lower the wage rate they receive in these industries. This is shown on figure 35.2.

Discrimination by consumers may actually lower the marginal revenue product of a particular group in comparison to other groups and thereby lower their wage rate. For instance, people prefer watching male track and field athletes and hence the price which can be charged for events featuring male athletes is higher than that for all-female meetings. So male athletes, on average, command higher appearance fees than female athletes.

Monopoly trade unions

Trade unions, by pushing the wage rate above the equilibrium level, may reduce employment. In Fig. 35.3 the free market wage is *OW* and at this wage the firm employs *OM* workers. A union is formed and negotiates a

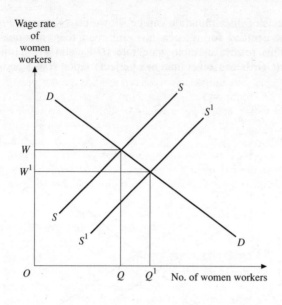

Fig. 35.2

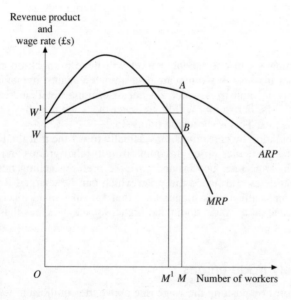

Fig. 35.3

wage of OW^1 which it has the power to enforce on all firms in the industry. According to our theory the effect of the union action will be to cause the firm to reduce employment to OM^1. Indeed if this were a profit-maximising firm and other things remained equal this is exactly what would happen. But unions, as we have seen, have the power to control the supply of labour and might react to any reduction of employment by threatening strike action. The line AB shows the scope for bargaining between employer and union. AB represents the surplus earned on each worker employed when the wage rate is OW and the number of workers employed is OM. It might well be that when the wage is raised to OW^1 and *employment remains at OM*, the firm is still making profits in excess of normal profits. In this case the union might be able to raise wages *and* resist any cut in the numbers employed.

We can present a similar picture for the industry as a whole. In Fig. 35.4 DD^1 and SS^1 represent the free market demand and supply curves for a particular type of labour. The free market wage will be OW and OM workers will be employed. A trade union negotiates a minimum wage of OW^1. This means that the dotted part of the SS^1 curve now has no relevance because, although some workers will be willing to work for less than OW^1, they will not be allowed to do so. The supply of labour to this industry is now represented by the line $W^1 XS^1$ and the equilibrium position is where the demand curve crosses this line. At this point OM^1 workers will be employed. The result of the union action, according to this representation, has been to reduce employment by MM^1 workers.

But this analysis assumes that other things remain equal and there is no change in the demand for labour. In fact, an increase in wages might

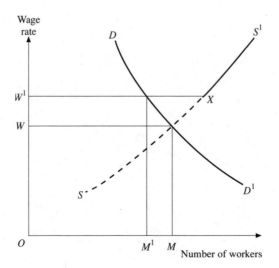

Fig. 35.4

well stimulate efforts to improve the productivity of labour and, if they are successful, the *MRP* curve will move upwards. The demand for labour will increase and there might well be no net reductions in the numbers employed. If this particular increase in wages is part of a general increase in wages there will be an incréase in the demands for most goods and services. Firms will be able to raise prices and the *ARP* and *MRP* curves of labour will move upwards. Again, the increased demand for labour might well offset the increased wages so that numbers employed are not seriously affected.

Monopsony and oligopsony employers

A monopsonist employer is the sole buyer, and an oligopsonist employer is one of only a few major employers of a certain type of labour. A local monopsonist would be the sole employer of a particular type of labour in a town or local area. Both are wage makers and may pay a wage rate below that which would operate in a perfect labour market. As monopsonists and oligopsonists influence the wage rate their marginal cost of labour exceeds the average cost of labour.

To employ an extra worker they have to pay a higher wage not just to the extra worker but to all the other workers as well. The number of workers employed will be determined by equating the marginal cost of labour with the marginal revenue product (*OL*). The wage rate paid is found from the average cost of labour (the supply curve). The wage rate paid is below the marginal revenue product. In a competitive labour market the wage rate would be higher (*OW*¹) and the level of employment would also be higher (*OL*¹).

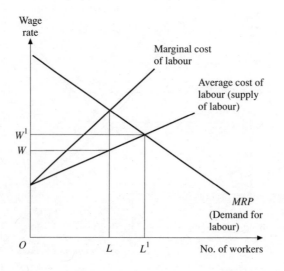

Fig. 35.5

Bilateral monopoly

It is possible that a monopsonist employer may face a monopolist trade union. This situation is referred to as a bilateral monopoly. In this case the level of wages and employment will depend on the relative bargaining strengths and skills of unions and employer representatives. However, it is likely that the wage rate and employment will be higher with a union presence than without. This situation is illustrated in Fig. 35.6. Without union intervention the wage rate would be OW and OQ number of workers will be employed. However, if a union raises the wage rate to OW^1, the supply curve becomes W^1 XY. The marginal cost of labour now becomes OW^1, up to OQ^1 number of workers. The employer will hire the number of workers when $MRP = MC$. So now a higher number of workers, OQ^1, are employed at a higher wage rate.

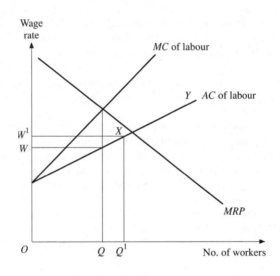

Fig. 35.6

Attachment between workers and employers

In a perfect market there would be no attachment between workers and employers so that a worker would feel free to move to a higher-paid job and an employer would feel free to dismiss existing workers if demand fell. However, in practice a worker may stay with an employer due to familiarity, pleasant atmosphere and other non-monetary advantages. Employers may hoard labour, during downturns, hoping that demand will pick up in the future and wishing to keep workers who have been trained in the ways of the firm. In practice, the attachment which exists between workers and employers reduces labour mobility.

36 Government action to correct labour market imperfections

A government can seek to improve labour market efficiency by removing the imperfections which occur in the labour market.

Education and training

For labour markets to work effectively, workers have to be occupationally mobile and possess the skills in demand. To achieve this a high level of education and training is required. The private sector will tend to under-provide both education and training. As we have seen education is a merit good but so is training. A better-educated and trained workforce provides benefits to society in the form of a more productive and adaptive workforce and higher national income.

Firms tend to underprovide training, in part because they fail to appreciate all the benefits of training, but also because they expect that some of the benefits will go to other firms if workers leave the firm soon after a period of training.

The current government is seeking to raise the skills levels of the workforce by raising the standards of school leavers, increasing the numbers who enter higher education and increasing the quality and quantity of training the employed and unemployed receive. However, its critics claim that the resources devoted to education and training are inadequate, that unlike many of our rivals a majority of UK citizens receive no formal education or training after the age of 16, and UK firms still devote a smaller percentage of their turnover to training than not only our EU competitors but also many newly industrialised countries.

Providing labour market information

Increasing information about job vacancies, wage rates and required skills should lower unemployment, increase the mobility of labour and create a more appropriate use of labour resources.

Government job centres provide information to the unemployed and some who are seeking to change jobs and put employers in touch with potential employees.

Trade union legislation

Conservative governments in the 1980s passed a series of Acts (including the Employment Acts of 1980, 1982 and 1988 and the Trade Union Act of 1984) relating to trades union. These reduced trade unions' bargaining power and restrictive practices by lowering trade unions' legal immunities and requiring unions to carry out secret ballots before taking industrial action. The conservative governments implemented this legislation in the belief that the actions of trade unions raise the real wage rate above the competitive market level and lower productivity, thereby reducing domestic competitiveness and increasing unemployment. However, trade unions can provide benefits to society including acting as a counterbalance to the bargaining power of employers.

Legislation against discrimination

Discrimination against any group of workers can result in the wage rate and the employment level being below the efficient levels. The government has passed two major Acts concerned with discrimination in employment. The Race Relations Act of 1976 makes it illegal to discriminate directly on the grounds of colour, race, nationality or ethnic or national origins or indirectly by providing conditions which, although they apply equally to everybody, have an adverse effect on one or more racial minorities. This Act gives people who have experienced discrimination at work the right to bring a complaint before an industrial tribunal. In addition to discrimination in employment the Race Relations Act also covers discrimination in education, housing and the provision of goods, facilities and services. This is also true of the Sex Discrimination Act 1975 which makes it illegal to discriminate on the basis of gender. Again, it covers direct discrimination, where, for example, a person fails to be given the offer of a job on the basis of their gender and indirect discrimination where, for example, a requirement of employment is made which one gender is unlikely to achieve. There are a number of exemptions including firms which employ fewer than six people and people working in private households.

Equal pay legislation

One of the most marked differentials in the national pay structure is that between the average earnings of men and the average earnings of women. In 1994 the average earnings of full-time women were about 79 per cent of those of full-time men.

This difference exists despite the Equal Pay Act which was passed in 1970 and came into force in December 1975. This Act requires that a woman receive equal treatment to a man within the same firm when she is employed on work of the same or a broadly similar nature to that of men, or in jobs which, though different from those of men is of equal value.

There are a number of reasons why a discrepancy continues to exist between the hourly wages of men and women. As Fig. 36.1 shows, women tend to be over-represented in the low-paying occupations. In

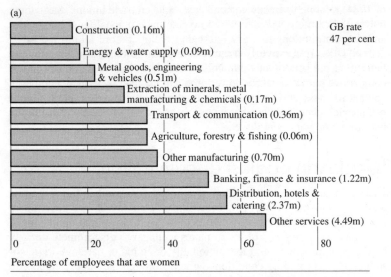

Industries are coded according to the Standard Industrial Classification
( ) The figures shown in brackets are the number of women employees in each industry.

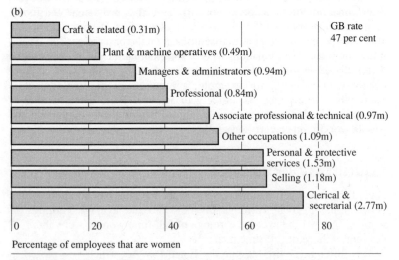

Industries are coded according to the Standard Occupational Classification
( ) The figures shown in brackets are the number of women employees in each occupation.

Source: *Employment Gazette*, February 1993

Fig. 36.1 (a) *Percentage of employees that are women by industry (Great
                 Britain, summer 1992, not seasonally adjusted)*
             (b) *Percentage of employees that are women by occupation (Great
                 Britain, summer 1992, not seasonally adjusted)*

1992 23 per cent of all women employees were employed in the distribution, hotels and catering industry. Women also form 75 per cent of all clerical and secretarial workers.

Women's average hourly wage rates are also lower than men's because there is a disproportionate number of women in jobs at the lower end of the pay scale. For example, of the 144 000 managers in large companies in 1993 only 8 per cent were women and whilst women make up 46 per cent of all university students only 3 per cent become professors or principal lecturers.

Women's promotion chances are affected by their level of education, by the fact that some leave the labour force for several years and hence accumulate less experience and miss out on training, and because prejudice still exists. Women workers, too, are less well organised in unions and tend to predominate in areas where trade union organisation has proved difficult (e.g. shops, hairdressing, small offices, etc.).

Women's average earnings are even further below men's than their hourly wage rates are. This is because women are less likely to be able to earn overtime and shift payments and, more significantly, because a much larger proportion of women work part time than men.

National minimum wage

A national minimum wage may be introduced to help raise the living standards of poorly paid workers, a high proportion of whom are likely to be female. Although most European countries have a national minimum wage, the current UK government is resistant to the idea. The government believes that a national minimum wage would result in higher un-employment and reduce, rather than improve the efficiency of the labour market.

A national minimum wage would be likely to be set above the current level of pay given to low-paid workers. The government believes that whilst this will cause the supply of labour to expand, demand for labour will contract and unemployment will increase. This is shown in Fig. 36.2, where employment falls from Q to QD.

Fewer workers may be employed because the cost of labour has risen. The workers who may be made redundant are likely to be from the most vulnerable groups including older workers, the disabled and the less skilled workers.

A national minimum wage may raise wages further by stimulating those who had previously earned near the minimum wage to press for a wage rise to retain their wage differentials. So the government opposes the introduction of a national minimum wage on the grounds that it will make UK firms less price competitive and will raise unemployment. However, supporters of a minimum wage claim that these two events will not necessarily occur. In labour markets where there is a monopsonist employer, a minimum wage may increase employment (see Ch. 35).

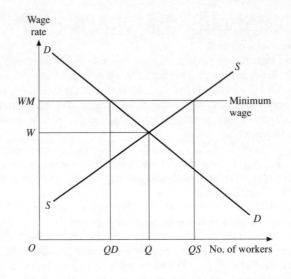

Fig. 36.2

Even in markets where monopoly does not exist a minimum wage, they claim, may increase employment and output. The basis of their argument is that a minimum wage will raise incomes thereby increasing demand. They also argue that a minimum wage may increase workers' morale and stimulate labour productivity. They point to the widespread existence of national minimum wage legislation in other countries as evidence that it does not threaten international competitiveness.

Labour market reforms

The present government is trying to increase the efficiency of the labour market by removing regulations and lowering the overhead costs of employing workers. The government has lowered employers' national insurance contributions, has made it easier to dismiss workers, abolished wage councils and is resisting pressure from the EU to introduce limits on working hours, work councils and paternity leave, etc. For this reason the UK government has not signed the Social Chapter of the Maastricht Treaty.

37 Distribution of wealth and income

The wages and other forms of income a person can earn, for example, dividends, influence the wealth they can accumulate and in turn the amount of wealth a person has can influence their earning capability.

The distribution of wealth

Comprehensive details of the distribution of income and wealth in the UK became available for the first time in 1975 when a Royal Commission, set up to examine the subject, presented its report. It showed that the distribution of wealth was very unequal, but that the degree of inequality has been declining.

Personal wealth is held in many forms, the most important of which is the ownership of dwellings. Other important forms of personal wealth are land, stocks and shares, consumer durable goods, deposits in banks and building societies, and other financial assets. It is now common practice to distinguish two kinds of personal wealth.

Marketable wealth consists of those assets which can be bought and sold, or which have an exchange value. It is composed of the types of item listed above. *Non-marketable wealth* consists primarily of pension rights. People contributing to pension schemes – both occupational schemes and the state retirement scheme – are building up rights to an income in the future. The Royal Commission considered it legitimate to include these pension rights as part of personal wealth (although, of course, they are not marketable).

Table 37.1 shows the distribution of marketable wealth amongst the top half of the population. The distribution has not changed much since

Table 37.1 UK Distribution of wealth

Marketable wealth	1976	1981	1986	1991
Percentage of wealth owned by				
most wealthy 1%	21	18	18	18
most wealthy 5%	38	36	36	37
most wealthy 10%	50	50	50	50
most wealthy 25%	71	73	73	71
most wealthy 50%	92	92	90	92

Source: CSO Social Trends, 1994

1976 although the share of the richest 1 per cent declined slightly between 1976 and 1981 and then stabilised. When pension rights are included
as part of personal wealth the inequality in the distribution is reduced.

Wealth is distributed unequally for many reasons. Two obvious reasons
are the inequality in the distribution of income which affects people's
ability to save, and the fact that people have different propensities to
save. Age, too, is a factor. Older people generally hold more wealth than
younger people because they have had more years to accumulate wealth.
One factor emerging from the report of the Royal Commission is that
about one half of all corporate dividends, and one half of interest payments to individuals, go to pensioners. The fact that wealth can be
inherited and earns income also helps to explain why, over a period of
years, vast fortunes can be built up. Another source of wealth is private
enterprise. A man who starts a business and builds it up into a successful
enterprise not only increases his income, he also creates a marketable
asset (the firm itself), the value of which will be greater than his financial
investment in the business.

The distribution of income

If the distribution of income is to be used as a means of assessing economic
welfare, it is necessary to use a much wider definition of income than the
one used by the Inland Revenue, which is concerned mainly with income
earned from employment and from the ownership of wealth, i.e. income
in the form of wages, salaries, interest, rent and profits.

The distribution of income between factors of production looks at how
total (national) income is distributed between labour (wages), owners of
property (rent and interest) and entrepreneurs (profits). However, the
concept of *disposable income* is more relevant to economic welfare, and
this consists of the incomes derived from factor services mentioned
above, together with various forms of cash benefit (e.g. social security

Table 37.2 Distribution of disposable household income

| | *Percentage share of total disposable after housing costs* | |
	1979	*1990–1991*
Group of households		
Bottom fifth	10	6
Next fifth	14	12
Middle fifth	18	17
Next fifth	23	23
Top fifth	35	45

Source: CSO Social Trends 1994

payments) *minus* direct taxes (income taxes and national insurance contributions). Table 37.2 shows that the distribution of income has become more unequal since 1979.

This information can also be shown on a Lorenz curve. The 45° line shows the line of complete equality. The degree of inequality can be assessed by the extent to which the curve showing the distribution of income deviates from the 45° line.

The income of a household depends to a large extent on the number of economically active people it contains. Households in the bottom fifth of the distribution contain very few economically active persons, while those in the highest group contain an average of more than two. The aged, the sick and the disabled tend to be concentrated in the lowest income group. This group also contains a large number of one-parent families, families where the head of the household is unemployed, and families with children where the wage-earner is in a low-paid occupation.

Investment income and income from self-employment are important elements in the income of households in the top fifth of this distribution. The very unequal distribution of wealth is a major cause of the inequality in the distribution of income, since a fairly large percentage of the income of the highest income groups derives from the ownership of land, property, stocks and shares and other financial assets.

How much inequality?

Although economic analysis might *explain* the causes of economic inequalities, it does not *justify* them. Inequalities of income and wealth are still very great in absolute terms and there is no doubt that they generate widespread dissatisfaction. The economist must take note of these resentments because they have important effects on economic performance. The usual indicators of economic success such as the rate of economic growth, the stability of the price level, a balance of payments surplus, and even the level of employment, will not make much impact on, or excite a lot of interest from, the average citizen if he is convinced that the distributions of income and wealth are grossly inequitable. Such convictions can lead to serious social and economic stresses.

Gross inequalities in the distributions of income and wealth lead to feelings of 'unfairness' because, quite apart from creating inequalities in living standards, they lead to inequalities of opportunity. The wealthy can buy superior education and training for their children and there is no doubt that the possession of wealth confers certain social advantages. Inherited wealth provides an income to the recipient regardless of his abilities, aptitudes, or efforts.

In deciding what is an equitable distribution of income, the economist can offer no conclusive answers because it is a matter of personal judgement (i.e. a value judgement). On the assumption that the purpose

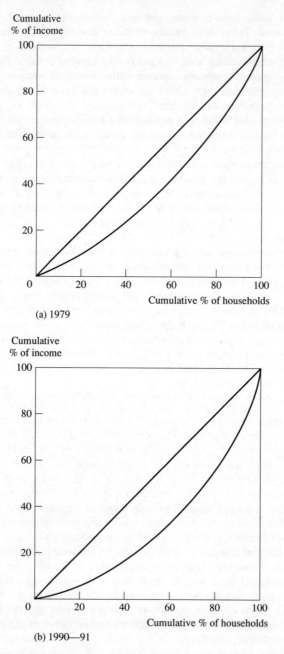

(a) 1979

(b) 1990—91

Fig. 37.1   The Lorenz curve

of economic activity is to maximise the satisfaction of wants, it might the argued that an equal distribution of income would be the ideal. This conclusion is based on the notion that the Law of Diminishing Marginal Utility applies to income and that everyone derives the same utility from a given amount of income. Let us assume that satisfaction can be measured in some units called, say, 'utils'. If, for each person, the satisfaction derived from the first £5 of income is 8 utils and this diminishes by 1 util for each additional £5 of income, then the total utility or satisfaction to be derived from £30 distributed among 3 people is maximised when each receives £10.

But incomes are also incentives to production. In order to get people to work harder, accept greater responsibility, develop new ideas, undertake long and difficult training or to carry out unpleasant tasks, it is usually necessary to offer higher rewards. If these incentives are not forthcoming, the amount of real income available for distribution will probably be reduced. The problem is to weigh these considerations against each other. Equal distribution may give the highest level of satisfaction from any given income, but probably would cause total income to be less than it would be under an incentive system.

Purely economic arguments about the desirability of different patterns of income distribution will be inconclusive. In any case, the economist's criterion of desirability (i.e. the satisfaction of wants) is only one of several possible ways of judging what is 'best'. There are many people who think that rewards should be strictly related to effort, or risk, or responsibility. Others believe that people's needs (e.g. family responsibilities) should be the deciding factor.

There is fairly general agreement that the distributions of income and wealth brought about by market forces are inequitable, and most governments have policies for reducing these inequalities. The main instruments for doing this are a system of direct taxation which is progressive, and a distribution of cash benefits and benefits in kind to raise the incomes of those most in need.

Redistributive effects of taxes and benefits

The Central Statistical Office carry out an annual study of the redistribution of income brought about by the effects of taxes and benefits. This analysis has three stages.

The starting point for the analysis is *original income*. This is the income in cash and kind of all members of the household before the deduction of taxes or the addition of any state benefits. This first stage looks at the redistributive effects of cash benefits. There is a large number of such benefits including retirement pensions, child benefit, job seekers' allowance, income support, widows' benefit, sickness benefit and so on. When cash benefits are added to original income we obtain the household's *gross income*.

Stage two deals with the effects of direct taxes on the distribution of household income. As far as households are concerned the relevant direct taxes are income tax and the employee's and self-employed national insurance contributions. The deduction of direct taxes from gross income gives us *disposable income*.

The third stage estimates the effects of indirect taxes and benefits in kind. A wide range of indirect taxes have effects on household income. These taxes include VAT, excise duties, motor vehicle duties, council tax, local authority rates and employers' contributions to the national insurance scheme. Taxes such as these are levied directly on consumers or are assumed to be fully passed on to consumers. The more important benefits in kind are the health and education services; school meals and housing subsidies are other examples of benefits in kind. When disposable income is adjusted to take account of indirect taxes and benefits in kind we are left with households' *final income*. To summarise:

Original income *plus* benefits in cash = Gross income
Gross income *minus* direct taxes   = Disposable income
Disposable income *minus* indirect
taxes *plus* benefits in kind   = Final income

The most important measure in the policy for redistributing income appears to be the payment of cash benefits, since these go largely to people who are not earning.

Direct taxes further increase *the share* of income going to the lower income groups but the net effect on distribution is much less than that due to cash benefits.

The effects of indirect taxation are less clear. These taxes take a higher percentage of the disposable income of the middle-income households than households at the extremes of the range. This is due to the fact low-income households spend a large proportion of their income on food, and rent (which are exempt from indirect taxes) while high-income households tend to allocate more of their income to savings, mortgage interest and insurance premiums which attract little indirect tax. The regressive effects of indirect taxes are offset to some extent by the progressive nature of the subsidies on housing.

The higher paid tend to receive more benefit in kind mainly because of free education. Households at the bottom of the income range have a smaller number of children than those at the top. Better off parents tend to be older and have older children. They have fewer children under school age and more in the secondary school than less well off parents with the same number of children. They also obtain proportionately more benefits from the more costly further and higher education schemes.

The highest health benefits go to households with retired people and young children.

The poverty and unemployment traps

The poverty trap arises when people become worse off when they seek to improve their living standards by working more hours or gaining higher paid employment. Their disposable income falls because they pay more tax and lose benefits. In effect they pay a marginal tax rate of over 100 per cent.

The unemployment trap affects a relatively small group of people, often with large families, who find that the amount they receive in benefits when unemployed exceeds what they could earn in employment.

The possibility of people experiencing either the poverty or unemployment trap were reduced in the UK in the 1988 budget. Now benefits are related to net income after tax and taking the previous benefits paid into account.

38 Measures of living standards

National income

Most traditional measures of living standards have concentrated on measures of material living standards i.e., the quantity of goods and services which people can enjoy. The most well-known indicator is national income. This is a measure of output. The output of goods and services is a continuous process so that in trying to measure what is produced we are in fact dealing with a *flow* and not a stock. We have to measure a flow of output over time and the time period used for this purpose is invariably one year. Note that the total national product includes *services* as well as goods, because production is defined as any economic activity which satisfies a want and for which people are prepared to pay a price.

The problems of measurement

Money values

The first problem which arises is that of valuation. Total output consists of a vast range of different goods and services whose quantities cannot be added together in physical units. We cannot add kilograms of wheat, to metres of cloth, to tonnes of coal in physical terms. The only possible common unit of measurement is money. If all commodities have money prices, the products of the quantities and prices will give us total money values. Although the use of money as a measuring rod is the only feasible way of measuring total output, it does give rise to difficulties. For example, we must assume that *relative* prices are a reasonable reflection of the relative amounts of satisfaction provided by the different commodities. If commodity A is priced at £5 while the price of commodity B is £2.50, it means that one unit of A counts for twice as much output (i.e. renders twice as much satisfaction) as one unit of B. Another problem arises when the value of money itself changes, so to compare the value of output in one year with that of another year the effects of inflation have to be taken out.

Public services

Difficulties are also encountered when goods and services do not have market prices. This is true of many public services such as defence, law and order, education and health services. They are certainly part of the national output since they satisfy wants and use up scarce resources. The solution adopted is to measure their values 'at cost'. The salaries of teachers and policemen are taken as a measure of the values of their outputs. The total money cost of providing public services is assumed to be a fair representation of the value of output.

Self-provided commodities

Similar problems are encountered with the goods and services which people provide for themselves. For example, farmers consume some of their own output, a great deal of repair and improvement work is carried out on a 'do it yourself' basis, and many people make their own clothes. In such cases there is no market measurement of the value of the output. Where similar goods and services are sold in the market it is possible to give self-provided goods and services an imputed valuation – an estimate of their values can be included in the national income figures. This method is used, for example, in the case of owner-occupied dwellings. The market rents of similar properties are used as guidelines for the imputed rents of premises occupied by their owners. Where there is no reliable market indicator, the assumed value must be an arbitrary estimate or it may be decided to omit the commodity from the calculations of the national output. This latter solution is adopted in the case of housewives' and househusbands' services. Rough estimates put the value of these services at about one-fifth of national income.

Double counting

Adding up the total outputs of all the enterprises in the economy will give us an aggregate many times greater than the true value of the national product. The problem here is one of 'double counting'. It arises because the outputs of some firms are the inputs of other firms. Suppose the annual output of the flour mills sells for £15 m. and the value of the output of the bakeries is £25 m. Added together they give a total output of £40 m., but the value of the flour has been counted twice. If we added together the value of the wheat output from the farms, the flour output from the mills, and the bread from the bakeries, we would be counting the value of the wheat three times!

There are two possible ways of dealing with this problem. National output can be measured by adding the values of the *final products*, or by totalling the *values added* at each stage of production. In the example used earlier the bakeries added £10 m. to the value of the flour they purchased from the mills – this is the true measure of their outputs. The total of the values added at each stage will be exactly the same as the total value of the final products. Table 38.1 should make this clear. We assume the whole process of producing bread begins with the farmer and

Table 38.1 The values added at each stage of the production of bread (£ m)

	Value of output	Cost of intermediate goods	Value added
Farmers	10	0	10
Millers	15	10	5
Bakers	25	15	10
Retailers	30	25	5
	—		—
			30

ends with the retailer. (In fact the seed will be part of a previous year's output.)

Intermediate goods and materials are the material inputs at the various stages of production – the goods each firm purchases from other producers. It can be seen that the value of the final product (which includes additions to stocks) is exactly the same as the total of the values added by the various production processes.

Factor cost

The value of the national output is measured at factor cost, that is, in terms of the payments made to the factors of production for services rendered in producing that output. Using market prices as measures of the value of output can be misleading when market prices do not accurately reflect the costs of production (including profits). Nowadays, most market prices contain some element of taxation and a few of them include an element of subsidy. Thus about two-thirds of the market value of tobacco purchased in the UK will consist of tax payments and only one-third represents payments to the makers and sellers of this tobacco. In order to arrive at the factor cost value, taxes on expenditure must be deducted and subsidies must be added to the market price valuations. It would be very misleading to use the figures for national income at market prices since it would mean that the value of national output could be increased by an increase in the rates of taxation.

Gross national product and national income

In the UK, the main official measurement of total output is described as the *Gross National Product (GNP)*. In 1993 its value was £546 933 m at current prices.

The word 'National' requires some explanation because GNP is *not* the value of the total output produced within the UK. The total product of all the resources located within the UK is known as the *Gross Domestic Product (GDP)*. The difference between GNP and GDP is largely a matter of ownership. Some of the UK output is produced by resources owned by foreigners and this leads to a flow of income (interest and profits) out of the country. On the other hand, British-owned assets abroad lead to a corresponding flow of income from overseas into the UK. The net difference between these flows is recorded as *net property income from abroad*. If this item is added to GDP we arrive at the GNP figure. Thus,

Gross Domestic Product + net property income from abroad =
Gross National Product

GNP, therefore, is the total output from resources owned by the residents of a country wherever these resources happen to be located. GDP is the total output from all the resources located in a country wherever their owners happen to live.

The word 'Gross' indicates that no deduction has been made for that part of total output which is needed to maintain the nation's stock of capital assets. The value of the output required to replace obsolete and worn-out capital is known as *depreciation*, or *capital consumption*. The total output of capital goods is described as Gross Investment and the net additions to the stock of capital is known as Net Investment. We have, therefore,

Gross Investment – Depreciation   = Net Investment

Gross National Product – Depreciation = Net National Product

Net National Product consists of all the goods and services becoming available for consumption together with the net additions to the nation's stock of capital. This is the total which is generally known as the *National Income*.

We should note, however, that it is extremely difficult to obtain an accurate estimate of the annual amount of depreciation and economists often use the figures for Gross National Product for purposes of analysis.

Measuring the national income

There are three possible approaches to this problem and they are based on three different views of the national income.

First of all the national income may be viewed as the total output from domestically owned resources during the course of one year (the *Output approach*).

Secondly, national income may be viewed in terms of the incomes earned by the factors of production engaged in producing the national output. Since the total product is valued at factor cost, it must be exactly the same as the total value of the incomes (wages, interest, rent and profits) which have been paid out to the factors of production. National income, then, may be measured by totalling these incomes (the *Income approach*).

Thirdly, national income may be looked at from the point of view of its disposal. The national output must either be bought for use or added to stocks. If we assume that net additions to stocks amount to 'expenditure' by the firm on its own output, we can measure national income by the amount of money spent on purchasing the national output (the *Expenditure approach*).

It should be apparent, therefore, that

National Output ≡ National Income ≡ National Expenditure

These totals are identically equal since they are merely different ways of looking at the same thing. We have defined the terms in such a way that they must be equal. There are, however, a number of possible pitfalls in measuring the national income by these different methods because the totals of income, output, and expenditure presented to us in real world statistics are, very often, not the factor cost valuations.

The output method

The most direct method of measuring the national output or income is to use the output figures of all the firms in the country. We have already noted the problem of double counting so we must either use the 'value added' method, or take the total value of all final products.

Exports are included because they are part of the national output, but imported materials and services must be excluded. If the value added method is used, imports will be automatically excluded since we only record the values added in this country. This will now give us the GDP and to this total must be added the net property income from abroad. This item may be negative but in the UK's case is usually positive.

If the general level of prices has been changing during the course of the year, it is necessary to make an adjustment for the purely monetary changes in the value of stocks. A rise in prices increases the value of existing stocks even when there is no change in their volume. In order to obtain an estimate of the *real* changes in stocks it is necessary to make a deduction equal to the 'inflationary' increase in value. This deduction is described as Stock Appreciation (this would be added when prices had been falling) in the official tables (see Table 38.2).

The income method

The main point to note here is the fact that *all* personal incomes are not included in the national income. We must only take account of those which have been earned for services rendered and in respect of which there is some corresponding value of output. In any advanced society a sizeable proportion of total personal income is made up of *Transfer Payments*. These payments take the form of social security payments such as unemployment pay, old age pensions, child benefits, and the like. All these are transfer payments *not* because they are paid out of taxes, but because they are not payments for services rendered – there is no contribution to current real output by the recipients. The test of whether an income payment is a transfer payment or not is quite simple. We ask, 'Is this a payment for services rendered during the period in which the income was received?' If the answer is 'No', then it is a transfer payment.

The official statistics record incomes in the form in which they are received. Thus we find figures for wages, rent, interest and profits, and a separate category for the incomes of the self-employed. It must be noted that factor incomes are recorded gross (i.e. before taxes are paid), because this is the measure of the factors' contributions to output.

We must also take account of the fact that all the income generated in production does not find its way into personal incomes. Some part of company profits may be added to reserves, and the profits of nationalised undertakings go to the government and not to persons. These *undistributed surpluses* must be added on to the totals of factor incomes received by persons.

We have already noted that some of the income derived from economic activity within the country will be paid to foreign owners of assets located here, while income from British-owned assets abroad will be moving in the opposite direction. The income account, therefore, must be adjusted by including the item 'net income from abroad'. Finally the stock appreciation adjustment must be made in order to eliminate the element of windfall gain in the profits received (see Table 38.2).

The expenditure method

In estimating the value of the national product by the expenditure method we must record only *final expenditures*. All the expenditure on intermediate goods and services must be excluded. It is the usual practice to break down total expenditure into five large categories: Consumption, Government Spending, Investment, Imports, and Exports. This classification is extremely useful for purposes of analysis. There are several adjustments to be made to the total national expenditure in order to arrive at a figure for the national income at factor cost.

The available statistics provide us with national expenditure at *market prices*. These prices differ from the factor cost values by the amount of taxes and subsidies they contain.

Thus,

National income at market prices – Indirect taxes + Subsidies
= National income at factor cost

We must be careful to include only that part of government expenditure which represents payments for goods and services – government spending on transfer payments must be excluded.

The expenditure method also necessitates some adjustments to take account of international transactions. Total *domestic expenditure* includes spending on foreign goods and services (imports) which does not generate factor income at home. On the other hand it does not include expenditures by foreigners on domestically produced goods and services (exports) which do generate income at home. Thus exports must be added and imports subtracted from total domestic spending.

The expenditure which actually takes place on capital goods (i.e. investment) must be supplemented by an estimated value of the additions to stocks, and work in progress. Incomes will have been earned in the production of these incomplete or unsold goods which have not yet reached the market. In order to arrive at the factor cost value of total output we include an imputed expenditure on these items. In other words we assume that the producer himself has 'purchased' the additions to stocks and the unfinished goods. (See Table 38.2.)

Using the information

The measurement of the national income by official sources was first carried out in 1941 and the information is now published annually in the publication *National Income and Expenditure*, more commonly known as the Blue Book.

National income figures are used for a number of purposes. Growth figures are based on changes in GDP and GNP (see Ch. 42). Governments use national income data in formulating and assessing economic policy. They also use national income figures to compare changes in living standards over time and internationally (see below).

Real income and money income

Using a monetary system of measurement gives rise to certain problems. Difficulties arise when we wish to compare the national income of one year with that of another because the value of money itself may change. When the general level of prices is changing, the value of money is changing and the standard of measurement becomes variable.

If the general price level has been changing during the period under consideration, the figures recorded for the different years will have to be adjusted to take account of the price changes. What is needed is a measure of what the national income would have been in the latter year, had prices remained constant. A simple example should make clear the manner in which the national income of one year may be compared *in real terms* with that of another year.

Table 38.2 UK National Income 1992 (£ million)

Output[1]	£	Income	£	Expenditure	£
Agriculture, forestry + fishing	9309	Income from employment	341 009	Consumers' expenditure	382 696
Mining + quarrying including oil extraction	9842	Income from self employment	58 060	General govt final consumption	214 855
Manufacturing	114 698	Gross trading profits of companies	64 574	Gross domestic fixed capital formation	92 892
Electricity, gas + water supply	13 717	Gross trading surplus of public corporations	1813	Value of physical increase in stocks	−1992
Construction	32 002	Gross trading surplus of general government enterprises	89	Total domestic expenditure	605 974
Wholesale + retail trade repairs, hotels + restaurants	72 549	Rent	46 846	Exports of goods and services	139 827
Transport, storage + communication	41 613	Imputed charge for consumption of non-trading capital	4207	Total final expenditure	745 801
Financial intermediation, real estate, renting + business activities	121 704	Total domestic income	516 598	Less imports of goods and services	−149 164
Public admin, national defence + compulsory social security	36 605	Less stock appreciation	−2216	Statistical discrepancy (expenditure adjustment)[3]	−472
Education, health, social work	52 509	Statistical discrepancy (income adjustment)[3]	212	GDP at market prices	596 165
Other services including sewage + refuse disposal	32 892	GDP at factor cost	51 454	Less taxes	−87 679
Total	537 440	Net property income from abroad	5777	Plus subsidies	6108
Less adjustment for financial services[2]	−23 058	GNP	520 371	GDP at factor cost	514 594
Statistical discrepancy (income adjustment)[3]	212	Less capital consumption	−63 984	Net property income from abroad	5777
GDP at factor cost	514 594	National Income	456 387	GNP	520 371
				Less capital consumption	−63 984
Net property income from abroad	5777			National Income	456 387
GNP	520 371				
Less capital consumption	−63 984				
National Income	456 387				

Notes

1 The contribution of each industry to the gross domestic product after providing for stock appreciation.

2 To avoid some double counting of interest paid on loans and interest received by financial institutions.

3 The estimates of GDP are built up largely from independent data on income and expenditure. The statistical discrepancy is the difference between these estimates.

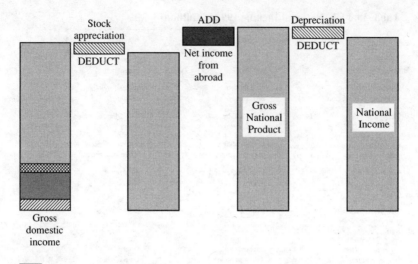

Income from employment

Income from self-employment

Profits of companies and public enterprises

Rent

Fig. 38.1   National income – income method

Table 38.3

Expenditure approach N.B. Use expenditure on final goods and services

C + I + G	*Total Domestic Expenditure at market prices*
C + I + G + X	*Total Final Expenditure at market prices*
C + I + G + (X – M)	*Gross Domestic Product at market prices*
add Net Property Income from Abroad	*Gross National Product at market prices*
subtract Taxes on Expenditure	
add Subsidies	*Gross National Product at factor cost*
subtract Capital Consumption	*National Income*

Differences between measures.

To get from	to		You must
gross	net	*subtract*	Depreciation
domestic	national	*add*	net property income from abroad
market prices	factor cost	*subtract*	Taxes on expenditure
		add	subsidies

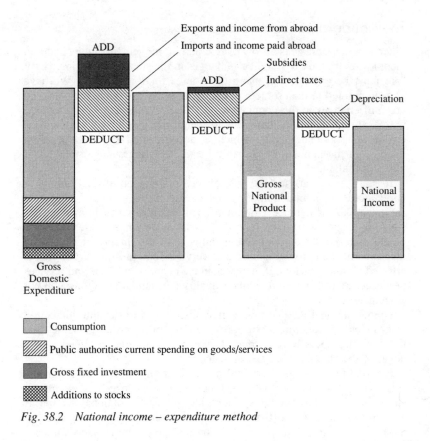

Consumption

Public authorities current spending on goods/services

Gross fixed investment

Additions to stocks

Fig. 38.2   National income – expenditure method

	Year 1	Year 2
National income (£ million)	10 000	12 000
Index of prices	100	105

National income of Year 2 expressed in terms of the prices ruling in Year 1

$$= \frac{12\,000}{1} \times \frac{100}{105}$$

$$= £11\,428.5\text{m.}$$

The example shows that, although the national income in monetary terms had increased by 20 per cent, in real terms the increase was only about 14.3 per cent.

The standard of living

Since income represents a flow of real output, movements in the national income are often used to indicate changes in the standard of living. Great care must be exercised in using the figures for this purpose. We have already pointed to the problem of changing prices. Account must also be taken of changes in the population because it is *income per head* which is relevant when living standards are being discussed. A 5 per cent increase in total real income which is accompanied by an 8 per cent increase in the population probably means that the average standard of living has fallen.

It is also necessary to take note of the composition of total output. A large increase in total output which is due to an increased output of capital goods or defence equipment will not mean any immediate increase in economic welfare. Indeed, national income figures are a measure of the material standard of living rather than the quality of life. They measure the quantity of goods and services but the quality of life is affected by many factors. If increases in the quantity of goods and services produced are offset by falls in their quality the standard of living will not have increased.

Higher national income figures may also give a misleading indication of changes in economic welfare if they have occurred at the same time that working hours have increased, working conditions declined and/or negative externalities have been created.

Externalities, both positive and negative are not accounted for in the calculations of the national income. Pollution, noise, congestion, and mental strain may be the by-products of a rapidly increasing national income. If a nation spends, say, £10 m. on increasing the output of some commodity and then has to spend £1 m. on mitigating the nuisances associated with this output, it would be rather misleading to say that 'output' had increased by £11 m.

Output may increase but if the distribution of income is very uneven only a few may experience a rise in their material living standards. It is also possible that official national income figures may understate the quantity of goods and services which people enjoy. Some goods and services which are produced and sold are not recorded in the official figures. Their sale is not declared because the activity is illegal or in order to avoid paying tax or losing benefits (the black economy). In addition, as we have already noted, a number of non-marketed goods and services, for example, child rearing by parents are not included in National Income figures, although they affect the quality of life.

International comparisons

Statistics of national income per head are the most frequently used bases for comparing living standards in different countries. There are many reasons why such comparisons must be used with caution. The levels of accuracy in measurement may differ very widely. In countries where subsistence agriculture is the main activity there is a large element of guesswork in the final compilation. There are great discrepancies in the patterns of income distribution in different countries. Two countries may have the same income-per-head figures but the standards of living will be very different if in one the income is fairly evenly distributed, while in the other income distribution is very unequal. The composition of total output may be different. For example, one country may devote a much greater proportion of its resources to defence than another country and yet the two countries may have very similar figures for income per head.

Externalities, the size of the black economy, working hours, working conditions and the quality of goods and services are also likely to differ between countries. Some differences arise from climate or geography. Inhabitants of cold countries have to spend a relatively large proportion of their incomes on keeping warm, while people living in sparsely populated countries will have to spend relatively more on communications and transport. It does not follow that living standards are lower where these expenditures are lower.

International comparisons also have to be undertaken in a common unit of measurement. For some time the most widely used unit has been the US dollar. The rate of exchange, however, may not be a good indicator of the relative domestic purchasing powers of the two currencies. For example, if £1 = $2, it does not follow that $2 in the USA will purchase more or less of the same volume of goods and services as £1 in the UK. The official exchange rate only takes account of the commodities entering into international trade and these may represent a very small selection of the commodities traded within each nation. The exchange rate may also be held at an artificially high level by government action. Since 1993 increasing use has been made by international organisations, including the United Nations, of purchasing power parity exchange rates. These seek to measure the cost of a typical basket of goods in different countries, both internationally traded goods and non-internationally traded goods, for example, housing. If the typical basket of goods costs £7000 in the UK and $21 000 in the USA, the ratio is 1:3 and the effective exchange rate to the used to convert the national income figures would be £1 = $3.

Alternative measures of living standards

The use of national income figures for the purpose of comparing standards of living over time and between countries needs to be supplemented by various social indicators such as the number of hospital beds and doctors per head of the population, numbers in further education, and the nature and quality of the different welfare measures. A number of measures have been developed to take at least some of these factors into account.

Measurable economic welfare

In 1972, William Nordhaus and James Tobin developed measurable economic welfare (MEW). This adjusts GDP and other measures of national income by adding leisure, unpaid housework, non-marketed goods, the value of services given by consumer durables over the year. Deductions are made for 'regrettables' such as expenditure on commuting to work, defence, the police, negative externalities including pollution and expenditure on consumer durables. This is an interesting approach which seeks to cover more of the aspects which affect economic welfare although it does encounter the difficulty of having to attach a monetary value to non-marketed goods.

Human development index

This also seeks to give a wider measure of economic welfare. It was introduced by the United Nations in 1990. The index is based on three sets of indicators. Real GDP (measured using PPP exchange rates) is one, adult literacy and mean years of schooling is another and life expectancy is the last. The idea is that human development depends on the quantity of resources available to people in a country, their ability to use the goods and services and the time they have to use these goods.

39 Models of national income determination

According to Keynes, the most important determinant of national income is the level of aggregate (total) demand. The higher the level of demand, the higher the level of output and employment. To examine this relationship we will make use of models of the economy.

We begin with an economy in which there is no government and no foreign trade. There are only two sectors, *firms* and *households*. Firms are the producing units which hire services provided by the people from the households. For these services firms pay wages (for labour), rent (for land), interest and dividends (for the services of loan and risk capital). There is, therefore, a flow of factor services from households to firms and a flow of income from firms to households. These flows are represented by the upper pipes in Fig. 39.1.

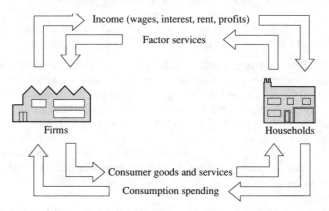

Income (wages, interest, rent, profits)

Factor services

Firms

Households

Consumer goods and services

Consumption spending

Fig. 39.1

In this model, households are also the purchasers of the national output. There is a flow of spending from households to firms and a flow of goods and services from firms to households. These flows are represented by the lower pipes in Fig. 39.1. This economy would remain in equilibrium since firms are selling their goods at prices which are made up of their various costs (including profits) and these costs represent the incomes paid to households. Thus, incomes received by households are always sufficient to buy the total output of firms. We are assuming that the economy has unemployed resources so that any change in planned spending leads to changes in output and employment.

In developing our model we need to understand the nature of a number of variables and we will examine three of these in more detail now. In addition, from here on we shall make some use of the common abbreviations: Y = National Income. C = Consumption. S = Saving. I = Investment. G = Government spending on goods and services. T = Taxation. X = Exports. M = Imports.

Consumption

Consumption is the amount households spend on goods and services to satisfy their current wants. The proportion of their disposable income, i.e., income after direct taxation plus any state benefits, is called the average propensity to consume. $APC = C/Y$. For example, if a person spends £1000 out of a monthly disposable income of £1500 their APC will be £1000/£1500 = 0.66.

As income rises the total amount spent is likely to increase. However, the proportion spent tends to decline. For instance a person with an income of £100 a week may have to spend all of their income to meet basic requirements (i.e., an APC of 1). Whereas a person with a disposable income of £20 000 a week may spend £8000 (APC of 0.4).

Influences on consumption

Income. The main influence on consumption is income. However, there is some controversy over this relationship. Keynesians argue that people's spending is based on their current income. Whereas the monetarist, Milton Friedman argues that consumption is based on their lifetime income so that, for example, a medical student may spend extravagantly now in the expectation of a future high income. Duesenberry's relative income hypothesis suggests that people's spending decisions are influenced by how their current income compares with their previous income and, more significantly, by how much other people are spending (keeping up with the Jones's).

Availability and cost of credit. The easier and cheaper it is to borrow, the more people are likely to spend. When people spend more than they earn they are said to be dissaving.

Distribution of income. A less even distribution may reduce spending. This is because the rich who receive higher incomes will not significantly increase their spending whereas middle- and lower-income groups experiencing reductions in their income will reduce their spending by quite large amounts.

Age structure. Middle-aged people tend to spend a lower proportion of their income than the young.

Inflation. The effects are uncertain. People may be tempted to bring forward their purchases of cars, washing machines and other items if they expect their prices to continue to rise. However, this tendency may be more than offset by a desire to save more to maintain the real value of savings – see p. 332.

Indirect taxes. A rise in indirect taxes will be likely to reduce consumption.

Range of goods and services. The greater the range of goods and services and the higher their quality the more people are likely to spend.

Saving

It is important to distinguish between saving and savings. Saving is income which is not spent. So it is $Y - C$. It is a flow as it represents how much is saved over a given period of time. For example, a person may save £50 a week whereas savings is a stock concept and represents an accumulation of past saving. If the person had savings of £2000 initially they would now have £2050. The proportion of income which is called the average propensity to save. $APS = S/Y$.

As income rises both the total amount saved and the proportion saved tend to increase. So a person with a disposable income of £1000 a month may save £100 ($APS = 0.1$), whereas a person with a disposable income of £4000 a month may save £1000 ($APS = 0.25$).

Influences on savings

Income

The most obvious requirement is the ability to save and this depends upon the level of income. No one can save until the level of income is sufficient to cover what are considered to be the necessities of life. As income rises beyond this level so does the ability to save. As we have seen, as we earn more, we spend more, the *proportion* of income which is devoted to consumption spending tends to fall. What is true of the individual is also true, in this case, of society as a whole. The rate of saving in rich countries is much higher than that in poor countries.

Social attitudes

The prevailing social attitude towards thrift has a significant influence on the level of saving. Where thrift is regarded as a virtue, more will be saved. In Victorian times, hard work and careful saving were regarded as admirable personal characteristics, and they were important contributors to the rapid industrial progress during that period. Other communities place a higher value on leisure and consumption and in such societies the thrifty person might be despised as a mean person. Where this is the case, the level of savings would obviously be relatively low.

The financial framework

In the developed countries, all kinds of institutions for the safe deposit of savings are available. Savings banks, commercial banks, insurance companies, and building societies are all widely known, easily accessible, and have the confidence of the people. By prudent investment of the funds they obtain they are able to offer potential savers both security and income. This range of opportunities not only stimulates savings but ensures that most of the potential saving is made available to borrowers. In less developed countries there are few such institutions, they are not widely known or easily accessible, neither do they have the confidence of the majority of the people, who lack knowledge and experience of institutional forms of saving.

The rate of interest

There is great uncertainty about the influence of the rate of interest on the level of savings. The reasons for this uncertainty should be fairly clear when we have looked at the nature of savings in our type of economy.

Inflation

Inflation tends to reduce the real value of money wealth. So people tend to save more when inflation rises in order to maintain the real value of their savings. In the mid 1970s and early 1980s both inflation and the savings ratio were high whilst between 1984 and 1988, when inflation was relatively low, the savings ratio fell.

Much saving is habitual

Many people firmly believe that saving is a good moral habit, that is, people *ought* to save. Others like to have the feeling of security which comes with the possession of 'something in the bank'. Changes in the rate interest are not likely to affect this type of saving.

A large part of total saving is contractual

This type of saving is carried out through insurance companies, pension funds, and building societies. The individual saver puts himself under a contractual agreement to pay a fixed annual sum (e.g. the insurance premium or superannuation contribution). Variations in the rate of interest will have little or no effect on existing contracts, although they might alter the nature of future contracts.

Many people save in order to achieve some definite objective

Many savers have a definite target such as the deposit for a new house, the purchase price of a motor cycle, or the cost of a holiday abroad. Saving in order to accumulate a fixed and known sum of money is not likely to be influenced greatly by changes in the rate of interest. In fact, an *increase* in the rate of interest might well *reduce* the level of such saving since, at the higher interest rate, the required sum will accumulate at a faster rate.

A large part of total saving is carried out by companies

Companies save in order to build up reserves which will act as a cushion against future business fluctuations and provide funds for future expansion. Company savings are not likely to vary with the rate of interest since the main purpose of such saving is not to achieve income in the form of interest.

A part of total saving is made up of government saving

When government revenue from taxation exceeds government expenditure we have a form of public saving. This will occur when the government feels that the purchasing power of the community is excessive in relation to the available supply of goods and services at current prices. Public saving of this type will not be varied to take account of any changes in the rate of interest.

The motives for, and nature of, saving provide sufficient evidence to support the view that the rate of interest and the rate of saving are not linked in any simple straightforward manner. Very high and very low rates of interest might well have some marked effects on the level of saving, but any 'normal' changes in the rate will probably have very little effect.

Government policies

Governments encourage saving by, for example, giving favourable treatment to saving. For instance, the introduction of TESSA (a tax exempt saving scheme) in 1989 promoted saving in the UK.

Investment

There are a number of influences on investment.

Rate of interest.   As we saw in Chapter 32, one influence is the rate of interest. An increase in the rate of interest will tend to reduce investment and vice versa.

Changes in technology.   Firms may undertake more investment if new machines will lower production costs.

Changes in cost of capital.   If capital becomes cheaper to buy and install more is likely to be purchased.

Expectations.   These can be referred to as 'animal spirits' and can have a significant influence. If entrepreneurs are optimistic about the future they are likely to invest more.

Corporation tax.   Lower corporation tax will increase post-tax returns and stimulate investment.

Government incentives.   An increase in government grants and investment tax allowances will be likely to increase investment.

Profit levels.   Higher profit levels will encourage firms to invest and will provide them with the finance to do so.

Rate of change of income.   This is one of the main influences on investment and its significance is explored below.

The accelerator theory

The accelerator theory states that net investment is related to the rate of change of national income. For instance, if the growth of national income increases, consumption will rise and firms will seek to increase their productive capacity. According to the accelerator theory a change in the rate of growth of demand for consumer goods will cause a greater percentage change in demand for capital goods. For example, if in one year demand for consumer goods from one firm with eight machines rises from £800 to £900 (one machine makes £100 worth of output and there is no depreciation) the firm will order one machine. If then demand rises at a faster rate from £900 to £1200 the firm will now order an extra three machines. So whilst in the second period demand for consumer goods rises by $33\frac{1}{3}$ per cent, demand for capital rises by 300 per cent. The accelerator theory emphasises how volatile investment can be and how it can accentuate changes in national income, both increases and decreases.

A change in the rate of growth of national income will not always cause a greater percentage change in demand for capital goods for a number of reasons. Entrepreneurs may not be convinced that the resulting change in demand will last and so will not adjust their productive capacity. Firms might initially have had spare capacity so they would be able to expand output, if demand is rising, without having to buy more machinery, etc. In contrast, the capital goods industry may not have any spare capacity and so may not be able to supply more capital goods. A change in technology may mean that output can be increased with a smaller percentage rise in investment. The accelerator theory concentrates on private-sector investment. Whereas private-sector investment will tend to increase as income level rises, public-sector investment may fall to offset possible inflationary effects.

Leakages and injections

Having examined consumption, saving and investment in some detail we can now return to our model.

The model as it stands is very unrealistic because even in the simplest economy all the income received by households is not spent – some of it is saved. *Saving represents a leakage* from the circular flow of income because it is part of the income paid out by firms which is not returned to them through the spending of households. When saving takes place, firm's expenses will be greater than their receipts and some of their output will remain unsold. They will react by reducing output so that income and employment will fall. If we assume that households always save some fraction of their income and there are no other expenditures to offset this leakage, income must eventually fall to zero.

Fortunately there is an offsetting expenditure in the form of investment. Our first model of the economy assumed that firms only produced consumer goods and services which were in turn bought by households. In fact, some firms produce capital goods for sale to other firms. This expenditure on capital goods adds to the circular flow of income; it has the opposite effect to a leakage and causes output and income to expand. We can say, therefore, that *investment is an injection.*

Figure 39.2 shows a more realistic model of the economy which incorporates the saving leakage and the investment injection. This diagram concentrates on money flows; for purposes of simplification the real flows (i.e. goods and services) have been omitted.

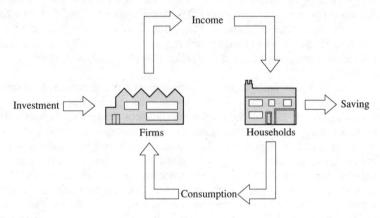

Fig. 39.2

A more realistic model

In order to bring our model of the economy nearer to reality we must take account of the fact that governments play an important part in determining the level of economic activity and that all countries take some part in international trade. It is not difficult to introduce these additional sectors into the circular flow of income analysis.

Foreign trade

Some part of the expenditure of households does not flow back to domestic enterprises because households buy foreign goods as well as home-produced goods. These *imports are a leakage* from the circular flow because they represent income paid out by firms which does not flow back to them. *Exports are an injection* into the circular flow because this spending by foreigners on home-produced output is an additional source of income which is not generated within the domestic system. For purposes of this particular analysis, exports and imports may be treated in the same way as investment and saving. If exports exceed imports there will be an expansionary effect on income while an import surplus will have a depressing effect on income.

Government

Government spending takes several forms, but we are only concerned with that part of it which directly creates income for factors of production. *Public spending on goods and services is an injection* because it adds to real output and creates employment. Transfer payments do not, directly, generate output and income. When they are spent they will increase demand but this will show up as an increase in the propensity to consume. *Taxes are a leakage* because they remove purchasing power from the system. The importance of G and T lies in the fact that they can be deliberately manipulated by the authorities in order to influence the level of output and employment. A budget deficit will have an expansionary effect and a budget surplus a depressing effect on income.

Figure 39.3 provides a highly simplified picture of the circular flow now that we have taken account of the government and international sectors. According to Fig. 39.3 all the leakages originate in the household sector. In the real world, of course, this is not the case, because the same leakages take place at different points in the circular flow. Firms pay taxes on their income, they save (i.e. they retain profits), and they buy foreign materials and machines. Taxes are levied on expenditures as well as incomes so that the tax leakage also applies to the streams of consumption and investment spending. Figure 39.3 would become very complicated if we tried to show the locations of the injections and leakages more accurately – the important point is to identify the nature of these leakages and injections and to understand just how they affect the flow of income.

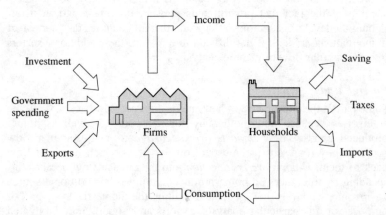

Fig. 39.3

The equilibrium level of income

Expenditure = output

The national output or national income will be in equilibrium when total planned expenditure is just equal to the output that is actually produced. Total expenditure consists of several elements:

- consumer spending on goods and services (C),
- investment spending by firms (I),
- government spending on goods and services (G), and
- exports (X), i.e. spending by overseas residents on the national output.

However, some part of the spending on C, I and G is not used to purchase the national output: the money is spent on goods and services produced by overseas countries. To find out how much is spent on the national output, therefore, we must deduct the value of imports (M) from spending in the home market. This will give us the total planned spending in the home market, plus exports, minus imports. Thus

Total planned expenditure on the national output
$$= C + I + G + X - M$$

The value of the national output is equal to the national income (Y), so the economy will be in equilibrium when

$$Y = C + I + G + X - M$$

Figure 39.4 shows what is known as the 45° diagram. National income is measured on the horizontal axis and total planned expenditure, at different levels of national income, is measured on the vertical axis. National income is inequilibrium at OY level of national income (NY). If all the output produced is sold there is no reason for producers to change their output.

Leakages = injections

Figure 39.3 can be used to derive another formula for the equilibrium condition. It is apparent from the diagram that the circular flow of income will only be stable when the total planned leakages are equal to the total planned injections. In an economy with a government sector and a foreign trade sector, it is not a necessary condition for equilibrium that S, should be equal to I, or that G be equal to T, or X be equal to M. The national output will be in equilibrium when

Total planned injections = Total planned leakages
$$I + G + X = S + T + M$$

Thus an excess of saving over investment may be offset by a budget deficit or an export surplus.

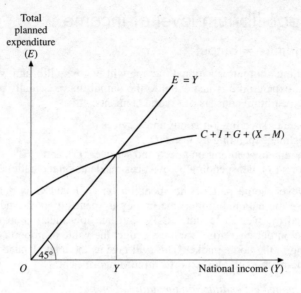

Fig. 39.4

It must be pointed out, however, that an equilibrium level of income is not, in itself, a desirable state of affairs: an economy can settle into an equilibrium position when there is large-scale unemployment, as, in fact, many economies did during the Great Depression of the 1930s.

40 Aggregate demand and supply

In the previous chapter we discussed total planned expenditure which can also be referred to as aggregate expenditure. This is the amount which will be spent at different levels of income. In this chapter we start by examining aggregate demand. This is the amount which will be spent at different values of the general price level.

The aggregate demand curve (AD)

This shows the quantity of goods and services which households, firms, overseas buyers and government are prepared to buy at different values of the general price level. It is drawn on the assumption that other things (e.g. the money supply, rates of taxation, the marginal propensity to consume) remain unchanged.

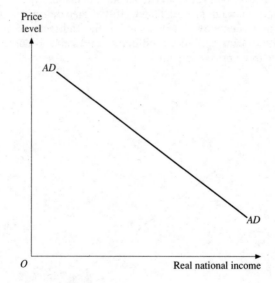

Fig. 40.1   Aggregate demand curve

There are three main reasons why there is an inverse relationships between the general price level and aggregate demand and hence why the AD curve slopes down from left to right.

- A rise in prices reduces the real value of people's income and wealth and hence decreases their ability to consume.
- Higher prices increase people's and firms' demand to hold money for transaction purposes. This increase in the transactions demand for money is likely to raise the rate of interest and thereby reduce demand for consumer goods (consumption) and demand for capital goods (investment).
- An increase in the general price level will make domestic goods and services less competitive against foreign goods and services. This will reduce demand for domestic products from both domestic and foreign consumers.

Movements along the aggregate demand curve

As with a demand curve for a particular product, the cause of a movement along an aggregate demand curve will be a change in price, in this case a change in the general price level. A rise in the general price level will cause a contraction in aggregate demand and a fall in the general price level will cause an extension in demand. Figure 40.2 shows an extension in aggregate demand. If the general price level falls people's purchasing power will increase, the transactions demand for money will fall causing a reduction in interest rates and domestic goods will become more price competitive.

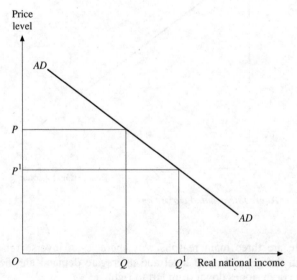

Fig. 40.2   Extension in aggregate demand

The shape of the aggregate demand curve

One group of economists, Keynesians, believe the aggregate demand curve is steep. This is because they think that a rise in the price level will have only a small impact on the rate of interest and this in turn will have only a small impact on consumption and investment. They argue that the demand for money is dominated by the speculative motive. This is interest elastic so that an increase in demand for money will cause only a small rise in the rate of interest. In their view the main influence on both consumption and investment is income and not the rate of interest. The implication of the aggregate demand curve being steep is that a change in the price level will not significantly alter aggregate demand.

Monetarists, a group of economists who believe that changes in the money supply are the main determinant of aggregate demand, take a different view. They believe the aggregate demand curve is shallow. They think the main component of the demand for money is the transactions demand and that this is interest inelastic so if a rise in the general price level leads to an increase in demand for money there may be a large rise in the rate of interest. Again, contrary to the Keynésian view, monetarists believe a change in the rate of interest can have a significant impact on consumption and investment. In their view, changes in the price level can have a large effect on aggregate demand.

Shifts in the aggregate demand curve

The aggregate demand curve will shift to the right (an increase in aggregate demand) or shift to the left (a decrease in aggregate demand) if there is a change in an influence on aggregate demand other than a change in the price level.

An increase in aggregate demand will cause more to be demanded at any given price level. An increase in aggregate demand is illustrated in Fig. 40.3.

Causes of shifts in aggregate demand

The aggregate demand curve will shift if households, firms, the government and/or foreigners alter the amount they wish to spend at any given price level. There are a number of factors which can cause a change in desired expenditure on consumption, investment, government spending and/or net exports. An increase in aggregate demand, for example, may be caused by any of the following:

- An increase in the money supply will increase demand directly as people and firms will have more money to spend and indirectly by lowering the rate of interest.
- A rise in optimism will increase both consumption and investment.

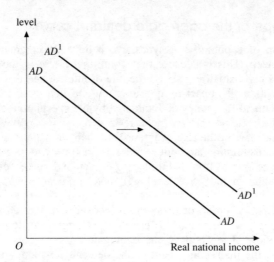

Fig. 40.3   Increase in aggregate demand

- A fall in the exchange rate will be likely to increase demand for net exports.
- Government policy resulting in a reduction in taxes and/or an increase in government expenditure will raise aggregate demand.
- An increase in the expected rate of inflation will be likely to increase consumption as people bring forward their spending plans.
- If incomes rise abroad, demand for exports will likely to increase.
- Following a rise in population, the greater the number of people the higher the level of demand is likely to be for a wide range of goods and services.
- A fall in the rate of interest will probably stimulate demand for consumer durables and capital goods.
- As the population becomes wealthier, following a rise in aggregate wealth, consumption usually rises.

The aggregate supply curve

Aggregate supply is the total amount all firms wish to supply at each given price level.

Economists distinguish between the short-run and the long-run supply curves. We will look at the short-run supply curve first.

The short-run supply curve

The short-run supply curve slopes up from left to right as illustrated in Fig. 40.4. In the short run it is assumed that the prices of all factors of

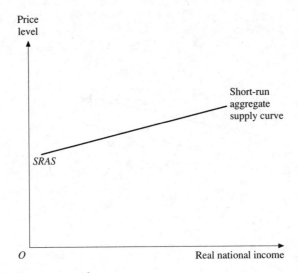

Fig. 40.4   Short-run supply curve

production are fixed. Nevertheless, an increase in output is likely to be associated with higher unit costs. This is because overtime may have to be paid, less efficient machines may be used and less efficient methods of production may have to be employed. As higher output is associated with higher unit costs firms will only supply more goods if they can be sold at higher prices, resulting in an upward sloping supply curve. Whilst unit costs do rise with output they rise by small amounts, making the short-run aggregate supply curve elastic.

Shifts in the short-run aggregate supply curve

The short-run aggregate supply curve will move to the right (an increase) and to the left (a decrease) as a result of a change in an influence other than a change in the price level. Shifts in the short-run aggregate supply curve are often referred to as supply side shocks.

A decrease in the short-run aggregate supply curve will mean that firms will offer less for sale at any given price level. Figure 40.5 illustrates a decrease in the short-run aggregate supply curve.

Among the factors which can cause a decrease in aggregate supply are:

- A rise in wage rates will increase firms' costs of production at any level of output, causing firms to reduce aggregate supply.
- A rise in raw material costs will again raise firms' costs of production.
- A rise in corporation tax will not only raise firms' costs of production but also may discourage entrepreneurs and reduce their willingness to produce.

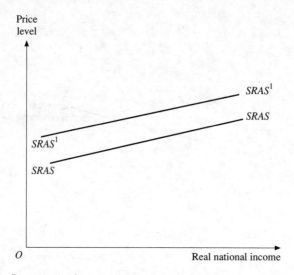

Fig. 40.5   Decrease in short-run aggregate supply curve

- Unfavourable weather will affect agricultural output and construction work.
- Natural disasters, for instance, a widespread fire, may damage a number of firms' productive capacity.
- A decrease in factors of production resulting in a decrease in productivity will raise costs of production and lower supply.

The long-run aggregate supply curve

The classical view is that the long-run aggregate supply curve is vertical as shown in Fig. 40.6. This is because it is defined as the aggregate quantity of goods and services supplied when the economy is operating at full employment (natural rate of unemployment). It indicates the maximum potential output possible with given resources and given technology.

The Keynesian view is that even in the long run there can be unemployment so that they think the long-run aggregate supply curve will have a different shape. Figure 40.7. illustrates this version. At low levels of output the long-run aggregate supply curve is horizontal. This is because with a resulting high level of unemployment output can be increased without a rise in costs. Then at higher levels of output it slopes upwards as firms begin to experience rises in costs of production as resources become scarcer. At the full employment level the curve becomes vertical. Again this represents the maximum potential output.

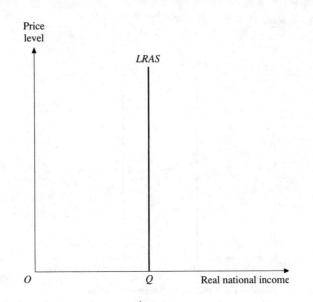

Fig. 40.6   Long-run aggregate supply curve

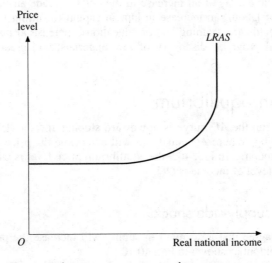

Fig. 40.7   Keynesian long-run aggregate supply curve

Shifts in the long-run aggregate supply curve

Over time, an economy's maximum potential output can change as a result of a change in the quantity and/or quality of factors of production. An increase in the curve is shown in Fig. 40.8.

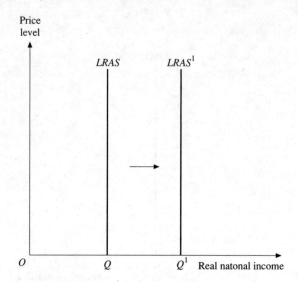

Fig. 40.8   Increase in long-run aggregate supply curve

The specific causes of an increase in the curve include an increase in the supply of labour, an increase in human capital (resulting from, e.g., improved healthcare, training and/or education), increase in investment, technological progress, discovery of raw materials, and greater incentives to work.

Short-run equilibrium

In the short run the *AD* curve is downward sloping and the *AS* curve is upward sloping. Where *AD* equals *AS* will determine the price level and the level of income. In Fig. 40.9 the equilibrium price level is *OP* and the equilibrium level of income is *OQ*.

Effects of supply-side shocks

Economists agree that a decrease in supply will increase the price level and reduce output as shown in Fig. 40.10.

Long-run equilibrium

New classical economists, who include monetarists and supply-siders, consider that free market forces result in an optimal allocation of resources. They believe that in the long run labour markets will be in equilibrium and the economy will operate where aggregate demand

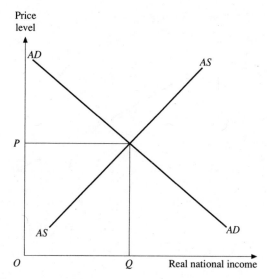

Fig. 40.9   Short-run equilibrium

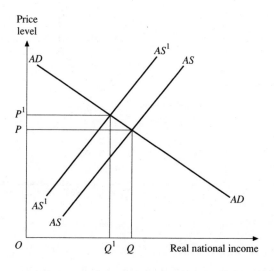

Fig. 40.10

equals aggregate supply at the full employment (natural rate of
unemployment) level. This is shown in Fig. 40.11(a). Keynesians argue
that the long-run equilibrium level of real *Y* can occur at any level of
employment. Figure 40.11(b) shows the economy operating at less than
full employment.

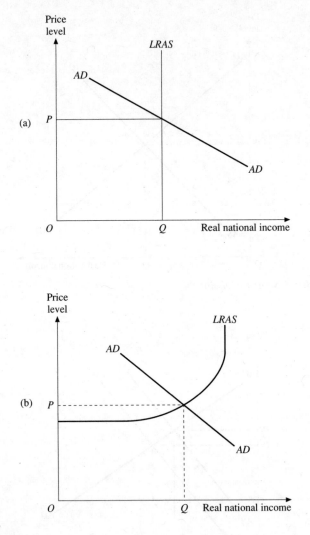

Fig. 40.11

The different views on the long-run equilibrium lead economists to different conclusions about the effects of an increase in aggregate demand. Supply-side supporters believe an increase in aggregate demand, without any increase in the long-run aggregate supply will result solely in a rise in prices. This is shown in Fig. 40.12(a).

Keynesians agree that an increase in aggregate demand will be purely inflationary if it occurs at the full-employment level. However, they argue that if it occurs at less than full employment, both output and

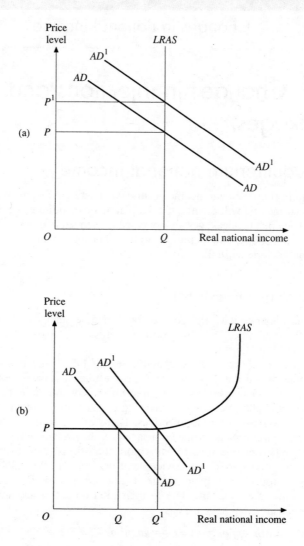

Fig. 40.12

prices may rise or there may be a rise solely in output. Figure 40.12(b) shows an increase in aggregate demand raising output but having no effect on prices.

41 Changes in injections and leakages

Disequilibrium national income

Disequilibrium national income occurs when national income is changing. National income will change if total planned expenditure is not equal to output and planned leakages are not equal to planned injections. If leakages exceed injections, and output is higher than total planned expenditure, national income will fall.

Savings and investment

We can illustrate why and how national income changes when leakages do not equal injections by examining a simple two-sector economy (households and firms).

In this model the injection is investment and the leakage is savings. In any time period the amount which people plan to save is not likely to match the amount which firms plan to invest. By and large the decisions to save and the decisions to invest are taken by different groups of people who have different objectives. There will be some limited amount of overlapping because firms both save (i.e. they retain some profits) and invest. When people plan to save more than firms plan to invest, total expenditure on goods and services will be less than the value of firms' current output. Firms' payments for factor services (wages, rent, interest and profits) are equal in value to their total output. These incomes are either consumed or saved. Thus

Income (= value of output) = Consumption + Saving

Firms receive revenue from the consumption spending of households and the spending of other firms on investment goods. Thus

Total expenditure = Consumption + Investment

It should be clear, therefore, that when saving is greater than investment, total planned expenditure will be less than the value of total output. Firms will be receiving less in revenue than they are paying out in incomes to the factors of production. They will cut back production, and income and employment will fall.

When firms plan to spend more on investment goods than people plan to save, the opposite will happen: total planned spending will exceed the value of the national output. Stocks will be run down and firms will increase production, and employment and income will rise.

Only when the amount which people plan to save is equal to planned investment will the economy be in equilibrium and planned expenditure be just sufficient to purchase the planned output of firms. There will be no tendency for income and employment to rise or fall. In summary:

When planned I > planned S, income will rise
When planned I < planned S, income will fall
When planned I = planned S, income will not change

The paradox of thrift

Keynes argued that what people *plan to save* and what in fact they *do save* are quite different things. An increased desire to save does not necessarily result in a higher level of saving. It could, indeed, cause the total level of saving to fall! The immediate effect of an increased desire to save is a fall in consumption. A fall in consumption spending reduces the incomes of those who produce and sell consumer goods and this fall in incomes, as explained in the next section, develops into a cumulative process. The fall in the propensity to consume will lead to an eventual fall in total income much greater than the initial fall in consumption spending. It could be so great in fact that although people are *trying to save* more, the ability to save is reduced to such an extent that total savings actually fall. This effect is known as the *paradox of thrift*.

The full model

Using all injections and leakages, national income will rise when

$$I + G + X > S + T + X$$

and hence when

$$Y < C + I + G + (X - M)$$

National income will fall when

$$I + G + X < S + T + X$$

and hence when

$$Y > C + I + G + (X - M).$$

The multiplier

As we have seen, discrepancies between the rate of leakage and the rate of injection cause movements in income but these upward and downward movements will not continue for ever. The expansions or contractions of income will gradually peter out because there are forces at work which tend to bring the economy into equilibrium. Changes in income bring about changes in saving and investment until the plans to save and the plans to invest are made compatible. This adjustment process is explained by the theory of the multiplier.

Let us assume that initially an economy is in equilibrium when $Y = £10\,000m.$, $S = £4000m.$, and $I = £4000m$. Now suppose that investment increases to £5000m. due to an increase in housebuilding. The income received by those engaged in the building industry will rise by £1000m., but this is not the end of the matter. If the saving habits of the community remain unchanged (i.e. they continue to save 0.4 of their income), then £600m. of this additional income will be spent and £400m. will be saved. The recipients of this extra spending will have additional income equal to £600m. They will spend £360m. of this income and save £240m., and so it will go on. The increase in the rate of investment will set up a series of rounds of spending and saving. The total income and total saving will gradually increase, and at each stage the increments are getting smaller and smaller until they become immeasurably small. The series looks like this:

Increase in income = £1000m. + £600m. + £360m. + £216m. + + +
Increase in saving =   £400m. + £240m. + £144m. + + +

Series of this type can be summed by using the very simple formula

$S = \dfrac{a}{1 - r}$ where S = the sum of the series, a = the first term, and r = the

common ratio (i.e. the fraction by which we multiply each term in order to get the next term).

Using this formula we get the following results:

Increase in income = £2500m. Increase in saving = £1000m.

The value of the multiplier must be $2\frac{1}{2}$, because an increase in investment has caused income to rise by an amount equal to $2\frac{1}{2}$ times the increase in investment.

In the two-sector economy, the multiplier is equal to the eventual change in income divided by the initiating change in investment.

Note that the economy is once again in equilibrium.

Income = £12 500m. saving = £5000m., and investment = £5000m.

The increase in investment causes income to rise until the level of saving is once again equal to the level of investment. This arithmetical example of the multiplier is illustrated in diagrammatic form in Fig. 41.1.

The multiplier, however, works both ways. A fall in investment has downward multiplier effects and income falls until saving is equal to the new and lower level of investment. We use the same formula and series

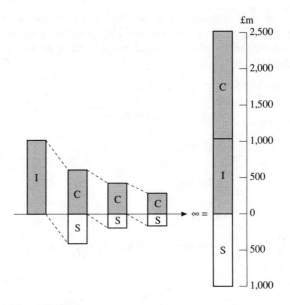

Fig. 41.1   The multiplier

to calculate the effects of a cut in investment spending. The only difference will be the signs in the spending and saving series; they will now be minus signs.

The determinants of the multiplier

The size of the multiplier depends upon the proportion of any increase in income which is spent (i.e. passed on within the circular flow). In the example above, 0.6 of each addition to income was spent and 0.4 was saved. Clearly if 0.8 of any additional income had been spent, the final increase in income would have been much larger. Another way of looking at it is to say that the size of the multiplier depends upon the proportion of any increase in income which leaks out of the system. Thus, the smaller the fraction saved, the larger the multiplier.

The Marginal Propensity to Consume (MPC)

The MPC is that fraction of any small increase in income which is spent on consumer goods and services. If an extra £1 of income leads to an increase of 70p in consumption spending, the MPC is 0.7. Empirical evidence indicates that the MPC declines as income increases. In other words, although consumption rises as income increases, *the rate of increase* of consumption tends to decline. As we become more affluent we spend more on consumer goods and services, but we spend a smaller proportion of our income on these things. It is the MPC which determines the size of the multiplier. This may be demonstrated by returning to the arithmetical example used a little earlier, where we assumed the MPC was 0.6.

Using the formula $S = \dfrac{a}{1-r}$ we have

Increase in income $= \dfrac{\text{Increase in investment}}{1-r}$

$$= \frac{£1000\text{m.}}{1-r}$$

$$= \frac{£1000\text{m.}}{1-0.6}$$

$$= £2500\text{m.}$$

Now, $\dfrac{£1000\text{m.}}{1-0.6}$ may be written as $£1000\text{m.} \left(\dfrac{1}{1-0.6}\right)$ or,

$£1000\text{m.} \left(\dfrac{1}{1-MPC}\right)$.

The expression in the last parentheses is the multiplier since this is the quantity by which we multiply the increase in investment in order to obtain the increase in income. Thus,

The multiplier $= \dfrac{1}{1-MPC}$

The Marginal Propensity to Save (MPS)

The MPS is that fraction of any small increase in income which is saved. In the simple model of the economy which we are now using, income can only be disposed of in two ways – it can be consumed or saved. Thus, if, of every extra £1 of income, 70p is spent and 30p is saved, the MPS will be 0.3. Since consumption rises more slowly than income, the MPS will increase as income increases. In a two-sector economy, $MPC + MPS = 1$, and $1 - MPC = MPS$. We can, therefore, rewrite the formula for the multiplier *in a two-sector economy* as,

The multiplier $= \dfrac{1}{MPS}$

Worked example 1

In a two-sector economy, $MPS = 0.2$, $I = £5000\text{m.}$, and $Y = £25\,000\text{m.}$
a Assuming investment remains constant,
i What is the equilibrium level of saving?
ii What is the value of the multiplier?

b If investment were to increase by £100m. what would be the new equilibrium level of income?

a i   In equilibrium $S = I$, so that if investment remains constant at £5000m., the economy will settle in equilibrium where $S = $£5000m.
   ii If $MPS = 0.2$, then $MPC = 0.8$

$$\text{The multiplier} = \frac{1}{1-MPC} \quad \text{or} \quad \frac{1}{MPS}$$
$$= \frac{1}{1-0.8} \quad \text{or} \quad \frac{1}{0.2}$$
$$= 5$$

b   Increase in income   = The multiplier × increase in investment
                          = 5 × £1000m.
                          = £5000m.
    New level of income = £25 000m. + £5000m. = *£30 000m.*

The multiplier in the more complex economy

The multiplier is still governed by the proportion of any marginal change in income which consumers spend on domestic output. The expression $\frac{1}{1-MPC}$ still gives us the value of the multiplier, but the proportion of additional income which is 'passed on' within the system is now reduced by three leakages, namely, saving, imports and taxation. This means that $1 - MPC$ is no longer equal to MPS. In fact $1 - MPC$ is equal to that proportion of any increase in income which leaks out of the circular flow. As a fraction of additional income this leakage is equal to $MPS + MPM + MPT$, where MPM = the marginal propensity to import, and MPT = marginal rate of taxation. We can now rewrite the formula for the multiplier in an economy with government activity and foreign trade,

$$\text{The multiplier} = \frac{1}{1-MPC} \quad \text{or} \quad \frac{1}{MPS + MPM + MPT}$$

The multiplier takes effect whenever there is a change in the planned rate of spending. Thus a change in I, or G, or X will have multiplier effects on income. There will also be multiplier effects when there is a change in consumption spending which is independent of changes in income. A change in the *propensity to consume*, therefore, will have multiplier effects. We have illustrated the multiplier process by talking about increases in planned spending, but remember that the multiplier also applies when there are decreases in planned spending. Income will fall by a multiple of the fall in planned expenditure.

Worked example 2

Out of every extra £1 of income, a community saves 20p, spends 15p on foreign commodities, and the government takes 15p in taxation. What is the value of the multiplier?

Out of each extra £1 of income, consumption spending on domestic output accounts for £1 – (20p + 15p + 15p) = 50p.
Therefore, $MPC = 0.5$, $MPS = 0.2$, $MPM = 0.15$, and $MPT = 0.15$

$$\text{The multiplier} = \frac{1}{1 - MPC} \quad \text{or} \quad \frac{1}{MPS + MPM + MPT}$$

$$= \frac{1}{1 - 0.5} \quad \text{or} \quad \frac{1}{0.2 + 0.15 + 0.15}$$

$$= 2 \qquad \qquad = 2$$

The workings of the multiplier can be shown graphically. Figure 41.2 shows the effect on national income of a rise in exports.

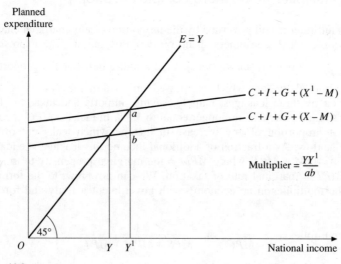

Fig. 41.2

Changes in aggregate demand

The preceding analysis showed how changes in planned spending bring about changes in the national income which are much greater than the initial changes in the rate of spending. The effect of an increase in aggregate demand can also be analysed by using aggregate demand supply curves.

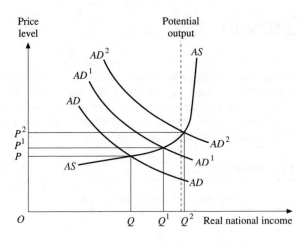

Fig. 41.3

In Fig. 41.3, equilibrium occurs where the *AD* curve intersects the *AS* curve because at this point the output which businesses are prepared to supply is equal to the amount of goods and services which spenders are willing to buy. When aggregate demand is *AD*, equilibrium occurs at the price level *OP* and the output level *OQ*. However, at this point the economy is in equilibrium at well below its potential output, and many of its resources will be unemployed.

An increase in aggregate demand from *AD* to AD^1 leads to a relatively large increase in output (and employment) but a relatively small increase in prices – supply is relatively elastic. A further increase in aggregate demand from AD^1 to AD^2 has a much greater effect on prices because firms now have much less scope for increasing production; many of them will be approaching their maximum potential outputs. Any further increases in aggregate demand end up as price increases rather than output increases.

42 Growth

Insistent demands for higher standards of living have put great pressures on governments to achieve faster rates of economic growth. One of the most publicised aspects of economic activity in recent years has been the 'league table' showing the growth rates achieved by different countries. Table 42.1 is an example of this type of thing.

Table 42.1 Growth in GDP

	Percentage change on previous year (1994*)
China	10.6
France	0.8
Germany	1.6
The Netherlands	1.9
Italy	0.6
Japan	0.0
Russia	−17.0
Singapore	11.0
South Africa	3.2
UK	3.3

* Based on figures for first and second quarters of 1994
Source: *The Economist*, 13 August 1994

In the more affluent societies there has been some reaction against the pressures for more rapid growth. Opponents of growth maintain that the costs of growth in terms of damage to the environment and the 'quality of life' are disproportionately high. Nevertheless, the demands for more consumption *and* more leisure are strong enough to make growth a major objective of economic policy.

The meaning of economic growth

In general usage, economic growth is taken to mean any increase in the gross national product (GNP) or gross domestic product (GDP), but for several reasons this is a rather misleading use of the term. First of all, GNP is measured in terms of money values so that inflation will increase the figure from one year to another. If we are to use the concept of growth to indicate changes in real income, the annual GNP figures must be corrected for price changes before any valid comparisons can be made. Secondly, changes in real GNP do not necessarily indicate corresponding changes in economic welfare. These are more accurately indicated by changes in real income per head so that changes in GNP should be related to changes in population. We should also take account of the composition of total output when relating growth to living standards. A massive increase in defence spending would show up as a large increase in GNP, but it would be misleading to use this as an indication of an improvement in material living standards.

There is one further important distinction to be made. When an economy is functioning with excess capacity, GNP may be increased by putting the unemployed resources to work. Economists do not usually describe an increase in GNP which arises from a fall in unemployment as economic growth because the extra output is a once-and-for-all gain. The problem of economic growth is how to increase output when all resources are fully employed; it refers, therefore, to an increase in the country's productive potential. This means that economic growth can only be measured between periods when the utilisation of resources, or rates of unemployment, were very similar.

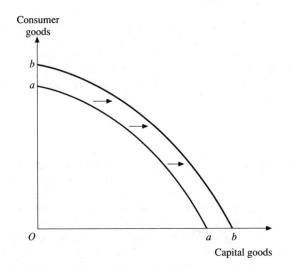

Fig. 42.1

The causes of growth

Economists have identified several factors which determine the rate of growth, but there is a lot of disagreement on the relative importance of these factors. It is fairly obvious that, on the supply side, economic growth will depend upon the increase in the quantity and quality of the factors of production and the efficiency with which they are combined. But the demand side is also important. The incentives to increase capacity and output will clearly depend upon the level of aggregate demand. The object of demand management is not merely to bring planned spending up to a certain level and hold it there, it must be steadily raised to take account of the desired or attainable rate of growth. More is said about this later. In the meantime, we can look at some of the ways in which a nation's productive potential can be increased.

Increased skills and education

Education and training are often described as 'investment in people' and there is no doubt that they have an important part to play in raising the productivity of the labour force. The lack of these facilities provides a serious barrier to more rapid economic progress in the developing countries.

Economies of scale

We have already explained how larger scale production can raise productivity (see Ch. 9). The scope for improved growth rates on this particular basis depends very much on the size and stage of development of the economy. There is obviously much more scope for growth through economies of scale in the developing world than in the larger industrialised societies.

Investment

In this context we are mainly concerned with net investment; that is, the additions to the national stock of capital. There are two ways in which the stock of capital may increase. When the labour force is increasing, an equivalent amount of investment is likely to be made otherwise the amount of capital per worker would be falling. This process is known as 'capital widening' and need not necessarily lead to any increase in output per worker. Increasing the amount of capital per worker is known as 'capital deepening' and this process should lead to increasing labour productivity.

Although investment is recognised as a factor in economic growth, there is much dispute as to the way in which the two are linked. While it is true that no country has achieved a very fast growth rate without a high rate of investment, there are several examples of countries which have invested heavily and failed to achieve high growth rates. Much depends on the type of investment being undertaken. The construction of schools, houses, hospitals, and other forms of social capital does not have a direct influence on productive efficiency in the same way as manufacturing, commercial, or agricultural investment. One must look at the type of investment as well as its volume when assessing the likely effects on economic growth. In this connection a piecemeal modernisation of industry is not likely to be so effective as a complete rebuilding.

The extent to which new capital is used efficiently is also an important consideration. When improved machinery is installed, fears of redundancy may cause unions to insist on unchanged manning schedules so that the full potential gains in labour productivity may not be realised. The average age of the capital stock is another important determinant of productivity. If one country *replaces* its capital more frequently than another, it will have better and more efficient equipment even though the *net* investment figures may be the same for both countries.

New technology

Many economists believe that the introduction of new techniques may be a more important cause of growth than an increasing stock of capital. 'New technology', however, is a rather vague term and it is taken to include such things as new inventions, new techniques of production, improvements in the design and performance of machinery, better organisation and management, more efficient factory layouts, better training facilities, and more efficient systems of transport and communication. It is unrealistic to separate technical progress and investment completely, because much of the new technology tends to be 'embodied' in new kinds of equipment. When an old lathe is replaced by a more efficient new model, there has been no increase in the volume of investment, but there has been an increase in the industry's productive potential.

Reallocation of resources

Changes in output per head are very much influenced by changes in the distribution of the labour force. As economic development takes place, there is a tendency for labour to shift first from primary production (agriculture, mining, etc.) to secondary production (manufacturing) and later to the service industries. Normally, output per worker tends to grow more rapidly in agriculture and manufacturing than in the service industries since it is more difficult for people such as doctors, teachers, and civil servants to raise their productivity. It is also the case that productivity has tended to rise more rapidly in manufacturing than in agriculture.

Thus, in Japan and continental Western Europe where, since the Second World War, there has been a substantial movement of labour from agriculture to manufacturing, there have also been some very high growth rates recorded until the 1990s.

The desirability of economic growth

Growth is an important objective of economic policy because it is the key to higher standards of living. It is economic growth which has made it possible for millions of people to escape from the miseries of long hours of back-breaking toil, deplorable living conditions, a low expectancy of life, and other features of low income societies. Furthermore, people have come to expect economic growth – we expect our children to have a better life (in the material sense) than we have had.

From the government's point of view, economic growth is desirable because it brings in increasing revenues from a given structure of tax rates. It means that more and better schools, hospitals, and other social services can be provided without resorting to the politically unpopular measure of raising the rates of taxation. Economic growth also makes it easier (politically) to carry out policies of income distribution which favour the less well off. If real income per head is increasing, a more than proportionate share of the increment can be allocated to the lower income groups and a less than proportionate share to the higher income groups. No one need be worse off.

Of great importance is the cumulative nature of economic growth. We must use compound interest calculations to work out the longer term effects of particular growth rates. For example, a country which maintains a growth rate of 3 per cent per annum will achieve a doubling of real income in 24 years. It is this aspect of growth which explains why relatively small differences in national growth rates can, in a matter of 10 or 15 years, lead to large absolute differences in living standards. It also explains why the differences in real income between a rich country and a poor country can widen even when they are both experiencing the same rate of growth. A 3 per cent increase on £1 m. is a much greater increase in absolute terms than 3 per cent on £1000.

The benefits and costs of economic growth

There are a variety of ways in which the benefits of economic growth may be enjoyed. By maintaining the same labour force working the same number of hours, the community may enjoy the gains from its increasing ability to produce in the form of higher levels of consumption. Alternatively, since any given output can now be produced with a small labour input, workers may decide to take part of their improved living standards in terms of increased leisure. It would also be possible to maintain consumption levels *and* reduce the proportion of the population at work by extending the provisions for full-time further education and/or reducing the age of retirement. Economic growth, as pointed out earlier, also makes it possible to devote more resources to the social services without having to cut private consumption.

Nevertheless, in whatever form society chooses to take the future benefits, economic growth imposes a sacrifice in terms of current living standards. In a fully employed economy a higher rate of investment can only be carried out by allocating more resources to the production of capital goods; the current output of consumption goods, therefore, will be less than it might otherwise be. It is true that a much greater annual output of consumer goods will be forthcoming in the future, but it may be many years before there is any *net* gain. Is it worth it?

Economic growth also gives rise to a variety of social costs. Rising incomes make it possible for more people to own cars, but this could lead to problems of pollution and traffic congestion. Natural resources, including the rainforests, may be depleted at a rapid rate.

Huge modern steel plants, chemical works, oil refineries, and generating stations may be very efficient on the basis of purely commercial assessments, but they could impose costs on society by destroying natural beauty and other amenities. Modern methods of agriculture may greatly increase yields per acre, but they could have damaging effects on wildlife. On the other hand we must remember that it is economic growth which makes it possible to devote more resources to the search for safer and cleaner methods of production.

Perhaps the most disturbing social costs are those associated with a rapid pace of economic change. The technical progress which makes machines and production methods obsolete also makes people redundant. Labour will have to learn new skills, adopt new methods of working, and accept more frequent changes of occupation. While programmes of retraining with adequate financial grants can deal with the problem to some extent, there still remains the social cost in terms.

Economic policy and growth

The policy measures already discussed can be used to influence the various factors which determine growth. Fiscal and monetary measures can be used to stimulate private investment and public investment, research and development may be encouraged by grants and tax allowances, and the government can enlarge and improve educational and training facilities. It also has the ability to maintain demand at levels which will encourage firms to expand their capacities.

If growth were the only objective of economic policy, there is little doubt that it could be achieved. But we know that governments are faced with the problem of conflicting objectives. In the UK, these conflicts have been particularly acute and for much of the post-war period aggregate demand has been managed with a view to dealing with balance of payments problems and escalating inflation. In fact, for much of this period output has grown at a slower rate than the country's productive potential.

The use of demand management techniques to deal with inflation and external deficits resulted in a series of 'stop-go' phases. Deflationary measures were applied to slow down the rate of inflation or to reduce the level of imports and they were relaxed when unemployment rose to politically unacceptable levels. Stop-go policies however are not likely to encourage those attitudes and expectations which are conducive to economic growth. If business people become convinced that any expansionary phase will be short-lived, they will not undertake the longer term investment projects which would increase the nation's productive capacity. When there is a lack of confidence in the ability of the government to carry out a sustained programme of expansion, any increase in aggregate demand is likely to increase short-term speculation in shares and property rather than industrial investment.

Workers too are unlikely to be receptive to changing practices and techniques, many of which cause redundancies, unless they are convinced that sustained growth will generate new job opportunities.

The government may also find it difficult to persuade people to accept the sacrifices which a faster rate of economic growth demands. If people have a very strong time preference it will require very high rates of interest to persuade them to forgo current consumption (i.e. to save and lend more). Likewise a movement of resources from the creation of social capital to the production of more industrial capital may be strongly resisted. If the economy is fully employed, any attempt to raise the rate of economic growth must entail some sacrifice in terms of present living standards, otherwise measures designed to increase investment will simply give rise to inflation.

Countries like the UK, which are heavily dependent on imported materials, face another serious problem when trying to raise the rate of economic growth. An expansion of investment brings about an immediate increase in imports (materials and machinery) and since there is unlikely to be an immediate increase in exports, then, unless the country is enjoying an export surplus, the likely effect is a deficit on the current account of the balance of payments. If a deficit does arise and is not offset by inward investment from abroad or if the foreign currency reserves are inadequate to deal with it, or the government is not prepared to allow the necessary depreciation of the currency, imports will have to be cut and the growth objective abandoned.

43 Business cycles

Definition

The business cycle (or trade cycle) is a periodic fluctuation in economic activity and it occurs as the economy moves away from its trend path. The general trend in economic activity is upward but actual real GDP can deviate, sometimes quite significantly, from trend real GDP.

The business cycle was first identified in 1862 by the French economist, Clement Juglar. In the 1960s some economists began to think that business cycles were a thing of the past. However, the swings in economic activity from the 1970s onwards have resulted in business cycles becoming a topical issue again.

The phases of the cycle

The downturn (or contraction)

This is when economic activity slows down. Consumption rises more slowly and then starts to decline. Entrepreneurs become more cautious, cancelling expansion plans and not undertaking net investment. Some firms will close, causing unemployment to rise. The lower consumption and rising unemployment are likely to reduce inflationary pressure, lower government tax revenue and raise government expenditure on unemployment related benefits.

If a downturn lasts long enough it can turn into a recession. A recession is defined as a fall in GDP over two or more successive quarters.

The trough

This is characterised by a high level pessimism amongst entrepreneurs, negative net investment (firms not replacing worn out machines), falling demand for consumer goods as well as capital goods, high unemployment and usually a low level of imports.

A deep trough is called a slump or depression. Where the trough bottoms out and the economy begins to expand is referred to as the lower turning point.

The upturn (or expansion or recovery)

In this period consumption increases, production expands, profits rise and net investment becomes positive. Entrepreneurs and workers become more confident. Unemployment falls which further stimulates demand for consumer and capital goods. Inflationary pressures may begin to develop.

The peak (or boom)

During a peak or boom period employment is high as are expectations, profits and imports. There is a high level of demand for capital and consumer goods. Indeed, the high level of demand may result in a shortage of some of the factors of production, the development of bottlenecks and inflation. The peak can occur before real GDP reaches its potential level or at a point beyond the full employment level. In the latter case the economy is said to be overheating. During this period of high demand risky investments may be undertaken and some inefficient firms may be able to survive. The upper turning point is reached where a peak turns into a downturn. Figure 43.1 illustrates a business cycle with its four phases.

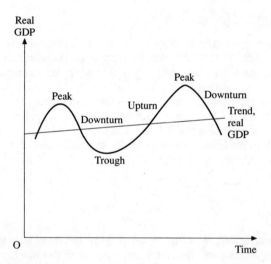

Fig. 43.1   A business cycle

During the peak period the economy is supply constrained whereas during the trough period the economy is demand constrained.

Duration of cycles

A number of cycles may be identified, distinguishable by their different durations and sometimes causes.

The Kitchin inventory cycle

This lasts approximately three to five years from peak to peak and is associated with stocking and destocking in industry.

The Juglar or investment cycle

This lasts approximately seven to eleven years and as its name suggests is connected now with changes in net investment.

The Kuznets cycle

This is thought to last between fifteen and twenty-five years and is caused by fluctuations in activity in the construction and allied industries.

The Kondratieff cycle

This lasts from forty-five to sixty years and because of the long duration of these cycles they are sometimes referred to as long waves. Kondratieff, a Russian economist writing in the 1920s, argued that short waves or cycles occur within long cycles. The long cycles, he suggested, are caused by technological innovations, wars, revolutions, opening up of new countries and discoveries of gold. All of these events will have impacts on economies which can take decades to work through. For example, the introduction of the microchip is still resulting in the creation of new products, new industries, new skills and new work methods and patterns of employment.

Explanations of business cycles

These can be divided into two broad categories. One type of cause is called internal or endogenous and these arise from changes within the economy itself, for instance, changes in stocks.

The other type is called external or exogenous. This category includes causes arising from factors outside the particular economy, for example, the supply-side shocks which can arise from rises in the price of oil and war. We can now examine some of the explanations.

Fluctuations in the money supply

Monetarists argue that when the money supply increases and the rate of interest is low the economy expands and moves into a boom. However, the higher level of demand increases demand for money, both by firms and consumers, for transaction purposes. This raises the rate of interest which in turn reduces investment and consumption and leads to a downturn.

Bursts of technological innovation

As we have seen above, technological innovation, such as the development of railways, increase the range of products, number of industries and demand.

Stop-go cycles

To stimulate growth and employment a government may increase aggregate demand. This reflationary action will increase activity but as the economy expands the government may become concerned about inflationary pressures and balance-of-payments difficulties developing. As a result the government may adopt deflationary policies. These may cause a downturn which will continue until the government again becomes concerned about the low level of output and employment.

Political cycles

These are linked to stop-go cycles. A government is more likely to take harsh deflationary measures after a general election and may seek to boost the economy before a general election in order to win political popularity.

Multiplier-accelerator theory

This emphasises the cumulative nature of business cycles. If there is a rise in exports, national income will rise by a multiple amount. This in turn will cause investment to rise (the accelerator) which will generate a further rise in national income. A ceiling will be reached as shortages in labour and other resources are experienced and when income grows more slowly investment will fall. This will set in motion a downward movement in national income.

The fall in national income does not continue indefinitely. A floor will be reached where firms have to replace at least some of their worn-out machinery. Consumption cannot fall to zero and again a point will come where people will have to replace consumer durables and where they will resist any further falls in their consumption, even if this means using up their savings.

The inventory cycle

This is linked to the accelerator. Inventories are stocks of raw materials and finished products held by producers and finished products held by retailers. If there is a rise in demand for consumer goods, retailers will initially run down their stocks. They will then order more goods from producers who in turn will order more raw materials. When retailers and producers are again content with their stock levels they will reduce their orders which will slow down the economy. This fall in economic activity will continue until firms have reduced their stocks to such an extent that they have to replenish them.

Forecasting business cycles

Companies and the government seek to forecast business cycles by using surveys, such as the regular CBI survey, and by examining economic statistics. There are three types of indicators.

Leading indicators

These react ahead of the cycle and so indicate changes in activity in advance. They include the FT 500 share index, new car registrations and gross trading profits of companies.

Coincident indicators

These occur with the cycle, and provide evidence that the cycle is occurring. The most important is obviously changes in real GDP. However, others include the index of the volume of retail sales, the index of production industries and changes in stocks.

Lagging indicators

These react after the changes in economic activity and confirm the turning points in the cycle. The two best known are unemployment and investment. For instance, it may be a year or more before a rise in economic activity is reflected in a rise in employment and investment. This is because firms will want to see that the rise in demand will last before they increase the number of workers and machines they employ.

Recent history

In the 1960s there were only small fluctuations in the economy. In the 1970s the fluctuations became more pronounced and the decade ended with the economy in a downturn which developed into a trough in 1981. The level of economic activity slowly picked up in the mid 1980s and in the period 1986–88 there was a consumer boom. This was stimulated by a rise in the availability and fall in the price of credit, a fall in income tax and rises in confidence. Between 1990 and 1992 the economy experienced a recession due to the rise in interest rates, the high value of the pound and the fall in confidence among other factors. The economy came out of the recession very slowly and concerns are expressed that downturns are becoming more severe whilst peaks are being reached at lower levels of economic activity. The rate of structural change is increasing and advanced countries are facing increased competition from the Pacific Rim countries.

44 Unemployment

Measuring unemployment

Unemployment can be measured in a number of different ways. The main official measure in the UK is the claimant count. This includes as unemployed anyone between the ages of 18 and 60 receiving an unemployment-related benefit such as job-seekers' allowance.

The Employment Department also measurers unemployment by means of a labour force survey. This uses the International Labour Organisation's definition of unemployment which counts as unemployed all those who are actively seeking and available to start work, whether or not they are claiming benefit. Each measure has its advantages and disadvantages. These are outlined in Table 44.1.

Table 44.1 Survey-based ILO unemployment and administrative claimant unemployment compared

ILO unemployment

Advantages	Disadvantages
• internationally standardised	• relatively costly to compile
• usable for inter-country comparisons	• normally less timely
• considerable potential for analysis of other labour-market characteristics, or of particular sub-groups	• subject to sampling and response error
• articulated with data from the same source on employment and the economically inactive	• not always suitable for small areas due to sampling limitations

Claimant unemployment

Advantages	Disadvantages
• relatively inexpensive	• not internationally recognised
• available frequently (normally monthly)	• coverage changes whenever administrative system changes, although recalculation of consistent series allows meaningful comparisons over time
• available quickly	• coverage depends upon administrative rules; may not be suitable for other purposes
• 100 per cent count gives figures for small areas	• limited analysis of characteristics of unemployed people

Source: *Employment gazette*, July 1994

Accuracy of the claimant count

There are some people in the claimant count who are working in the black economy, and some who, whilst claiming and receiving benefits, are not actively looking for work. However, there are others who might be considered as unemployed but who do not appear in the official claimant count. These include those who are looking for a job but who are aged under 18 or over 60, or who are not entitled to benefits or who do not claim benefits. If this group is larger than those working in the black economy or those not looking for work but claiming benefits the official figures will understate the level of unemployment.

Stocks and flows

Unemployment is a stock. It is a measure of the number of people unemployed at a particular point of time. However, this stock of unemployment is influenced by the flow of people into the stock and the flow of people leaving the stock. New people entering the stock of unemployment will not only be those losing jobs but also previous non-participants in the labour force who are now seeking employment, for example, students finishing degree courses who cannot find employment. People who leave the stock may have found employment, may have given up looking for work, may have retired, may have joined a government training scheme or may have entered higher education.

Unemployment will rise if the number entering the stock exceeds the number of new jobs.

Duration

In examining unemployment it is important to consider not only the numbers unemployed but also how long they have been unemployed, i.e., how long it is after they enter the stock that they leave it. For example, an unemployment rate of 12 per cent with an average duration of three months unemployed may be considered to be less of a problem than an unemployment rate of 8 per cent if the average duration is three years.

Unemployment rate

The unemployment rate is the number of people on the claimant count expressed as a percentage of the labour force.

$$\frac{\text{registered unemployed}}{\text{labour force}} \times \frac{100}{1}$$

The labour force includes all those who are economically active i.e. willing and able to work. So it consists of those in employment and the unemployed. This contrasts with the working population which is those of working age i.e. those between 16 to 60 in the case of women and 16 to 65 in the case of men. Not all of those in the working population are in the labour force. Students, those who have retired early, some handicapped people and housewives and househusbands are in the working population but not in the labour force.

Types and causes of unemployment

Unemployment can be categorised in a number of ways. One way is in accordance with its causes.

Residual unemployment

In all societies there is an element of residual unemployment because there will always be some people who are virtually unemployable on a permanent basis. These are people who find it difficult or impossible to cope with the demands of modern production methods and the disciplines of organised work.

Frictional unemployment

This arises from immobilities in the labour force. Labour is not perfectly geographically or occupationally mobile. So people can remain unemployed despite the fact that there are jobs available, either in other parts of the country, or requiring skills they do not have.

Search unemployment

This is a form of frictional unemployment. It occurs when people who are unemployed do not take the first job on offer but search for better-paid employment.

Casual unemployment

This is again a form of frictional unemployment. There are certain groups of people who are out of work between periods of employment. For instance, opera singers, actors, roof repairers.

Seasonal unemployment

This occurs in those industries which experience marked seasonal patterns of demand. Industries such as farming, building and tourism are affected in this way.

Structural unemployment

This is unemployment which arises from a fundamental change in the structure of industry. For example, the decline of mining in the UK has resulted in a large number of former coal-miners becoming unemployed.

Regional unemployment

This is linked to structural unemployment. It arises when the declining industry is concentrated in one area. The region dependent upon the industry may suffer particularly heavy unemployment because there will be a local multiplier effect arising from the decline in the income generated by the major industry.

Technological unemployment

This arises from the introduction of new technology. For instance, the increasing use of cashpoint, switch and other plastic cards has reduced the number of bank clerks.

International unemployment

This arises when workers lose their jobs due to a fall in demand for domestically produced goods.

Cyclical unemployment

This is also referred to as demand deficiency unemployment. It arises due to inadequate demand. Figure 44.1 shows that the level of aggregate expenditure is insufficient to achieve full employment (Y_{fe}). There is a deflationary gap of *ab*.

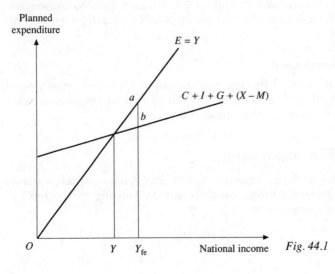

Fig. 44.1

The non-accelerating inflation rate of unemployment

In the 1960s and 1970s, attempts to reduce the level of unemployment by increasing aggregate demand led to sharp increases in the rate of inflation and to balance of payments problems. This experience led economists, and governments, to pay increasing attention to the concept of *a natural rate of unemployment*. More recently it has come to be known as the non-accelerating inflation rate of unemployment (NAIRU) as it can also be defined as that rate of unemployment which is consistent with a stable rate of inflation.

NAIRU is an essential feature of the monetarist theory of inflation, which holds that increases in aggregate demand *can* reduce unemployment below its natural level, but the effect will only be temporary. In the longer run, unemployment will return to its natural level and the net effect of an increase in demand will be a higher rate of inflation. NAIRU is the rate of unemployment which exists when an economy is producing its potential output and is associated with an equilibrium situation in the labour market. At this level of unemployment, the demand for labour is equal to the supply of labour at the existing *real wage rate*.

Equilibrium unemployment

Equilibrium unemployment is the unemployment which exists when the aggregate demand for labour is equal to the aggregate supply of labour and vacancies match the number unemployed. Whilst there may be macro-economic equilibrium at the current real wage rate, people may still be unemployed. This may be because they are unaware of the vacancies, unsuitable to take up the vacancies, unable to take up the vacancies or unwilling to take up the vacancies.

Figure 44.2 shows equilibrium unemployment. The *ADL* curve shows the aggregate demand for labour. The *ASL* curve shows the aggregate supply curve of labour consisting of those workers willing to accept jobs at each wage rate. The curve *ALF* represents the total labour force. The macroeconomic labour market is in equilibrium at a wage rate of *OW* but there is unemployment (equilibrium unemployment) of *LLX*. As the real wage rate rises the gap between the total labour force and those willing and able to work at the wage rate narrows. This is because people become more willing to accept jobs at higher wage rates. The NAIRU is not zero and the types of equilibrium unemployment which exist include voluntary (i.e., those who choose to live on benefits rather than work), search, residual, frictional, seasonal, casual, structured, and technological.

In all these cases there may be vacancies in some occupations, industries and geographical areas whilst unemployment exists in other occupations, industries and different parts of the country.

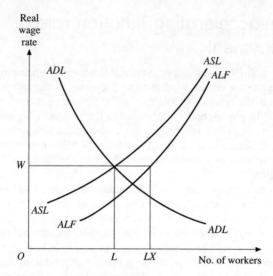

Fig. 44.2   Equilibrium unemployment

Disequilibrium unemployment

This occurs when there is disequilibrium in the labour market, specifically when aggregate supply exceeds aggregate demand at the current wage rate. This is shown in Fig. 44.3. At the wage rate *OW* there is disequilibrium unemployment of *LLZ*.

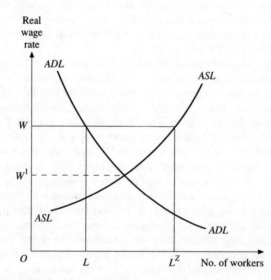

Fig. 44.3   Disequilibrium unemployment

If the wage rate were to fall to OW^1 the disequilibrium unemployment would disappear. So for disequilibrium unemployment two conditions have to hold. One is that the aggregate supply of labour must exceed the aggregate demand for labour. The other is that wage rates are not flexible downwards. This is often referred to as wages being sticky downwards.

Causes of disequilibrium unemployment

There are a number of reasons why the real wage rate may be higher than the market clearing (equilibrium) rate. One possible reason is the wage rate being driven up above the equilibrium rate either by trade union power or a government-set minimum wage rate. However, the effects are somewhat uncertain. This is because the higher wage earned may stimulate increased expenditure and a rise in demand for labour.

Another possible reason is a growth in the labour supply not matched by a rise in the aggregate demand for labour. Figure 44.4 shows the market initially in equilibrium. When the supply of labour increases from ASL to ASL^1 the wage rate, being sticky downwards, remains at OW and unemployment of LLZ arises.

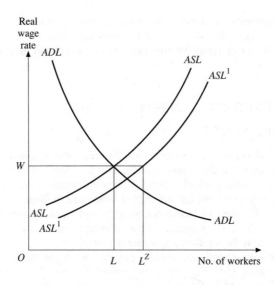

Fig. 44.4

The most significant cause of disequilibrium unemployment is a fall in aggregate demand. As we have seen this is cyclical unemployment. Figure 44.5 again shows the labour market initially being in equilibrium. Then a fall in aggregate demand shifts the aggregate demand curve to the left, i.e., from ADL to ADL^1. The wage rate does not fall and LLZ unemployment is created.

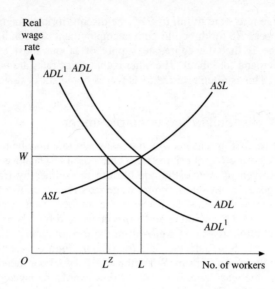

Fig. 44.5

When aggregate demand falls, cyclical unemployment could occur even if the wage falls to the equilibrium level. This is because falling wages will lower demand for consumer goods which, in turn, will lower demand for labour.

Equilibrium and disequilibrium unemployment

New classical supporters believe that the real wage adjusts relatively quickly to changes in the supply and demand for labour. Hence they think that the unemployment which exists is of an equilibrium nature. In contrast, Keynesians argue that the labour market is usually in disequilibrium with the demand and supply of labour not being brought into equality with quick adjustments in real wages. They consider the main cause of unemployment to be a fall in aggregate demand.

Some economists take the middle ground and argue that it is possible for equilibrium and disequilibrium unemployment to occur simultaneously. Figure 44.6 shows equilibrium and disequilibrium unemployment occurring at the same time. The total unemployment experienced is *LLX*, with *LZ* being disequilibrium unemployment and *LZLX* being equilibrium unemployment.

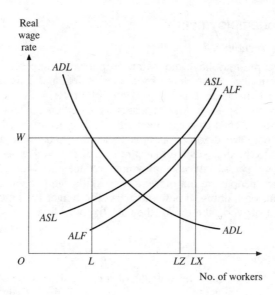

Fig. 44.6

The effects of unemployment

Unemployment has consequences for the unemployed themselves and for society as a whole.

Benefits of unemployment

Benefits to those unemployed

It may seem strange to discuss the benefits of being unemployed. For most people the disadvantages of being unemployed far exceed the benefits. Nevertheless there may be benefits. One is the time it gives people to explore job opportunities and apply for jobs (frictional and search unemployment). Being unemployed may also provide people with more time to pursue their leisure activities.

Benefits to society

Unemployment creates greater flexibility. An economy will be able to expand relatively quickly and easily if there is a pool of suitably qualified unemployed workers. It is also argued that unemployment reduces cost-push inflation by lowering wage claims, makes workers more willing to accept new methods of production and more reluctant to take industrial action. Most economists, however, argue that the costs of unemployment exceed any possible benefits.

Costs of unemployment

Costs to the unemployed

Although people may have more time to pursue leisure activities they may be constrained in so doing by a lack of income. This is because most people experience a fall in income, often a significant fall. The unemployed also suffer a loss of status as a certain amount of social stigma is still attached to being unemployed. The unemployed are more likely to experience divorce, nervous breakdowns, bad health and are more likely to attempt suicide than the rest of the adult population. In addition, long periods of unemployment reduce the value of human capital. When people are out of work their skills can become rusty, and they miss out on training in new methods. The longer the time a person has been out of work, the harder they are likely to find gaining another job.

Costs to society

The main cost to society is the output which is lost. This is the opportunity cost of unemployment. The output is lost for all time. Even if unemployment later falls, the lost output can never be regained. People will enjoy fewer goods and services than they could have consumed with higher employment. The country will be producing inside its production possibility curve as shown in Fig. 44.7.

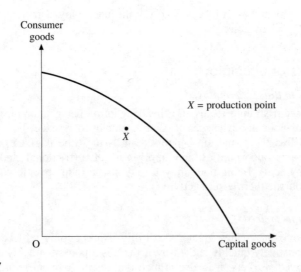

Fig. 44.7

Unemployment depresses incomes and thereby deprives the government of both direct and indirect tax revenue. Whilst government revenue will fall as unemployment rises it will have to increase its spending on unemployment related benefits.

In recent years there has been increased evidence of a link between crime and unemployment, particularly in the case of young unemployed men. The burden of unemployment is not borne evenly by society. The young, people from ethnic minorities and those lacking skills are more likely to experience unemployment.

45 Money

In the absence of some form of money, exchange must take the form of *barter* which is the direct exchange of goods and services for goods and services. Barter will serve man's requirements quite adequately when he provides most of his needs directly and relies upon market exchanges for very few of the things he wants. As the extent of specialisation increases, the barter system proves very inefficient and frustrating. In the simplest society each family will provide by its own efforts most of its needs and perhaps some small surpluses. A farmer will exchange any small surplus of food, wool, or hides for the surpluses of other producers. But this system of exchange becomes very cumbersome as economic activities become more specialised. A specialist metal worker must seek out a large number of other specialists in order to obtain, by barter, the variety of goods he needs to satisfy his daily wants.

The great disadvantage of barter is the fact that it depends upon a 'double coincidence of wants'. A hunter who wants to exchange his skins for corn must find, not merely a person who wants skins, but someone who wants skins *and* has a surplus of corn for disposal. The alternative is to exchange his skins for some other article and then carry out a series of similar exchanges until he finally gets his corn. Time and energy which could be devoted to production is spent on a laborious system of exchange.

Quite early in his history man discovered a much more convenient arrangement. The use of some commodity as a medium of exchange makes exchange triangular and removes the major difficulty of the barter system. If a commodity is generally acceptable in exchange for goods and services, it is money. A producer now exchanges his goods for money and the money can then be exchanged for whatever goods and services he requires.

The functions of money

Money has several functions and these are outlined below.

A medium of exchange

As we have already explained, the use of money as a medium of exchange makes possible a great extension of the principle of specialisation. In an advanced society the use of money allows us to exchange hours of labour for an amazing variety of goods and services. We can exchange, for example, two weeks' labour for a holiday abroad just as easily as we can exchange it for a piece of furniture or a year's rent on a television set. Such exchanges are taken for granted yet they would be inconceivable without the use of money.

A measure of value

The first step in the use of money was probably the adoption of some commodity as a unit of account or measure of value. Money, most likely, came into use within the barter system as a means whereby the values of different goods could be compared. The direct exchange of goods for goods would raise all sorts of problems regarding valuation. For example 'How many bushels of corn are equal in value to one sheep, if twenty sheep exchange for three cows and one cow exchanges for ten bushels of corn?' This problem of exchange rates is easily solved when all other commodities are valued in terms of a single commodity which then acts as a standard of value. Money now serves as such a standard and when all economic goods are given money values (i.e. prices), we know, immediately, the value of one commodity in terms of any other commodity.

A store of value

Once a commodity becomes universally acceptable in exchange for goods and services, it is possible to store wealth by holding a stock of this commodity. It is a great convenience to hold wealth in the form of money. Consider the problems of holding wealth in the form of some other commodity, say wheat. It may deteriorate, it is costly to store, it must be insured, and there will be significant handling costs in accumulating and distributing it. In addition, its *money value* may fall while it is being stored. The great disadvantage of holding wealth in the form of money has become very apparent in recent years – during periods of inflation its *exchange value* falls.

A means of making deferred payments

An important function of money in the modern world, where so much business is conducted on the basis of credit, is to serve as a means of deferred payment. When goods are supplied on credit, the buyer has immediate use of them but does not have to make an immediate payment. The goods can be paid for three, or perhaps six, months after delivery. In the case of hire purchase contracts, the buyer takes immediate delivery but pays by means of instalments spread over one, two, or three years.

A complex trading organisation based upon a system of credit can only operate in a monetary economy. Sellers would be most unlikely to accept promises to pay in the future which were expressed in terms of commodities other than money. They would have no idea how much of the commodities they would need in the future, and if they do not want them, they face the trouble and risks involved in selling them. Sellers will accept promises to pay expressed in terms of money because, whatever the pattern of their future wants, they can be satisfied by using money.

The characteristics of money

To serve as money and to carry out its functions efficiently an item must possess certain characteristics.

The essential characteristic of money is that it must be *generally acceptable*. Unless the medium of exchange is freely acceptable by everyone, no producer is going to take the risk of accepting it in exchange for his products. He must have confidence that the 'money' will, in turn, be accepted by the sellers of the things he wishes to buy.

An efficient medium of exchange must be *portable* by having a high ratio of value to bulk and weight. It would be very inconvenient to use large, heavy, and bulky objects as money.

The commodity must also be *divisible*, that is, capable of subdivision into smaller units without any loss in value. Suppose hides are being used as money and two sheep are worth one hide. How does one buy one sheep? When the hide is cut into two equal parts, the value of the two halves is less than the value of the whole hide.

A most essential characteristic of whatever is to serve as money is *durability*. People will not accept anything which is subject to rapid deterioration and hence loses value while it is in their possession.

Finally the commodity must be *limited in supply*. Unless there is some limitation on supply, either natural or artificial, people will have no confidence in the value of the commodity.

Forms of money

Precious metals

This list of desirable qualities enables us to see why, at all times and in all places, people have adopted the precious metals, gold and silver, as the commodities to serve as money. Gold and silver are portable since they have a very high commodity value and it is very easy to produce them of uniform fineness. They are divisible without loss in value and they are easily recognisable. These metals can be stored without risk of deterioration and, most important, they are limited in supply. Gold especially is difficult and costly to extract. Since the annual additions to the existing world stocks are relatively very small there is virtually no risk of a large increase in supply destroying the value of gold.

Coins

The precious metals were first used as money on the basis of weight. We read in the Bible, 'And Abraham weighed unto Ephron the silver' (Gen. 23:16). The shekel and the pound are units of currency and also units of weight. The inconvenience of weighing out the metals each time a transaction took place led to the introduction of coins. It was appreciated that exchange would be greatly facilitated if the pieces of metal to be used as money carried some clear indication of their weight and fineness. Coins are shaped pieces of metal bearing some authoritative imprint which certifies their money value.

There is, however, always a temptation for rulers to enrich themselves by reducing the commodity value of the coinage below its declared money value. They do this by reducing the precious metal content and adding some metal of lower money value. By this means any given weight of gold and silver can be used to produce more coins. The declared money value of the coins is not changed and the additional coins can be used to swell the royal coffers. In the middle of the sixteenth century the debasement of the coinage, which was seriously affecting the acceptability of money, led to the formulation of *Gresham's Law* which stated that *bad money drives out good*. Where a variety of coins are circulating some of which have a higher gold or silver content than others (of the same money value), people will hoard the coins with a higher commodity value and try to use the debased coins.

Banknotes

Development

The next great step forward in the history of money was the introduction of paper money. Banknotes first came into use in Britain during the seventeenth century. The essential feature of the new development was that people began to use *claims* to precious metal as money instead of the metal itself. The dangers of theft and the lack of security in the average home meant that gold and silver were deposited in goldsmiths' vaults – the depositors receiving some written acknowledgement of their ownership. If these receipts were stolen no loss was suffered because the gold and silver would not be withdrawn without the depositor's signature. It became a common practice for a person to pay his debts by endorsing his receipts with an instruction to the goldsmith (the embryonic banker) to transfer his deposit to some other person. Thus, bankers' receipts were endorsed and passed from hand to hand in settlement of debts. A further and important step forward came when bankers made out the deposit receipts, or 'promises to pay', as *payable to bearer* instead of to some named person. These claims to gold and silver could now be transferred without endorsement and the person in possession had a full legal claim to the amount of money specified on the receipt. These notes came to be issued in convenient denominations (e.g. £5, or £10) instead of being a single receipt for the full deposit. Bearer notes were the first fully-fledged banknotes.

Fractional backing

Initially the banknote would be accepted as a claim to gold or silver, used for one transaction and then 'cashed'. But, in time, the banknote itself came to be regarded as money and was passed from hand to hand financing numerous transactions. As long as people were absolutely certain that they could, at any time, convert the notes into gold (or silver) they would be quite happy to accept them in payment for goods and services. In the early stages of banking the value of the notes issued was exactly equal to the value of precious metals held in the strongrooms. In other words the banknotes had a *100 per cent backing* in the form of precious metals.

As the public gradually acquired more confidence in them, banknotes began to circulate more and more freely and it became apparent to the bankers that the greater part of their holdings of precious metal (specie) was lying idle. Every day some notes would be presented for conversion into gold or silver, but at the same time other people would be depositing specie. Only a small proportion of the metallic 'backing' would be required to meet any daily *net* demand for precious metal. It became fairly obvious that bankers could issue notes to a total value well in excess of the value of the gold and silver they were holding, and still meet all the likely demands from those who wished to convert their notes. Suppose a banker found by experience that over a period of time the maximum net withdrawal of gold and silver was equal to 20 per cent of the average value of his stock of these metals. This would indicate that his stock of specie would support a note issue equal to five times its own value. The cautious banker would be aware of the fact that he might at some time be called upon to meet unexpectedly heavy demands for conversion of his notes and he might allow for this by issuing notes equal to twice the value of his stock of precious metals.

When bankers began to issue notes in excess of their holdings of gold and silver they were, in fact, creating money. When notes are backed 100 per cent by specie, no money has been created – the public have merely changed the form in which they are holding money. But *fractional backing* implies the creation of money since the value of banknotes issued exceeds the value of the precious metal supporting them. Bankers issued these additional notes as loans on which the borrower had to pay interest.

Main forms of money today

We have now reached the stage where our banknotes, while still carrying a 'promise to pay' printed on their faces, are no more than *token money*. This is also true of the coinage; the commodity value of the coins is but a tiny fraction of their money value. Nevertheless the notes and coins are universally acceptable; the fact that they have no real commodity value, and are not backed by gold, in no way affects their ability to serve as money.

Banknotes and coins are not the most important form of money in developed economies. In the UK about 90 per cent, by value, of all transactions are settled by means of cheques, credit and switch cards. But these are not themselves money, they are merely orders to bankers to transfer money from one person to another. The money so transferred consists of bank deposits. If there is no money in the form of a bank deposit then any cheques drawn on that account will be worthless.

The greater part, in value terms, of the payments made each day are carried out by adjustments made to the totals in different bank deposits. A payment from one person to another merely requires that the banker reduces the amount in one deposit and increases it in another. Transferring money, therefore, has become little more than a kind of book-keeping exercise; the money itself does not consist of some physical tangible commodity.

Measures of the money supply

The way in which money in the UK is measured has changed over time. The most recent change occurred in 1989 and was undertaken to reflect the increased similarity between bank and building society deposits.

Currently, the two measures which receive the most attention by the government are M0 and M4. M0 includes notes, coins and clearing banks' operational balances at the Bank of England (see Chapter 47). M4 consists of notes and coins in circulation and UK sight and time deposits (current and deposit accounts) held in UK banks and building societies.

M0 is known as a narrow measure of the money supply and it is concerned with forms of money used as a medium of exchange. Conversely, M4 is a broad measure since it includes forms of money which are used both as a medium of exchange and as a store of value.

Legal tender

Not all money used in the UK is legal tender. Indeed the main form, bank deposits is not. Legal tender is actually any form of money that must by law be accepted in settlement of a debt. All UK banknotes and £1 coins are full legal tender, and coins up to certain values. For instance, 10p coins are legal tender up to £5 but people have the right to refuse amounts above that.

Near money

This can also be referred to as quasi-money. It consists of financial assets which are held mainly as a store of value rather than as a medium of exchange.

Near money items fulfil some but not all the functions of money and usually have to be converted into true money before they can be spent. However, these items, for example, postal orders, Treasury bills, are close to true money as they can usually be converted quickly and at little or no cost.

46 Financial institutions

Financial intermediaries

The main function of the financial institutions which make up the British banking system is to collect deposits from those with surplus cash resources and to lend the funds to those with an immediate need for them. This is the function of a *financial intermediary*. There are many advantages of the funds being channelled through a financial institution rather than being loaned directly by savers to borrowers.

Many savers want to save relatively small sums. They will also want liquidity – the ability to withdraw their money when they want it. Most borrowers want to borrow for definite periods of time – often for quite long periods. Financial intermediaries can aggregate many small sums of savings and make relatively large loans. They can offer savers liquidity by borrowing for short periods of time and lending for long periods. Depositors can be allowed to withdraw funds because such withdrawals are likely to be matched by new deposits. If such an institution retains the confidence of its depositors there is no reason why the funds available for lending should fall significantly.

Savers will tend to look for security – they want to feel that their money is 'safe'. By spreading its loans over many different types of borrower, a financial intermediary greatly reduces the risk of losses. It can take account of likely losses in the rate of interest it charges to borrowers.

Financial intermediaries can use their size and expertise to offer savers a wide range of savings schemes and to offer borrowers several different types of loan.

Building societies

Since the 1986 and 1988 Building Society Acts there has been a considerable extension of the range of financial services offered by building societies. Their most important functions are still those of collecting retail deposits and providing mortgage loans. However, the fact that they can now supply cheque books, cheque guarantee cards, credit cards and cash-dispenser facilities means that a building society deposit can now be used in very much the same way as a current account in a bank. Building societies now have the freedom to supply a percentage of their total lending in the form of unsecured loans for purposes other than the purchase of houses. They can also offer a range of other services connected with the buying and selling of houses.

In 1989 Abbey National was reclassified as a bank. The 1990s have witnessed a series of mergers between building societies, and between building societies and clearing banks.

The clearing banks

The clearing banks are so called because they operate a clearing system. This system enables cheques, direct debits, standing orders and other methods of payment to be cleared, i.e., exchanged so that money is moved out of the deposit of the person making the payment into the deposit of the person receiving the payment. The business is dominated by the 'Big Five', Abbey National, Barclays, Lloyds, the Midland and the National Westminster.

The strength of a large bank with many branches derives from its ability to obtain economies of scale, which have become significant with the increased application of advanced technology. In addition, with a large number of depositors, no single depositor can embarrass the bank by withdrawing their funds. With many branches, the bank has a geographical spread of risks which enables it to withstand losses due to a slump in any one industry or region.

The functions of the clearing banks

Attracting deposits

The banks attract deposits from the public in three main forms.

Current accounts (sight deposits) are deposits which can be withdrawn on demand and which are subject to transfer by cheque. Traditionally, sight deposits have not earned interest, and banks can make a charge for handling the cheques drawn on these accounts. In recent years, however, several banks have decided to pay interest on balances held in current accounts.

Deposit accounts (time deposits) are deposits which earn interest but which cannot be transferred by cheque or withdrawn on demand. Normally some period of notice of withdrawal is required, but banks may waive this requirement subject to some loss of interest.

Large fixed-term deposits. The banks offer higher rates of interest on large sums of money deposited for fixed periods of time. In order to attract such deposits, the banks offer *certificates of deposit*, which are marketable securities.

Lending

Clearing banks are profit-seeking enterprises, and their main source of income is the interest they charge on their loans. These banks lend to all types of enterprise in all types of industry, as well as to the government and other public authorities. They also have a large market in personal loans. The banks have traditionally concentrated on short-term loans for the provision of working capital. However, they are now much more flexible in the length and purpose of their lending. In the personal sector the banks now compete in the mortgage market, offering secured loans for house purchase. Medium – and long-term loans are provided for industry for periods of up to 20 years.

Money transmission services

One of the most important services provided by the clearing banks is the operation of the country's main payments system. Cheques are the most important method of bank payments, but other methods include standing orders, direct debits and credit cards.

In spite of the growing use of payments methods involving banks, a huge quantity of cash is still needed by the public. Virtually all the nation's cash distribution is undertaken by the clearing banks.

Other services

The banks provide a wide range of other financial services, such as the provision of foreign currency, investment advice, management of funds, executor and trustee services, insurance services, and unit trusts.

The Bank of England

Most countries have a central bank, which is responsible of the operation of the banking system. The central bank in the UK is the Bank of England, which was taken into public ownership in 1946. It has many re-sponsibilities, which are summarised below.

- It is the government's bank. It handles the income and expenditure of the Exchequer and other government departments.
- It is the bankers' bank. The clearing banks maintain accounts at the Bank of England. The final cash settlements within the banking system and between the banking system and the Bank of England take place through these accounts. The Bank is also a banker for about 100 overseas central banks and international monetary institutions.
- It is the central note-issuing authority for the UK and the sole note-issuing authority for England and Wales. Some banks in Scotland and Northern Ireland still issue their own notes but these are largely backed by Bank of England notes.
- It manages the national debt. This is a major responsibility which involves making repayments on government securities when they mature, undertaking new issues of long-term securities, making regular payments of interest to holders of existing government securities, and handling the weekly issues of Treasury bills. The management of the national debt, as we shall see later, has important effects on the supply of money and the rate of interest.
- It is the lender of last resort. The Bank of England stands ready to come to the assistance of the banking system in times when it is threatened by a shortage of cash.

- It acts as the government's agent in the foreign exchange market, in which it can intervene to influence the value of sterling against other currencies.
- It has the responsibility for carrying out the government's monetary policy.
- It has legal powers to supervise the operations of other banks. All banks are expected to supply the Bank of England with information about their business, and they have to respond to directives given to them by the Bank.

Independence for the Bank of England?

There is currently a debate about whether the Bank of England should be given independence. This means independence not in the sense of being removed from government ownership and overall control but in the sense of being free of direct, day-to-day control by the Treasury. Independence would mean that the Bank of England would be given clear policy goals and be required to give regular reports to parliament. There has already been a step in this direction with the Bank of England being given the right to decide the exact timing of interest rate changes still at the moment decided on by the government.

Those in favour of greater independence argue that the Bank would be able to introduce longer-term policies and would be less subject to political pressure to change the rate of interest and the money supply. However, other economists warn that an independent Central Bank might pursue price stability at the cost of higher unemployment and that granting independence would reduce the government's policy options.

The central bank of Switzerland, the Bundesbank and the Reserve Bank of New Zealand are among the central banks which have a significant degree of independence from government control. In other countries the trend is towards giving central banks greater independence in their conduct of monetary policy. One driving force behind this movement in the European Union is the Maastricht Treaty which requires member states to make their central banks independent before they can proceed to full monetary union.

The merchant banks

Several merchant banks date back to the nineteenth century, when they were simply merchant houses trading in various parts of the world. Some of them grew in reputation and turned to the finance of trade as a specialised business. The finance of international trade remains an important function but other activities have tended to become more important. The main activities of the merchant banks are summarised below.

Acceptance business

The principal merchant banks, including Kleinwort Benson, Morgan Grenfell and Rothschilds, are members of the Accepting Houses Committee. In this connection their work consists of 'accepting', that is, adding their names to 'promises to pay' issued by merchants in home and overseas trade. By accepting an IOU, the bank guarantees payment if the person or firm promising payment defaults.

Financial advisors to companies

The best-known activity of the merchant banks is the handling of mergers and take-overs, in which they advise and act for the parties concerned in the negotiations. They will, however, advise on any aspect of a company's financial affairs.

Share issues

The merchant banks also act as Issuing Houses. As well as advising companies on methods of raising finance, and the government on privatisation they will usually carry out all the work involved in floating a new issue of shares or debentures.

Investment management

In addition to their advisory role, merchant banks will take on the active management of investments on behalf of other institutions. They operate investment and unit trusts.

Wholesale banking

The merchant bank's main deposit-taking activity is the acceptance of wholesale deposits (i.e. deposits of very large sums) for periods ranging from one day to a year. They are active in the money market, lending mainly to banks and other financial institutions. In the capital market they provide finance for companies. Much of their business is in foreign currencies, and they are very prominent in the Euro-currency market.

The discount houses

The London discount market is an important part of the banking system. It is basically concerned with dealings in short and very short-term loans. The main institutions operating in the market are the ten discount houses which are members of the London Discount Market Association, although some banks run money-trading departments which operate in ways similar to discount houses.

The main function of a discount house is to 'discount' a variety of IOUs or 'promises to pay' which are issued by the government, local authorities, banks and companies.

Discounting is the process of buying a security for less than its face value (or redeemable value). For example, if a security which promises to pay £100 in 3 months' time is bought (discounted) by a discount house for £99, the discount house has, in effect, provided the seller of the security with a loan of £99 for 3 months. If it holds the bill for 3 months, until it becomes due for repayment, the discount house will be entitled to a payment of £100 from the person who signed the promise to pay. It will have earned interest equal to £1 for making a loan of £99 for 3 months. The *rate of interest* on this loan is therefore

$$\frac{1}{99} \times \frac{100}{1} \times \frac{4}{1} = 4.04 \text{ per cent per annum}$$

Although this is the true rate of interest (i.e. the yield), the rate of discount is normally based on the face value of the security. Thus, in this example, the *rate of discount* is

$$\frac{1}{100} \times \frac{100}{1} \times \frac{4}{1} = 4 \text{ per cent per annum}$$

Discount houses borrow money on a very short-term basis from various banks in the City of London. Much of this money is borrowed *at call* (i.e. it is repayable on demand) or overnight. The discount houses use these funds to discount a variety of securities including commercial bills and Treasury bills and make profits (or losses) on the difference between the rates of interest they pay on the money they borrow and the rate they charge for discounting securities.

Commercial bills are issued by firms and are a way of financing trade. They are issued for one to twelve, but usually three months. Discount houses are the main buyers of these bills. They sell many of them, at a higher price to the clearing banks. Treasury Bills (see Fig. 46.1) are government securities with a life of 91 days and are the instruments by which the government carries out its short-term borrowing. Each week the government borrows large sums of money by offering Treasury Bills for sale in the money market. They are government promises to pay which do not carry a fixed rate of interest. The system used is one of tendering and each week various financial institutions (e.g. discount houses, branches of overseas banks) are invited to submit bids for the following week's offer of Treasury Bills. The higher the bid price, the lower the rate of interest which the government has to pay for its borrowed funds. For example, if the bid price is £97$\frac{1}{2}$ (per £100 face value), the government is paying slightly more than 10 per cent per annum for a 3-month loan.

The discount houses obtain only a part of the weekly issue although they guarantee to take up the total issue at the prices they offer. Other financial institutions usually outbid them for part of the total issue.

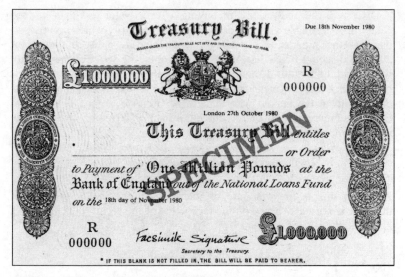

Fig. 46.1   Treasury Bills are issued in denominations of £5000, £10 000, £25 000, £100 000, £500 000 and £1 000 000

Importance of the discount houses

The discount houses perform several useful functions.

- They provide the banks with a convenient form of liquidity. When banks have a temporary surplus of funds they can add to their deposits with the discount houses, and when they are short of funds they can call back their loans to the discount houses.
- They act as market makers in Treasury bills and other short-term securities. They stand ready to buy or sell these items on a regular basis; in other words, they ensure that these credit instruments are liquid assets.
- The discount houses assist the government with its borrowing requirements since they are prepared, if necessary, to take up the entire weekly issue of Treasury bills.
- They provide a vital link between the Bank of England and the rest of the banking system. By operating in the discount market, the central bank can eliminate shortages and surpluses of liquidity in the banking system and can exert an influence on the market rate of interest.

47 Assets and liabilities of the banking sector

Assets are the items a bank owns, for example cash, whereas its liabilities are items which include an obligation to pay out money to the holders in the future, for example, deposits.

The assets and liabilities of the Bank of England

The Bank of England is divided into two departments, the Issue Department and the Banking Department. The Issue Department is responsible for the issuing of notes, and the Banking Department carries out all the other functions. The Bank publishes a weekly return which gives details of the assets and liabilities of the two departments and each year a balance sheet. Table 47.1 shows a copy of one year's balance sheet.

Table 47.1 Bank of England
Balance sheet at 28 February 1994 (£ m.)

	Issue Department		
Liabilities	£	*Assets*	£
Notes in circulation	17 163.5	Government securities	1047.2
Notes in Banking Department	6.5	Other securities	16 122.8
	17 170.0		17 170.0
	Banking Department		
Liabilities		*Assets*	
Public deposits	5402.3	Government securities	1157.1
Special deposits	–	Advances + other accounts	7063.8
Bankers' deposits	1731.8	Premises, equipment + other securities	1545.7
Reserves and other accounts	2624.6	Notes and coin	6.7
Capital	14.6		
	9773.3		9773.3

Source: adapted from Bank of England report and accounts 1994

The Issue Department

Liabilities

The Issue Department's liabilities consist of Bank of England notes in circulation, together with those held in the Banking Department for issue to the clearing banks.

Assets

Government securities include British government securities and government-guaranteed securities, Treasury bills and loans to the National Loans Fund.

Other securities include commercial bills of exchange, local authority bills and some company securities.

Note that the UK note issue is entirely fiduciary – there is no gold backing for UK banknotes.

The Banking Department

Liabilities

Public deposits are the balances held by the central government at the Bank of England.

The government keeps two main accounts at the Bank of England. One is the Exchequer Account. Taxation receipts go into this account and government spending is paid out of this account. The other account is the 'National Loans Fund'. Government borrowing and lending pass through the National Loans Fund.

Special deposits. These are deposits called from other banks when the monetary authorities wish to reduce the liquidity of the banking sector. They are held in a special account because they are not part of the banks' liquid assets – they are 'frozen' assets. No calls for special deposits have been made in recent years.

Bankers' deposits. This item consists of two elements:
a Operational deposits – these are the working balances kept mainly by the clearing banks.
b Cash-ratio deposits – these are the obligatory, non-interest-bearing, non-operational deposits which all recognised banks must maintain at the Bank of England. These deposits must be equal to 0.35 per cent of each bank's eligible liabilities.

Reserves and other accounts include deposits of overseas central banks, some local authority and public corporation accounts, and the Bank's reserves.

Capital is a vestigial item – it is the share capital taken over when the Bank was nationalised.

Assets

Government securities consist of both long-term securities and Treasury bills.

Advances and other accounts are the short-term loans made to the discount houses and loans to other customers.

Premises, equipment and other securities include ordinary shares, local authority bills, and bonds and commercial bills, together with the value of the Bank's physical assets.

Notes and coin are held for issue to the clearing banks. When a clearing bank wishes to obtain a further supply of cash it simply withdraws part of its operational deposit. The following example shows what happens when this takes place.

Example: The effects of a withdrawal of £2 million by the clearing banks would be:

In the Banking Department's account
• Notes and coin in the Banking Department would fall by £2 million.
• Bankers' deposits would fall by £2 million.

In the Issue Department's account
• Notes in circulation would increase by £2 million.
• Notes in the Banking Department would fall by £2 million.

The banking mechanism

A banking problem – liquidity or profitability?

Since banks are joint stock companies, they have an obligation to their shareholders to operate as profitably as they can. They also have an obligation to their depositors which requires them to meet all the depositors' demands for cash. This latter obligation means that the banks' assets must contain an adequate reserve of cash and, additionally, some extremely liquid assets to deal with unexpectedly heavy demands for cash.

These different obligations present the banks with a dilemma because the need for liquidity conflicts with the objective of profitability. The more liquid an asset, the lower its earning power. Cash, the most liquid of assets, earns no income. Short-term loans are liquid assets but they earn lower rates of interest than long-term loans, which are illiquid assets. (Remember that liquidity refers to the ability to convert an asset into cash quickly and easily with little risk of a capital loss.)

Since cash earns no income, banks will try to keep their cash reserves to a minimum. Just how small this cash reserve can be depends upon the banks' ability to obtain income-earning assets which are very liquid. The existence of the money market enables British banks to acquire a variety of such income-earning assets. Loans to the discount houses, to brokers in the money market and to dealers on the Stock Exchange can be recalled immediately or at very short notice. The banks also hold supplies of Treasury bills, commercial bills, and government securities nearing maturity which can be sold to money market institutions at any time with little risk of capital losses.

Liquid assets

The traditional liquid assets of the banks are:

• Cash, i.e. notes, coins and operational balances held at the Bank of England.
• Money market loans.
• Treasury bills, local authority bills and commercial bills.

Less liquid assets

The more profitable, but less liquid, assets held by the banks are:

• Investments. These consist of long-term government securities, although the banks normally buy such securities when they have 5 years or less to run to maturity. These securities earn higher rates of interest than short-term securities and they can be sold at any time on the Stock Exchange. Heavy sales of such securities, however, would drive down their market prices and might cause the banks to suffer capital losses.
• Advances. These are the banks' loans to individuals, firms and the public authorities. They are the most profitable of the banks' assets, and the ones which banks seek to maximise. Interest rates on these loans vary according to the duration of the loan and the credit-worthiness of the borrower.

Table 47.2 is a simplified balance sheet of the UK *retail banks*. These are the familiar High Street banks which offer a full range of banking services. Officially, retail banks are defined as banks which either have extensive branch networks or participate directly in a UK clearing system.

The importance of the banks' balances at the Bank of England

The clearing banks' operational balances at the Bank of England are current accounts from which cash can be withdrawn on demand. The banks therefore include these balances as part of their cash reserves.

The government banks with the Bank of England, and this means that payments between the government and the rest of the economy have direct effects on the banks' operational balances. When households and firms make payments to the government (e.g. payments of taxes), they will do so with cheques drawn on their own banks. This means that the

Table 47.2 An example of a combined balance sheet of the UK retail banks, May 1993 (£ bn)

Liabilities	£	Assets	£
Sterling		*Sterling*	
Notes issued	1.9	Notes and coins	3.3
Sight deposits	182.7	Balances with the	
Time deposits	228.2	Bank of England:	
Certificates of deposit	52.8	Operational deposits	0.1
		Cash ratio deposits	1.4
Other currencies		Loans to discount houses	7.7
Sight and time deposits	72.2	Certificates of deposit	21.3
Certificates of deposit	18.0	Other money market loans	36.1
		Treasury bills	1.6
Sterling and other currencies		Eligible bank bills	81.4
		Other bills	9.4
Capital and other		Advances	379.3
liabilities	829.0	Investments	40.7
		Other currencies	
		Mainly inter-bank loans in UK and loans overseas	773.4
		Sterling and other currencies	
		Miscellaneous assets	29.1
	1384.8		1384.8
Eligible liabilities	405.9		

Source: CSO Financial Statistics 1994

Notes

Many of the items in this balance sheet have been explained earlier.

The *liabilities* consist almost entirely of deposits in sterling and other currencies, together with certificates of deposit issued by the banks. The item 'notes issued' refers to banknotes issued by banks in Scotland and Northern Ireland. The banks are joint stock companies and their capital, which consists of loans from shareholders, is a liability.

On the *assets* side of the balance sheet, balances at the Bank of England consist of the obligatory cash-ratio deposits and the bankers' operational deposits.

Treasury bills and other bills are purchased from the discount houses and bill brokers, and eligible bank bills are those which have been accepted by an eligible bank. The certificates of deposit are those which have been discounted (i.e. purchased) by the banks. Other currency assets are loans made in other currencies; they are claims on borrowers denominated in foreign currencies. In recent years, foreign currency business has grown quite rapidly as a share of total business.

Eligible liabilities are a measure of each bank's sterling resources. They consist mainly of a bank's sterling deposits, excluding those with an original maturity of more than two years.

banks owe money to the government, which the Bank of England settles by reducing the banks' operational deposits. When this happens, the banks' cash reserves are reduced. When the government buys goods and services from households and firms, it does so with cheques drawn on its account at the Bank of England. Households and firms will pay these cheques into their bank accounts, and the Bank of England will owe money to the commercial banks. This debt will be settled by increasing the banks' balances at the Bank of England, and the cash reserves of the banks will increase.

A knowledge of these procedures is important to an understanding of open market operations and of the work of the discount houses, both of which are explained later. Each day, payments between the government and the rest of the economy amount to hundreds of millions of pounds. These flows will not balance – sometimes they leave the banks with a shortage of cash, sometimes with a surplus. The Bank of England can take steps to reduce what it considers to be a surplus of cash in the banking system or to relieve a shortage. It does this through a special relationship with the discount houses.

Operations in the discount market

The discount houses use money borrowed for very short periods of time (much of it 'at call' or 'overnight') to buy the credit instruments described earlier – they are, in fact, making loans. They can normally make profits by charging a higher rate of interest for their loans than the rate they pay for the money they have borrowed. The discount houses are able to do this because they take the risks involved in borrowing 'short' and lending 'long'.

For example, 'call money' may be used to discount 91-day bills. This means that money which is repayable on demand has been used to make a 3-month loan. Now, if the banks are running short of cash, they will react by calling back some of their loans to the discount houses and these houses must honour their promises to repay. But the money they have borrowed is now 'locked up' in bills. The discount houses must find some way of obtaining new loans in order to repay the banks the loans they are recalling.

If only one or a few banks are 'calling', the problem may be solved by borrowing from other banks which happen to have funds to spare. If, however, all the banks are running short of cash and making calls on the discount market, the discount houses will be obliged to borrow from the Bank of England. The central bank will always come to the aid of the discount houses by buying some of their bills or by providing loans against the security of bills. But it will only deal in *eligible bills*.[1]

NOTE 1 Eligible bills consist of Treasury bills, certain local authority bills, and commercial bills accepted by eligible banks.

Although the Bank of England will always meet the discount houses' demands for funds, it is free to set the rate of interest it charges for this assistance. The terms on which the Bank deals with the discount market depend upon its present policy with regard to interest rates.

If it wishes to see an upward movement in the short-term market rate of interest, it will charge a rate of interest higher than the current market rate. Under these circumstances the discount houses will be making some losses on the assistance they obtain from the Bank. In order to repay their loans from the banks, they will have to pay the central bank a higher rate of interest than they have been earning on their own lending. If the discount houses are forced to borrow from the Bank of England at penal rates of interest, they will take steps to correct the situation by raising their own discount rates. Correspondingly, other short-term rates of interest will rise; for example, the banks will raise the rates they charge for call money. If, however, the market is short of cash and the Bank of England does not wish to see any upwards pressure on interest rates, it will tend to supply funds to the discount houses at the current market rate of interest.

If there is a surplus of funds in the banking system, the central bank can reduce it by selling Treasury bills to the discount houses, which will lead to a reduction in the bankers' balances at the Bank of England.

The creation of bank deposits

Bank deposits are created by the banks and not by the state, although the state, as we shall see later, has various ways of controlling the commercial banks' ability to create deposits. Bank deposits come into being in three ways:

1 When a bank receives a deposit of cash (notes and coin).
2 When a bank makes a loan, (advance). This is referred to as credit creation. Since it involves the creation of money.
3 When a bank buys securities with cheques drawn on itself.

1 When a person deposits cash (say £1000) in his bank he receives a bank deposit of the same money value. The value of his personal supply of money has not changed, it has simply changed its form; he now has a bank deposit whereas he previously held notes and coin. The effect of this transaction in the bank's accounts may be represented as follows:

Liabilities	*Assets*
Deposits £1000	Notes and coin £1000

The bank's assets and liabilities have increased by equal amounts. A bank's liabilities consist of claims against the bank. A bank's deposits are liabilities to the bank because it is committed to meet all depositors' demands for cash and to honour all cheques drawn on these deposits. The cash (notes and coin) is an asset because it is a claim against the central bank.

2 The second and more important method by which bank deposits come into being is by means of a bank's lending operations. Lending is the most profitable of a bank's activities (it charges interest on its loans). When a bank makes a loan, say £1000, it credits the account of the borrower with the amount of the loan. In this case the bank has created a bank deposit without any prior deposit of cash. The effect on the bank's accounts will be as follows.

Liabilities	*Assets*
Deposits £1000	Loans £1000

The money supply in this case *has* increased. What has taken place, in fact, is an exchange of claims. The banker has exchanged a claim against himself (i.e. a deposit of £1000) for a claim against the borrower (i.e. a loan of £1000). If you lend me £10, then I acquire an asset together with an equal and opposite liability to repay you the £10. The bankers' loans represent assets because they are claims against the borrowers and banks usually safeguard themselves as far as possible by requiring borrowers to provide some kind of security to cover the value of the loan. This security may take the form of a legal charge against the borrower's property or some good evidence of his ability to repay.

3 Banks may also create deposits by purchasing securities (usually government bonds) with cheques drawn on themselves. The seller of the security will pay the cheque into his bank account and his deposit will increase by the amount he has been paid for his security, say, £1000. There has been no transfer of funds from any other depositor – the total of bank deposits will increase by the amount paid by the bank for the securities. In the bank's books the transaction will have the following effect:

Liabilities	*Assets*
Deposits £1000	Securities £1000

Again, the bank's assets and liabilities have increased by equal amounts.

Cash and liquid assets ratios

The banks cannot create deposits to an unlimited extent. Bank deposits are convertible into cash either immediately (in the case of current accounts) or at relatively short notice (in the case of most time deposits). Banks, therefore, must always be in a position to meet depositors' demands for cash (notes and coin). Deposit banking is based on the principle that all depositors will not simultaneously exercise their rights to withdraw their funds in the form of cash.

Just as the goldsmith-bankers discovered that only a small part of their note issue was likely to be converted into gold on any one day, so modern deposit-bankers realise that, on any one day, only a small part of their total deposits is likely to be 'cashed'. Every day a large number of people will be withdrawing cash from the banks, but it is likely that, at the same time, many other people will be depositing cash. It is the possible *net* withdrawal of cash which concerns the bankers.

Although confidence in modern banks is so great that by far the greater part of total payments (by value) takes the form of transferring deposits by means of cheques, bankers must maintain some safe ratio between their cash reserves and total deposits. In a developed country where cash payments account for a very small percentage of the total value of all transactions, this ratio will be very small and banks will be able to create deposits to a much greater money value than the amount of cash they are holding.

For example, suppose the banks decide that a 5 per cent cash ratio is more than adequate to meet all likely demands for cash. This means that they can create deposits (by making loans) equal to 20 times the value of their cash reserves (since $5\% = 5/100 = 1/20$). In other words, if this banking system is holding £10 million in notes and coin, it can allow its deposits to increase to a maximum value of £200 million. Thereby increasing the money supply by £190 million. Since lending money is the most profitable of a bank's activities, we assume that banks will always try to expand their deposits to the maximum level.

$$\text{Maximum level of bank deposits} = \frac{1}{\text{Cash ratio}} \times \text{Cash reserves}$$

Thus if the cash ratio is 5 per cent,

$$\text{Maximum level of bank deposits} = \frac{1}{\frac{5}{100}} \times \text{Cash reserves}$$
$$= 20 \times \text{Cash reserves}$$

The amount by which deposits (money supply) can change as a result of a change in cash (liquid assets) in the banking system is known as the credit creation (or credit or bank) multiplier. In our example it is 20. In the developed countries one of the main reasons why the banks can operate with such very small cash reserves is the availability of very liquid assets which the banks are able to hold as secondary reserves (see page 394). Unexpectedly heavy demands for cash can be met by converting these liquid (or reserve) assets into cash. Under these conditions, therefore, the amount of cash held by the banks is not the strict regulator of the total value of banks deposits. Banks can always replace any net outflow of cash by converting some of their liquid assets. It does not follow, therefore, that a loss of cash will force the banks to reduce their total lending (i.e. deposit creation). What is critical for the banks is their ability to obtain liquid or reserve assets.

If there is a conventional or legal ratio between the value of the banks' liquid assets and the level of bank deposits, it is the availability of liquid assets which determines the total value of bank deposits. Thus, if the banks are obliged to maintain a supply of specified liquid assets equal to *at least* 10 per cent of total deposits, then bank deposits cannot exceed ten times the value of the liquid assets. More formally we can say that under this system,

$$\text{Maximum value of bank deposits} = \frac{1}{\text{Liquid assets ratio}} \times \begin{matrix}\text{Value of}\\\text{liquid assets}\end{matrix}$$

Thus, if the liquid assets ratio is 10 per cent

$$\text{Maximum value of bank deposits} = \frac{1}{\frac{10}{100}} \times \begin{matrix}\text{Value of}\\\text{liquid assets}\end{matrix}$$

$$= 10 \times \text{Value of liquid assets}$$

Limits on banks' ability to create credit

In addition to the liquidity ratio they keep there are a number of other limits on a bank's ability to create money by making loans (advances).

Banks may have the liquid assets to support advances but they cannot lend if creditworthy individual firms do not want to borrow.

Banks' ability to lend can also be restricted by government policy. There are a number of ways in which the government, through the Bank of England, can seek to influence bank lending and these are discussed in Chapter 61.

48 The value of money

The intrinsic value of money may be negligible; the £5 note regarded as a piece of paper is practically worthless, and its only value arises from its acceptability in exchange.

The value of money to us can only be expressed in terms of what the unit of money will buy and this is determined by the prices of goods and services. When the price of the goods and services we buy rises the value of money falls and likewise falling prices indicate an increase in the value of money so domestic inflation will reduce purchasing power and hence the value of money. A rise in the exchange rate will have the same effect by raising the price of imported goods.

Measuring changes in the value of money

This task would be easy if all prices moved proportionately and in the same direction, but prices do not move in this way. In any given period of time some prices will rise, others will fall and others remain unchanged, and those prices which do move in the same direction will not all move to the same extent. As we have already indicated, different groups of buyers and sellers are interested in different groups of prices. Statisticians deal with this problem by providing measurements of movements in export prices, import prices, commodity prices, wholesale prices, and so on.

We will look at a number of measures of changes in prices (and hence the value of money) but we will devote most attention to the best-known one which is the index of retail prices (more commonly known as the retail price index (RPI), which is a weighted price index.

Index numbers

Index numbers deal with *percentage changes* rather than with absolute changes. The price change of each commodity is expressed in percentage terms and the average of these percentage changes is then calculated. The index number 100 is given to each price in the year on which we base our comparisons. Subsequent price changes are expressed as movements from 100 and then averaged. A simple arithmetic average of the percentage changes in prices indicates that prices in Year 2 are 31.6 per cent higher than they were in Year 1. Prices in subsequent years would be expressed as percentages of those in Year 1 (the base year) and averaged in a similar manner.

Example:

	Year 1		Year 2	
Commodity	Price	Index	Price	Index
A	5p	100	10p	200
B	$12\frac{1}{2}$p	100	15p	120
C	100p	100	75p	75
	3)300		3)395	
	Price Index = 100		Price Index = 131.6	

The index numbers resulting from these calculations would be misleading since each of the commodities is assumed to be of equal importance. In other words a 10 per cent change in the price of Commodity A would have exactly the same impact on the index as a 10 per cent change in the price of Commodity C or Commodity B. In the real world we know that the prices of those things on which we spend a large proportion of our income are far more important to us than the prices of those things we rarely purchase. Changes in the price of bread are of much greater relevance to the mass of consumers than changes in the prices of fur coats. It is possible to overcome this particular difficulty by using a system of weights whereby each commodity is given a weight proportional to its importance in the general pattern of consumer spending. Referring back to the example above, let us suppose that 50 per cent of total consumer spending is devoted to Commodity A, 30 per cent to Commodity B, and 20 per cent to Commodity C. Weights are now allocated in the proportions 5:3:2. The price indices for each year are multiplied by the appropriate weights and the average is obtained by dividing the total of these weighted indices by the total of the weights.

The weighting of the commodities has produced a different result from that obtained in the earlier calculation. The average price movement is now revealed as an increase of 51 per cent, as against 31.6 per cent in the earlier example. This is due to the fact that Commodity A, which had the

Table 48.1 Calculating price indices by weighting commodities according to their importance in consumer spending

Commodity	Weights	Price	Index	Year 1 Weighted index	Price	Index	Year 2 Weighted index
A	5	5p	100	500	10p	200	1000
B	3	$12\frac{1}{2}$p	100	300	15p	120	360
C	2	£1	100	200	75p	75	150
	10			10) 1000			10) 1510
				Price index = 100			Price index = 151

largest percentage price increase, is the commodity which is most heavily weighted.

The index of retail prices

In the United Kingdom official attempts to measure movements in the cost of living began in 1914 with the Cost of Living Index. This was restricted in its coverage since its construction was based on a sample of 2000 'typical working-class' households. It was compiled on the same basis until 1947 when the name was changed to the *Index of Retail Prices*. Subsequently the index has been revised in 1952, 1956, 1962, 1974 and in January 1987. The basic features of the construction of this index are as follows:

- A representative sample of the population is selected and asked to maintain a careful budget of their expenditure over some period of time, usually 1 month.
- These budgets are analysed to provide information on the pattern of consumer spending. From this information we derive a picture of the spending patterns of the 'average family'.
- In the light of the data derived from the expenditure surveys decisions are taken on the range of goods and services to be included in the index and on the weights to be allocated to each class of goods.
- Some particular date is now chosen as the base date and the prices at this date are expressed as 100.
- The prices of the selected commodities are checked each month and the new prices are expressed as percentages of those ruling at the base date.
- The price index is then calculated as shown in Table 48.1.

The earlier indices had weights which were based upon some single prior sample survey of consumer spending. The current index has weights which are revised every year and which are based upon a continuous survey of family spending. The sample of households used for this purpose is now 7000 .

As time has gone by the samples used in the surveys have become more and more representative of the entire population and it is held that the current index is based upon an expenditure survey which is representative of 88 per cent of the whole population. Likewise the list of goods and services included in the index has been gradually extended and now includes more than 350 separate items for many of which information is collected for several different varieties.

The Department of Employment, which is responsible for the calculations, carries out, through its local offices, price checks in some 200 towns of different sizes, distributed geographically according to population densities. Prices are collected from the whole range of retail outlets – small shops, supermarkets, chain stores, department stores, cooperative societies, mail order firms, and so on. The Index of Retail

Prices divides the goods and services covered into 14 main groups, each of which contains a variety of goods and services. For example, the item 'Housing' records changes in the costs of rent, mortgage interest, property insurance, water charges, rates, repair and maintenance and do-it-yourself materials, and the item 'Catering' includes price changes which affect the costs of restaurant meals, canteen meals, take-away foods and snacks. Table 48.2 gives details of the weights used to calculate the index in 1993.

Table 48.2 UK Index of Retail Prices

	Weights used in 1993
Food	144
Catering	45
Alcoholic drinks	78
Tobacco	35
Housing	164
Fuel and light	46
Household goods	79
Household services	47
Clothing and footwear	58
Personal goods and services	39
Motoring expenditure	136
Fuel and other travel costs	21
Leisure goods	46
Leisure services	62
	1000

Source: CSO Annual Abstract of Statistics 1994

Notes
Since the weights add up to 1000, it is easy to express the relative importance of each item as a percentage, by dividing its weight by 10. For example, food accounts for 14.4 per cent of the total weights.

This index was introduced in 1987. Subsequent price changes will be related to the value of 100 in January 1987.

The previous index, based on the prices ruling in 1974, reached a value of 394.5 in January 1987, when it was discontinued.

Coverage of the index of retail prices

In the 1990s increasing use has been made of different versions of the index of retail prices. These versions differ in their coverage.

The headline rate of inflation is the RPI. Whereas RPIX, sometimes referred to as the underlying rate of inflation, is the RPI excluding mortgage interest payments, RPIX is the government's target measure for inflation. RPIY is RPIX excluding indirect and local authority taxes. This is sometimes called core inflation.

Limitations of the index of retail prices

Some of the problems associated with its use are discussed below. The index only attempts to measure changes in retail prices as they affect the *average* family, but are there any such families?

The pattern of consumer spending is always changing. As incomes, tastes, and fashions change, so do the demands for various goods and services. This raises problems with regard to weighting and it is for this reason that the current index allows for a frequent adjustment of the weights.

Many commodities are subject to frequent changes in design, or quality, or performance. Where a price change accompanies the introduction of a new model or an improved design, it is extremely difficult to assess the real nature of the price change. Can we really say what has happened to the prices of furniture, washing machines, television sets, or motor cars over the past 10 years? The price comparisons would not be related to the same products. If the price of a particular make of car increases by 10 per cent, but the quality and performance of the new model is much superior to that of the older model, has the exchange value of the car increased or decreased?

New materials and new products are continually coming into use and causing significant shifts in consumer demand. The introduction of, for example, video recorders and micro-wave ovens has changed spending patterns. In recent years a whole new range of plastics has transformed the nature of household appliances and fittings available to the great majority of households. These changes call for frequent modifications of the weighting structure.

Consumers' shopping habits change. In recent years there has been something of a revolution in the retail trade with the introduction and rapid growth of supermarkets and hypermarkets. Families with deep freezers now undertake bulk buying of many foodstuffs. Nowadays a greater weight must be given to the prices of goods sold in the supermarkets and chain stores and a smaller weight to the prices in the small independent shops.

Other measures of price changes

The Tax and Price Index (TPI)

This was introduced in August 1979. It shows how purchasing power is affected not only by changes in prices but also by changes in direct taxes. In the construction of the index price changes have a weighting of $\frac{3}{4}$ and changes in direct taxes (including National Insurance contributions) have a weighting of $\frac{1}{4}$. The TPI is designed to show the increase in gross income (i.e. income before direct taxes) needed in order to maintain the same level of real net income after taking account of changes in both prices and tax rates and allowances.

The GDP deflator

As we have seen this is used to convert national income figures from current to constant prices taking the effects of inflation out of the figures. The GDP deflator has a wide coverage. It measures changes in consumer goods and, unlike the RPI, changes in capital goods and exports.

The Producer Price Index (PPI)

This measures changes in the price of goods purchased and manu-factured by the UK industrial sector. As it represents the price of goods in their earlier stages of production it is taken as an indicator of future changes in the RPI.

Price movements

We have seen that it is possible, by means of index numbers, to obtain some approximate idea of the extent of the changes in the value of money. The forces which change prices tend to change *all* prices although there will be deviations from the general pattern (e.g. a change of fashion leading to a temporary surplus and hence a lower price when other prices are moving upwards). There are great differences in the flexibility of different prices. The most variable prices are those of raw materials and other primary products which are traded on world markets. A glance at any table of commodity prices (mining and agricultural products) will reveal just how extensive the price variations can be over relatively short periods of time. The explanation lies in the fact that both the demands for and the supplies of these commodities tend to be inelastic. Quite small changes in demand or supply lead to relatively large changes in price. It is significant that most major government schemes to stabilise prices are concerned with primary products.

The prices of manufactured goods tend to be much more stable. The prices of many of these goods are controlled by very large firms and stability of price is important from the point of view of advertising campaigns and production planning. There is also the point that the supplies of manufactured goods tend to be fairly elastic and output can be more easily adjusted to changes in demand.

The long-term tendency is for prices to rise. Over the past seven centuries the average trend of British prices has been an increase of about $1\frac{1}{2}$ per cent per annum. But it would be misleading to interpret this statement as indicating a smooth steady upward movement in prices. There have been periods when prices have been falling and several periods of comparative price stability. The general picture seems to be one of a series of periods when there was a strong upward movement in the price level followed by periods of stable prices or periods when prices were falling. This pattern changed after the Second World War, however. In the post-war period prices have risen continuously. There have been periods when prices were rising quite sharply and periods when prices were rising very slowly, but the movement of prices has always been upwards, albeit with a significant fall in the inflation rate in the mid 1990s. Figure 48.1 shows the average annual percentage increases in the Index of Retail Prices in recent years.

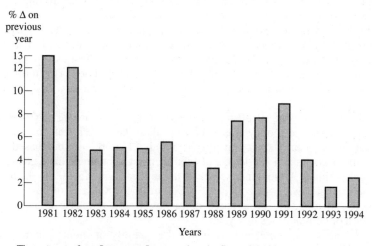

The years run from January to January; thus the figure for 1981 covers the period from January 1980 to January 1981

Source: CSO Monthly Digest of Statistics, August 1994

Fig. 48.1   Annual percentage increase in the Index of Retail Prices, 1981–94

In seeking to explain the cause of changes in the general level of prices some economists make use of the quantity theory of money.

The quantity theory of money

The earliest formulation of the quantity theory of money held that changes in the value of money could be explained by changes in the supply of money. It assumed that the spending habits of the population and the output of goods and services were fairly stable so that the demand for money was also stable. In this situation changes in the value of money could be explained by changes in the quantity available. If we represent the quantity of money by the symbol M and the general price level by the symbol P, the older quantity theory may be expressed in the form,

$M \propto P$

It holds that price changes are directly proportional to changes in the quantity of money. A 10 per cent increase in the money supply would cause a 10 per cent increase in prices.

It should be obvious, however, that changes in the quantity of money may or may not have an influence on prices. It is the act of *spending* which influences prices and, if any increase in the money supply is not spent, it will not influence the prices of goods and services. In this early theory M is seen as the actual stock of money, in the form of coin, notes, and bank deposits. There is, however, another aspect of the supply of money which is much more relevant; namely, the rate at which the supply is used over a given period of time, say 1 year. During a period of 1 year each unit of money may be used several times. The term the *Velocity of Circulation* (V) is used to describe the rate at which money changes hands.

If the total value of all transactions during one year was £20 000 m. and the stock of money was £5000 m., then the velocity of circulation must have been 4 since, on average, each £1 of money purchased £4 worth of goods and services, and each £1 must on average have changed hands 4 times. Although the stock of money was only £5000 m., the total purchasing power was equal to £20 000 m. If the velocity of circulation increased to 5, the same stock of money would purchase £25 000 m. worth of commodities in 1 year.

We have, therefore, two views of the quantity of money. It may be regarded as a stock (M) or as a flow, that is, as a stock of money moving at some given rate. It is the latter view which is important since it is this flow of money which determines the level of spending. The flow of spending will be equal to MV; that is, the quantity of money multiplied by the number of times each unit changes hands.

The value of total expenditure (MV) must be equal to the value of goods and services sold by businesses. If we designate P to stand for the average price level and T to represent the total volume of transactions, PT represents the value of goods and services bought and sold.

The Equation of Exchange

Since MV and PT are simply two different ways of looking at the same thing – the total spending on goods and services – the relationship can be expressed in the form of an equation:

$MV = PT$

This is known as the Equation of Exchange and represents a refinement of the older, or crude, quantity theory. It does not represent a theory but a statement of fact. It is a truism because by definition MV must be equal to PT. It is not a theory because it tells us nothing about the causes of changes in the various quantities. The Equation of Exchange is useful, however, because it identifies and calls our attention to the factors which influence the value of money. The following examples illustrate some of the possible relationships between M, V, P and T.

If we assume that V is constant

- A change in M must lead to a change in P or T, or both.
- If full employment conditions exist, an increase in T is not possible in the short run, so an increase in M will cause an increase in P.
- If unemployed resources are available, output can be increased. An increase in M, therefore, will cause an increase in T, so that P could well remain unchanged.

If we assume that V is not constant

- An increase in M might be accompanied by an increase in V. This would cause total spending to increase by much more than the increase in M. This is one of the causes of very high rates of inflation. When prices begin to rise fairly rapidly, people become reluctant to hold money – they exchange it for goods as quickly as possible.
- It is possible that an increase in M might be accompanied by a fall in V, as people might hold much of the increase in M in idle balances. In this case, an increase in M might have little effect on P or T.

The early quantity theory was based on the assumption that both V and T were constant. It was believed that the pattern of income payments and expenditure changed very slowly and that the economy always tended towards full employment. In other words, changes in M could be related directly to changes in P.

However, the idea that changes in the price level are due entirely to changes in the money supply is very much disputed. Nevertheless certain long-term trends can be partially explained by the quantity theory. Major changes in the price level during the nineteenth century were closely related to movements in the supply of gold (to which the money supply was linked at that time). The great inflations in Germany in the 1920s and in Hungary in the 1940s were both characterised by massive increases in the supply of money.

The revival of the quantity theory

In the 1960s there was a great revival of interest in the quantity theory of money. This was due largely to Professor Friedman and his associates at Chicago University. Friedman's studies and research showed that fluctuations in the national income appeared to follow the fluctuations in the rate of growth of the money supply quite closely. Those economists generally described as Monetarists believe that this relationship is causal; that is, that changes in the money supply *cause* the changes in the level of income.

Opponents of this view say that, if there is such a close relationship, it need not be causal. For example, suppose that firms become more optimistic and decide on programmes of expansion. They approach the banks for loans to finance new investment. They are granted these loans and carry out their plans to increase production. As a result of these developments the statistics will show an increase in GNP and an increase in the money supply. But which was the cause and which was the effect? Monetarists would probably argue that the increase in bank lending was the cause of the increase in GNP. Their critics might argue that the increase in investment demand was the cause of the increase in GNP, and that the increase in the money supply was an effect rather than a cause.

Monetarism and the velocity of circulation

Monetarists believe that there is a fairly stable relationship between the demand for money and total income (nominal GNP). The demand for money is seen as being determined mainly by the transactions motive and for this reason it will be closely related to the level of income.

If we say that the demand for money is a stable function of GNP, we are also saying that V is a stable function of GNP. For example, let us assume that, at any moment of time, people wish to hold money balances equal to 25 per cent of nominal GNP and that the money supply is, in fact, equal to 25 per cent of GNP. This means that the demand for money is equal to the supply of money. In the situation we have described, V will be 4. (This must be so because, if the supply of and demand for money is equal to a quarter of nominal GNP, then, on average, each unit of money must change hands 4 times during the course of the year.) Now assume that the money supply increases and that the demand for money is stable (i.e. a quarter of nominal GNP). People will find themselves holding excess money balances because the money supply is greater than a quarter of nominal GNP. The supply of money is greater than the demand for money, and V will be less than 4. People will try to reduce their money holdings by increasing their rate of spending on goods and services. The effect of this increased expenditure will be to increase nominal GNP. The rate of spending will continue to increase until nominal GNP is once again equal to 4 times the supply of money. The demand for money will then be equal to the supply of money, and V will again be equal to 4. The increase in nominal GNP may be due to an increase in output, an increase in prices, or an increase in both.

The important point here is that a stable V means that a change in the money supply will have a direct and significant effect on the aggregate demand for goods and services, very much as the quantity theory predicts.

There is no clear evidence that V *is* stable. In the short run it appears to be quite unstable, but in the longer run it seems to follow a much more stable trend.

Monetarist and Keynesian theories – some points of difference

Monetarists' views on the effects of changes in the supply of money are rather different from Keynesian ideas on this subject (explained in Chapter 32). In the Keynesian theory, the effects on aggregate demand are indirect – they come about via changes in the rate of interest. For example, an increase in the money supply will cause the rate of interest to fall and this, in turn, will lead to an increase in investment (i.e. spending on capital goods). Keynesians expect this effect to be relatively small, however, because they believe that investment is not very responsive to changes in the rate of interest.

A further reason why Keynesians think that changes in the supply of money will have a relatively small effect on nominal GNP is based on the belief that changes in the rate of interest will have a relatively large effect on the demand for money. For example, an increase in the money supply will lower the rate of interest and this, in turn, will increase the speculative demand for money (see Chapter 32). This means that more of the money supply will be held in idle balances, so that, on average, each unit of money will be used less frequently, i.e. V will fall. Monetarists, on the other hand, think that a change in the rate of interest will have little effect on the demand for money, i.e. that V will remain relatively unaffected.

49 Inflation

Types of inflation

Inflation is a situation in which the general price level is persistently moving upwards.

In an extreme form of inflation, prices rise at a phenomenal rate and terms such as *hyperinflation*, runaway inflation, or galloping inflation have been used to describe these conditions. Germany experienced this kind of inflation in 1923 and by the end of that year prices were one million million times greater than their pre-war level.

Under conditions of hyperinflation people lose confidence in the currency's ability to carry out its functions. It becomes unacceptable as a medium of exchange and other commodities, such as cigarettes, are used as money. When things have become as bad as this the only possible course of action is to withdraw the currency and issue new monetary units.

Another type of inflation is described as *suppressed inflation*. This refers to a situation where demand exceeds supply, but the effect on prices is minimised by the use of such devices as price controls and rationing.

The most common type of inflation is that experienced since the war in Britain and most other developed countries. This is *creeping inflation* where the general price level rises at an annual rate between 1 and 6 per cent.

Traditionally Keynesians have classified the causes of inflation as demand-pull or cost-push.

Demand inflation

Demand inflation may be defined as a situation where aggregate demand persistently exceeds aggregate supply at current prices so that prices are being 'pulled' upwards.

Full employment

All economists agree that once the nation's resources are fully employed, an increase in demand must lead to an upward movement of prices. This is illustrated in Fig. 49.1 which shows that the increase in aggregate demand from AD to AD^1 occurring at the full employment level of real national income results in a rise in the general price level from OP to OP^1.

Conditions of excess demand when there is full employment can arise in several different ways. Wartime conditions provide a good example. War brings full employment, a large increase in the numbers at work,

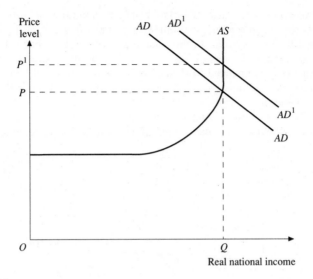

Fig. 49.1

and a great deal of overtime working. The net result is a large increase in total income and hence in potential demand. On the other hand, the supply of consumer goods and services will fall as resources are diverted to meet military demands. In the markets for consumer goods, demand will be much greater than supply at current price levels. During wartime the excess demand is not allowed to exert its full effect on the price level. The government imposes price controls on essential commodities and supports these price controls with a system of rationing. Large-scale savings campaigns and heavy taxation are also used to remove some of the excess demand.

A situation of excess demand may arise when a country is trying to achieve an export surplus, in order, perhaps, to pay off some overseas debt. Exports are inflationary because they generate income at home, but reduce home supplies. Imports, of course, can make good this deficiency of home supplies, but if exports are greater than imports there will be excess demand in the home market unless taxes and savings are increased to absorb the excess purchasing power.

Demand inflation might develop when, with full employment, a country tries to increase its rate of economic growth. In order to increase the rate of capital accumulation, resources will have to be transferred from the production of consumer goods to the production of capital goods. Incomes will not fall since the factors of production are still fully employed, but the supply of the things on which these incomes may be spent will fall. Unless taxation and/or savings increase there will be excess demand and rising prices.

Another possible cause of inflation under conditions of full employment is an expansion of government spending financed by borrowing from the banking system. In this case the expenditure is being financed by an increase in the money supply. Even where the additional government spending is financed from taxation the effect may still be inflationary since the additional taxes might reduce private saving rather than private spending.

Figure 49.2 shows planned expenditure increasing above the full employment level of income and an inflationary gap of *ab* being created.

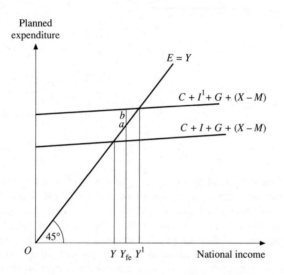

Fig. 49.2

Less than full employment

It is possible that increases in aggregate demand can result in a rise in the general price level at less than full employment, if output cannot be adjusted proportionately. Supply constraints can arise due to shortages of skilled labour, lack of availability of raw materials and components and a shortage of skilled entrepreneurs. Figure 49.3 shows an increase in aggregate demand causing a rise in both output and the general price level as bottlenecks begin to be experienced.

We have shown how excess aggregate demand can cause prices to rise but why should they continue to rise? An inflationary process of the demand-induced type is usually explained in terms of the conditions in the markets for the factors of production, especially those in the labour market.

When firms can sell more goods and services than they are producing, they will increase their demands for the factors of production and since these are already fully employed their prices will rise. For example, firms

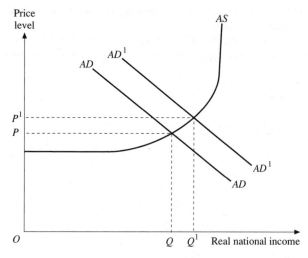

Fig. 49.3

will have to bid up wages in order to tempt workers away from their existing jobs. If, as is most likely, the rise in wages exceeds any increase in productivity, costs will rise and business people will pass on these higher costs in the form of higher prices. Where demand persistently exceeds supply, firms will have little fear that the higher prices will reduce the demands for their products. But the increases in wages, salaries, and other factor incomes will mean that aggregate demand will also rise, so that once again we have excess demand – and so the process will go on. Prices in the markets for goods and in the markets for factors of production are being pulled upwards.

Cost-push inflation

Initiating factors

Cost-push inflation describes a situation where the process of rising prices is initiated and sustained by rising costs which push up prices. It must not be confused with a situation where excess demand is causing entrepreneurs, faced with shortages, to bid up the prices of factors of production. In such cases the passing on of the higher costs in the form of higher prices is a feature of demand inflation.

Cost inflation occurs when prices are forced upwards by increases in factor prices (i.e. costs) which are *not* caused by excess demand. There are several ways in which costs may rise independently of the state of demand.

One example of a supply shock which will shift the short run supply curve is a rise in the price of imported materials. Under these circumstances domestic costs, and hence prices, are increased whatever the level of domestic demand.

This is illustrated in Fig. 49.4 which shows the rise in costs of production moving the aggregate supply curve to the left and pushing up the general price level.

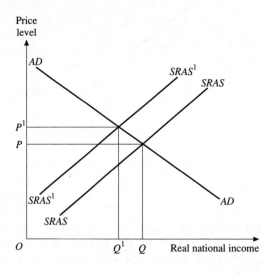

Fig. 49.4

An increase in indirect taxation (i.e. taxes on goods and services) is another way of giving the general price level an inflationary 'push'. Again prices would rise regardless of the state of demand. Possibly the most common cause of cost-push inflation, however, is an *increase in wages which exceeds any increase in productivity*. Any of these events may initiate a rise in prices – we have to explain why that rise continues.

The inflationary process

An increase in indirect taxes will lead to a once-and-for-all rise in prices. Import prices may rise for several months, but eventually they level out or begin to fall. These things cause prices to rise, but they do not explain the continuous process of rising prices.

It is the wage-price spiral which is the most common feature of cost inflation. An increase in wages which is designed to compensate for an increase in prices will generate a further increase in prices which in turn leads to another round of wage increases and so it goes on. The compensating wage rise which exceeds the growth in productivity appears to be the main explanation for the persistent rise in prices which is the feature of cost inflation.

Cost inflation continues of course because the increases in costs which lead to price increases are also increases in income. Factor prices are costs to the entrepreneur, but incomes to the factors of production, so that although prices increase so does the ability to pay these higher prices. An increase in costs is followed by an increase in demand.

It can be shown that if wages were to increase by no more than the amount strictly necessary to compensate for the increase in the price level, the inflationary sequence would gradually peter out. Wages make up only part of total costs so that an increase in wages would not lead to a corresponding increase in prices. For example, if wages make up 70 per cent of total costs, a 10 per cent increase in wages (no change in productivity) would cause prices to rise by 7 per cent. A compensating wage increase (an attempt to maintain real income) would now lead to a price increase of 4.9 per cent and so on. There must be other elements contributing to the price increases if the inflationary process is to continue. Either wages must be increasing by far more than is necessary to offset the price increases or the other elements in prices (e.g. profits) must be increasing proportionately with wages.

A comparison of demand and cost-push inflation

Demand inflation is likely to be associated with either full employment or rising employment, whereas it is possible that cost-push inflation may be associated with rising unemployment. Figure 49.3 shows output declining which is likely to be matched by a rise in unemployment. The appropriate policies to be adopted will also be influenced by the cause of inflation.

Monetarist explanations of inflation

Monetarists believe that the main cause of inflation is the growth of the money supply. Many of them think that this is the sole cause. They argue that excess demand or rising costs are symptoms of inflation and not the cause. Monetarist theory holds that there is a strong direct connection between the supply of money and total spending. This means that if the money supply is allowed to grow at a faster rate than the output of goods and services (real GNP), the inevitable effect will be inflation. Nominal GNP will be increasing at a faster rate than real GNP.

The monetarist theory is based on the quantity theory which we discussed in Chapter 48. Monetarists assume that V and T are constant so that a change in the money supply has a direct and proportionate effect on the price level.

Monetarists believe a rise in the money supply will increase aggregate demand. In the short run this will increase output (and employment). Figure 49.5 shows the aggregate demand curve shifting to the right AD^1 and aggregate supply extending. However in the long run, as wages and costs rise, the short run aggregate supply curve will move to the left to $SRAS^1$. There is a move up the vertical long run aggregate supply curve and output returns to its previous level but at a higher price level. (This is discussed in more detail in Chapter 50.)

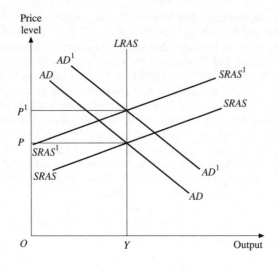

Fig. 49.5

Keynesian views of inflation and the money supply

Economists agree that inflation is a monetary phenomenon in the sense that it will be combined with an increase in the money supply. However, whilst monetarists believe that inflation is caused by increases in the money supply, Keynesians believe that inflation causes an increase in the money supply. If the general price level is rising, firms and individuals will borrow more to meet higher costs and prices, and the resulting higher bank lending will increase the money supply.

The effects of inflation

Inflation can have a number of effects, many of which are considered undesirable.

The effects on the distribution of income

Inflation leads to an arbitrary redistribution of real income. Although a rise in the general price level produces a corresponding rise in money incomes, all prices do not rise to the same extent and different income groups will be affected in different ways. There will be some 'gainers' and some 'losers'.

The losers are those whose incomes are fixed, or relatively fixed, in money terms. This group will include people whose income is derived from fixed interest securities, controlled rents, or some private pension schemes. Income recipients in this category will experience a fall in their real incomes.

When incomes are directly related to prices, real income will remain relatively unchanged. The incomes of sales people, and professional groups such as architects, surveyors, and estate agents whose fees are expressed as a percentage of the value of the work undertaken, fall into this category. A large number of wage earners also come into this group since many workers have agreements which link their money wages to the Retail Price Index.

The effects on incomes derived from profits depend largely upon the kind of inflation being experienced. During demand-pull inflation, profits tend to rise. The prices of final goods and services tend to be more flexible in an upwards direction than many factor prices, some of which are fixed on fairly long-term contracts. The margins between the two price levels tends to widen because of this time lag. When there is cost-push inflation, profits may be squeezed. Since there is no excess demand some firms may find it rather difficult to pass on the full effects of rising costs in the form of higher prices.

Wage earners generally more than hold their own when the price level is rising. In the UK and most other industrial countries wages in most years have risen faster than prices, but, as already mentioned, there tends to be some redistribution effect as those with superior bargaining power gain at the expense of the weaker groups.

Inflation tends to encourage borrowing and discourage lending because debtors 'gain' and creditors 'lose'. Debtors repay in monetary units which have less purchasing power than those which they borrowed. If a person borrows a sum of money for 2 years during which time inflation is running at 10 per cent per annum, the same sum repayable at the end of the term will be worth about 17 per cent less in real purchasing power than the sum of money borrowed. It is for this reason that lenders demand higher rates of interest during periods of inflation.

There can be a transfer of income from taxpayers to the government if fiscal drag occurs. Fiscal drag is when tax payers are dragged into higher tax brackets when their money incomes rise and as a result experience lower real incomes. However, governments now usually adjust tax brackets in line with inflation to prevent this occurring.

Effects on production

Demand-pull inflation is associated with buoyant trading conditions and sellers' markets where the risks of trading are greatly reduced. These easy market conditions might give rise to complacency and inefficiency since the competitive pressure to improve both product and performance will be greatly weakened. This is not likely to be the case in a cost-push inflation where trading conditions are likely to place a premium on greater efficiency. Where firms cannot absorb some of the higher factor prices by improving productivity they may find it difficult to survive. It is possible that employers seeking to hold down costs will react to rapidly rising wage costs by devising means of economising in their use of labour and hence raise the level of unemployment.

Demand inflation, it is sometimes argued, is conducive to a faster rate of economic growth since the excess demand and favourable market conditions will stimulate investment and expansion. The falling value of money, however, may encourage spending rather than saving and so reduce the funds available for investment. It may also lead to higher interest rates as creditors demand some additional return to compensate for the falling value of money. Nevertheless relatively high nominal rates of interest may not be a deterrent to investment. If the nominal rate of interest is 10 per cent, but the rate of inflation is 8 per cent, the 'real' rate of interest is only 2 per cent.

Inflation can raise firms' costs. There may be menu costs (i.e., costs included in altering prices), shoe-leather costs (costs experienced in moving money around to gain high interest rates and estimating what is a 'fair' price) and costs involved in calculating the future prices that will have to be paid for raw materials, etc.

Effects on the balance of payments

In economies such as the UK which are dependent upon a high level of exports and imports, inflation often leads to balance of payments difficulties. If other countries are not inflating to the same extent, home-produced goods will become less competitive in foreign markets and foreign goods will become more competitive in the home market. Exports will be depressed and imports will rise. If this process continues it must lead to a balance of payments deficit on the current account. The problem will be a particularly difficult one where inflation is of the demand-pull type, because in addition to the price effects the excess demand at home will tend to 'draw in' more imports. These balance of payments effects apply particularly where a country is operating a fixed rate of exchange. As we shall see in Chapter 56 a floating rate of exchange means that the rise in home prices does not have such an unfavourable effect on the volumes of exports and imports.

Although there is the risk that a vicious spiral can develop with inflation lowering the exchange rate, which in turn, raises the price of imported goods and thereby further contributes to inflation.

Counter-inflationary policies, which themselves will affect firms and consumers, are discussed in Chapter 64.

50 The relationship between inflation and unemployment

For a number of decades now politicians and economists have debated whether a relationship exists between inflation and unemployment and if so what form the relationship takes.

The traditional Phillips Curve

Work by an economist Bill Phillips, at the London School of Economics published in 1958 suggested that a stable relationship existed between unemployment and money wages. He based his findings on figures for unemployment and money wages over the period 1861 to 1957.

This work was developed to suggest a trade-off between unemployment and inflation (as measured by changes in money wages). This relationship is illustrated by the Phillips Curve.

The Phillips Curve shows that when unemployment is low inflation is high and when unemployment is high inflation is low, i.e., an inverse

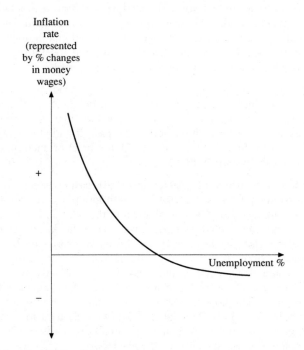

Fig. 50.1   The Phillips Curve

relationship. When unemployment is low workers will be in a strong position to press for wage rises. Whereas when unemployment is high more workers compete for each job and wage rises are held down. It also shows that money wages are sticking downwards. Once the curve passes below the horizontal axis it flattens out since even if unemployment rises to high levels workers will resist cuts in their money wages.

The Phillips Curve implies that a government can choose its preferred combination of unemployment and inflation. For example, it can decide to aim for low unemployment if it is prepared to accept high inflation.

Reaction against the Phillips Curve

In the late 1960s and throughout the 1970s the Phillips Curve came in for considerable criticism. This was based on two grounds, one theoretical and the other empirical.

Milton Friedman, the American monetarist economist, argued that workers are concerned with real and not money wages and that whilst there may be a short-term trade-off relationship between unemployment and inflation there is no long-term relationship. He developed the expectations-augmented Phillips Curve to explain this difference between the short- and and long-run positions. His analysis led him to conclude that governments could not reduce unemployment by increasing demand. This view was taken up by the Labour Government in 1976 and in a famous speech the then Prime Minister, James Callaghan, rejected the Phillips Curve relationship and the Keynesian solution to unemployment

It used to be thought that a nation could just spend its way out of recession and increase employment by cutting taxes and boosting government spending. I tell you in all candour that, that option no longer exists. In so far as it existed in the past, it had always led to a bigger dose of inflation, followed by a higher level of unemployment. (Speech to Labour party conference).

The period of the late 1960s, 1970s and 1980s cast considerable doubt on the inverse relationships suggested. Both inflation and unemployment rose. Keynesians explained this breakdown in the relationship by calling attention to the unexpected external inflationary shock caused by the OPEC oil price rises in the mid 1970s and early 1980s and by labour market imperfections. It was claimed that labour markets changed with the labour force being divided into two groups, the insiders and the outsiders. The insiders were those in work and the unskilled who had recently become unemployed. Whereas the outsiders were the long-term unemployed lacking skills. This latter group were thought to have little influence on pay so that as their number increased it did not have the effect of moderating wage claims by the insiders.

The expectations-augmented Phillips Curve

Milton Friedman's view that workers and employers will not suffer from money illusion in the long run but that it will take time for peoples' expectations to adjust to changes in prices and money wages is illustrated in his expectations-augmented Phillips Curve. This is shown in Fig. 50.2.

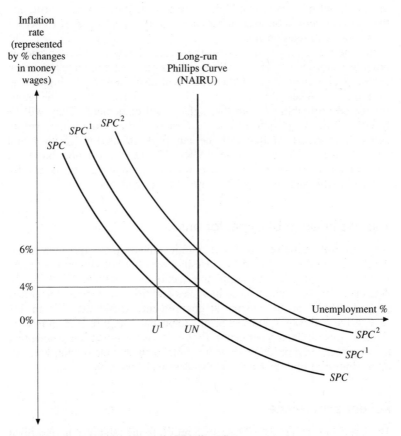

Fig. 50.2   Expectations-augmented Phillips Curve

Let us assume that unemployment is at the NAIRU level (see Chapter 44) and that the rate of inflation is stable at 4 per cent per annum. This will be the *expected* rate of inflation, and wage settlements will be linked to it so that real wage rates will be constant. Now assume that the government tries to reduce the level of unemployment to U_1 by increasing aggregate demand. The effect will be an increase in prices, and production will become more profitable because many costs will not change immediately: wages, for example, are normally adjusted annually.

The expected and actual rate of inflation differ

The increase in demand, therefore, will lead to an increase in prices, an increase in output and an increase in employment. Unemployment may fall to U_1 but now there is a higher rate of inflation, say 6 per cent, and the economy moves on to a higher short-run Phillips Curve, SPC^2 with a worse trade-off relationship.

In time 6 per cent will become the expected rate of inflation and, in order to restore the level of real wages, workers will negotiate 6 per cent increases in money wages. Other costs will also adjust to the higher rate of inflation. When this happens, firms will have lost all the gains (increased profitability) from the higher level of demand. They will be faced with the same ratio of costs to prices as they experienced before demand increased. Output will be cut back to its former level and unemployment will return to the NAIRU. The rate of inflation, however, will remain at 6 per cent because wages and other costs have fully adjusted to this annual rate of increase in the price level.

The importance of expectations

If people fully anticipate that a change in government expenditure (and the money supply) will lead to a rise in prices but not output, then there will be no long-run and no short-run effect on employment. Workers will demand a proportioate increase in wages and firms will raise their prices proportionately. So the change in government expenditure will, in this case, leave real wages and real profits unchanged. Figure 50.3 shows the economy operating at 5 per cent inflation. A rise in government spending has no effect, short or long run, on unemployment and the economy moves up the long-run Phillips Curve, in this case to 10 per cent.

Recent experience

The late 1980s and early 1990s saw a return to the relationship described in the traditional Phillips Curve. As Table 50.1 shows, inflation and unemployment moved in opposite directions. In the consumer boom of the late 1980s increased spending reduced unemployment whilst contributing to inflation. In the early 1990s the effect of the recession and the reduction in expectation of inflation resulted in unemployment rising and inflation falling.

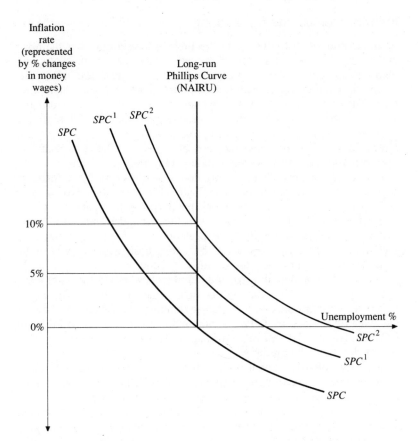

Fig. 50.3

Table 50.1 Inflation and unemployment

Year	Inflation % (ΔRPI)	Unemployment %
1986	5.5	11.1
1987	3.9	10.0
1988	3.3	8.1
1989	7.5	6.3
1990	7.7	5.8
1991	9.0	8.1
1992	4.1	9.8
1993	1.7	10.3
1994	2.5	9.9

Source: CSO *Annual Abstract of Statistics* 1994, *Monthly Digest of Statistics* August 1994

Inflation versus unemployment

From the mid 1970s to the end of the 1980s price stability was the price objective of UK governments. However in the 1990s with continuing high unemployment and low inflation many economists and some politicians shifted their focus from reducing inflation to reducing unemployment. The costs of unemployment are very evident, not evenly spread and whilst, in theory, it is possible to cushion the unemployed from the financial costs, it is very difficult to protect them from the psychological effects. Whereas not only may the costs of moderate inflation be relatively low, there may be costs in lowering inflation further.

Zero or a very low level of inflation is not necessarily a desirable objective. It may change consumers' attitudes. Instead of buying now before prices rise they may postpone purchases in the hope that prices will fall. Firms which had previously benefited from demand pull inflation (expanding and innovating in the expectation of rising profits) may now seek to improve their profit margins by cutting costs which may be at the expense of employment and the quality of products.

The real debt burden of firms, and individuals who had taken out loans in the expectation of inflation will be higher than anticipated. There may be a reverse money illusion with people thinking that the returns they are receiving on savings are falling as nominal interest rates fall in line with inflation, leaving the real rate unchanged. This may encourage them to seek higher but riskier returns.

Very low inflation may also make it more difficult for firms to adjust their costs in the face of falling demand. With inflation it may be possible to cut real wages but with zero or very low inflation, money wages may have to be cut. This may provoke industrial unrest and if it proves difficult to reduce wage rates, employers may take the alternative option of making some workers redundant.

51 The nature of international trade

Unique features of international trade

International trade involves the exchange of goods and services across international boundaries. It differs from internal trade in a number of ways. There may be restrictions imposed by governments and international organisations on the movement of products into, and sometimes out of, countries. Communication may be difficult during the trading process. Higher costs may also be involved including possibly greater transport costs, the need to translate advertising messages and related literature into other languages, the need to explore and keep up to date with changes in tastes in foreign markets and the need to change currencies. Firms may also face differences in technical and legal requirements in overseas markets. There are also extra risks involved in international trade including wars and famines abroad.

Benefits of trade

As well as the costs and uncertainty involved in international trade there are benefits. Indeed, firms engage in international trade because they believe that the benefits outweigh the costs. Engaging in international trade gives firms access to larger markets enabling them to take greater advantage of economies of scale. They may also be able to purchase raw materials and component parts more easily and more cheaply.

Consumers can also gain from international trade. They are able to purchase goods not made in their own countries, have access to a greater variety of products and can benefit from increased competition in the form of lower-priced and better-quality products.

The overriding benefit claimed for international trade is that, by enabling the principle of division of labour to be extended to the international arena, it increases world output and hence raises the material standard of living.

The pattern of UK trade

The UK exports and imports mainly finished manufactured products and trades mainly with countries possessing similar markets to our own. Table 51.1 and Fig. 51.1 show that most of our trade is now with other members of the European Union, although a number of non-members including the USA and Japan also figure prominently.

Table 51.1 The UK's main trading partners 1993

	Most important providers of imports to the UK	*Most important recipients of exports from the UK*
1	Germany	Germany
2	USA	USA
3	France	France
4	Netherlands	Netherlands
5	Japan	Belgium & Luxembourg
6	Belgium & Luxembourg	Irish Republic
7	Italy	Italy
8	Irish Republic	Spain
9	Switzerland	Sweden
10	Norway	Japan

Source: CSO *Monthly Digest of Statistics* July 1994

The basis of trade

International trade arises because the production of different kinds of goods requires different kinds of resources used in different proportions and the various types of economic resources are unevenly distributed throughout the world. The international mobility of resources is extremely limited. Land is obviously immobile in the geographical sense. The international movement of labour is restricted by barriers of language and custom and most nations now impose restrictions on immigration. Capital is more mobile geographically but it only crosses international boundaries when particularly favourable conditions exist (e.g. political stability, no threats of confiscation, no barriers to taking profits out of the country, etc.).

Since it is very difficult to move resources between nations, the goods which 'embody' the resources must move. Nations which have an abundance of land relative to labour will concentrate on 'land-intensive' commodities such as wheat and meat. They will exchange these goods for 'labour-intensive' products such as manufactures made by countries which have an abundance of labour and capital relative to land. Just as our individual abilities and aptitudes fit us for different occupations, so the different resources and the historical development of nations equip them for the production of different products. Unlike individuals, nations do not specialise completely in one process or in one product. They tend to concentrate on certain types of activity, but even the greatest importers of food grow some of their own requirements, and importers of manufactured goods carry out some manufacturing.

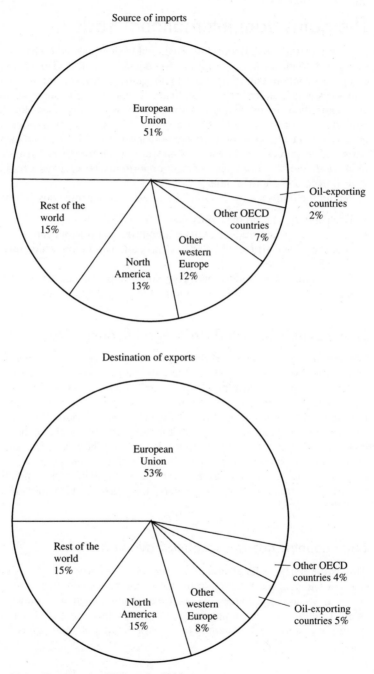

Source of imports

European
Union
51%

Oil-exporting
countries
2%

Rest of the
world
15%

Other OECD
countries
7%

Other
western
Europe
12%

North
America
13%

Destination of exports

European
Union
53%

Rest of the
world
15%

Other OECD
countries 4%

North
America
15%

Other
western
Europe
8%

Oil-exporting
countries 5%

Fig. 51.1   The pattern of UK trade, 1993

The gains from international trade

We know that in the real world international trade is carried on by a large number of countries in a vast range of goods and services. This is a very complex situation but it is possible to gain an understanding of the principles which underlie this complicated economic structure by using a very simplified model. For this purpose we assume that there are two countries, Country A and Country B; only two commodities are produced, tractors and wool; there are no barriers to trade and no transport costs and resources within each country are easily transferred from one industry to another. There are constant opportunity costs as resources are moved from one use to another.

Within the limits set by this model we can consider three possibilities.

- Each country can produce only one of the commodities.
- Each country can produce both commodities, but tractors can be produced more efficiently in one country and wool more efficiently in the other.
- Each country can produce both commodities, but one of the countries can produce both commodities more efficiently than the other.

Each country can produce only one commodity

We need not spend much time discussing this first possibility because the gains from trade are self-evident. International trade greatly increases the variety of goods available to each country. These particular circumstances were the basis for most of the earlier examples of international trade and they still explain a great deal of present-day trade. Britain, for example, must rely on foreign trade for some of her raw materials and part of her food supply. It does not, however, explain the major part of international trade, because this takes place between countries which could well produce for themselves the goods which they import. The greatest producer of cars, the USA, is also the greatest importer of cars.

Each country has an absolute advantage

This is the fairly realistic situation where each country is more efficient than the other in the production of one of the commodities. Country B, we will assume, produces wool more efficiently than Country A, while Country A has the advantage in producing tractors. We can use a simple arithmetical example to illustrate the potential gains from trade.

	Tractors		Wool (bales)
With x resources Country A can produce (per annum)	20	or	100
With x resources Country B can produce (per annum)	10	or	150

It is fairly easy to show that greater specialisation will increase total output. Suppose Country A moves 2x resources from wool production to tractor production and Country B moves 2x resources from tractors to wool. The effect on total output would be,

	Tractors	Wool
In Country A	+40	−200
In Country B	−20	+300
Net gain	+20	+100

Let us now suppose that each of these countries has 10x resources and in the absence of international trade each country devotes half it resources to each industry.

	Tractors		Wool
Country A will produce	100	and	500
Country B will produce	50	and	750
Total output	150	and	1250

Now if international trade were possible these countries would tend to specialise. We shall assume that they specialise completely.

	Tractors		Wool
Country A now produces	200	and	0
Country B now produces	0	and	1500
Total output	200	and	1500

As one would expect, total output is much greater when the countries specialise. In order to obtain the benefits of specialisation these countries must exchange some part of their individual outputs, but the rate at which they exchange wool for tractors must be beneficial to *both* countries. We cannot specify the exact rate of exchange, but we can identify the limits within which the exchange rate must lie. It will be somewhere between the *domestic opportunity cost ratios* of the two countries.

In Country A the 'cost' of 1 tractor is 5 bales of wool since this is the output of wool which must be forgone in order to produce 1 tractor. Country A, therefore, will not accept less than 5 bales of wool for each tractor since she can obtain wool on these terms by transferring resources at home. Similarly, Country B will not offer more than 15 bales of wool for 1 tractor since she can obtain tractors at this 'price' by using her own resources. The domestic opportunity costs ratios are,

	Tractors		Wool
In Country A	1	:	5
In Country B	1	:	15

In order to be favourable to both countries, the exchange rate must lie between these ratios. Let us suppose that it settles at 1 tractor for 10 bales of wool and 70 tractors are exchanged for 700 bales of wool. After trade, therefore, the position is as follows.

	Tractors		Wool
Country A now has annual supply of	130	and	700
Country B now has annual supply of	70	and	800
Total output	200	and	1500

Both countries are clearly better off than when they were operating on a basis of self sufficiency. A now has 30 more tractors and 200 more bales of wool. B now has 20 more tractors and 50 more bales of wool. In Fig. 51.2 we have used the figures from the above example to provide a diagrammatic representation of the situation in Country B before and after specialisation and trade.

Each country has a comparative advantage

We now turn to the third of the possibilities mentioned earlier. One country is more efficient than the other in the production of both commodities. We shall assume that Country A is the more efficient country; it has an *absolute advantage* over Country B in both industries. It can be shown that even in these circumstances it is possible for specialisation and trade to benefit both countries. The principle involved is known as the *Principle of Comparative Costs*. This states that even

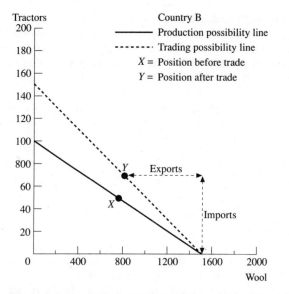

Country B can produce any combination of tractors (T) and wool (W)
on the line joining 100 tractors and 1500 wool. It chooses the
combination represented by (50T and 750W) when trading possibilities
are not available. When trading opportunities arise, Country B specialises
in wool which exchanges internationally at the rate of 10W for 1T.
It now chooses position Y.

Fig. 51.2

where one country has an absolute advantage over the other in both
industries, specialisation and trade can benefit both countries providing
each country has a *comparative cost advantage*. Comparative cost relates
to the opportunity costs of producing the commodities and not the
absolute costs. The best way of explaining the idea is to make use of a
simple arithmetical example.

	Tractors		Wool (bales)
With x resources Country A can produce either	20	or	200
With x resources Country B can produce either	10	or	150

Quite clearly in terms of resources used, the costs of production in both
industries are lower in Country A. If we look at the opportunity costs,
however, the picture is rather different. In Country A the 'cost' of 1

tractor is 10 bales of wool, while in Country B it is 15 bales of wool. Country A has a *comparative advantage* in tractors. In Country A the cost of a bale of wool is 1/10 of a tractor, while in Country B the cost is 1/15 of a tractor. In terms of the output of tractors forgone, wool is cheaper in Country B than in Country A. Country B has a *comparative advantage* in wool.

Let us now assume that each country has 10x resources and in the absence of international trade devotes half its resources to each industry.

	Tractors		*Wool*
Country A produces	100	and	1000
Country B produces	50	and	750
Total output	150	and	1750

If trading possibilities arise, each country will tend to specialise, but in this case if they specialise completely, we find that the total output of tractors increases, but the output of wool falls. Each country will specialise in that industry in which it has a comparative advantage so that complete specialisation would give us, 200 tractors and 1500 bales of wool. It is possible to show that the increase in the output of tractors, in value terms, more than offsets the fall in the output of wool, but this is not really necessary because by partially specialising the more efficient country can have more of both commodities. Thus if Country A devotes 2x resources to wool and 8x resources to tractors while Country B specialises completely in wool we have the following situation.

	Tractors		*Wool*
Country A produces	160	and	400
Country B produces	0	and	1500
Total output	160	and	1900

We now have a greater total output of both commodities than that which obtained when both countries were producing only for domestic consumption. As explained earlier the fact that the opportunity cost ratios are different in the two countries means that beneficial trade is possible.

Some qualifications

1 The gains from trade are modified by the existence of transport costs and tariffs. The economic effects of these are very similar since in both cases the cost of moving the goods is increased. In the case of transport costs the increase in price is unavoidable, whereas in the case of tariffs the cost increase is 'artificial' because it is the result of a policy decision and, therefore, reversible.

2 The theory outlined above is based on the unrealistic assumption that the opportunity cost ratios remain ûnchanged as resources are moved from one industry to another. In the last example we assumed that every time Country A moved x resources from wool production to tractor production, the output of wool fell by 200 bales and the output of tractors increased by 20 units. This is not very likely since some resources will be more efficient in one industry than the other. In other words, as the degree of specialisation increases we are likely to encounter the law of diminishing returns.

3 As opposed to the preceding point it is very possible that increasing specialisation will yield advantages in the form of economies of scale. This is most likely in the manufacturing industries.

4 Comparative cost advantages are always changing. New methods of production, the use of newer types of raw materials, improvements in transport, and changes in market conditions will change the relative efficiencies of different countries in different types of economic activity. In the nineteenth century a substantial world lead in technology gave the UK a very great comparative advantage in the production of cotton cloth. In the later twentieth century she has become a net importer of cotton cloth.

5 The shifting nature of comparative cost advantages points to a major danger of over-specialisation and of too great a dependence on foreign trade. A country which concentrates most of its resources on a very narrow range of industries is very vulnerable to economic change.

6 International trade leads to greatly enlarged markets and increases the extent of competition. It should, therefore, stimulate efficiency.

7 In practice the exchange rate may not lie within the opportunity cost ratios and may benefit developed countries at the expense of third-world countries.

52 Protectionism

Protectionism is the restriction of international trade. It prevents consumers and sellers reaching the equilibrium price and quantity that would prevail in a free market. Every major trading nation operates some form of restriction on its trade with the rest of the world.

Methods of protection

Tariffs

The tariff is the most well-known barrier to trade. It acts in exactly the same way as a tax by artificially raising the price of the foreign product as it enters the country. Tariffs may be *ad valorem*, that is, a percentage of the monetary value of the import, or *specific*, that is, a tax per unit of weight or physical quantity.

Figure 52.1 shows the effect of a specific tariff. Domestic demand is shown by the domestic demand curve (*DD*) and domestic supply by the domestic supply curve (*DS*). When the country engages in free trade the price is set where domestic demand equals the world supply (*WS*). In this situation domestic consumers purchase *OM* amount at a price of *OP*. *OJ* quantity is supplied by domestic producers and *JM* quantity is imported. The imposition of a tariff shifts the world supply to WS^1. This raises the price to P^1 and reduces the quantity bought and sold to *OL*. However, domestic production rises by *JK* to *OK*, and imports fall to *KL*.

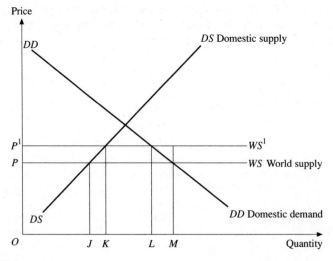

Fig. 52.1

Traditional non-tariff measures

Quotas

A quota takes the form of a physical limitation on the quantity of the commodity which is allowed to enter the country in a given year. Quotas bring in no revenue to the state and foreign producers cannot overcome them by reducing prices, as they might do in the case of a tariff.

A quota may be set on the value or volume of imports. The effect of the imposition of a volume quota is shown in Fig. 52.2. The government sets an import quota of Q^1. This makes the supply curve vertical at Q^1 and raises price to P^1.

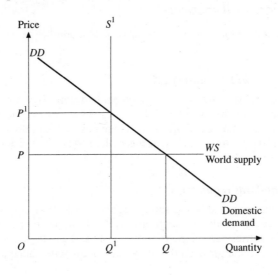

Fig. 52.2

Embargoes

This is the most extreme form of quota since it places a physical limit on imports of zero. It is a complete ban. It may be placed on imports from particular countries (e.g., Iraq during and after the Gulf War) or on imports of certain of goods (e.g. drugs).

Exchange control

Importers require foreign currencies in order to buy goods abroad. American firms will require payment in dollars, German firms in marks and so on. A country obtains its supplies of foreign currencies by means of the efforts of its exporters. A thorough-going system of exchange control will require the foreign currencies earned by exporters to be surrendered to the central bank which will pay for them in the home currency. Importers requiring foreign currency must apply to the central bank which can thus, very effectively, control the variety and volume of imports by controlling the issue of foreign currency. Exchange control was abolished in the UK in 1979.

Import deposit schemes

A government can seek to limit imports be requiring importers to place, in advance, a deposit usually with the Central Bank before they can buy goods from abroad. This makes importing more time consuming and more expensive as it reduces the importing firms' liquidity.

Newer non-tariff measures

The 1970s and 1980s witnessed the growth of a number of new methods of trade restriction.

Voluntary Export Restraint (VERs)

A voluntary export restraint is an agreement between two countries where the government of the exporting country agrees to restrict the volume of its exports of a certain good or goods. Japan has entered into a number of VERs with EU members and with the United States in the international trade in cars.

Product standards regulations

A country can use health and safety regulations to limit imports. Harsh health and safety standards which often differ from those operating in the exporting countries can raise exporters' costs and can be used to directly limit imports on the grounds that they have not reached adequate quality standards.

Complex customs procedures

Imposing the need for laborious and difficult paperwork to pass through customs borders and creating frontier delays, increases the difficulty and cost of exporting.

Government contract policy

A government may have a policy of placing orders with domestic producers in preference to importers even if their goods are cheaper or of a better quality. In this case the demand for imports is likely to fall but their price may remain unchanged as shown in Fig. 52.3.

Indirect measures

The measures we have discussed so far seek to limit imports directly. Protection from competition from overseas can also come from trying to make domestic products more attractive.

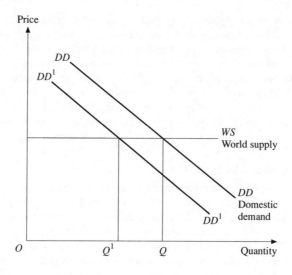

Fig. 52.3

Subsidies

A nation may decide to subsidise certain domestic industries as a means of protecting them from the competition of lower-priced foreign goods. The subsidy will reduce the price of the domestic product and hence make it more difficult for the foreign producer to sell a similar product in the home market. There will be a redistribution of income towards the producers and consumers of the subsidised good because the cost of the subsidy will fall on taxpayers.

Campaigns

Governments can seek to switch consumption from imports to domestic products by running campaigns extolling the virtues of buying home produced goods and emphasising their quality.

Arguments advanced for protection

Revenue purposes

The use of customs duties as a means of providing the state with revenue has a long history (more than 300 years in Britain). This is one of the motives, albeit not the main one, of the EU common external tariff.

Protecting employment and countering the effect of a general depression

During the Great Depression of the 1930s, most countries resorted to increased protection of home industries in an attempt to maintain employment at home by diverting expenditure from foreign to domestic products. The philosophy is simple enough – money spent on home-produced goods creates employment at home while that spent on imports does not. But the imports of one country are the exports of another and restrictions on imports creates unemployment and distress in other countries. They are very likely to retaliate by protecting their own industries. A cumulative effect is inevitable; the barriers to trade become higher and higher and more and more widespread. As world exports decline all trading nations must, to some extent, be worse off.

Protecting particular industries

The best-known argument for protection is the 'infant industry' or 'sunrise industry' argument. A nation may be relatively late in developing a particular industry and yet be favourably endowed with the basic economic requirements for the effective operation of such an industry. If the industry were to be established on a small scale in conditions of free trade, it would not survive the competition from fully developed large-scale producers abroad who would be operating at much lower costs. It is necessary, therefore, to protect the infant industry until it reaches a scale of production large enough to allow its costs to fall to a level which is competitive with its foreign rivals. Many developing countries have had to resort to severe protectionist policies in order to establish domestic industries. Unfortunately, once imposed, these tariffs are difficult to remove. Even when they have achieved large-scale production, industries do not welcome the removal of the protective barrier – there is always strong pressure on governments to retain the tariff.

As mentioned earlier, the comparative advantages enjoyed by different countries in the production of different commodities are always changing. The country which was the first to establish a major cotton industry may find eventually that a faster rate of technical progress in other countries has moved the advantages in this industry to other parts of the world. Other producers may be nearer the source of the raw materials, or to the major markets, or they may have much cheaper supplies of labour.

These changes in the comparative costs of production will mean that particular industries (sometimes referred to as sunset industries) will be declining in some countries and expanding in others. Ideally, a country should be moving its resources from those industries where it is losing its cost advantages to those newer industries where it is enjoying cost advantages, but economic resources are usually not sufficiently mobile for this transfer to take place without some hardship. Capital and labour cannot be moved quickly and easily from say the cotton industry to the computer industry; specialised labour and capital are very immobile. When industries come under pressure from the lower-priced goods of the more efficient foreign competitors there is usually a strong political demand for some measure of protection. Tariffs or quotas are advocated as a means of protecting an industry while some adjustment to the new situation takes place. Lancashire asked for protection from the low-priced cotton goods from India, Pakistan, and Hong Kong while the industry was being scaled down in size and the remaining firms modernised and merged into larger units. Without some degree of protection it is unlikely that private investment would be forthcoming for projects such as these.

A strong argument can be advanced to protect industries against dumping. Foreign producers may be selling their products at less than cost in order to get rid of surplus stock and to gain a monopoly position in the export market by driving out domestic producers.

Safeguarding the interests of workers

The basis of this particular argument is that imports from countries where wages are relatively low represent 'unfair' competition and threaten the standard of living of the more highly paid workers in the home industries.

In the 1990s concern has been expressed about the UK's ability to compete against the new Asian Tigers, China and India. However, a policy of restricting imports from low-wage countries will simply reduce the demand for these products, increase unemployment in these countries and drive wages there even lower. It will also increase the cost of living at home and lessen the incentives to move resources out of the industries which have lost their cost advantages. It is an argument which could well be used against the country imposing the restrictions. For example, the USA might use such an argument to restrict the entry of British goods, since, relative to the USA, Britain is a low-wage country.

Strategic reasons

Some industries such as iron and steel, agriculture, chemicals, and scientific instruments are regarded as strategic industries which are absolutely essential to a nation at war. It is regarded as most desirable that such industries should be maintained so as to reduce a nation's dependence on foreign supplies of strategic materials. Where they have not been competitive in world markets these industries have normally been protected by means of tariffs or quotas.

Preventing or eliminating a balance of payments deficit

A country may find that it is persistently spending more on foreign goods and services than it is earning from the sale of its exports. When it has made every effort, without success, to eliminate this deficit by increasing its exports and substituting home products for imported goods, it has little alternative to the use of import controls. However, a major trading nation would only use protection as a last resort in dealing with a balance of payments problem.

Protectionism versus free trade

On purely economic grounds it is difficult to support most of the arguments for the restriction of international trade. Tariffs distort the true cost relationships and reduce the differences in comparative costs. The extent of international specialisation is reduced and so is the potential level of world output. Consumers in the home country are obliged to pay higher prices for the protected home-produced goods and for the imported goods. The erection of trade barriers also invites retaliation and increases the probability of a general reduction in world trade. Industries operating behind tariff walls are protected from foreign competition and this could lead to a lower level of efficiency.

On the other hand we can be too enthusiastic in advocating any move towards freer trade, particularly where the gains are heavily weighted in favour of a particular group of countries. It seems that liberalisation of world trade has generally benefited the wealthier industrialised countries and done little to narrow the gap between the rich and poor countries. Some limitation on free trade may be necessary in order to assist the developing countries. They could be allowed, for example, to impose restrictions on imports to protect their infant industries while being granted access to markets in the developed world on very favourable terms. We must also remember the point made earlier about the vulnerability to change which results from over-specialisation.

General Agreement on Tariffs and Trade

In 1947 some 23 major trading nations made an agreement on certain rules in respect of international trade and began a series of conferences with a view to reducing tariffs and dismantling other barriers to trade. This arrangement survived and was known as the General Agreement on Tariffs and Trade (GATT). Member nations met at regular intervals and negotiated agreements to reduce quotas, tariffs and other restrictions.

The Uruguay Round

GATT operated through a series of negotiated rounds between member countries. There were eight such rounds. The last round was the Uruguay Round, signed in April 1994, which after prolonged negotiation covering a period of seven years, reduced restrictions on agricultural products, reduced the number of voluntary export restrictions and made services, including financial services, the subject of agreement for the first time.

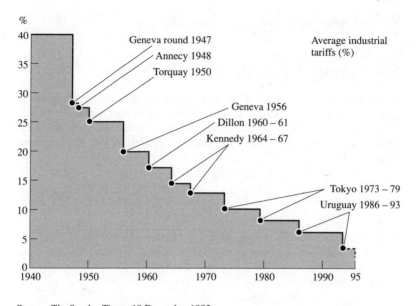

Source: *The Sunday Times,* 19 December 1993

Fig. 52.4   GATT and industrial tariffs

The World Trade Organisation

The World Trade Organisation (WTO) came into existence on 1 January 1995, replacing GATT. It has enhanced powers for the settlement of trade disputes and is a multilateral trade organisation, covering goods, services and intellectual property rights with a common disputes procedure.

53 Trade blocs

Economic integration

Since the Second World War there have been many examples of groups of countries joining together for the purpose of stimulating trade between themselves and to obtain other benefits of economic co-operation. Economic integration between countries can take several forms.

Free trade areas

These consist of groups of countries which have abolished tariffs and quotas on trade between themselves. Each of the member countries, however, maintains its own independent (and different) restrictions on imports from non-member countries. An example is provided by the North American Free Trade Association which was formed in 1993 consisting of the USA, Canada and Mexico.

Customs unions

Customs unions are a closer form of economic integration. There is free trade between member countries, but all members are obliged to operate a common external tariff on imports from non-member countries. An example is the central American Common Market consisting of Guatemala, El Salvador, Honduras, Nicaragua, Costa Ricca and Panama.

Common markets

These are customs unions which, in addition to free trade in goods and services, also allow the free movement of factors of production (labour and capital) between member states.

Economic unions

These organisations include all the features of a common market, but also require member states to adopt common economic policies on such matters as agriculture, transport and taxation. The European Union is moving some way towards economic union.

The European Union

Aims

As set out in the Treaty of Rome, the basic aims of the EU are as follows:

1 The elimination of customs duties and quotas on the import and export of goods between member states.
2 The establishment of a common customs tariff and a common commercial policy towards non-member countries.
3 The abolition of obstacles to the free movement of persons, services and capital between member states.
4 The establishment of common policies for agriculture and transport.
5 The prohibition of business practices which restrict or distort competition within the common market in ways which are considered to be harmful.
6 The association of overseas countries and territories in order to increase trade and development.

Membership

The European Union came into being in January 1958, with a membership of six countries. The membership has since been enlarged to include Denmark, Ireland and the UK (in 1973), Greece (in 1981), and Spain and Portugal (in 1986), Austria, Finland, and Sweden (in 1995).

The enlargement of the Union has created a problem, in the sense that there is now a major difference between the living standards of the less prosperous members (mainly the Mediterranean countries but also including Ireland) and the other, more industralised members of the EU.

The institutions

The Commission

The Commission is based in Brussels. The Commissioners are independent: they are not in Brussels to represent the interests of their own national governments, but are committed to European policies. The role of the Commission is to draft policies and present them to the Council of Ministers for decision. It also has the important tasks of implementing and administering the Union's policies, and for this purpose it has considerable executive powers.

The Council of Ministers

This is the body which takes policy decisions. It is the only Community institution whose members (one from each country) directly represent their national governments. Different ministers attend: most frequently they are the foreign ministers, but agricultural ministers might attend when farm policies are being decided, and finance ministers when financial matters are being considered. Unanimity is required for 'essential' or major decisions, but there is provision for majority decisions on other matters.

The Court of Justice

The Court sits in Luxembourg. It consists of 13 independent judges who are appointed by mutual consent of the member states. Its function is to settle any disputes about the interpretation and application of the Treaty of Rome. Individuals, institutions and member governments may appeal to the Court. Its decisions become binding on member states.

The European Parliament

The European Parliament is based in Strasbourg. The commission and the council are answerable to it and it has the power to veto the Union's budget.

The European Parliament may, at the request of a quarter of its members, set up a committee of inquiry to investigate allegations of maladministration. Any citizen of the Union and any person living or doing business in a member state has the right to address a petition to the European Parliament.

The Court of Auditors

This examines the accounts of all revenue and expenditure of the Union, and all bodies set up by the Union. It provides the European Parliament and the council with a statement of assurance regarding the reliability of the accounts.

The Economic and Social Committee

This is a largely advisory body which looks at all commission proposals. It can issue an opinion which is sent to the Council and than the Commission.

The Committee of the Regions

This again has an advisory status. Where it considers that specific regional interests are included, the Committee of the Regions may issue an opinion on the matter and can issue an opinion on its own initiative.

The European Investment Bank

Its purpose is to contribute, by borrowing and using capital subscribed by member countries, to the balanced and steady development of the Union. It is a non-profit-making institution and provides loans for projects which stimulate development in the less-prosperous regions, develops resources for energy, protects the environment, improves communications, expands the use of technology and funds projects of common interest to several member states which they cannot finance alone.

The Common Agricultural Policy (CAP)

The aims of the CAP are, briefly,

- to increase agricultural productivity
- to ensure a fair standard of living for the agricultural community
- to stabilise the markets in farm products
- to provide adequate supplies of foodstuffs, and
- to ensure supplies to consumers at reasonable prices.

For the main agricultural products the system works in the following manner.

Each year the Council of Ministers sets a *target price* for the product for the next agricultural year (April to March). This is the price which is considered to be most appropriate to meet the CAP objectives set out above.

An *intervention price* is then set a few percentage points below the target price. If the market price falls below this intervention price, farmers can sell their output to EU agencies at the intervention price; these purchases will be placed in store. In theory, such periods should be offset by others when demand exceeds supply and in which the shortage can be met by selling supplies held by the intervention centres. In fact, in many cases, supply has continued to exceed demand at the intervention prices, which has given rise to the so-called 'food mountains'.

A *threshold price* is also set. This applies to imports of food entering the Community and ensures that the price of imports is equal to or greater than the target price. Since world prices of foodstuffs tend to be lower than those in the EU, this means a levy is placed on imports equal to the difference between world prices and threshold prices. The system acts as a form of protection for EU farmers.

If world prices are below the intervention prices, then farmers will clearly prefer to sell to the EU authorities rather than export their products. In this case, in order to encourage exports, the EU will pay export refunds (a subsidy) to encourage farmers to export their surpluses. On the other hand, if there is a shortage of foodstuffs in the Union it can be relieved by reducing the threshold price and by reducing the subsidies on exports.

Increasing productivity in agriculture and the fairly stable demand for foodstuffs have led to the accumulation of large surpluses of certain farm products (e.g. cereals and dairy products). These surpluses are costly to store and export. If they are sold overseas at relatively low prices, they tend to reduce world prices and hence reduce the incomes of producers in other countries. The problem with the EU system of guaranteed prices for agricultural products is that it makes farmers' incomes dependent upon their outputs, i.e. there is an incentive to increase output – hence the surpluses. In more recent years, the EU has attempted to reduce these surpluses by slowing down the rate of increase of intervention prices, fixing output quotas for certain products (for example milk), and proposing to introduce 'guarantee thresholds', i.e. production levels beyond which guaranteed prices will be cut. A set-aside scheme has also been introduced whereby farmers are paid a subsidy for not using a proportion of their land.

Assessment of CAP

There is no doubt that the CAP has ensured adequate supplies of good quality foodstuffs, but it has proved to be a costly system. However, it must be borne in mind that all the EU governments are committed to supporting agriculture. Dismantling the CAP would not mean the creation of free markets in farm products – member governments would then be obliged to spend large sums of money protecting their agricultural industries. Before the UK entered the EU, for example, British citizens enjoyed relatively cheap food because it was sold in the UK market at world prices. These prices, however, were lower than the costs of production on British farms. The government, therefore, supplemented farm incomes with subsidies which covered the difference between British costs of production and market prices.

The EU budget

The EU's budget is financed by revenues from a number of sources.

- Customs duties on imports from non-EU countries. These are the proceeds of the common external tariff and are paid over to the EU by all member countries
- Agricultural levies, which are charged on imports of certain foodstuffs
- An amount equivalent to 1.2 per cent of each country's GNP, as an annual transfer
- A VAT contribution equal to 1.4 per cent of VAT on a standard basis of charging VAT.

The UK is a net contributor to the EU budget but since 1984 it has received a rebate on its payments.

The effects of membership of the EU

When a country joins the EU or another trade bloc it may experience trade creation or trade diversion. Trade creation occurs when the removal of trade barriers results in greater specialisation according to comparative advantage and hence a shift in production from higher cost to lower-cost production.

Trade diversion results in consumption shifting from lower-cost producers outside the trade bloc to higher-cost producers inside the trade bloc. Trade creation is obviously advantageous whereas trade diversion is not. These are static effects. They occur once but there are other possible advantages and disadvantages which occur over a period of time.

Possible dynamic gains of EU membership

Greater specialisation and economies of scale

Supporters of the EU argue that the creation of a greatly enlarged 'home' market enables the more efficient producers to achieve a much larger scale of production and hence produce at lower costs. Within the EU, industries can operate on a Union rather than on a national scale. It is also pointed out by the supporters of the EU that the exploitation of the results of technological development and research in areas such as nuclear energy, space, aviation, and computers is extremely costly and probably beyond the resources of any single European country. If such industries are to be efficient and capable of competing with those of the industrial giants such as the USA and Japan, smaller countries will have to collaborate, pool their research facilities and operate joint development programmes. Economic integration makes it much easier to operate joint industrial programmes of this sort.

Greater competition

The removal of trade barriers allows more scope for the application of the principle of comparative advantage. Regional cost differentials will reveal themselves as differences in market prices and these differences will enable the more efficient firms to expand at the expense of the less efficient who will no longer enjoy the protection afforded by tariffs and quotas. The allocation of resources will be determined by the relative efficiencies of producers within the EU as a whole. This argument assumes, of course, that competition within the Union will not be distorted by the formation of monopolies and cartels.

Increased exports

The increased efficiency of producers within the Union brought about by more competition and larger-scale production will, it is believed, enable them to compete more effectively in world markets.

More investment

If the formation of a trade bloc does generate a faster rate of economic growth then the rising prosperity of the group as a whole will make it possible to provide more funds to help the less developed parts of the Union and to provide more aid to developing countries in other parts of the world.

Raised expectations

Knowledge that they are operating in a significant and powerful market may make entrepreneurs more optimistic and may encourage them to undertake more investment both for purposes of modernisation and expansion.

Possible dynamic losses

Diseconomies of scale

Access to a large market may cause firms to expand too far and experience rising unit costs.

Unemployment

A less efficient country may suffer as firms move out to the more prosperous parts of the trade bloc. This departure can lead to a downward multiplier effect.

Administrate costs

Running a trade bloc can involve high costs. There is a danger that the organisation can become too bureaucreatic and too slow to respond to changing economic and political events.

The European Monetary System (the EMS)

The EMS was introduced in 1979 in an attempt to obtain a greater degree of stability in the exchange rates between member countries of the EU. There are three separate aspects of the scheme.

The European Currency Unit (the ECU)

This is a unit of account (or numéraire) made up of a basket of fixed amounts of EU currencies weighted according to the importance of the economies they represent (the Deutschmark accounts for about one-third of the total weights). When the dollar equivalents of all the components of the basket have been calculated, they are added together to give the dollar value of the ECU.

The exchange rates and intervention mechanism

The value of each member's currency is declared in terms of the ECU and this automatically gives the parity between any pair of currencies. Each participating central bank is required to intervene in the foreign exchange market to keep the rate for its own currency against every other participating currency within 15 per cent of the agreed parity or central rate. Although the currencies of countries which are members of the

EMS are thus linked together, as a block they are floating against third currencies.

In order to ensure that a country whose currency is divergent takes action at an early stage there is a kind of early warning system known as 'the divergence indicator' which signals the fact that the value of a currency is getting out of line. This second mechanism is based on a currency's value in terms of the ECU, not in terms of other participating currencies. Each currency has a given permitted percentage divergence from its central value in terms of the ECU; these limits are described as 'divergence thresholds'. If a currency crosses its divergence threshold, it is presumed that the central bank will take steps to correct the situation (i.e. it will buy or sell the currency in the foreign exchange market).

Credit arrangements

The ECU is used as a denominator for expressing debts and claims between central banks. It is also an instrument for settlement between Community central banks; in this role the ECU functions as an asset.

The Single Market

On 1 January 1993 the single market came into existence removing most of the restrictions on the movement of goods, services, capital and people within the community. Its key features included the removal of non-tariff barriers including technical barriers and the awarding of state contracts, mutual recognition of health and safety standards and professional qualifications and a movement towards harmonising VAT rates in member countries.

The Maastricht Treaty

This was signed on 7 February 1992 and represents a move towards economic, political and social union. It sets out a common foreign and security policy, a common interior and justice policy and a common social policy. It also outlined a detailed programme and timetable for monetary union.

The Social Chapter

This is an agreement on social policy. The stated objectives are to promote employment, improve living and working conditions, implement proper social protection, improve dialogue between management and labour, combat social exclusion and develop human resources with a view to lasting high employment. The social provisions include a minimum wage, equal pay for male and female workers for equal work, minimum standards for health and safety at work and the setting up of workers' councils.

Eleven of the twelve members signed the social chapter. The UK opted out and so does not participate in the deliberations or adoptions of proposals. Acts adopted by the council do not apply to the UK. This has displeased the other eleven members who have accused the UK of seeking an unfair competitive advantage, 'social dumping'.

The European Monetary Union

Economic and Monetary Union (EMU) would eventually mean that the European Union would have a single currency, a single central bank and a single monetary policy.

The Delors Committee Report, presented in April 1989 recommended a three-stage route to monetary union. Stage 1 occurred between 1 July 1990 and 31 December 1993. This involved freeing movements of capital, strengthening competition policy and increasing economic and monetary policy co-ordination.

Stage 2 began on 1 January 1994. This is a transition period, preparing for the third stage. During this stage the aim is for member countries to achieve greater monetary convergence by avoiding excessive budget deficits, keeping inflation rates and interest rates in line with other members and maintaining exchange rates within the normal bands for at least two years with no realignments or excessive intervention. At the start of this stage the European Monetary Institute (EMI) was established at Frankfurt a. M. The EMI coordinates and monitors monetary policies throughout the EU. It has responsibility for preparing the technical ground for the establishment of the European System of Central Banks (ESCB) and the introduction of the single currency in Stage 3. Its role also includes overseeing the development of the ECU, monitoring the functioning of the EMS and holding foreign exchange reserves of any national central bank which wishes to deposit their reserves with the EMI.

Stage 3. This will begin at the earliest on 1 January 1997 if at least seven member countries have achieved sufficient monetary convergence. However, if this does not occur and if no date has been set by the end of 1997, Stage 3 will begin automatically on 1 January 1999 for the member countries who have met the necessary conditions. Stage 3 will involve the participants fixing their exchange rates against each other and the ECU, and a move towards the introduction of a single currency. The EMI will be replaced by the ESCB and the European Central Bank (ECB). The ESCB and ECB will operate monetary policy including determining exchange rate policy, managing foreign exchange reserves, issuing ECUs and taking decisions on interest rates.

Britain and the EMU

A Protocol attached to the Treaty recognises that the UK shall not be obliged to move to the third stage without a separate decision to do so by its government and parliament. If the UK decides not to change its mind and continues its opt out it will retain its powers in the field of monetary policy according to national law. The commitment to a single currency, the conduct of monetary policy by the ESCB, the ECB's rights to issue currency, the rules on national central banks and the fixing of currency rates will not apply to Britain. The UK government opted out on the grounds that it wishes to maintain an independent monetary and exchange rate policy. This does have advantages but also involves an opportunity cost as the UK will not be able to benefit from the advantages of monetary union including the elimination of costs of converting currencies, removing exchange rate uncertainty and, possibly, lowering inflation.

54 The terms of trade

Definition

The rate at which one nation's goods exchange against those of other countries is referred to as the Terms of Trade. In the examples used earlier the concept can be seen very clearly because the terms of trade could be expressed as 'so many bales of wool per tractor'. In the real world things are more complex. Countries import and export a great variety of goods and services and it is not possible to express the terms of trade as a simple ratio between physical units of commodities. Although the reality of international trade is the exchange of goods and services for other goods and services, all these items have money prices and it is possible to measure their exchange values in terms of these prices. The method adopted makes use of two important index numbers – the Index of Import Prices and the Index of Export Prices.

The terms of trade are given a numerical value which is equal to:

$$\frac{\text{Index of Export Prices}}{\text{Index of Import Prices}} \times 100$$

Measurement

The index of export prices and the index of import prices are weighted price indexes. They are constructed from a sample of prices of more than 200 export and import commodities respectively.

In the base year each of the two index numbers will be 100 so that the terms of trade will be 100. If, subsequently, export prices rise relative to import prices the numerical value of the terms of trade will rise. The terms of trade index will fall if import prices rise relative to export prices. There are a number of ways in which such changes might come about. Export prices and import prices could be moving in opposite directions, one set of prices could be stable while the other is changing or export and import prices could be moving in the same direction but one of them could be rising or falling faster than the other.

Movements in the terms of trade

A rise in the numerical value of the terms of trade is described as a *favourable* movement since it indicates that any given volume of exports is now exchanging for a greater volume of imports. Similarly a fall in the terms of trade index is said to be *unfavourable* because any given volume of exports now exchanges for a smaller volume of imports. We must be careful not to interpret the words 'favourable' and 'unfavourable' too literally when talking about movements in the terms of trade. While the price movements may be favourable the movements in the values of exports and imports may be unfavourable because these depend upon quantity changes as well as price changes. Likewise an unfavourable movement in the terms of trade may well have a favourable effect on the balance of payments.

Causes of movements in the terms of trade

Changes in demand and supply conditions, and changes in the external value of the currency can alter the terms of trade. For example, a decrease in overseas demand for a country's product is likely to lower the price of its exports and hence cause an unfavourable movement in the terms of trade. An increase in supply of major export products will also lower export prices and lead to an unfavourable movement in the terms of trade. A fall in the value of the country's currency will also lower the price of exports relative to imports and hence lead to an unfavourable movement in the terms of trade.

Effects of changes in the terms of trade

The effects of changes in the terms of trade will be influenced by their cause. An increase in export prices arising from an increase in demand

Table 54.1 The UK terms of trade (1990 = 100)

Year	Index of export prices	Index of import prices	Terms of Trade
1981	76.2	73.7	103.4
1982	81.4	79.9	101.9
1983	86.3	84.2	102.5
1984	93.1	91.8	101.4
1985	98.1	96.3	101.9
1986	88.4	91.9	96.2
1987	91.5	94.6	96.7
1988	92.4	93.7	98.6
1989	96.6	97.7	98.9
1990	100.0	100.0	100.0
1991	101.4	101.2	100.2
1992	103.5	102.1	101.4
1993	115.0	111.0	103.6

Source: CSO *Annual Abstract of Statistics* 1994, and CSO *Monthly Digest of Statistics* June 1994

will have a more beneficial effect on the balance of payments position than an increase arising from inflation. The effects will also be influenced by the elasticity of demand for exports and imports. For example, if the prices of UK exports rise by 5 per cent due to an increase in the costs of production it will earn more foreign currency only if the quantities sold remain unchanged or fall by less than 5 per cent (i.e. if demand is inelastic). If the foreign prices of imports fall by 5 per cent less foreign currency will be spent only if the quantities imported expand by less than 5 per cent (i.e. if demand is inelastic). If the demands for exports and imports were elastic, the 'favourable' movement in the terms of trade would *worsen* the balance of payments because expenditures on foreign commodities would rise while revenues from exports would fall.

There is also the income effect to consider. Lower prices for imports could mean that foreign countries are earning less from *their* exports and hence their abilities to buy from other countries will be correspondingly reduced. In the case cited above, the UK might find that she is selling less abroad because the prices of her imports have fallen.

For countries which engage in world trade on an extensive scale, as the UK does, movements in the terms of trade are of great significance. When the volumes of imports and exports are very large, quite small changes in the terms of trade can make a large impact on the balance of payments. With imports running at about £134 600 million per annum (1993) even a 1 per cent fall in import prices could mean, for the UK, a saving of some £1346 million in foreign currency, or alternatively, the existing level of exports could buy additional imports worth £1346 million.

55 The balance of payments

Definition

A country engaging in foreign trade will be making payments to foreign countries and receiving payments from them. Each nation keeps an account of its transactions with the rest of the world which it presents in the form of a balance sheet described as the *balance of payments*.

In the UK full details of these transactions are given in the annual balance of payments statement, while estimates of the overseas payments position are provided quarterly. International payments arise from a variety of transactions.

The export and import of goods is referred to as visible trade and the differences between the values of exports and imports of physical items is known as the balance of visible trade.

Since 1993 the UK has made use of the European Intrastat System to calculate the value of its trade with the European Union. This relies on VAT returns from companies rather than on records from H.M. Customs and Excise. This has raised questions about the accuracy of the import figures as VAT returns are collected only every three months and because VAT reporting is staggered with only a proportion of companies filing each month.

The purchase and sales of services (invisible trade)

In addition to the international trade in visible items there is a considerable trade in services. London, New York, and Zurich, for example, provide financial services for countries all over the world. Some countries have large merchant navies which earn foreign currencies by providing shipping services for other countries. British insurance companies insure property and people all over the world. Countries such as Italy, Switzerland, Spain, and Greece have very large tourist industries which sell a variety of holiday services to foreigners. A company providing services to foreign households and firms is earning foreign currency just as effectively as the firm selling machinery or motor cars to foreigners. Capital invested abroad earns foreign currency in the form of interest, profits, and dividends. Britain, like most developed countries, earns a great deal of foreign currency by selling services to overseas residents, but she also spends a great deal in buying such services from foreign residents. Britain also spends large sums in purchasing local services for the armed forces stationed overseas. This international trade in services is described as *invisible trade*.

Capital movements

International payments also arise from the movements of capital from one country to another. These capital transactions are usefully distinguished as long-term and short-term.

Long-term capital movements are those which arise from overseas investments in shares or long-term securities, or from the establishment of factories in foreign countries. If an American firm decided to build a plant in Britain, there is a movement of foreign currency to the UK. Britain receives dollars which she exchanges for the pounds necessary to carry out the work. Typical long-term capital movements are:

- Long-term lending between governments or between governments and international institutions.
- The purchase of stocks and shares in foreign companies or the purchase by foreign residents of shares in home-based companies.
- The setting up of plantations, mines, or factories abroad, or the establishment of similar enterprises by foreign companies in the home country.

Short-term capital movements reflect the transfer of liquid assets from one country to another. These funds are held in bank accounts or in very short-term securities such as Treasury Bills or local authority bills. They can, therefore, be withdrawn at very short notice. As an international banker the UK holds a very large amount of money on short-term deposit for foreigners. Since sterling is a *key currency* and is used to finance a relatively large share of world trade, many nations maintain working balances in London. In recent years a large volume of short-term capital or 'hot money' has been moving from one country to another seeking greater security (e.g. against depreciation) or higher interest rates. A movement of short-term capital to a country represents an inflow of foreign currency and there is a corresponding outflow when such funds are withdrawn by foreign holders of domestic financial assets.

The balance of payments account

The UK balance of payments account classifies transactions into two main groups

Current account transactions

These transactions cover

- visible trade – the exports and imports of goods, and
- invisible trade – the exports and imports of services, together with investment income (interest and profits) and most transfers (i.e. gifts and grants).

Transactions in external assets and liabilities

This section covers capital transactions of the kind explained earlier. The main components are

- inward and outward investment,
- transactions between UK banks and overseas residents,
- borrowing and lending overseas by UK residents other than banks and government,
- drawings on and additions to the official foreign currency reserves, and
- other government transactions in external assets and liabilities.

External assets represent financial claims on overseas residents. They are acquired when UK residents purchase securities issued by foreign governments or shares in foreign companies, for example, and when British banks make loans to overseas residents.

External liabilities are financial claims on UK residents which are held by overseas residents. Typical examples are the purchase by overseas residents of shares issued by UK companies and securities issued by the UK government, deposits in UK banks held by overseas residents, and borrowings by UK residents from banks overseas.

Table 55.1 gives details of the main sections of the UK balance of payments.

Table 55.1 Summary of the UK balance of payments in 1993

		£ m
Current account		
Visible trade		−13 680
Invisible trade		
Services		+5145
Interest, profits, dividends		+2718
Transfers		−5110
	Current balance	−10 927
UK external assets and liabilities		
Transactions in assets		−162 768
Transactions in liabilities		+171 668
		+8900
Balancing item		+2027

Source: CSO *Monthly Digest of Statistics*, July 1994

The current account

The current account is of great importance because it shows the country's net surplus or deficit on its day-to-day trading with the rest of the world. If a country has a surplus on its current account, it has acquired foreign assets in the form of financial claims on the residents of other countries. These financial claims may be used to acquire property abroad, to buy shares in foreign companies, to make loans to overseas residents or to increase the official foreign currency reserves. Alternatively, the surplus may be used to reduce external liabilities, for example, by repaying loans from overseas residents. The important point is that a current account surplus will increase the *net* external assets of a country.

A current account deficit will increase a country's external liabilities (e.g. by borrowing abroad) or reduce its external assets (e.g. by running down the foreign currency reserves). A current account deficit, therefore, will reduce the *net* external assets of a country.

External assets and liabilities

The way in which plus and minus signs are used in the account which records transactions in external assets and liabilities can be rather puzzling. They are as follows:

assets: *increase –*   *decrease +*
liabilities: increase +   decrease –

An increase in external assets has a minus sign because the *financial* transaction when the asset is acquired causes an outflow of foreign currency (to buy the asset). When an external asset is disposed of, the transaction is given a plus sign because there is an inflow of foreign currency (from the sale of the asset).

An increase in external liabilities (e.g. by borrowing abroad) has a plus sign because it leads to an inflow of foreign currency. When external liabilities are reduced (e.g. loans are repaid), the transactions are given minus signs because there is an outflow of foreign currency.

Deficits and surpluses

The balance of payments account is presented as a balance sheet and, like all balance sheets, it must balance. The total outflow of money must equal the total inflow. The account shows the outflows of money as debit items, and they are given minus signs. Inflows of money are credit items and are given plus signs. This means that, because 'the balance of payments always balances', the sum of the credit and debit items must be zero.

At first sight this may be difficult to accept because we are always hearing about countries having surpluses or deficits on their balance of payments. There is, however, no contradiction here. The terms 'surplus' and 'deficit' refer to the manner in which the account has been balanced. If, in a particular period of time, a family's payment (debit items) are greater than its receipts (credit items), it will be in deficit. But it cannot spend more than its income unless it borrows, reduces it savings, or sells some of its assets. When these transactions are included in its balance sheet as credit items, the account will balance. Similarly, if a family's receipts are greater than its payments, it will be in surplus. But a balance sheet will record the manner in which the surplus has been distributed, for example, to increase savings or to repay loans. When these items are included as debit items, the balance sheet will balance.

Exactly the same principles apply to the balance of payments. If outflows exceed inflows (i.e. there is a deficit), the account will be balanced by withdrawals from the foreign currency reserves, by borrowing overseas, or by the sale of external assets. These items are counted as inflows (i.e. credit items). If inflows exceed outflows (i.e. there is a surplus), the account will be balanced by items which show how the surplus has been distributed, for example, by additions to the foreign currency reserves, the repayment of overseas loans, or the purchase of external assets. These items are treated as outflows (i.e. debit items).

Notice that the transactions which bring about the overall balance in the balance of payments are capital items. They are recorded in the section of the account which is headed *UK external assets and liabilities*. This account includes changes in the foreign currency reserves.

Although the overall balance of payments must balance, the different sections of the balance of payments need not balance. However, since the total outflow of money must equal the total inflow, it follows that a deficit in one of the sections must be balanced by a surplus in the other. A country can only increase its net overseas assets by new investment, if it is running a surplus on the current account.

The balancing item

In spite of what has been said in the previous section the details in Table 55.1 show that the balance on current account is *not* offset by an equal and opposite balance on the net transactions in external assets and liabilities. The sum of the two balances is *not* zero.

This is a result of the fact that it is impossible to obtain a complete and accurate record of the millions of individual transactions which go to make up the balance of payments account. There are numerous errors and omissions which are due to payments not being recorded and to delays in obtaining information. It is for this reason that, as more information becomes available, the balance of payments figures are subject to revision in the months following their original publication.

The balancing item represents the total of the errors and omissions; it is the amount which is required to bring the *recorded* balance of pay-

Table 55.2 UK balance of payments in 1992 (£ million)

Visible trade			
Exports	+107 047		
Imports	−120 453		
		Visible balance	−13 406
Invisible trade			
Services	+3440		
Sea transport	−3837		
		−397	
Civil aviation	+4422		
	−4969		
		−547	
Financial & other services	+16 841		
	−6269		
		+10 572	
Travel	+7686		
	−11 090		
		−3404	
Interest, profits & dividends			
General government	+1584		
	−2144		
		−560	
Private sector & public	+69 211		
corporations	−62 874		
		+6337	
Transfers			
General government	+2888		
	−7673		
		−4785	
Private sector	+1975		
	−2250		
		−275	
		Invisible balance	4786
		Current balance	−8620
UK external assets and liabilities			
Transactions in assets			
UK investment overseas	−42 242		
Loans to overseas			
residents by banks	−25 837		
Other private			
lending overseas	−17 620		
Changes in official reserves	+1406		
Other external assets of government	−682		
	−84 975		
Transactions in liabilities			
Overseas			
investment in UK	+31 733		
Overseas borrowing by UK banks	+24 300		
Other private borrowing from			
overseas	+38 831		
Other external liabilities of government	−1569		
	93 295		
		Net transactions	
		in assets &	+8320
		liabilities	
Balancing item			+300

Source: CSO: *The Pink Book*, 1993

ments into balance. The inclusion of the balancing item makes the sum of the credit and debit items equal to zero. A positive balancing item means that there has been an unrecorded net inflow of foreign currency.

Table 55.2 presents a more detailed picture of the UK balance of payments. The figures in the account are expressed in pounds sterling, but it must be remembered that the transactions referred to involve receipts and payments in foreign currencies.

Equilibrium in the balance of payments

Although the balance of payments always balances this does not mean that it is always in equilibrium. It is a commonly held belief that the balance of payments situation is satisfactory when it shows a surplus. But it should be clear that *world* exports and *world* imports must be identically equal. If one nation is in surplus there must be a corresponding deficit somewhere in the world, assuming, that is, other things remain equal. All nations cannot achieve a surplus simultaneously.

A country can only run a persistent deficit on current account if it has unlimited reserves of gold and foreign currencies or if it can persistently borrow these resources from the rest of the world. Neither of these possibilities is very realistic. A country may, however, run a deficit on current account for several years if it is being balanced by long-term capital inflows (loans or grants) which are financing new productive capacity in industry or agriculture. This new capacity hopefully will in time generate additional exports to earn the foreign currency required to repay the loans. Where there are no such loans, and the foreign currency reserves and temporary borrowing facilities are strictly limited, the existence of a persistent deficit means that the balance of payments is in disequilibrium. A country faced with this situation must introduce policy measures to restore equilibrium. We shall deal with these measures later when discussing foreign exchange because they depend very much on whether the country is operating a floating or fixed exchange rate.

But the idea of an equilibrium situation in the balance of payments being considered solely in terms of external balance is probably much too limited. For example, a low level of exports may be balanced by a low level of imports simply because the country is experiencing heavy unemployment. If the country moved to a full employment level of output there would probably be a sharp rise in imports (raw materials, fuel, and finished goods) which would put the balance of payments in deficit. Imports may be in balance with exports because the country has imposed severe trade restrictions in the form of tariffs, quotas, and exchange control. Equilibrium in the balance of payments can only be considered in relation to the other objectives of economic policy. If full employment and trade liberalisation are objectives of that policy neither of the situations cited above could be considered satisfactory because the equilibrium in the balance of payments is being achieved (*a*) at the cost of heavy unemployment and (*b*) by imposing severe trade restrictions.

Causes of deficits on the current account balance

Whilst, as we have stated, the overall balance of payments must balance, sections may be in deficit or surplus.

Most attention is usually paid to the current account position and particularly to current account deficits. A deficit on the current account may arise from high income levels in the home country. This is because when incomes are high people will usually buy more goods and services. Some of these will come from abroad, thereby increasing imports, and some from domestic producers, thereby possibly reducing exports. In addition to increasing the imports of finished manufactured goods, high incomes may also increase expenditure on imported raw materials as domestic firms expand output to meet higher home demand. In contrast, it is when income levels abroad are low that a deficit may arise. This is because overseas countries are likely to import less and to compete more vigorously in the export market. An overvalued exchange rate will also lead to problems with exports being relatively high in price and imports being relatively cheap.

There are, however, more significant problems which can cause a deficit. The country may be producing products of a low quality, its costs of production may be higher and it may be producing products in low world demand.

Effects of deficits and surpluses on the current account balance

The effects will depend on the size, cause and duration of the deficit or surplus.

In the short term a deficit will increase living standards. This is because the country will be consuming more goods and services than it is producing. However, if the deficit is not covered by an inflow of overseas investment, it will have to be financed by drawing on reserves or by borrowing. Reserves are not finite and it may be difficult to find willing lenders. In addition, borrowing and attracting overseas investment will involve an outflow of interest, profits and dividends in the future, thereby weakening the invisible balance.

A deficit on the current balance will reduce the money supply if it is not offset by changes in monetary policy or net transactions in assets and liabilities. It will reduce inflationary pressure as it involves a net leakage of demand.

In contrast, a surplus involves a net injection of extra demand in the economy. It is often taken to be a sign of economic strength. However, it is not completely beneficial. It involves an opportunity cost since the country is forgoing the opportunity to consume more goods and services.

It may also add to inflationary pressure as it involves a net inflow of money and a net outflow of goods and services. A surplus may be unpopular with countries in deficit. Diplomatic pressure can be put on a country to reduce such a deficit, however, it will not be the same strength of pressure as can be placed by creditors on deficit countries.

56 Exchange rates

Currencies are exchanged in the foreign exchange market, but what determines the rates at which they exchange for one another? This is really a question of prices – we are asking what determines the price of one currency in terms of another. The key issue which dominates the debate on this subject is whether currencies should stand in a fixed relation to each other or whether their values should be allowed to fluctuate in response to the free operation of the forces of supply and demand.

Free, fluctuating or floating exchange rates

In principle, this means the existence of a free or competitive foreign exchange market where the price of one currency in terms of another is determined by the forces of supply and demand operating without any official interference. In this type of market the value of the pound in terms of the dollar would depend upon the demand for pounds from holders of dollars and the supply of pounds from holders of sterling who are wanting to buy dollars. British residents trying to buy foreign goods and services will be *supplying pounds* to the foreign exchange market (and demanding foreign currencies) while overseas residents wishing to buy British goods and services will be *demanding pounds* (and supplying foreign currencies). There will be some equilibrium price (i.e. exchange rate) which equates these two forces. The price of pounds, of course, will be expressed in terms of foreign currencies. These can also be referred to as free or fluctuating exchange rates. Figure 56.1 shows the equilibrium price of pounds in terms of US dollars.

If the demand for the pound increases, due for example to an improvement in the quality of UK goods and hence their popularity, its price will rise. This is turn will cause supply to extend as foreign exchange dealers will become more willing to sell the currency at a higher price. This is illustrated in Fig. 56.2.

Thus, the foreign exchange value of a national currency will be closely related to that country's balance between exports and imports. It will also be influenced by the capital transactions between that country and the rest of the world. In addition to the normal commercial transactions, however, there are the activities of speculators to consider. Speculators buy and sell foreign currencies with a view to making a capital gain. They buy when the value of a currency is expected to rise and sell when it is expected to fall. If the exchange value of the pound is expected to rise and in fact does rise from, say, from £1 = $1.5 to £1 = $2, then someone who transfers $15 000 into pounds at the lower rate and moves back into dollars at the higher rate will make a profit of $5000. These transactions, when carried out on a large scale, can have a significant influence on exchange rates.

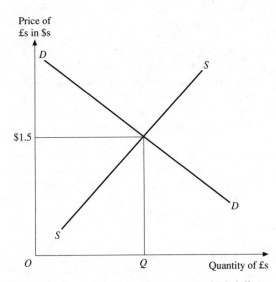

Fig. 56.1   The equilibrium price of sterling in terms of US dollars

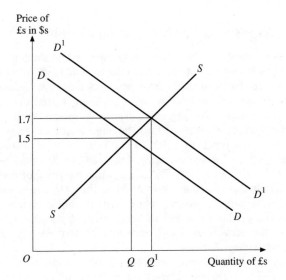

Fig. 56.2

Advantages of floating exchange rates

The great attraction of a floating rate is that it provides a kind of automatic mechanism for keeping the balance of payments in equilibrium. Suppose the pound sterling is floating and Britain is importing goods and services of greater value than her exports. At the current exchange rate the supply of pounds will exceed the demand for them and the exchange value of the pound will fall (i.e. the pound will *depreciate*). Let us suppose it falls from £1 = $2 to £1 = $1.5. British goods now become cheaper in foreign markets (a £1000 machine will fall in price from $2000 to $1500) and the volume of exports will rise. In the home market foreign goods will become more expensive *in terms of pounds*, because the pound will buy less foreign currency, and the volume of imports will fall. What happens, of course, is that the changes in the exchange rate alter the terms of trade, but whether these relative price changes can bring about the necessary changes in the volumes and values of exports and imports quickly and smoothly depends upon the elasticities of the demand for and supply of exports and imports. Nevertheless it is clear that movements in the exchange rate will tend to bring the balance of payments back into equilibrium. The reader should be able to reason out the sequence which would result from a balance of payments surplus.

If a government is confident a floating exchange will ensure a balance of payments equilibrium it will not have to hold reserves of foreign currency. Another advantage of operating a floating exchange rate is that it stops the exchange rate being a target. The government will not have to introduce measures to protect the value of the currency at a fixed rate which might threaten its other objectives.

Disadvantages of a floating exchange rate

A major disadvantage of free or floating rates is that they add a further element of uncertainty to international trading. The world prices of many commodities are far from stable (look at the indices of world commodity prices) and traders are obliged to accept a high degree of risk on this account. A system of floating rates, however, injects another variable element into the cost structure of firms buying goods from abroad. Buyers now have two price levels to watch – the foreign price of the commodity, *and* the price of the foreign currency. For example, it would be possible for the dollar price of cotton to be falling while the price of cotton to the Lancashire importer is rising. This would be the case where the value of the pound falls proportionately more than the dollar price of cotton. Some authorities believe that this added element of uncertainty is a major deterrent to the growth of world trade and in particular it discourages long-term contracts.

The type of speculation mentioned above is a further cause of instability. There is however a type of speculation which reduces the risks of trading. Some foreign currency dealers provide a *forward market* whereby they will quote fixed prices for foreign currencies for future delivery. Importers buying raw materials from abroad, for which payment is due several months hence, can be certain of the prices they must pay by buying 'future' dollars, marks, francs, etc., in the forward market. They will, on average, pay prices rather higher than those which will be ruling at the time their payments are due but the differential may be regarded as a kind of insurance premium for the risks taken by speculators who could, of course, lose heavily if they seriously misjudge the future course of exchange rates. The current prices quoted in the foreign exchange market are known as *spot* prices.

Critics of floating rates say that the *external* prices of home-produced goods will be subject to constant change and this will lead to a very unstable pattern of demand. This makes production planning very difficult because economic resources are not sufficiently mobile to cope with this type of situation without imposing some kind of hardship (e.g. a much greater uncertainty about employment prospects).

Under a system of floating exchange rates, a balance of payments surplus or deficit is automatically adjusted by movements in the exchange rate. This is very attractive to governments who are relieved of the unpleasant task of dealing with a deficit by using tariffs or quotas, or by taking measures to restrict home demand. But there are dangers in this greater freedom. If a country is suffering from inflation, a floating rate may remove some of the pressure on the government to deal with the problem, because the higher prices of home produced goods will not prejudice exports (the rate of exchange will fall and the *foreign prices* of exports will not rise). But the depreciation of the currency in the foreign exchange market will make imports dearer and this could well lead to cost-push inflation. A floating exchange rate cannot insulate the home economy from external forces.

Managed exchange rates

Although market forces are the main determinant of floating exchange rates, in practice there are times when the central banks try to influence the market rates. They can do this by adjusting interest rates (to influence the flows of funds into and out of the country), for example, or by intervening directly in the foreign exchange market. In the latter case they will be reducing or increasing the foreign exchange reserves.

If the central bank does not intervene in the market, it is described as *clean floating*; if the central bank does intervene, it is described as *dirty floating*. Governments attempt to 'manage' the exchange rate in order to smooth out fluctuations around what is believed to be the equilibrium rate of exchange.

Freely floating exchange rates have not proved capable of moving easily and quickly to levels which would correct payments imbalances.

They have shown a tendency to 'overshoot' their equilibrium values and then, after some time, to move to the opposite extreme. Such large changes in exchange rates can be very disturbing to international trade: it is estimated that profit margins on exports can be halved or doubled if exchange rates change by 10 per cent. Some official intervention in the foreign exchange market may be designed to offset this overshooting to some extent.

Fixed exchange rates

Definition

In a typical fixed exchange rate system the countries must fix the values of their currencies in terms of some common standard. In order to maintain a currency at a fixed value, the monetary authorities of a country must stand ready to buy and sell the currency at the fixed price. This means that they must have large supplies of their own currency, gold, and convertible foreign currencies in order to remove any excess demand or supply at the fixed price. Figure 56.3 helps to explain this problem.

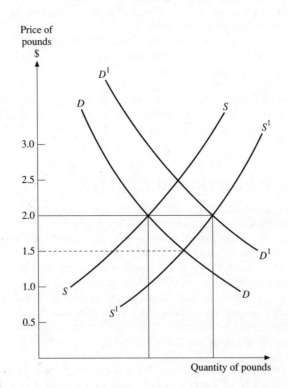

Fig. 56.3

We assume that the UK authorities have agreed to maintain a fixed exchange rate of £1 = $2. Initially the market is in equilibrium at this price. Imports now increase and the supply curve moves from SS to S^1S^1. In the absence of any intervention by the authorities the price would fall to £1 = $1.5. The authorities, however, enter the market and buy pounds raising demand from DD to D^1D^1 and maintaining the exchange rate at £1 = $2.

When the authorities are intervening, as in the case above, to buy the domestic currency, they are, of course, spending the official reserves of foreign currency and gold. In the example above the Bank of England would be buying pounds with gold, or dollars, or marks, or some other convertible currencies. Thus, when we read that 'the pound had to be supported' we know that the official reserves have been depleted. Similarly when the demand for the currency exceeds its supply at the fixed price, the monetary authorities will be selling the home currency on the foreign exchange market and hence replenishing the reserves of foreign currency.

Advantages of a fixed exchange rate

The great advantage of a fixed exchange rate is that it removes the uncertainty associated with floating rates. The negotiation of long-term contracts, the granting of long-term credits, and the undertaking of long-term investment overseas are less risky when there is some confidence in the stability of the exchange rate.

A fixed exchange rate is also said to impose discipline on a country to avoid inflation. This is because it will not be able to rely on a fall in the exchange rate to regain competitiveness lost through inflation.

Disadvantages of a fixed exchange rate

The major disadvantage of fixed exchange rates is that while with the floating rate the burden of adjusting a balance of payments disequilibrium falls on the exchange rate itself, under a fixed rate system this burden tends to fall on the domestic economy. A country with a persistent deficit would soon exhaust its foreign currency reserves and indeed any temporary borrowing facilities in trying to hold up the exchange value of its currency. It must take steps to remove the cause of the deficit. The necessary measures to reduce imports and stimulate exports will inevitably have some adverse effects on the home economy. Monetary and fiscal measures will be used to reduce home demand so that the demands for both home-produced goods and imports will fall. The use of tariffs and quotas will inevitably raise home prices. The reduction of demand in the home market will provide domestic firms with more resources and more incentive to increase their export sales. Higher interest rates may be used to attract short-term capital from abroad. This will improve the balance of payments, but it will also raise home costs and discourage investment. It is because the fixed exchange rate puts the official reserves at risk and hence puts the burden of adjustment on the home economy that most governments favour some more flexible system.

There may arise situations when the exchange rate cannot be held and if an adjustment has to be made it may not be of the correct magnitude.

Revaluation and devaluation

Situations arise when the exchange rate cannot be held. A persistent surplus or deficit indicates that the fixed rate is being held at well below or well above its true market rate of exchange. A persistent surplus might be dealt with by measures which increase home demand so as to encourage more imports and, perhaps, raise home prices making exports less competitive. A reduction in the restrictions on imports would also help to reduce the surplus. A persistent deficit might be eliminated by measures to reduce home demand and/or increase the restrictions on imports. When these measures prove ineffective, or, more likely, when governments are not prepared to impose them on the domestic economy, the only solution is to change the rate of exchange. Countries with surpluses would revalue by moving the exchange values of their currencies to higher parities. Countries with deficits would devalue by lowering the exchange value of their currencies in terms of other currencies.

Revaluation makes exports relatively dearer (in terms of foreign currencies) and imports relatively cheaper in terms of the home currency. Since a balance of payments surplus is widely regarded as a sign of success, surplus countries are usually reluctant to revalue, but if they do not, they are perpetuating the imbalance of world trade and other countries in persistent deficit may be forced to resort to the use of trade restrictions.

Effective exchange rates

Throughout this chapter, we have used the term *the* exchange rate. In fact, of course, for any given currency there is a large number of exchange rates. The external value of the pound may be expressed in terms of dollars, marks, francs, yen, and so on. Effective exchange rates are a way of measuring a currency's external value in terms of other currencies, in much the same way as a price index measures its internal value.

An effective, or trade-weighted, exchange rate is a weighted average of the individual exchange rates. The weight given to each country's currency reflects the importance of that country both as a trading partner and as a trading competitor. Sterling's trade-weighted exchange rate is calculated by the Bank of England using a 'basket' of 17 different currencies. Based on 1985 = 100, its value in July 1994 was 79.1.

The Exchange Rate Mechanism

The exchange rate mechanism (ERM) is part of the European Monetary System (see Chapter 53). It is an adjustable-peg system with member countries having to maintain the value of their currencies within a set band. If a currency begins to move outside this band the country is expected to take action to bring it into line. For instance if the exchange rate is falling near to its lower limit a country would be expected to buy its currency, and if this failed, to raise its domestic interest rate. Figure 56.4 shows how an increase in the supply of the currency, arising for instance from an increase in demand for imports, would lower the price of the currency and place it outside the set band. To avoid this, the government of the country concerned, possibly with the support of other member governments, steps in and buys the currency. This shifts the demand curve to D^1D^1 and keeps the value of the exchange rate within the set band.

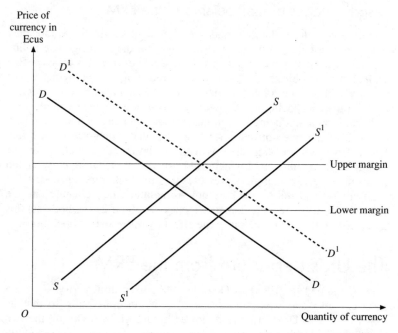

Fig. 56.4

If there are serious pressures on the currency, either up or down, its value will have to be adjusted or the currency will have to leave the system. The ERM does allow for realignment of the members' currencies with the agreement of the member countries, although the aim is to avoid realignments if possible. The currencies of the member countries are allowed to float against non-members.

Advantages of membership of the ERM

Countries gain the advantages of a fixed exchange rate. The greater predictability of exchange rates can promote trade and reduce destabilising speculation. There will be greater pressure put on governments to reduce inflation as the exchange rate cannot be changed regularly. There may also be a convergence in the inflation rates of member countries.

The more EU countries which are in the ERM, the easier it is to co-ordinate exchange rate and monetary policy and to move towards Economic and Monetary Union. This may or may not be viewed as an advantage (see Ch. 53).

Disadvantages of membership of the ERM

Membership reduces the independence of a country's fiscal and monetary policy. For instance, as we have seen, to prevent the exchange rate falling a government may have to raise its interest rate even if this may conflict with domestic objectives, for example, reducing unemployment. The country will also no longer be able to use the exchange rate as a policy tool, for instance, deliberately lowering it to stimulate employment.

In addition to not being able to make frequent changes in the rate there is a risk of the rate not being set at a sustainable long-run equilibrium level. If it is set too high there is likely to be an adverse effect on the exporting industries, employment and growth. Whereas if it is set too low it may create inflationary pressures through high import prices.

In buying and selling the currency to maintain the exchange rate the government may affect the domestic money supply. If it does not want this to occur it will have to neutralise the effect by open-market operations.

The UK's departure from the ERM

The UK joined the ERM in October 1990. Its central parity was 2.95 Deutschmarks and was permitted a 6% margin either side so that its upper limit was DM 3.13 and its lower limit DM 2.78. During the two years of membership the value of the pound was relatively stable. However, on 16 September 1992, Black Wednesday, the pound was forced to leave the ERM.

There were a number of reasons for this departure. Many economists believe that the rate was set too high. In addition the government, becoming increasingly concerned about the duration of the recession wanted to reflate the economy but was finding itself handicapped by membership of the ERM. However, a number of events coincided in

September 1992 to precipitate the UK's departure. The German interest rate was high. It had been expected that this would be cut but when on 14 September it was announced that the German interest rate was to be reduced by only 0.25%, funds continued to flow from sterling into Deutschmarks. There was concern that the French would vote 'no' in a referendum on the Maastricht Treaty. This created uncertainty in the foreign exchange markets with dealers selling what were considered the weaker ERM currencies and buying the stronger ones. The statement by the Bundesbank president, Helmut Schlessinger, that the value of the pound was too high put further downward pressure on sterling. Speculators witnessing these events sold sterling and bought German marks. The UK government purchased large quantities of the pound, spending more than £13 billion of foreign currency on 16 September, alone. It also raised the interest rate, in two stages from 10% to 15%. However, faced with such large-scale selling of the pound, the government was unable to sustain its value above DM 2.78 and at 7.40 pm on 16 September 1992, suspended its membership of the ERM.

The government has stated it will not rejoin the ERM until three conditions have been met. These are a greater convergence of monetary policy in the UK and Germany, particularly in terms of interest rates, a healthy UK economy and a stronger mechanism for assisting currencies which are coming under pressure.

57 International liquidity

Definition

If central banks are to intervene effectively in the foreign exchange market, either to maintain a fixed rate or to influence a floating rate, they must have the necessary reserves of acceptable liquid assets. International liquidity is the name given to those assets which the central banks use to finance their activities in the foreign exchange market. So it is a form of international money which is held in reserves, used to support the value of currencies and in settlement of international debts.

Forms of international liquidity

There are four main types of international liquidity
- Gold.
- Convertible national currencies.
- Borrowing facilities.
- International reserve assets.

Gold

Gold has a long history of use as a money commodity and has almost universal acceptability. The great advantage of gold as an international currency is the confidence people have in its ability to maintain its exchange value. This stems mainly from the knowledge that world supplies of gold cannot easily and quickly be augmented. Nevertheless it is clearly wasteful to employ vast resources of men and capital to produce gold merely in order to store it away in central banks.

Convertible national currencies

There are several advantages in using a particular national currency as an international standard of value and as an international reserve asset. Unlike gold, its costs of production and storage are negligible and the reserve asset is in the same form as the currency used by traders and investors. The supply can easily be increased or diminished to meet the needs of world trade. There are however some serious disadvantages in using the currency of a particular country as a form of international liquidity. Other countries can only build up their official reserves if the reserve-currency country is running a large and persistent deficit. But a prolonged deficit will cast doubt on the ability of that country to maintain the exchange value of its currency. The devaluation of a reserve currency imposes a financial penalty on foreign holders of that currency since the purchasing power of their reserves will fall, and the attempt to avoid such a devaluation will impose a heavy burden on the domestic economy of the reserve-currency country.

Borrowing facilities

Borrowing facilities are rather different from gold and reserve currencies because they are conditional – they have to be repaid. Borrowing facilities as a source of liquidity have the advantage that they can be expanded to meet growing demands, but the drawback is that lenders can dictate terms to the borrowers.

International reserve assets

Because of the disadvantages of using gold and national currencies and the objections raised to conditional borrowings there has been a growing awareness that the world's need for liquidity can best be met by the creation of an international reserve asset which would be costless to create, and whose supply and acceptability can be internationally controlled and enforced. Progress towards this objective has been rather slow because the creation of money is regarded as a matter for *national* governments and they are very reluctant to surrender this right. Nevertheless we now have such an international reserve asset in the form of the Special Drawing Rights (SDRs) issued by the IMF.

The International Monetary Fund

Establishment and aims

In 1944 the representatives of the allied nations met at Bretton Woods in the USA to discuss plans for promoting world recovery after the Second World War. This conference led to establishment of two very important institutions, The International Monetary Fund (the IMF) and the International Bank for Reconstruction and Development (the World Bank).

The IMF began operations in 1947 with 40 members; there are now more than 160 member countries.

The aims of the IMF were to encourage the growth of world trade by working for the full convertibility of national currencies, promoting stability of exchange rates and providing short-term financial assistance to members in balance of payments difficulties. These are still the main purposes of the IMF.

Convertibility

Currencies are convertible when holders can freely exchange them for other currencies. Convertibility is an important requirement for the full

End year, $ bn

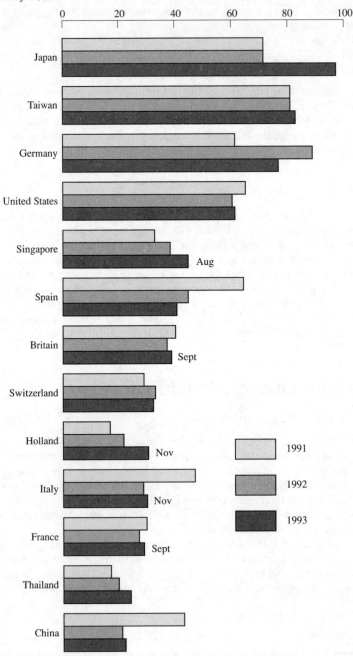

Source: *The Economist Magazine*, 26 February 1994

Fig. 57.1   Official reserves excluding gold

development of multilateral trade because it means that a country does not have to strike a trading balance with each of its trading partners. A deficit with one country can be offset by a surplus with another country. Figure 57.2 provides a simple arithmetic example to illustrate this important point.

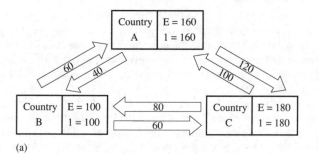

(a)

Each country's trade is in balance (exports = imports), but no pair of countries have balanced trade. Balance is achieved because currencies are convertible, e.g. Country B will exchange her surplus of Country A's currency for that of Country C in order to finance her deficit with C.

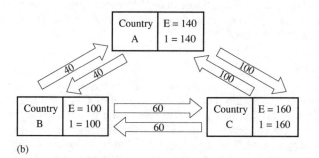

(b)

Currencies are not convertible – the lower of the two demands will determine the volume of trade between any pair of countries, e.g. Country C can only purchase 100 from Country A, because Country A only wishes to purchase 100 from Country C.

Fig. 57.2   (a) Multilateral trade (b) bilateral trade

The aim of convertibility proved difficult to achieve, because, for many years after the Second World War, the only currency in strong demand was the US dollar. The USA was the only major source of foodstuffs, raw materials and machinery and all countries were desperately short of dollars. Any movement towards general convertibility would have soon exhausted the other members' meagre supplies of dollars. Not until 1958 was there any real progress. In this year some 15 Western European countries made their currencies fully convertible for current transactions. By 1965 all the major currencies were convertible for current account transactions. In more recent years, most of the controls on capital transactions between developed countries have been removed.

Stability of exchange rates

The architects of the IMF were looking for a system of exchange rates which would be more flexible than the gold standard while providing a high degree of stability. They chose the *adjustable peg system*. All members were obliged to define the values of their currencies in terms of gold. (In fact, the values were expressed in terms of the US dollar since, at that time, the dollar was convertible into gold.)

Exchange rates were to be held within 1 per cent of the declared parities. This meant, for example, that if the declared parity of the pound had been £1 = $2.0, the rate would have been allowed to fluctuate between £1 = $2.02 and £1 = £1.98. It was the job of the central bank to hold the rate of exchange between these limits by intervening in the foreign exchange market.

The system was not rigid, however, because the IMF permitted devaluations and revaluations. A country might change the *par value* of its currency by up to 10 per cent without obtaining permission from the Fund. Devaluations or revaluations of more than 10 per cent required permission of the Fund. This system operated from 1947 to 1971, but it was subject to severe strains in the 1960s.

Financial assistance

All members contribute to a large pool of foreign currencies. The size of each member's contribution (i.e. its quota) is determined by the size of its national income and its share of world trade. The original arrangement was that a quota was payable 75 per cent in the member's own currency and 25 per cent in gold. This smaller proportion is no longer payable in gold; it may be paid in foreign currency or SDRs and may, in fact, be less than 25 per cent.

The purpose of this pool of currencies is to assist members in balance of payments difficulties. When a member country draws currencies from the IMF, it pays for them with an equivalent amount of its own currency. Members, therefore, do not 'borrow', they 'purchase'; conversely they do not 'repay', but 'repurchase'. When a country makes a drawing on the Fund, therefore, the Fund's holdings of that member's currency increase.

Drawings on the Fund are split into *tranches*. The reserve tranche equals the amount by which a member's quota exceeds the Fund's holdings of its currency. Purchases of currencies in the reserve tranche can be made automatically. For example, if the UK's quota was £2000 million and the IMF was holding £1700 million of sterling, the UK could purchase £300 million of foreign currencies without any conditions being attached to the transaction. In addition to the reserve tranche, there are four credit tranches, each equal to 25 per cent of the quota. Drawings in the credit tranches are conditional. In considering an application for drawings in the credit tranches the IMF will take into account the country's economic position and its likely ability to overcome its problems within a short period. The country must reach agreement with the IMF on the suitability of the policies it proposes to put into effect. A member is expected normally to repurchase as its balance of payments and reserve position improves; it will of course repurchase its own currency with foreign currencies. IMF assistance is essentially short-term and members are expected to repurchase within 3 to 5 years.

A member's drawing rights expire when the IMF is holding, in that member's currency, an amount equal to twice the value of its quota. There are, however, as explained later, special facilities available which allow drawings in excess of this amount.

Early achievements

The main function of the Fund is to provide temporary financial assistance. A nation experiencing a serious balance of payments deficit might, in the absence of such help, be forced to impose restrictions on its imports. This could lead to retaliation and a general increase in the barriers to trade. In the two decades following the end of the Second World War, there was an enormous expansion of world trade and the world experienced unprecedented rates of economic growth and unparalleled levels of prosperity and consumption. The work of the IMF (together with GATT) in helping to reduce the barriers to trade (e.g. exchange control and the use of quotas and tariffs) and in promoting international cooperation in the monetary and financial fields undoubtedly made an important contribution to these developments.

Emergence of problems

The dollar problem

The main reserve currency is the dollar and the supply of this currency as a reserve asset is dependent upon the size of the balance of payments deficits experienced by the USA. If the USA runs a deficit then other countries' holdings of dollars will increase. The very large US deficits in the 1960s undermined confidence in that country's ability to maintain the exchange value of the dollar. At this time the dollar was convertible into gold (for official) holders and the volume of dollars held outside the USA began to exceed the size of the US gold reserve. There were real fears that foreign holders would exercise their right to convert their dollars into gold on a large scale and force the USA to suspend the convertibility of the dollar into gold, and this eventually happened in 1971. This convertibility had formed the basis of the IMF system of stable exchange rates.

Parity adjustments

Although the IMF system allowed for the adjustments of parities (revaluation and devaluation), governments displayed a reluctance to use these measures. Devaluation, especially for countries such as the UK whose currencies were important reserve assets, was regarded as an admission of economic weakness and political failure which would further weaken confidence in the currency, act as a deterrent to foreign investment and encourage further speculation against the currency. Under an adjustable peg system, speculators have what amounts to a one-way option. The balance of payments figures over a period of time provide of fairly clear indication of whether a currency is over-valued or under-valued. A series of deficits would indicate over-valuation and if the exchange rate is to be moved it will be in a downward direction. Speculators, therefore, face little risk of loss. They sell the currency; if devaluation does take place, they make a profit (by buying back the currency at a lower rate); if devaluation does not take place, their losses will be limited to the costs of the currency transactions. Countries running balance of payments surpluses were reluctant to revalue because it would have been politically unpopular with the successful exporting industries and with producers who would have to face competition from cheaper imports. It was also argued that any falling off in the level of exports would reduce the rate of economic growth.

This unwillingness of governments to revalue or devalue meant that currencies were often over-valued and under-valued in the foreign exchange markets. This is a situation which can rapidly lead to a crisis as speculators and investors move their short-term balances from one currency to another in anticipation of changes which seem more and more inevitable the longer they are delayed.

Movements of short-term capital

There has been a progressive internationalisation of banking operations in the post-war years. This together with the removal of restrictions on convertibility means that the working balances of multinational corporations and other short-term balances can now be switched from one currency to another easily and quickly. International flows of funds were massively augmented by the recycling of the huge surpluses accumulated by the oil-exporting countries (OPEC), which resulted from the large increases in the price of oil during the 1970s. The size of these mobile funds and the speed with which they can be switched from one currency to another in response to interest rate differentials or anticipated changes in exchange rates means that individual nations are extremely vulnerable. In the 1960s and 1970s many governments found it extremely difficult to defend fixed exchange rates when massive flows of short-term capital could so quickly transform the balance of payments situation. In 1992 speculation put serious pressure on the European Exchange Rate Mechanism (see Ch. 56) causing the UK to leave the system in September 1992.

Measures to deal with the liquidity problem

Against the problems which occurred in the 1960s and 1970s several steps were taken to supplement the supplies of world liquidity.

- *Increased quotas*. Members' quotas in the IMF were increased on several occasions.
- *Stand-by credits*. These allow a member country the right to draw on a stated amount of foreign currency from the IMF and they are valid for a limited period of time. The availability of these resources (which it may not be necessary to use) helps to restore confidence in a member's currency when it has a deficit and is under severe pressure from speculators.
- *Currency swaps*. These involve the direct exchange of national currencies between central banks under an agreement to reserve the transactions at the same exchange rate at some future date (usually 3 months). Normally swap arrangements are used to restore confidence in a currency which is under heavy speculative pressures.
- *The General Arrangement to Borrow (GAB)*. This arrangement was set up by ten of the larger and richer IMF members after a currency crisis in 1961. These ten countries agreed to lend their currencies to the IMF should the latter run short of one of their respective currencies. This assistance does not become available automatically; its use requires the prior approval of the lending country and the aid is likely to be conditional.
- *Special Drawing Rights (SDRs)*. These represent an entirely new form of reserve asset. Their supply, their value and the interest payable on them are all determined by the IMF. SDRs are issued by the IMF to member countries in proportion to their quotas and represent claims or rights which are honoured by other members and by the IMF itself. By joining the scheme a member accepts an obligation to provide currency, when designated by the Fund, to other participants in exchange for SDRs. It cannot, however, be obliged to accept SDRs to a greater total value than three times its own allocation. Participants whose SDR holdings are less than their allocation pay interest on the difference between their allocation and their actual holdings and members holding SDRs in excess of their allocation receive interest.

    The value of the SDR is calculated daily as a weighted average of the exchange values of five major currencies (the US dollar, the Deutschmark, the French franc, the Japanese yen and the pound sterling). The value obtained is then expressed in dollars. SDRs are increasingly used as a unit of account by official organisations and in financial markets.

- *Special facilities*. In addition to the drawing rights on the reserve and credit tranches the IMF has made further funds available to meet special circumstances. Compensatory facilities allow drawings mainly by primary producing countries whose exports are adversely affected by factors beyond their control. Buffer stock facilities allow members to obtain financing for their contributions to international buffer stocks of primary products.

Recent developments

The IMF has responded to changing conditions in the world's monetary system in several ways.

It has accepted the fact that member countries should be free to adopt floating exchange rates if they so desire. The IMF, however, has laid down principles and practices which member states should follow in managing floating rates. It has been given authority to act as a watchdog to ensure that countries are not managing their exchange rates to the disadvantage of other countries.

Lending policies have been liberalised by increasing the resources available to members and extending the periods for which assistance is available. The annual access to the Fund's resources has been increased to 150 per cent of a country's quota, extending over a period of three years to 450 per cent. More special facilities have been introduced to provide assistance to members with balance of payments deficits which are large in relation to the size of their quotas.

The IMF has increased its resources by increasing members' quotas and by undertaking borrowing from the wealthier member countries.

Attempts have been made to increase the attractiveness of SDRs as financial assets by removing several restrictions on their use and increasing the rate of interest payable on them.

The IMF has broken the links with gold. Member countries do not have to pay part of their quota (or increase in their quota) in gold and they cannot use gold in transactions with the IMF.

The IMF now lends principally to developing countries and to east European countries. Developed countries borrow from each other's central banks.

The international debt problem

The oil price rise in 1973 increased the import bills of those developing countries which did not produce oil. It also slowed down the growth of their export markets as these countries were adversely affected by the increase in the price of oil. Many developing countries tried to maintain their growth rates by borrowing from commercial banks in the developed countries. These banks had funds to lend because many oil-exporting countries placed their surpluses in bank deposits. Some oil-producing countries also borrowed heavily to finance programmes of expansion.

After the second oil price rise in 1979, developing countries increased their borrowings to finance larger and larger current account deficits. The share of bank borrowing in total finance rose to over 70 per cent and became increasingly short-term as banks became more reluctant to lend. Industrialised countries reacted to the 1979 rise in oil prices by restricting demand in order to reduce inflationary pressures, and interest rates were increased. Export earnings of developing countries were restricted, and the costs of servicing their external debts were increased. The total external debt of developing countries rose to $670 billion in 1983. The five largest debtors (Mexico, Brazil, Argentina, South Korea and Venezuela) accounted for half of the total.

In 1982 a number of the debtors announced that they were unable to meet their repayment schedules. This led to fears of a collapse of the international capital market. With the commercial banks severely restricting lending the developing countries turned to the IMF for assistance. This caused serious problems because the scale of assistance required was greater than the current resources of the IMF, and loans were required for relatively long periods, whereas the IMF was designed to provide short-term assistance.

The IMF responded by prescribing adjustment programmes for the debtor countries. These programmes included the following features.

- A rescheduling of debts – extending the period for repayment and, in some cases, postponing the payment of interest.
- The IMF increased its resources by borrowing.
- IMF assistance was made conditional on more loans being provided by the commercial banks.
- The financial assistance provided under these schemes was made conditional on the debtor countries carrying out major changes in their economic policies.
- The conditions imposed by the IMF were an important factor in persuading the commercial banks to continue their lending to developing countries.

The 1980s also saw a number of East European countries, particularly Poland and Hungary, getting into debt. However, recently international debt problems have eased due to a fall in interest rates and oil prices.

58 Development Economics

Development economics is concerned with how developing countries can improve their economic welfare. Developing countries are those where the real income per head and the general standard of living are much lower than in the developed countries of, for example, North America, Western Europe, Australia, New Zealand and Japan.

Measures of development

There is no completely satisfactory way of measuring the level of economic development. National income per head is normally taken as the indicator for official purposes, but, as pointed out in Chapter 38, this may be misleading. As a result a number of other measures are used including the Human Development Index (HDI) and Measurable Economic Welfare (MEW) – discussed in Chapter 38. HDI and MEW come close to the approach adopted by some economists who argue that a country can only claim to be developed when certain basic needs are fulfilled. These include availability and access for all to education, health and employment, an adequate supply of food and shelter and sufficient free time. Figure 58.1 shows that a significant proportion of people living in developing regions of the world do not have access to basic facilities.

However it is measured there is no doubt about the very great differences between living standards in the developed world and standards in the developing world. As most of the developed countries are in the Northern Hemisphere and most of the developing countries are in the Southern Hemisphere, this gap is often referred to as the North–South divide.

Some common characteristics of developing countries

Every country has its special problems and rates of progress vary widely between different countries but there are some features which are common to the majority of the developing countries.

1 High birth rates, relatively high death rates and a low expectancy of life. The application of improved medical standards has reduced death rates whilst birth rates have remained high. Most of these countries are experiencing a rapid growth of population and a high dependency rate.
2 Concentration on agriculture. It is common to find 70 per cent or more of the labour force engaged in agriculture, but, in spite of this high degree of 'specialisation', productivity is extremely low.

3 A very low capital to labour ratio. All developing countries are suffering from a grave deficiency in the supply of capital.

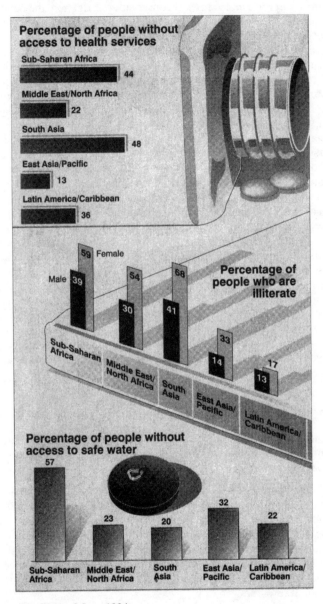

Source: *The Times*, 8 June 1994

Fig. 58.1   (a) Percentage of people without access to health service
(b) percentage who are illiterate (c) percentage without access to safe water

4 A poor natural resource endowment. Many of the developing countries are in tropical and sub-tropical regions where soils are fragile and climatic conditions unfavourable to many agricultural activities. Massive investment in programmes for soil conservation, irrigation, the control of pests and the use of fertilisers are needed in order to raise the productivity of the land.

5 Massive underemployment. Most people do some work but most are underemployed. Peasant holdings are very small and the system of land tenure often means that all the members of the peasant's family work on the family plot. Under these conditions the marginal productivity of labour is probably zero. There is often little activity between planting and harvesting.

6 Social, religious, and cultural patterns of life often act as serious barriers to change and development. Where people are strongly attached to customary ways of doing things, it is extremely difficult to improve the mobility of labour and introduce new techniques.

7 A low-quality labour force. Workers are lacking in education and technical skills and the relatively low standards of health often mean a low level of physical performance.

8 A heavy dependency on one or two export products (invariably primary products). Foreign currency earnings will be subject to large variations because the world prices of primary products are notoriously unstable.

9 A totally inadequate industrial and social infrastructure. Rapid economic development needs a basis in the form of good communications, adequate power and water supplies, an educated and trained labour force, and so on. The returns on this type of investment are of a very long term nature so that private investors are not likely to supply the resources for social overhead capital (or infrastructure). This is a task for public enterprise.

Conditions for development

To achieve a sustained growth in income per head and advancement in economic welfare the quality and quantity of factors of production will have to be improved.

- Human resources. The quality of human resources can be increased by improvements in education, training and health.
- Capital resources. Output per head will increase with capital deepening and with improved technology.
- Natural resources. Fertile land, a favourable climate and a good supply of minerals and fuels are obviously beneficial. However, a number of advanced countries, for example Israel, do not possess a good supply of natural resources.
- Allocation of resources. To increase income per head, resources should be moved from low-productivity industries to high-productivity industries.

- Innovation. Economic development will be stimulated by the adoption of new methods, improved technology, better communications and advanced management techniques.

Underdevelopment traps

As developing countries often lack the conditions necessary for development they can become caught in 'the vicious circle of poverty'. The rate of capital accumulation can only be increased if there is an increase in the rate of saving, but an increase in savings requires an increase in income and an increase in income requires an increase in investment! The current levels of income cannot possibly provide the necessary savings. One alternative is to raise the necessary funds by means of taxation (i.e. forced savings), but taxes are difficult to collect in most developing countries and, in any case, the tax base is very narrow. There is a temptation for governments to finance investment by expanding the money supply, but this would only lead to inflation which is simply another form of taxation (real incomes are reduced by rising prices).

Development strategies

There is a debate about the most effective way for developing countries to advance. Among the strategies considered are:

- Increasing primary production. If the developing countries concentrate on increasing their efficiencies in primary production, they face the problem that most of these products have very inelastic demands. A large increase in world supplies might well reduce the incomes of the poorer countries. Primary products also tend to fluctuate significantly in price because both their demand and supply are usually inelastic.
- Industrialising through import substitution. The aim here would be to allow infant industries to grow and establish a comparative advantage behind a protective wall of import controls. Imports would be replaced by domestic goods and the industrial structure would be diversified. There is a risk with this method that the domestic industries may come to rely on the protection and not improve their efficiency.
- Promoting export-led growth. As an economy develops its exports are likely to change from primary products, to labour-intensive, low-quality manufactured goods and later to high-quality manufactured goods. Competing in world markets will generate income and stimulate firms to increase their efficiency and competitiveness. Indeed, this approach relies on the firms being able to compete against countries which have already achieved low unit costs and in markets which are witnessing increasing levels of protectionism imposed mainly by developed countries.

- Borrowing from abroad. Funds borrowed from overseas countries can be used to invest in physical and human capital thereby raising productivity. However, developing countries have often run into problems following this approach. For instance, in the 1980s a number of countries got into serious debt problems for a variety of reasons including a fall in the price of primary products and a rise in interest rates.
- Relying on foreign aid. Assistance from abroad can enable developing countries to improve their infrastructure, their capital stock and their education, training and health systems. However, aid has not always been appropriate and has not always improved living standards. For instance, providing high-technology capital to a very poor, agricultural and over-populated country may not be very useful as it will need an educated and trained labour force to operate it and it is not going to generate a large demand for labour. (The question of aid is discussed in more detail below.)

Balanced approach

All the methods discussed above have been used by countries at the early stages of their development. For instance, Australia in the first half of the twentieth century concentrated largely on primary production whilst Japan at the turn of the twentieth century provided substantial protection for its industries. However, in practice countries in the past and now use a combination of strategies. For example, improving productivity in primary production should free resources to move into the manufacturing sector and increase manufactured exports.

Population policy

As we have seen many of the developing countries have large and growing populations. This means they must either accept the growth of population as inevitable and try to do something about the consequences, or make some attempt to limit the growth of population. The first alternative means giving priority to increasing the output of food and to job creation by concentrating on labour-intensive industries. It will be extremely difficult to raise real income per head because any increase in output must be devoted to feeding and housing the increasing numbers of people rather than to increasing the productivity of labour. The second alternative calls for a massive campaign to encourage family limitation, and the provision of low-cost birth-control facilities. However, this policy may run into strong religious and ideological resistance.

Foreign aid

Motives for giving aid

There are three motives for providing economic aid to the developing world.

Humanitarian motives

The plight of hundreds of millions of people living in abject poverty must strike the consciences of those whose lot is so much better. Humanitarianism demands that the fortunate minority should give some of their income to those who have so little.

Political motives

Both the communist and non-communist worlds have given some economic aid in the hope that it will help to win the political allegiance of the recipients.

Economic motives

If the developing countries succeed in escaping from 'the poverty trap' and achieve faster rates of economic growth, they will be able to enter more fully into international trade and provide growing markets for the outputs of other countries.

Forms of aid

The United Nations considers that economic aid consists of outright grants and long-term loans for non-military purposes. The chief aid-giving countries, however, take a much broader view and include private capital investment and export credits. In fact the term 'aid' is being increasingly replaced by the term 'development assistance'. Economic aid may take several forms.

Gifts of consumer goods

This form of aid has consisted mainly of the free distribution of American and EU stockpiles of foodstuffs (e.g. wheat). However, the large-scale release of such commodities may upset world prices and affect the earnings of other producers.

Loans and grants

Loans may be arranged on commercial terms (i.e. at market rates of interest) or on concessionary terms (i.e. at interest rates well below market rates). Grants and loans may be allocated to a specific project, or 'tied' to exports from the donor country, or without any such conditions. Grants and concessionary loans tend to take the form of *official assistance*, that is, they are supplied on a government to government basis (bilaterally) or via multilateral organisations. The main multilateral agencies are the World Bank and its two affiliates, the IDA and the IFC (explained later); the IMF; the regional development banks related to areas such as Latin America, Asia and Africa; the United Nations; the EU institutions and the Arab/OPEC funds.

Direct investment

This as the name implies, consists of the establishment of factories, mines, plantations, hotels, etc., in developing countries by firms which are based in developed industrialised countries. In some cases direct investment takes the form of a joint venture, the government of the developing country acquiring part ownership of the new installations.

Technical and direct assistance

The advanced nations provide technical experts to advise and assist the developing countries in their efforts to achieve growth. In many cases the industrial nations have undertaken the building of such projects as steelworks and power stations as a direct form of aid. They also provide technical training programmes for students from developing countries.

Education

Most of the wealthier nations provide facilities for overseas students to attend universities and colleges and provide them with scholarships. In addition they send teachers and instructors overseas.

Specialist services

The World Bank, The IMF, and the United Nations as well as individual countries carry out economic surveys for, and offer a variety of financial, technical, and advisory services to, developing countries.

Trade

Efforts to increase the productive capacity of the poorer nations will only be effective if these nations are able to increase their exports. It does not make much sense for the advanced nations to assist the economic development of the poorer countries and then to exclude their exports on the grounds that they are the products of low-wage labour. If these countries are to 'earn their way out of poverty' rather than become permanent recipients of aid, they must be granted wider opportunities to sell their products in overseas markets. There is a strong case, on economic grounds, for granting them preferential treatment in world markets. Such policies run into trouble when exports from developing countries cause redundancies in the developed countries.

The International Bank for Reconstruction and Development

The IBRD or *World Bank*, as it is commonly known, was established as a result of the Bretton Woods conference and is a sister institution of the IMF. While the purpose of the IMF is to provide short-term assistance to nations in balance of payments difficulties, that of the World Bank is to provide long-term assistance for reconstruction and development purposes. The IBRD has grown steadily since its establishment and there are now some 148 members. It is the world's largest multilateral source of development finance. Member nations are required to subscribe to the capital stock of the Bank, each being given a quota which is related to the member's national income and position in world trade. This capital stock, however, is not the major source of the Bank's lending ability. Each member is only called upon to pay a small part of the amount it has agreed to pay. For example, if the member countries are only called upon to pay 10 per cent of their agreed subscription, the remaining 90 per cent constitutes a guarantee fund; the Bank has the right to request payment of the outstanding amount. The existence of this guarantee fund provides the Bank with a security which enables it to borrow the majority of its funds in the world's capital markets.

The IBRD tends to set fairly stringent conditions on its lending, but because it has a reputation for investing only in soundly conceived projects and because its securities are backed by the capital subscribed (or guaranteed) by its members, it is able to attract investors who might otherwise have never become involved in the financing of projects in developing countries. Interest is charged on the loans, but the interest rate is set as low as is compatible with the Bank's ability to borrow.

In the early years of the Bank's existence, the major part of its lending was to European countries for purposes of reconstruction. Since the early post-war years, World Bank loans have gone increasingly to the developing nations.

Initially these were mainly for infrastructure projects such as road systems, electric plants, railways, irrigation, water supply, and industrial undertakings. More recently fewer loans have been given for infrastructure and more for education and health care. Loans are made to member governments, government agencies, or to private enterprise providing the latter can obtain a government guarantee.

The borrower's application for a loan is carefully examined by World Bank experts who must be satisfied that the project is designed to strengthen the economy and forms part of a sound economic development plan. One of the most valuable services rendered by the Bank is the advice it makes available to member countries from its teams of experts who have great experience of, and maintain a continuous research into, the problems of economic development. Technical assistance is an important part of the Bank's operations. It runs a staff college which trains personnel from developing countries.

The Bank will generally finance only part of the cost of project, insisting that the borrowing country should have some financial stake in the enterprise.

International Development Association

A general feeling that finance on somewhat easier terms should be made available to the poorer areas of the less-developed world led to the formation of the *International Development Association* (IDA). This is an affiliate of the World Bank. The Bank and the IDA operate with the same staff and the same standards, but the IDA makes funds available on very much easier terms. Loans by the IDA are free of interest although they carry a service charge. The repayment period is longer than that for IBRD loans. A country's economic condition determines whether it qualifies for World Bank or IDA loans, the weaker countries qualifying for IDA loans. Whereas the World Bank borrows most of its funds in the capital markets, the IDA is almost entirely dependent on the contributions of 18 of its wealthier members.

International Finance Corporation

Another member of the World Bank Group is the *International Finance Corporation* (IFC), which operates on more commercial lines. Its main function is to encourage the flow of domestic and foreign funds into productive private investment in developing countries. It can supply capital in any form – long-term loans, equity subscriptions, or both, and it can invest without government guarantee of repayment. Its capital is subscribed by member countries and these resources are supported by the income on its investments and by the revolving of its funds. It sells off its successful investments and reinvests the funds in other projects.

59 The nature of government policy

The objectives of government policy

Economic analysis is concerned with the means of achieving particular economic objectives. The choice of the objectives – how people want economic resources to be used in order to satisfy their wants – is a matter for political decision. While governments will differ in the emphasis they give to particular objectives and in the ways in which they try to achieve them, there seems to be broad general agreement on the main aims. They are:

- A high and stable level of employment.
- Price stability.
- A satisfactory balance of payments position.
- An acceptable rate of economic growth.
- An equitable distribution of income and wealth.

The framework of economic policy

The first task is to determine the objectives. Then the target has to be selected. Targets are the variables through which the government attempts to achieve its objectives. The next task is to choose the *instruments* of policy to be used in pursuit of the objectives and these instruments are based upon some available range of *measures*. For example, the government might decide that its immediate objective is to reduce the level of unemployment. For this purpose it may seek to influence (target) aggregate demand. To do this it might choose to use the instruments of taxation and government spending. The particular measures adopted might be a reduction in income tax and an increase in public spending on housing and roads.

Table 59.1 gives examples of government objectives and the instruments which can be used to achieve these.

Conflicts in government policy

It is important to realise that objectives may be incompatible. In order to achieve one goal governments have often been obliged to sacrifice another. Policies designed to bring about full employment have sometimes generated unacceptable levels of inflation; policies aimed at eradicating a balance of payments deficit have restricted the rate of economic growth, and so on. Policy-makers, therefore, are obliged to establish some scale of priorities.

Table 59.1

Objective	Target	Policy	Instrument
Reduction in unemployment	Aggregate demand	Fiscal	Taxation
Improvement in current balance	Price of exports and imports	Exchange rate	Devaluation
Promotion of growth	Investment	Monetary	Interest rate
Price stability	Bank lending	Monetary	Interest rate
Improved air quality	Emissions of CDCs	Fiscal	Taxation

Macroeconomic policies

There are a number of different forms of government macroeconomic policies. The two best known are probably fiscal policy and monetary policy. Fiscal policy includes any policy measure involving changes in the rate, timing or composition of government expenditure and/or taxation (see Ch. 60). Monetary policy is concerned with changes in the supply and/or price of money (see Ch. 61).

We discussed the other main forms earlier in the book. These include regional policy which covers any measure which influences the location of industry and/or people. Import controls, as we have seen, seek to reduce the volume of imports. Incomes policies are measures that include legislation which influence incomes, most often wages.

Government failure

Government failure occurs when government intervention fails to improve economic efficiency (welfare) or even reduces it. This is clearly not the aim of the government. It arises for a number of reasons.

One that we have just mentioned is that it is difficult for a government to achieve all its objectives simultaneously. Some economists argue that a government should have at least one instrument to achieve each objective. This is known as Tinbergen's rule.

In deciding which policy instruments to use a government will be making use of economic theory and of economic forecasts. There are conflicts of opinion on economic theory. For instance, monetarists argue that rises in the money supply cause inflation whereas Keynesians argue that it is changes in inflation which cause changes in the money supply.

In the last two decades there has been a growth in the forecasting groups. The government itself receives advice from the Treasury and from a panel of independent economists, who are known as the six wise men. The strength of the advice these economists give depends on the accuracy of the information gathered, and its interpretation in the economic models used.

Time lags

There are a number of delays involved in government policy. There is the time taken to recognise that there is a problem, the time taken to formulate policy measures, the time to introduce policies and the time for people and firms to react to the policies. From the time the problem is identified to the time the policy is implemented, economic circumstances may have changed. For instance, a government may decide that a rise in unemployment after the Christmas period is not just a seasonal rise but the start of an upward trend. As a result it may decide to stimulate economic activity by cutting tax rates. However, by the time this measure is introduced, demand may have been picking up anyway and the measure may instead add to inflationary pressures.

People and firms may also not react in the way the government expects. For instance, a reduction in tax rates may not cause consumers to spend more and firms to expand if there is a lack of confidence.

Policy constraints

There are also practical problems and international constraints. It is difficult to change much of government expenditure, particularly capital expenditure, taxation and legislation quickly. As a member of the European Union, the UK government cannot introduce import contracts against fellow members and has committed itself to keeping its VAT rate above 15%. The UK's ability to alter its rate of interest was limited whilst in the ERM (see Ch. 56).

Political influences

Governments, as we saw in Chapter 43, tend to introduce harsh measures just after an election and more popular ones near an election. Economic advisers may recommend a rise in taxation but if this is just before a general election a government may choose to ignore the advice.

Complexity

The real world is a complex and constantly changing place. For instance, with increasing mobility of money around the world, it is becoming more difficult to measure and control the money supply.

Civil servants' and politicians' self-interest

Civil servants and politicians may promote the growth of their own department to pursue their own advancement. As we have seen entrepreneurs' salaries and status are often closely linked to the size of the companies they run. Similarly a civil servant's pay, promotion chances and status and a politician's status and promotion chances may be influenced by the growth of their department even if it is not in the country's interest.

60 Fiscal policy

Definition

Fiscal policy is the deliberate manipulation of government income and expenditure so as to achieve desired economic and social objectives. The instruments of fiscal policy are taxation and government spending. Changes in the level, timing and composition of taxation and government spending can have a significant impact on people's lives.

Public expenditure

In the UK, public expenditure is officially defined as that expenditure which has to be financed from taxation (including local taxation), national insurance contributions, and government borrowing. This expenditure will include the current and capital expenditures of central and local government and any loans and grants to the nationalised industries. It does not include the trading expenditures of the nationalised industries nor any of their investment which is financed from internal sources.

In 1993–94 total planned public expenditure was £281 bn., equal to about 45 per cent of GDP. Public expenditure consists of two distinct types of outlay.

- *Spending on goods and services*. Central and local governments are large-scale employers and they also purchase a vast range of goods and services from firms in the private sector. This type of public spending makes a direct claim on the nation's resources.
- *Transfer payments*. These items consist of transfers of purchasing power from one section of the community to another. Transfer payments include social security benefits, subsidies, grants, and interest payments on the debts of central and local government. They represent a redistribution of income because they are financed from taxation. The main categories of public expenditure are shown in Figure 60.1.

The financing of public expenditure

Public expenditure is financed in various ways:

- taxes levied by central government,
- taxes levied by local authorities (i.e. local rates),
- national insurance contributions paid by employees, the self-employed and employers (these contributions are, in fact, a form of taxation),
- borrowing, and
- sales of assets.

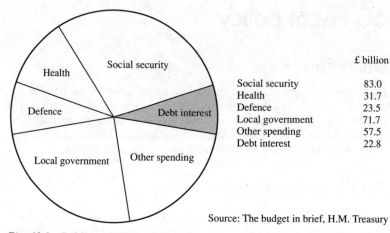

	£ billion
Social security	83.0
Health	31.7
Defence	23.5
Local government	71.7
Other spending	57.5
Debt interest	22.8

Source: The budget in brief, H.M. Treasury

Fig. 60.1   Public expenditure 1994–95

In the 1980s and 1990s the Conservative government raised large sums
of money from the sale of publicly-owned corporations to the private
sector (privatisation). The government accounts show these receipts as a
reduction in government spending rather than as an increase in government revenue. As Fig. 60.2 shows the main single source of government
revenue is income tax.

£ billion

	£ billion
Income tax	64.4
National insurance contributions	42.8
Corporation tax	17.6
Value added tax	43.1
Exise duties	27.1
Other receipts	57.4
Borrowing	37.9

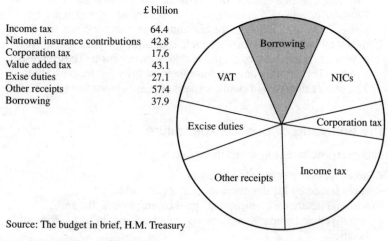

Source: The budget in brief, H.M. Treasury

Fig. 60.2   Public revenue 1994–95

Broad functions of public expenditure

To a certain extent both the total and pattern of public expenditure will depend upon the political philosophy of the government, but it is possible to identify the major functions of public spending.

The provision of public goods and services

As we saw in Chapter 25 these are goods and services for which there is clearly a demand but which must be provided on a collective basis.

The state subsidises some merit goods and provides others free at the point of use to increase their consumption. This policy is likely to assist in the redistribution of income because the cost is met out of taxation and if the tax system is progressive the benefits accruing to the lower income groups will be much greater than the contributions they make to the subsidies.

Social security

Social security is the largest single item of public spending in the UK. It embraces a wide range of benefits in the form of money grants (i.e. transfer payments), including retirement pensions, child benefit, income support, family credit, sickness benefit and widows' pensions. The state also provides a range of personal social services to assist the elderly and the disabled.

The broad objectives of the system of social security are to ensure that everyone is guaranteed some adequate minimum level of income and to prevent families from suffering undue hardship when their incomes fall due to some misfortune.

The regulation of economic activities

The state intervenes extensively in the economic activities of the private sector. It has set up a variety of supervisory and enforcement agencies to ensure that industrial and commercial activities are not conducted in ways which adversely affect the public interest. The Factories and Offices Acts lay down minimum standards for working conditions; The Public Health and Clean Food Acts control standards of hygiene in public and private premises; Town and Country Planning Acts regulate the development of land; Companies Acts enforce certain standards of commercial behaviour and the Monopolies and Restrictive Practices Acts regulate trading practices in the business world. This list could be greatly extended.

Influencing resource allocation and industrial efficiency

The state uses public funds and the instruments of fiscal policy such as taxes, tariffs, grants and subsidies to influence the structure, performance and location of privately-owned industry. It also still operates some business concerns itself, for example, the Bank of England, although privatisation has substantially reduced the number of industries owned by the state.

Influencing the level of economic activity

The income and expenditures of the public authorities are now so large that any changes in these variables have a great influence on the levels of output, employment, and prices.

The growth of public expenditure

Public expenditure has grown throughout the twentieth century. There are currently some strong upward pressures on public spending and the government is reviewing how some of these could be reduced.

Two of these pressures are the increased demand for higher education and the greater number of elderly people in the population. The government has already reduced maintenance grants to students in real terms and is looking at charging students tuition fees. It is also considering a wide-ranging review of state pension provision.

A more elderly population and a population with higher expectations of health care place pressure to raise spending on the health system. The continuing rise in car ownership and use also means existing roads have to be repaired more frequently and lead to calls for an increase in road building.

The structure of taxation in the UK

The Inland Revenue department

The taxes collected by this department are sometimes described as *direct taxes*. They are levied on income and capital and the burden of such taxes is borne by the person or company responsible for paying the taxes. Direct taxes are not usually passed on in the form of higher prices as is the case with indirect taxes (i.e. taxes on expenditure).

Personal income tax

The present system is a single graduated personal tax. The tax is not chargeable on a person's gross income because certain expenditures known as allowances can be offset against tax liabilities and there are also allowances according to a person's marital status. Thus
Gross Income – Allowances = Taxable Income.

In the UK the top rate of income tax is 40 per cent, the basic rate is 25 per cent, then there is a lower rate of 20 per cent and a certain level of income is tax free (tax allowance).

Corporation tax

This tax is levied on the profits of all companies resident in the UK whether the profits are earned at home or abroad. The tax is charged after allowances for such things as interest on loans and depreciation of capital. The main rate of corporation tax is 33 per cent with a lower rate of 25 per cent for small companies. Corporation tax is levied on all profits whether paid out as dividends or not. Dividends are subject to personal income tax but it is assumed that the basic rate of income tax has been applied to dividends before they are paid out (part of the corporation tax paid by a company is imputed to its shareholders). Corporation tax may encourage firms to raise funds in the form of loan capital rather than by an issue of shares, because interest on loan capital can be offset against cororation tax as a cost of production whereas dividends cannot.

Capital gains tax

This particular tax is levied on the increase in the value of certain assets between the time of their purchase and the time of their sale. Any increase in the value of most assets is taxable when the assets are disposed of. For basic rate tax payers, capitals gains are taxed at 25 per cent, and for higher-rate taxpayers they are taxed at 40 per cent. There are important exemptions for such things as personal private residences, private motor cars, winnings from gambling, and capital gains on government securities. In 1994–95 the first £5800 of an individual's capital gains in the year were also exempt.

Inheritance tax

This tax was introduced in 1986 to replace capital transfer tax, which had applied to all gifts of wealth above some given value. This tax is described as an inheritance tax because it applies to transfers of wealth made on death. In the 1988 Budget, inheritance tax was changed from a progressive to a proportional tax. A flat rate of 40 per cent is levied on all chargeable transfers of wealth. Transfers of amounts up to £15 000 are not subject to the tax.

The Customs and Excise Department

The taxes collected by this department are usually described as *indirect taxes* since the person who actually makes the tax payment to the authorities may pass on the burden of the tax to some other person. For example, the excise duties on petrol and beer are invariably passed on as higher prices although they are collected from manufacturers and distributors. The main indirect taxes on expenditure consist of excise duties on home produced goods and services and on goods imported from abroad, the value added tax and car tax, and the protective or import duties.

The excise duties

Most of the revenue from these duties is derived from three sources, tobacco, alcoholic drinks and hydrocarbon oil.

Tobacco. Cigarettes are subject to an *ad valorem* duty based on the recommended retail price and specific duty based on quantity. Other smoking products are charged by reference to their weight.

Alcoholic drinks. The duties on spirits, wines and beer are specific duties which vary according to the alcoholic strength of the liquids.

Hydrocarbon oil. These duties are also specific (i.e. related to quantity) and are levied mainly on petrol and diesel oils used in transport.

Betting and gaming. Most forms of betting and gaming in the UK are now liable to taxation. A proportional tax is levied on pool betting; casino gambling is taxed by means of licences and a similar system is applied to gaming machines.

Matches and mechanical lighters are also subject to an excise duty.

Value added tax (VAT)

VAT is a general sales tax which applies to a wide range of goods and services. The tax is charged to the sellers of output and their tax liability amounts to a percentage ($17\frac{1}{2}$ % in 1994–95) of the value added at that particular stage of production. The firms engaged in the production of a commodity add VAT to the value of their outputs, but they deduct from this figure the amount of VAT already paid on their inputs. In other words they pay VAT only on the value added by their particular activities.

Certain goods and services are given special treatment; they are either exempt or zero rated. When goods and services are exempt the trader does not charge his customer any output tax, but he cannot claim back any VAT already paid on his inputs. Exemption from VAT applies to land (including rents), insurance, postage, betting and gaming, finance, education, health services, burial and cremation.

Zero-rating means complete relief from VAT. A trader does not charge VAT on the goods and services he sells and he can reclaim any VAT which has been paid on his inputs. Zero-rating applies to exports, food (except meals out), children's clothing and footwear, books, newspapers, construction, passenger transport, drugs, and medicines on prescription and certain supplies to charities. In 1993 VAT at 8% was imposed on domestic fuel and power.

A major reason for the introduction of VAT in the UK was that it is a necessary condition of membership of the EU (then referred to as the EEC). Since VAT is not levied on exports (i.e. exporters can reclaim any VAT already paid on the goods) it should provide some incentive to exporters.

Car tax is a special tax on motor cars and motor caravans which is levied in addition to VAT. It applies to domestically manufactured and imported vehicles.

Protective duties are levied on imports into the UK from non-EU countries. The rates of duty are those which apply throughout the EU since membership of the EU obliges the UK to apply the common tariffs. Revenues raised by these duties are payable to the EU.

Motor vehicle excise duty. All motor vehicles in use in the UK have to be registered and licensed. The rates of motor vehicle duties vary according to the type of vehicle, heavier vehicles paying much higher duties.

Miscellaneous licences. Central government revenue is obtained from the issue of a variety of licences of which much the most important is the television licence.

Local taxation

Local tax revenue comes from firms which pay business rates and from households who pay Council Tax.

The uniform business rates are levied on firms by the central government which distributes the proceeds to local authorities on the basis of so much per adult. Extra financial assistance is available for those authorities with special problems.

The Council Tax replaced the Community Charge (often known as the poll tax) in April 1993. It is based partly on the value (in terms of sale price) of people's houses and partly on how much each council spends. Households in each local authority area are placed in one of eight bands (according to the value of their houses) with those in band A paying the least tax and those in band H, the most. The tax is based on two adults per household, although extra adults do not pay any more and households occupied by just one adult receive a 25 per cent discount.

The structure of taxes

Progressive taxes

A tax is progressive when it takes a greater percentage of income from the higher-income groups than it does from the lower-income groups. As taxable income increases, the increments become subject to higher rates of taxation; in other words, the marginal rate of taxation is higher than the average rate. This type of taxation is clearly illustrated in the example of UK income tax.

Proportional taxes

A tax is proportional when all taxpayers pay the same percentage of their income or wealth. In the UK, corporation tax is an example of a proportional tax.

Regressive taxes

Taxes are regressive when the poor are called upon to make greater sacrifices than the rich. If the first £1000 of income were taxed at 40p in the £, and the second £1000 at 30p in the £, the tax would be regressive. Flat rate taxes such as the excise duties on tobacco, beer, and petrol act regressively since the amount of tax included in the prices of these goods represents a greater percentage of the incomes of the lower paid groups.

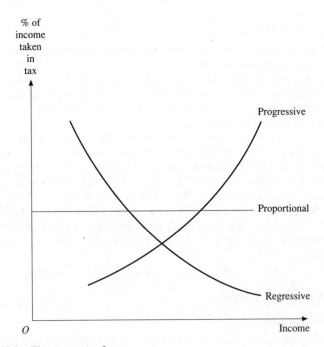

Fig. 60.3   The structure of taxes

We may summarise by saying that a tax is progressive, proportional, or regressive according to whether it takes from the higher income groups a larger fraction of income, the same fraction of income, or a smaller fraction of income than it takes from the lower income groups.

Canons of taxation

Adam Smith laid down certain canons of taxation which are still generally acceptable as basic principles for a system of taxation.

Equity

There must be equality of sacrifice. This implies that the burden of taxation should be distributed according to people's ability to pay. Smith thought that proportional taxes would satisfy this criterion, but nowadays it is generally accepted that progressive taxes are the most equitable type of tax. The argument is based on the idea that the principle of diminishing marginal utility applies to income. On this basis it might be argued that taking £30 per week away from the man earning £250 per week only deprives him of the same amount of satisfaction as would the removal of £5 from the wage packet of the man earning £100 per week.

The capital gains tax was introduced on grounds of equity. It was felt that a capital gain obtained by speculation in share or commodity markets should be subject to taxation in the same way as income earned on the factory floor.

Certainty

The taxpayer should know how much tax he has to pay, when it must be paid, and how it must be paid. He should be able to assess his tax liability from information provided and should not be subject to tax demands made in an arbitrary fashion. In theory, the British system of taxation satisfies these requirements – all the necessary information is available to taxpayers, but the tax laws have become so complex and extensive that it is sometimes difficult for the average man to be certain of all his rights and responsibilities.

Convenience

Taxes must be collected in a convenient form and at a convenient time. The Pay As You Earn (PAYE) system of tax collection is probably the most convenient method in general use. Under the previous system income tax was paid in arrears – the tax on the income earned in one period was payable in the following period. This system laid the onus of building up a tax reserve fund on each individual taxpayer. Taxes are paid in money and generally speaking this is the most convenient form of making tax payments. Some difficulties arise, however, when taxes are levied on wealth, the majority of which will not be held in the form of money. Problems arise in making accurate valuations of different assets and sometimes in realising these assets so that payments can be made in money. When wealth is held in the form of shares in a private company, for example, there might be difficulties in disposing of them – they cannot be offered for sale to the general public.

Economy

The costs of collection and administration should be small in relation to the total revenue. This requirement often conflicts with that of equity. The 'fairest' system of taxation would involve casting the net so widely and so carefully that collection costs would be disproportionately high.

The economic effects of taxation

On the distribution of income

Taxes will reduce the disposable income of firms and households. When the tax is progressive, the incomes remaining after tax must be less unequally distributed than incomes before tax. Only a proportional tax would leave the distribution of income unchanged. Indirect taxes also affect the distribution of income. The commodities which are subject to heavy taxation are widely consumed and have demands which are inelastic with respect to price. Since the lower income groups tend to spend a greater proportion of their incomes on some of these commodities the effect of the taxes can be regressive. For example, there is evidence that the tax on tobacco is regressive; it takes a higher proportion of the income of the poor than the rich. It appears, in fact, to be getting more regressive because tobacco consumption has fallen among the higher income groups. On the other hand the tax on alcohol seems to act progressively. The higher income groups consume relatively more wines and spirits which are subject to higher rates of tax.

On consumption

Direct and indirect taxes will affect both the total and the pattern of consumer spending. Direct taxes reduce disposable income, but the effect on consumption will depend upon the propensity to consume and the level of saving. If there is very little saving, direct taxes must reduce consumption. If, however, taxpayers are enjoying a relatively high standard of living which enables them to save, an increase in direct taxes may have relatively little effect on consumption. People may resist any cut in their living standards by reducing saving rather than spending.

Indirect taxes will also reduce the total demand for goods and services, especially where they are imposed on commodities with inelastic demands. Consumers will tend to maintain their consumption of these goods and so they will have less to spend on other goods and services. Again, much depends upon the propensity to consume and the existing levels of saving.

On incentives

Each time the Chancellor increases taxation voices are raised to proclaim the fact that the new levels of taxation will result in less effort, less investment, and less risk-taking, because taxation has now reached levels which make the *net* rewards for extra work and responsibility seem very unattractive. This argument applies particularly to progressive taxation where *additional* income is taxed at higher rates. There is obviously some level of taxation at which these disincentive effects will come into operation, but it is very difficult to determine that level. It might be argued that additional taxation will increase the workers' efforts. A person becomes accustomed to a certain standard of living and he might well react to an increase in taxes by working harder or longer hours in order to maintain the same disposable income.

On saving and investment

Heavy and steeply progressive taxation will reduce the ability to save; it might also reduce the willingness to save. As noted above, an increase in taxes might lead to a fall in saving rather than spending. Capital transfer and wealth taxes might also reduce the willingness to save because one of the incentives to accumulate wealth is the desire to pass on some of the results of one's efforts to one's children and grandchildren. It is difficult to determine the strength of these effects since so many factors influence the level of savings.

Private investment is determined largely by expected profitability so that we must expect the taxation of profits to have some disincentive effects. Much will depend upon the particular level of the tax, but the heavy taxation of profits will probably act as a disincentive as far as the more risky projects are concerned. Let us take as an example two projects, one fairly safe, one very risky, and assume a profits tax at the rate of 50 per cent.

| | *Estimated profits* | |
	Before tax	*After tax*
Project A (fairly safe)	£10 000 p.a.	£5 000 p.a.
Project B (very risky)	£30 000 p.a.	£15 000 p.a.

After tax, Project B still holds out the prospect of profits three times as great as those expected on Project A, but the absolute difference has fallen from £20 000 to £10 000. Is it worthwhile taking the much greater risks for a possible net gain of £10 000 as against the £20 000 which might be forthcoming without the tax?

On prices

Direct taxes fall on income and have no direct influence on the price level, but indirect taxes have an immediate impact on prices. An increase in direct taxes which led to a significant fall in demand could, of course, lead to a fall in prices, but in present-day conditions it is more likely to reduce output rather than prices.

INTERNATIONAL TRADE

An increase in indirect taxes

A potentially powerful generator of cost-push inflation. Much depends upon the weighting of the taxed commodities in the Retail Price Index. It is also possible that increases in direct taxes could stimulate wage demands and so lead to cost-push inflation.

Public finance and equity

One very important objective of government policy is to create a more equal distribution of income and wealth than that which would result from the uncontrolled exercise of market forces. Taxation which falls more heavily on the better-off groups is one policy instrument used for this purpose. The other aspect of the policy is the redistribution of this revenue in a manner which gives proportionately greater benefits to the poorer classes.

The budget

The budget since 1993 has been held in November. It is the occasion when the Chancellor of the Exchequer announces expenditure plans and taxation decisions. The Budget proposals are given legal force when passed in the Finance Act.

A budget deficit arises when government expenditure exceeds government revenue, whereas a budget surplus occurs when the government raises more in tax revenue than it spends.

Fiscal stance

A government may deliberately set out to run a budget deficit. In this case the government would be operating a reflationary fiscal policy, seeking to increase aggregate demand and thereby reduce unemployment and raise growth. This is referred to as a structural deficit. However, a budget deficit can also arise as a result of changes in the level of economic activity. This is referred to as a cyclical deficit. It occurs when a fall in economic activity lowers tax revenue and raises government expenditure, particularly on job seekers allowance.

To estimate the nature of the budget position, economists make use of the full employment budget concept. This measures what the budget position would be at full employment. Figure 60.5 shows three budget positions. Budget B shows no structural deficit since when there is full employment there is a budget balance. Any deficit or surplus would arise as a result of changes in national income. Budget position B^1 shows a deflationary or contractionary budget position. At the full employment level there would be a structural budget surplus. B^2 represents an expansionary budget position with a structural budget deficit at the full employment level.

Balancing the books 1994–5

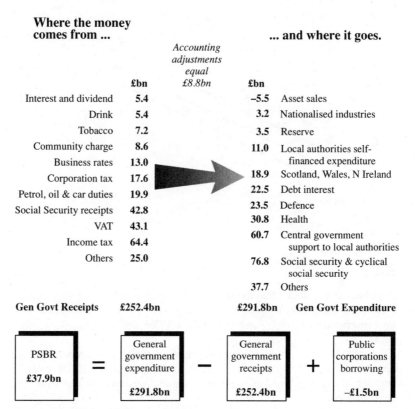

Where the money comes from ...

Accounting adjustments equal £8.8bn

... and where it goes.

	£bn		£bn	
Interest and dividend	5.4		−5.5	Asset sales
Drink	5.4		3.2	Nationalised industries
Tobacco	7.2		3.5	Reserve
Community charge	8.6		11.0	Local authorities self-financed expenditure
Business rates	13.0			
Corporation tax	17.6		18.9	Scotland, Wales, N Ireland
Petrol, oil & car duties	19.9		22.5	Debt interest
Social Security receipts	42.8		23.5	Defence
VAT	43.1		30.8	Health
Income tax	64.4		60.7	Central government support to local authorities
Others	25.0		76.8	Social security & cyclical social security
			37.7	Others

Gen Govt Receipts   £252.4bn   **£291.8bn   Gen Govt Expenditure**

PSBR £37.9bn	=	General government expenditure £291.8bn	−	General government receipts £252.4bn	+	Public corporations borrowing −£1.5bn

Source: *The Financial Times*, 1 December 1993

Fig. 60.4   Balancing the books 1994–95

PSBR and PSDR

A public-sector borrowing requirement (PSBR) arises when the public sector spends more than it raises in revenue. Public-sector finances are made up of the central governments' budget position, local authorities budget positions and the net trading surplus or loss of nationalised industries and public corporations. The largest component is the central government's budget position. A PSBR can be financed by borrowing from the banking sector, from overseas or from the non-bank private sector. It is this last source which is the most widely used with the government selling government securities to, for example, pension funds.

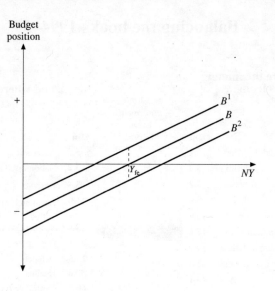

Fig. 60.5

PSDR

A public-sector debt repayment occurs when the public sector receives more in revenue than it spends. It is a negative PSBR as, in this case, the government instead of having to borrow will be able to repay some past debt.

In recent years public expenditure has usually exceeded public revenue. However, in the years 1987 to 1990 there was a PSDR mainly because of the high level of economic activity arising from the 1986–88 consumer boom.

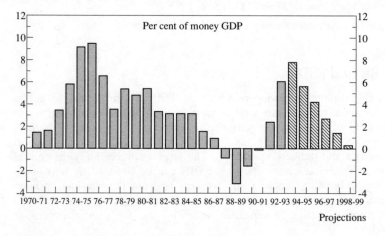

Source: The budget in brief, H.M. Treasury Nov. 1993

Fig. 60.6   Public-sector borrowing requirement

The national debt

The national debt is the accumulation of such government borrowings over past years. It is *not* the debt of the whole public sector; it is the debt of the central government. Until fairly recent years, the national debt grew most rapidly during the wars when governments found it impossible to finance all wartime expenditures from taxation. Since the Second World War a series of large budget deficits has increased the national debt considerably.

Composition of the national debt

The government borrows by issuing a wide range of different securities in an attempt to satisfy the requirements of different types of lenders (or 'savers'). An important distinction is that between marketable and non-marketable debt. Marketable debt consists of those government securities which can be bought and sold before the final maturity date. Such securities can change hands many times before the final date for repayment. Government stocks can be traded on the Stock Exchange and Treasury bills can be bought and sold in the money market. Marketability makes these securities liquid assets but their market values will depend upon the current rate of interest. Non-marketable debt consists of securities which must be held by the original purchaser until they are repaid. A major part of the non-marketable debt consists of National Savings Certificates.

Marketable debt represents about 70 per cent of the total debt and consists mainly of Government stocks (gilt-edged) which may be classified as follows:

Short-dated stocks. These are repayable by the government at some specified date within 5 years.

Medium-dated stocks. The government redeems these stocks at some specified date within 5 to 15 years.

Long-dated stocks. These securities mature at some specified date, but the securities have more than 15 years to run before that maturity date is reached.

Undated stocks. The government is under no obligation to pay back the money borrowed on undated stocks unless it so wishes. In other words there is no redemption date.

The majority of these securities carry a fixed rate of interest although since 1977 the government has issued stocks with a variable rate of interest which is linked to the market rate of interest on Treasury bills.

That part of the debt which consists of Treasury bills is often referred to as the *floating debt* because it represents short-term borrowing which has to be continually re-financed.

National savings securities include national savings certificates, defence bonds, premium bonds, national savings stamps, the index-linked saving certificates and the Save-As-You-Earn scheme.

The holders of the national debt

Official holdings account for about 9 per cent of the national debt. This part of the debt is held by government departments and the Bank of England. The relatively large holdings of the central bank consist of government securities held as a backing for the note issue and for the Bank's operations in the open market.

Another large slice of official holdings is held by the National Debt Commissioners who are responsible for the investments of the National Insurance Fund and the deposits of the National Savings Bank. A large proportion of the debt is held by financial institutions such as insurance companies, pension funds, building societies, and banks. Individuals and private trusts also hold a significant proportion of the national debt.

About 10 per cent of the UK national debt is held by overseas residents. As explained later, this external debt has important implications for the balance of payments.

The burden of the debt

Although the absolute size of the national debt has shown a striking increase in the years since the Second World War, taken by itself, the figure has little meaning. It must be judged in relation to the means of supporting the debt, that is, the ability to meet the interest payments to the holders of the debt. In 1946 the national debt was equal to approximately 290 per cent of the Gross Domestic Product whereas in 1992 this proportion had fallen to about 34 per cent.

It is often said that the practice of financing government spending by means of borrowed funds is 'unfair' because it transfers the liability for present spending to future generations who will be called upon to meet the interest payments and to repay the debt. This is not true. The financing of war by borrowings does not transfer the real burden of war. This has to be borne by the generation engaged in the war. It is they who have to go without the consumer goods, houses and so on so that war materials can be produced. We could not have increased the output of tanks in 1943 by reducing the output of motor cars in 1995. The same argument applies to the interest payments and the capital repayments in the years after the money was borrowed, because these transactions amount to a redistribution of income at the time when the payments are made. The generation making these payments is the same generation which is receiving them. Over the community as a whole the taxes are cancelled out by the interest received; the whole community does not experience any net gain or loss.

Since the national debt is simply a debt owed by the people collectively (i.e. the state) to the people individually, the community is neither richer nor poorer. If one brother borrows from another brother, the wealth of the family remains unchanged. If, however, the national debt were narrowly held (i.e. by relatively few rich people), the annual interest payments would amount to a fairly large redistribution of income from the taxpayers (most of the people) to the security holders (a small percentage of the people). The nation, however, is poorer to the extent of the debt held overseas. This is a real burden on the community because the interest payments and the repayments of capital must be made in foreign currencies and these, in turn, must be earned by exporting goods and services. The servicing and repayment of foreign debt involves a sacrifice of real output, that is, exports which do not exchange for imports.

Advantages of fiscal policy

The instruments of fiscal policy (taxation and government spending) act directly on the major economic variables (e.g. output, employment, prices); they are very powerful instruments. A budget surplus will remove purchasing power from the economy and reduce aggregate demand – a budget deficit will inject purchasing power and raise aggregate demand. But fiscal policy can be used in a discriminating manner to change the allocation of resources both industrially and regionally. The products of some industries can be taxed while other industries receive subsidies. Some industries may be selected for protection by means of tariffs while others may be allowed to compete with unrestricted imports. Some types of investment may be encouraged with investment grants or preferential tax treatment of profits. If the government wishes to encourage economic growth in particular regions it can apply such measures as investment grants, employment premiums, training grants, and so on, on a strictly regional basis. It may also deliberately bias its own spending by placing a disproportionate share of its own orders with firms in the selected regions.

Disadvantages of fiscal policy

A major disadvantage of fiscal policy is its relative inflexibility. Major changes in taxation and public expenditure cannot be carried out at frequent intervals – there is a great deal of administrative work involved. Changes in income tax, for example, involve the calculation and distribution of millions of new codes. Changes in public spending on goods and services take a long time to become effective. Much of this expenditure is tied to long-term contracts (e.g. the building of roads, power-stations, hospitals) which cannot be switched on and off as short-term regulators. There is often a serious time lag between the identification of the problem to be dealt with and the time when the fiscal measures begin to take effect. In this respect monetary policy may be a more efficient short-term regulator because it can be operated on a day to day basis.

Automatic stabilisers

Most fiscal arrangements have some features built into them which are known as *automatic stabilisers*. For example, as money incomes rise, a progressive system of income tax will automatically remove an increasing proportion of those incomes in taxation. Providing government spending remains unchanged there will be some restraining effects on inflationary tendencies. When incomes are falling the opposite effect occurs, proportionately less is taken in taxation, and if government spending is unchanged total demand will not fall as fast as gross money incomes.

Job seekers allowance and other social security benefits also act as automatic stabilisers. When unemployment rises and incomes fall, unemployment benefits increase and the opposite effect applies when unemployment is falling. Thus, a reduction in wages and salaries due to rising unemployment will not lead to a proportionate fall in aggregate demand.

61 Monetary policy

Definition

Monetary policy refers to the attempts to manipulate either the rate of interest or the supply of money so as to bring about desired changes in the economy. The aims of monetary policy are the same as those of economic policy generally. They are the maintenance of full employment, price stability, a satisfactory rate of economic growth, and a balance of payments equilibrium.

In the 1980s attention was focused on monetary policy following the monetarist view that the control of the money supply is probably the most important instrument for regulating total demand in an economy.

We have seen that the greater part of the money supply consists of bank deposits and that a large part of these deposits come into being as a result of bank lending. Total spending is very much influenced by the spender's ability to borrow from the banks either directly through loans or overdrafts, or indirectly through credit schemes. Any attempt to control the money supply therefore must be directed at controlling the bank's ability to lend, or to influencing firms' and households' willingness to borrow. We have already shown that the bank's ability to lend depends upon their supplies of liquid assets and some instruments of monetary policy are designed to act directly on the banks' supplies of these assets. But the willingness and ability to spend does not depend solely on the availability of bank credit – the price of that credit is also important. Even if the banks are willing and able to provide loans, some potential borrowers may not be persuaded to take up the bank loans if the rate of interest is so high that the prospective profits from the use of the loan, or the satisfactions from spending it on consumption, are scarcely higher than its cost.

The targets

The supply of money and the rate of interest are not independent variables. The monetary authorities cannot fix both the quantity *and* the price of money. If we refer back to Fig. 32.4 we see that if the demand for money (liquidity preference) does not change, any changes in the supply of money will alter the rate of interest (except at very low levels). Alternatively, if the supply of money remains fixed, any change in the demand for money will bring about changes in the rate of interest. Since the monetary authorities cannot determine demand they are in the same position as a monopolist; they can determine the quantity or the price – not both.

If the government chooses to fix a particular rate of interest then it must supply whatever quantity of money will be demanded at that rate.

As the demand for money changes, so must the supply; otherwise the rate of interest must change. If the authorities decide to fix the supply of money, the rate of interest will vary as the demand for money varies. The authorities are thus presented with a dilemma – should they try to influence demand by manipulating the rate of interest or control the supply of money by more direct means?

The effectiveness of the rate of interest as a policy instrument

There are very divergent views on the effectiveness of the rate of interest as a policy instrument. There seems no doubt that by raising the rate high enough it will reach a level which is a deterrent to borrowing and hence spending.

This was witnessed in 1989 when the sharp rise in the rate of interest significantly reduced borrowing and badly hit the housing market. But in times of boom when business people are very optimistic this level may be very high indeed, and such high interest rates may well conflict with other objectives of government policy. As the largest borrower in the country the government will be seriously affected by the greatly increased interest burden of the national debt. High interest rates will also be very unpopular in the politically sensitive housing market where interest charges are a major cost item. At the opposite extreme low interest rates are not likely to be very effective as a stimulant when the economy is depressed. Reducing interest rates to very low levels is not likely to encourage borrowing and spending when new investment offers little or no prospect of reasonable profits. When there is heavy unemployment lower interest charges are not likely to lead to any significant increase in borrowing on credit in the markets for consumer goods.

Nevertheless, changes in the rate of interest can be used in conjunction with other measures and the policy has the advantage that it is a flexible instrument which can be applied fairly quickly. In between the extremes of boom and slump it has effects on costs of production which can lead to changes in investment, especially in the holdings of stocks, which will, in turn, affect output and employment. Changes in the rate of interest also, it is believed, have important psychological effects on business people's expectations. They are also an important influence on the balance of payments position and the exchange rate.

It may be necessary at times to encourage an inflow of short-term capital or alternatively to ensure that there is not a large-scale withdrawal of balances by foreign depositors. This may be achieved by raising interest rates in the domestic market to levels which are more attractive than those in foreign money markets.

The instruments of monetary policy

The rate of interest

In recent years the short-term interest rate has been the instrument most widely used by the government. The rate of interest charged by the Bank of England was, until 1981, known as the Minimum Lending Rate and this rate was publicly announced so as to give the money market a clear signal of the Bank's intentions. The use of MLR was suspended in 1981 but was used briefly on 16 September 1992 in a vain attempt to support sterling. The idea now is that the central bank operates as a buyer and seller in the money market so as to influence the rate of interest. It can keeps the banking system short of money and then lend the required amount at an interest rate which it decides.

Open market operations

In addition to setting the terms on which it is prepared to lend, the central bank can act directly on the supply of financial assets in the banking system by means of its activities in the markets for securities. The Bank of England through its brokers buys and sells securities (Treasury Bills and other government securities) in the open market. On a daily basis the Bank of England seeks to avoid sharp fluctuations in interest rates. So if there is a shortage of funds it will purchase bills. However, if it wishes to restrict bank lending, it will instruct its broker to sell securities. The buyers will pay for these securities with cheques drawn on their accounts in the commercial banks. These cheques will be payable to the Bank of England which will then hold claims on the commercial banks. The debts will be settled by a reduction of the bankers' deposits at the Bank of England. A fall in these deposits represents a reduction in the banks' liquid assets ratio and they will be obliged to reduce the level of their total deposits in order to restore the required ratio of liquid assets to deposits. We should note, however, that this action will only force the banks to reduce their lending if they are operating with the minimum level of liquid assets. If the banks have a surplus of liquid assets, a reduction of their deposits at the central bank might still leave them with an adequate total supply of liquid assets and they will not be obliged to reduce their total deposits.

When the central bank wishes to see an expansion of bank lending it will enter the market and buy securities, making payment for them with cheques drawn on itself. The sellers of these securities pay the central banks' cheques into accounts at the commercial banks. The banks now hold claims on the central bank which will settle its indebtedness by crediting the outstanding amounts to the bankers' deposits. An increase in bankers' deposits at the central bank amounts to an increase in the liquid assets ratio. The banks will be able to expand their total lending by a multiple of the increase in their liquid assets.

Special deposits

The payment of special deposits deprives the banks of some of their liquid assets since they have been instructed that the funds for such payments should not be obtained from the sale of longer term securities. A call for special deposits, therefore, has the same effect as open market sales of securities, but it is a much more direct instrument. If the monetary authorities wish to encourage bank lending they can release any special deposits they are holding and thus increase the banks' supply of liquid assets. However, the last call for special deposits was made in 1979.

Funding

Although open market operations and calls for special deposits may be successful in changing the banks' liquid assets ratio, they will not be effective instruments for restraining bank lending when the banks are holding surplus liquid assets. Funding is a way of reducing the supplies of liquid assets available to the banking system. The policy requires the Bank of England to change the structure of the national debt by issuing more long-term securities and fewer short-term securities (Treasury Bills). This operation would make the banks more vulnerable to open market operations and calls for special deposits, because Treasury bills are liquid assets and long-term securities are liquid assets.

Quantitative and qualitative controls

A government, through its central bank can make use of quantitative controls (limits on bank lending) and qualitative controls (directives on who should receive loans). However, these have not been used in the UK since the 1970s.

Monetary policy stance

A restrictionist (or tight) monetary policy is one which seeks to reduce aggregate demand, often in an attempt to reduce inflationary pressures or correct a balance of payments deficit. It involves an increase in the rate of interest and/or a reduction in the growth of the money supply. In contrast, an expansionary monetary policy would be implemented to increase aggregate demand, probably to raise output and employment. In this case the rate of interest will be reduced and/or the growth of the money supply stimulated.

Monetary policy and the national debt

In addition to its responsibility for operating the government's monetary policy the Bank of England has the responsibility for the management of the national debt. These two responsibilities may present the central bank with conflicting objectives. As manager of the national debt the Bank of England has the task of raising large sums of money for the government every year. It must float new issues of securities to finance current government spending and to repay the loans which are maturing. The money and capital markets will only take up large issues of government securities if they are attractively priced, the risk of capital losses are not too great, and the yield is satisfactory. The central bank must operate in the open market by buying and selling securities in such a way as to maintain security prices and yields at attractive levels. The current rate of interest is a very important consideration because it influences the rate of interest which must be offered on new issues of securities, and with such a large national debt, it is desirable to minimise the interest burden.

But the central bank, as we have seen, is obliged to carry out open market operations with a view to controlling the lending activities of the commercial banks. It is very likely, therefore, that situations will arise where the objectives of debt management will conflict with those of monetary policy. For example, the central bank may be obliged to conduct open market sales of securities in order to reduce the banks' liquid assets. Heavy sales of securities, however, will depress security prices and the lowering of security prices has the effect of raising interest rates. Existing holders of government securities will suffer capital losses and this will not make the market very receptive to any new issue of securities which the central bank may be trying to float in order to finance government expenditure. There may also be occasions when monetary policy calls for a fall in interest rates (to stimulate private spending). If this occurs at the same time as the central bank has the responsibility for putting a large new issue of securities on the market, the Bank of England would be frustrating its debt policy objective since increasing the supply of securities would raise interest rates instead of lowering them.

Monetary policy and fiscal policy

Fiscal policy affects monetary policy and vice versa. If the government has a positive PSBR and finances it by borrowing from the banking system, then, other things being equal, there will be an increase in the money supply as bank deposits are created to supply the government with the necessary funds.

If the government borrows from the non-bank public, the money supply will not change because bank deposits are transferred from the private sector to the public sector. However, as explained below, the increase in government spending and borrowing will have some effect on the rate of interest.

Crowding out

One possible effect of an increase in government borrowing and spending has been described as the 'crowding-out' effect. It is believed, by some economists, to take place because the increase in government borrowing will increase the demand for loans and bid up the rate of interest. Furthermore, the increase in government expenditure will raise income and this will increase the demand for money for transactions purposes. This again will tend to raise the rate of interest.

The effect of the increase in the rate of interest will be to reduce private investment and consumption (e.g. the demand for durable consumer goods). In other words, the increase in government borrowing and spending will crowd out some private sector spending. Total expenditure, therefore, will increase by less than the increase in public expenditure. However, Keynesian's dispute that crowding out will occur. They claim that net government expenditure will raise national income and savings thereby creating extra funds for investment and obviating the need for the rate of interest to rise. Indeed, empirical evidence suggests that the rate of interest does not move in line with changes in the PBSR.

62 Balance of payments policies

For countries like the UK, which are heavily dependent on foreign trade (about 30 per cent of UK output is exported directly or indirectly), the foreign balance is a critical matter. While short-term deficits might be covered by the use of official reserves and overseas borrowing, in the longer run a country must pay its way in the world. But a satisfactory balance of payments position is not simply one in which income equals expenditure on foreign account. Equilibrium should not be achieved at the expense of the other objectives of economic policy.

Government policy in this area is subject to several limitations. While the manipulation of tariffs and other barriers to trade is a legitimate part of a balance of payments policy, the use of such measures is restricted by membership of bodies such as WTO and customs unions such as the EU. Secondly, membership of exchange rate systems such as the ERM puts some limitations on a country's freedom to use exchange rate adjustments as an instrument of policy. We must remember, of course, that membership of international institutions also confers substantial benefits. Thirdly, a country's balance of payments performance is determined by the economic policies adopted by other countries as well as by its own policies. An expansionary policy in the USA will lead to a marked improvement in the level of UK exports, while policies to protect infant industries in developing countries will have the opposite effect.

Influences on policies adopted

The policies a government will adopt to correct a balance of payments disequilibrium will depend on the cause of the disequilibrium, the type of exchange rate system being operated, the level of economic activity in the domestic market, government priorities and the constraints imposed by membership of international organisations, as outlined above.

Exchange rate systems

Fixed exchange rates

When countries are operating fixed exchange rates, national economies are closely linked and economic changes in one country will transmit their effects fairly quickly to other countries. Thus, a country experiencing a higher rate of inflation than its competitors will find its balance of payments position deteriorating because imports are becoming more competitive on the home market and exports less competitive in world markets. With a fixed exchange rate the immediate effect of any deficit falls on the official reserves of gold and foreign currency. When there is a persistent deficit, these reserves (plus borrowing facilities) will soon be exhausted so that, if the exchange rate is to be held, the government must take steps to eliminate the deficit.

Floating exchange rates

The main argument put forward in favour of floating rates is that they remove the burdens of policies to deal with deficits from the domestic economy. There is no need for a country to hold large reserves of foreign currency and no need to depress home demand when there is a deficit on the balance of payments. But floating rates do not remove balance of payments problems so neatly as the theory indicates, neither do they isolate the economy from external forces. Surpluses and deficits, it is true, will change the relative prices of imports and exports via changes in the exchange rate, and this movement will bring about an equilibrium in the foreign exchange market. It does not follow, however, that this will also bring about an equilibrium in the balance of payments. This latter situation will only come about if the volumes of imports and exports change by the correct amounts, and this depends upon the elasticities of demand for, and supply of, exports and imports. In any case, changes in the volumes of exports and imports take time, and the time lag between the change in the exchange rate and the changes in the quantities of exports and imports could be long enough for adverse effects to be felt in the home economy.

A change in the exchange rate

A country operating a fixed exchange rate which finds that its goods are not price competitive at home and abroad may decide to devalue its currency.

Devaluation

The immediate effect of devaluation is to change the relative prices of imports and exports. Exports become cheaper *in terms of foreign currency*, while imports become dearer *in terms of the home currency*.

Example: *Before devaluation* £1 = $2.0
A British car, price £10 000, costs $20 000 in the USA
An American machine, price $30 000, costs £15 000 in the UK
After devaluation £1 = $1.5
A British car, price £10 000, costs $15 000 in the USA
An American machine, price $30 000, costs £20 000 in the UK

The analysis from here on, of course is exactly the same as that for the depreciation of a currency on a floating exchange rate although a depreciation occurs as a result of market forces rather than government intervention.

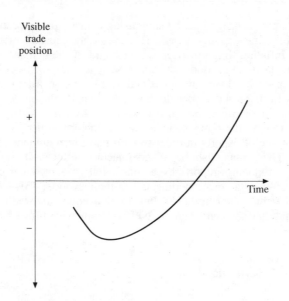

Fig. 62.1   The J effect

Before there is time for demand and supply to adjust, a fall in the exchange rate may cause a deterioration in the balance of payments position. This is known as the J curve effect and is illustrated in Fig. 62.1.

For a fall in the value of the currency to improve the balance of payments position, the combined price elasticities of demand for exports and imports must be greater than one. This is referred to as the Marshall–Lerner condition. Export volume will increase and the volume of imports will fall. But export *earnings* will only increase if the demand for exports is elastic, that is, if the volume of exports increases by a greater percentage than the percentage fall in their external prices. Since the foreign prices of imports do not change, any fall in the volume of imports must lead to a reduction in foreign currency expenditures.

There are several other factors which influence the effectiveness of devaluation as a remedy for a balance of payments deficit. It can only lead to favourable price movements if major trading rivals do not devalue their own currencies. The situation with regard to the supply of exports must also be considered. The full benefits of the increased demand for exports can only be realised if additional supplies of exports can be made available. If the devaluing country is operating at full employment, more goods can only be supplied to export markets by reducing supplies to the home market. It may be necessary, therefore, to increase taxation and restrict bank credit to reduce home demand in order to free supplies for foreign markets.

A fall in the exchange rate, by stimulating demand for domestic goods, will benefit domestic employment. However it may initiate or worsen a cost-push inflation. Import prices will rise and, if the demand for these goods is inelastic (e.g. foodstuffs and raw materials), this will raise the domestic price level and provoke claims for compensating wage increases. A further effect of devaluation is to increase the burden of overseas indebtedness. Since foreign debts are usually expressed in terms of foreign currency, the repayment of any given loan will now require a greater volume of exports in order to earn that given amount of foreign currency. There may also be adverse income effects. If devaluation succeeds in reducing imports by a substantial amount, other countries must be suffering a corresponding fall in their exports. This loss of income will reduce their ability to buy foreign goods and the devaluing country may find the beneficial price effects somewhat offset by this unfavourable income effect.

Import controls

Tariffs, quotas, exchange control and other methods can all be used to limit imports and direct demand to home-produced goods. However, as we have seen, membership of the EU prevents the UK from imposing import restrictions against member countries and membership of the WTO makes it difficult to impose them on non-EU countries. Import controls also have the potential to increase domestic inflation. Tariffs directly raise the price of imports on the domestic market and quotas, by limiting the supply of imports, are likely to push up their price. In addition, firms which use imported raw materials and components will experience a rise in their costs of production which they are likely to pass on to their customers in the form of higher prices. Domestic firms, seeing rival goods from abroad rising in price, may raise their own prices knowing they will be able to remain competitive.

Expenditure switching and expenditure reducing

Devaluation and import controls can be classified as expenditure switching measures. An expenditure-switching measure is any measure which seeks to direct spending from foreign goods to home-produced goods whereas expenditure-reducing measures are those which aim to reduce aggregate demand.

Deflation

By definition deflationary measures are expenditure reducing as they lower aggregate demand. This fall in demand may be achieved by a rise in taxation, a fall in government expenditure or a combination. This policy may be adopted when high income levels are sucking in imports and creating inflationary pressures. A fall in total planned spending should lead to a fall in expenditure on foreign goods and services. It might also lead to an increase in exports as domestic firms find it more difficult to sell in the home market and make greater efforts to sell in overseas markets.

There might, however, be an unfavourable 'feed-back' effect from abroad, because a cut-back in one country's imports reduces other countries' exports and, hence, other countries' income. The country carrying out the expenditure-reducing policy, therefore, might find that, although it has favourable effects on its imports, it also has unfavourable effects on its exports. The other major problem with these measures is that they tend to increase unemployment. If the deficit is a substantial one, expenditure-reducing measures would be very unpopular because it would require a relatively large reduction in aggregate demand in order to achieve the required cut in import expenditures. In other words, the 'cost' in terms of unemployment would be politically unacceptable.

Other measures to reduce a deficit

A lack of price competitiveness and a high marginal propensity to import are not the only possible causes of a deficit. Firms may be poor at marketing and in order to rectify this a government may promote trade fairs, give awards to top exporters and encourage university and other courses in marketing. The quality of goods may be poor and here measures may be undertaken to improve education, training, research and development. The country may also be producing products which are not in high world demand. In this case a government may give financial assistance to sunrise industries.

Balance of payments surplus

So far we have concentrated on measures to reduce a deficit. However, as we saw in Chapter 55 a balance of payments surplus can have disadvantages. To remove a surplus a government can again use expenditure-switching and, in this case, expenditure-increasing measures. In a fixed exchange rate system it can revalue its currency by moving the exchange value of its currency to a higher priority. This will make exports relatively dearer (in terms of foreign currencies) and imports relatively cheaper (in terms of the home currency). Another expenditure-switching measure to reduce a surplus would be to reduce or remove import controls. Expenditure-increasing measures would include cuts in income tax, increases in student grants, etc.

63 Measures to reduce unemployment

For some time in the 1980s it was thought the UK would never return to a situation of full employment. However, in the early 1990s economists began to discuss again not only the desirability but also the possibility of achieving full employment.

The meaning of full employment

Full employment cannot mean a situation where everyone wanting to work and able to work is constantly employed. It is not zero unemployment. There will always be some elements of frictional, structural, seasonal and residual unemployment. It is sometimes taken to mean a situation where the number of vacancies is at least equal to the numbers out of work. In this case aggregate demand is providing the right number of jobs, but they are not in the right place or of the right type to match the geographical distribution and occupational skills of the unemployed. This definition is not acceptable because it is possible to visualise a situation where there is a large number of unemployed and a correspondingly large number of vacancies. For this reason full employment is usually defined in terms of some politically acceptable level of unemployment. This level will vary according to the prevailing conditions and the experience of recent years. In the twenty-five years which followed the end of the Second World War people became accustomed to unemployment rates of $1\frac{1}{2}$ per cent to 2 per cent. At this time a rate of unemployment of something less than $2\frac{1}{2}$ per cent would probably have been regarded as a situation of full employment. Nowadays, full employment is usually taken to mean less than 3 per cent unemployed.

The Keynesian approach

Keynesians believe that unemployment is largely involuntary, will not be corrected by free market forces and results mainly from a lack of aggregate demand. Their analysis indicates that equilibrium at less than a full employment level of income is possible because total planned expenditure consists of spending decisions by households, firms and government which are not coordinated in any way. It is possible, therefore, that the amount which people plan to save plus the amount they plan to spend on imports *out of a full employment level of income* will be greater than the amounts which firms plan to invest and which other countries plan to spend on home-produced goods and services. In other words, if, at a full employment level of income, planned leakages are greater than planned injections, income will fall and settle in equilibrium at a level which is below the full employment level.

Demand management

Keynes suggested that the achievement of a full and stable level of employment required the government to play an active part in determining the level of total expenditure. This policy, known as *demand management*, was adopted by most governments in the post-war period.

If the government is to manage aggregate demand effectively, it must be capable of influencing the components of aggregate demand, i.e. C, I, G, X and M. Government spending and taxation will be important instruments for this purpose, and by running budget deficits or surpluses, the government can inject or withdraw purchasing power into or from the economy.

Reducing unemployment

As Keynesians believe that unemployment is caused principally by a lack of aggregate demand, they advocate increasing aggregate demand. Figure 63.1 shows that output is initially at Q. This is below the full employment level of QX and there is a deflationary gap. An increase in government expenditure shifts the aggregate demand curve from AD to AD^1, thereby raising output to the full employment level. It should be noted that the increase in government spending has a magnified effect on national income. This is because of the multiplier.

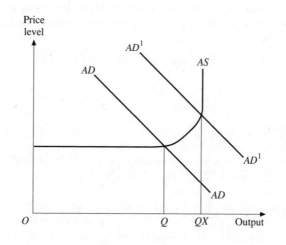

Fig. 63.1

Let us suppose that an economy is in equilibrium producing a less than full employment output. The task of government is to increase aggregate demand until all resources are employed. If the deficiency of income is estimated to be £10 000 million and the multiplier is believed to be 2, then one or more of the components of aggregate demand must be raised, in total, by £5000 m. There are a number of policies which can be employed to achieve this objective.

Fiscal policy

The government might act in a direct manner by increasing its own expenditures on goods and services while leaving taxation unchanged. Alternatively it might decide to stimulate private spending (both C and I) by reducing taxation, but the effects here are more difficult to estimate because some of the increase in disposable income will be saved rather than spent. An increase in social security benefits will be an effective way of bringing about an increase in C because the MPCs of the recipients will be very large. Private investment might be encouraged by more generous investment grants. In other words the government will budget for a deficit.

A worked example

In an economy, national income = £1000 m.
The injections are, G = £100 m., I = £80 m., X = £70m.
The leakages are, M = 0.05 of income, S = 0.1 of income, and T = 0.1 of income and these proportions are constant.
The government considers that it is necessary to raise national income to £1200 m. in order to achieve full employment. It decides to increase its own expenditure and leave the rate of taxation unchanged. By how much must G be raised?

a Since the consumption of home-produced goods is a constant proportion of income,

$$MPC = 1 - (0.05 + 0.1 + 0.1) = 0.75$$

The multiplier $= \dfrac{1}{1 - 0.75} = 4$.

In order to raise national income by £200m., therefore, government spending must increase by £50 m. (i.e. to £150 m.)

b Alternatively,
In equilibrium,   planned injections = planned leakages
i.e. $I + G + X$ $= S + T + M$
When the equilibrium level of income is £1200 m.,
I(£80 m.) + G + X(£70 m.) = S (£120 m.) + T(£120 m.) + M(£60 m.)
                    G = £150 m.

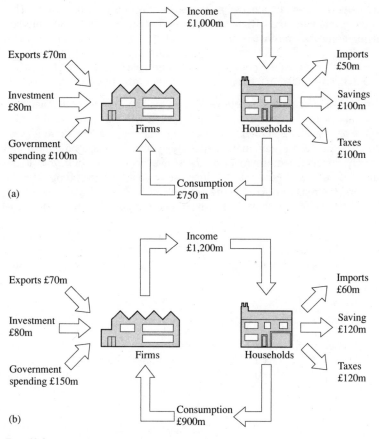

Fig. 63.2

The initial and final situations are illustrated in Fig. 63.2 where (a) shows the original equilibrium and (b) the equilibrium situation after the effects of the increase in *G* have worked themselves out.

Monetary policy

In this particular case, attempts will be made to encourage private investment and consumption spending by relaxing any restrictions on the commercial banks' lending activities and the authorities will take steps to bring about a fall in the rate of interest.

Exchange rate policy

To increase aggregate demand a government might decide to lower its exchange rate. This will make exports cheaper in terms of foreign currency and imports more expensive in terms of the domestic currency. This should switch demand from foreign goods to domestic goods thereby raising domestic employment.

The supply-side approach

New classical economists believe that increasing aggregate demand will not in the long run reduce unemployment but will cause inflation to rise. Figure 63.3 shows that unemployment is initially at UN and there is price stability. Increasing government spending, raises aggregate demand and initially lowers unemployment to U_1. However, the higher demand also raises inflation to 6 per cent. The increase in costs and the recognition by workers that real wages are being eroded causes unemployment to return to NAIRU. However, there is now 6 per cent inflation (see Ch. 50).

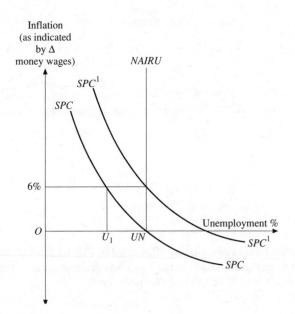

Fig. 63.3

New classical economists argue that the only way to reduce unemployment without increasing inflation is to increase aggregate supply. They advocate policies which are directed towards increasing the efficiency with which capital and labour are used in production. Such policies include measures which aim to reduce the imperfections in the labour market and the use of tax incentives to encourage more investment and improvements in productivity.

These measures include keeping a gap between the job seekers allowance and low wages so as to increase the willingness of the unemployed to take up jobs. They support trade union reform to reduce the tendency for trade unions to push up wages above their equilibrium levels and engage in restrictive practices, thereby making labour less attractive to employers. They also oppose minimum wage legislation.

To encourage people to take up employment and to encourage entrepreneurs to expand and employ more workers they advocate tax reform, increasing the gap between economic agents' earned income and their disposable income by lowering direct tax.

As well as potential workers being unwilling to take up employment, they may be unable to do so because of the lack of suitable skills so new classical economists advocate education and training as ways of increasing labour productivity and hence making employers more willing to expand their labour force. Improving labour flexibility, making it easier to 'hire and fire' workers and using less rigid work patterns including part-time and casual employment, they believe will also encourage employers to recruit more workers.

In addition, new classical economists argue that deregulation and privatisation improve efficiency and thereby raise output and employment. All these measures are aimed at increasing the economy's aggregate supply potential and lowering NAIRU. Figure 63.4 shows the long-run aggregate supply curve shifting to the right thereby increasing output and employment.

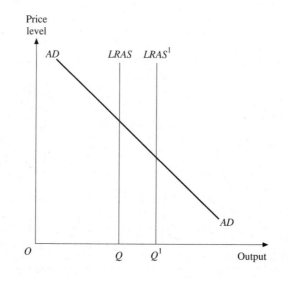

Fig. 63.4

Common ground

Keynesians and supply-side supporters both favour improving information, promoting labour mobility and training to reduce frictional and structural unemployment. They also agree that raising aggregate demand when the problem is one of regional unemployment is more likely to generate inflationary pressures in the prosperous areas while leaving the depressed regions largely unaffected – although they disagree about what alternative measures should be used.

Most economists now accept that to reduce unemployment both aggregate demand and aggregate supply may need to be raised. Improving the quality of the workforce, and making people more willing to take up employment will not be effective if demand for goods and services is insufficient to create an adequate number of jobs. Similarly, increasing demand without ensuring that the unemployed have the necessary skills and willingness to take up the vacancies created would be likely to cause inflation and a balance of payments deficit rather than a reduction in unemployment.

64 Anti-inflationary policies

Although opinion is divided on whether a low rate of inflation (2 or 3 per cent per annum) is undesirable, there is little disagreement on the undesirability of higher rates of inflation (more than 10 per cent per annum). Inflation creates serious tensions because it tends to redistribute income in favour of the more militant groups with strong bargaining powers and penalises those on fixed incomes and those with weaker bargaining powers. It usually leads to a deterioration in the balance of payments, and favours debtors at the expense of creditors. The most serious problem is the tendency for inflation to escalate. It creates expectations of further price rises and these expectations lead unions and firms to raise wages and prices by amounts which take account not only of past and present, but of future price increases. Once inflation becomes firmly established, the most important and the most difficult objective of any policy to cure inflation is to change these expectations. People must be convinced that the proposed measures will be effective. The policy measures adopted will depend on what is thought to have caused the inflation, its level, the state of the economy and the government's priorities.

Fiscal policy

Demand-pull inflation at full employment

To combat demand-pull inflation occurring at full employment a government can employ a deflationary fiscal policy. This will involve raising taxation and/or cutting government expenditure. Increasing income tax will be likely to lower consumer spending, raising corporation tax will tend to lower investment and reducing government spending directly lowers aggregate expenditure. A reduction in any or all of these components of aggregate expenditure will have a downward multiplier effect and may succeed in removing an inflationary gap. Figure 64.1 shows that a fall in government spending from G to G^1 removes the inflationary gap of AB.

All these measures have their limitations. Increasing income tax may cause prices to rise if it stimulates workers to press for wage rises to maintain their real disposable income. It may prove difficult to cut government spending and reducing public- and private-sector investment will lower future potential output.

Demand-pull inflation at less than full employment

If aggregate demand is moving ahead of current output at less than full employment a government may adopt rather different fiscal policy

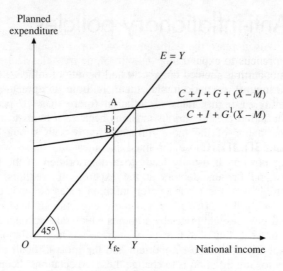

Fig. 64.1

measures. It may seek to correct the imbalance in aggregate demand and aggregate supply by raising aggregate supply rather than by reducing aggregate demand. Fiscal policy measures which may be used include government grants for firms setting up in development areas, cuts in corporation tax and subsidies to sunrise industries. It would be hoped that these measures would raise aggregate supply more than aggregate demand and make future aggregate supply more responsive to changes in aggregate demand. Figure 64.2 shows that an increase in aggregate supply to $LRAS^1$ lowers the price level to P^1.

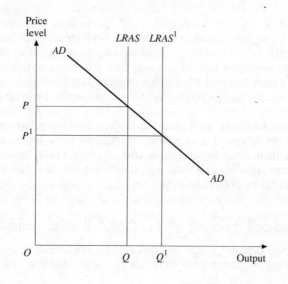

Fig. 64.2

To achieve the same objective new classical economists recommend cutting direct taxes. They believe that reducing income tax and corporation tax will increase the willingness of people to enter the workforce and entrepreneus to expand their output. Some new classical economists also favour cutting unemployment-related benefits to encourage the unemployed to seek work more actively. Increasing the numbers employed will raise aggregate supply.

Cost-push inflation

Some of the fiscal policy measures outlined above could also be employed to combat cost-push inflation. For instance, reducing corporation tax will lower firms' costs. Other possible fiscal policy measures include reducing indirect tax, cutting income tax in an attempt to lower wage claims, reducing the prices charged by government concerns, subsidising production costs and lowering wage rises in the public sector. If the government lowers its expenditure by more than it lowers tax, it may be able to reduce firms' costs without adding to aggregate demand.

Monetary inflation

Lowering expenditure by more than tax revenue is a fiscal policy approach which might also be adopted if the cause of inflation is thought to be the money supply growing faster than output because of government borrowing. Reducing a public-sector borrowing requirement will reduce a government's need to borrow. However, in practice most of the PSBR is normally financed by borrowing from the non-bank private sector and hence does not add to the money supply.

Monetary policy

As we have seen, monetarists argue that the cause of inflation is the growth of the money supply exceeding the growth of output. To combat this they argue that the solution to inflation is to reduce the growth of the money supply so that it matches output growth. Figure 64.3 shows that a fall in the growth of the money supply reduces aggregate demand and inflation. To achieve a reduction in the growth of the money supply, the government may adopt a number of policies including raising interest rates and limiting bank lending. However, Keynesians question the direct proportionate link and argue that the causal relationship runs the other way. They maintain that increasing economic activity creates a demand for more money and the money supply is increased to meet the growing demand for it.

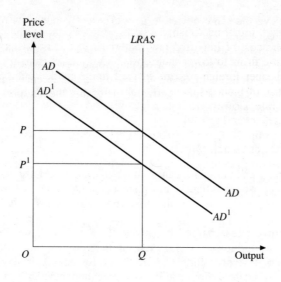

Fig. 64.3

Demand-pull inflation

Deflationary monetary policy may also be employed against demand-pull inflation. Raising interest rates and reducing bank lending will be likely to lower investment and reduce consumer spending, particularly on items bought on credit. However, the effectiveness of an increase in interest rates depends very much on the state of business and consumer expectations. If firms and people are optimistic that incomes will rise in the future they may be willing to borrow at high interest rates. In addition, with a high rate of inflation, high interest rates may not be a serious deterrent to borrowers because the real rate of interest may be quite low; indeed, it may even be negative. The alternative measure, controlling bank lending, has been found difficult to implement in practice with, for example, firms getting round limits by lending directly to each other.

Cost-push inflation

A government might adopt an expansionary rather than a restrictionary monetary policy in the case of cost-push inflation. In particular, it could reduce firms' costs by lowering interest rates.

Exchange rate policy

In the early 1980s the government encouraged a rise in the value of the pound on foreign exchange markets as part of its anti-inflationary policy.

A higher exchange rate can reduce inflation in three main ways. It lowers the price of imported finished goods which count in the RPI and it reduces the cost of imported raw materials. In addition it puts pressure on domestic firms to lower their costs and prices to remain competitive against cheaper foreign imports in their home market and to offset the rise in price of their goods in foreign markets resulting from the higher exchange rate. However, a high exchange rate can have an adverse effect on employment and growth.

Membership of a fixed exchange rate regime, such as the ERM, can also be used as an anti-inflationary measure. As the value of the currency is fixed within margins, a competitive advantage lost by higher domestic costs, cannot be regained by a fall in the value of the currency. This will put pressure on domestic firms to keep their costs and prices low.

Incomes policies

The main aim of an incomes policy is to link the growth of incomes to the growth of productivity so as to prevent the excessive rises in factor incomes which raise costs and hence prices. It also has the important objective of preventing a redistribution of income towards those groups with powerful bargaining positions. By focusing attention on the need to raise productivity in order to justify wage increases, an incomes policy may lead to a greater awareness of the need to increase industrial and commercial efficiency. Although an incomes policy must embrace all forms of income – wages, interest, rent, and profits – it will tend to concentrate largely on wages because these account for about two-thirds of the value of final output.

Structure

There are three fundamental steps in establishing and operating an effective incomes policy. First, a decision must be taken on the permitted (or recommended) percentage increase in aggregate income for the period ahead (normally one year). This figure is referred to as the *norm* and is usually based on the anticipated increase in total output. In the sequence of incomes policies which were tried in the UK from 1965 onwards, the norms varied from zero to about 10 per cent.

The next step is to decide the manner in which the total increase in income is to be distributed among the various income groups.

The third and most difficult task is to give effect to these decisions by setting up some machinery for enforcement and supervision.

Major difficulties arise when the second stage is reached. Even if we assume that general agreement is reached on the *average* wage increase, it does not mean that all workers will receive the same percentage increase in wages. If this policy were adopted, existing wage differentials would be frozen and the major incentive to labour mobility would be removed. If the government is anxious to encourage labour mobility it will have to allow industries which are short of labour to offer something higher than the norm while industries trying to shed labour will pay something less than the norm. There will also be demands from other groups for 'exceptional' treatment. Workers who feel that they have been left behind in previous wage-price spirals will press for special treatment. It might also be necessary to allow some exceptions in order to encourage greater efficiency by permitting increases above the norm where workers have made a substantial contribution to increased productivity.

It is very difficult to introduce flexibility into an incomes policy without causing resentment among those who do not qualify for special treatment. When it comes to justifying a wage increase we all feel that we have a special case to plead. Movements away from existing differentials are often regarded as 'unfair'. Such feelings also arise because increases in productivity vary enormously as between different industries. Some industries, especially those which are science-based (e.g. chemicals) and those which can obtain important technical economies (e.g. the motor industry), are capable of achieving annual increases in productivity well above the national average. Workers in such industries may feel that their wage increases should be related to movements in productivity in their own industries and not to the national average.

Perhaps the most difficult task of all is that of enforcement and supervision. In a society where the traditional method of wage negotiation is that of freely conducted collective bargaining and where powerful trade unions are determined to retain their freedom to negotiate on behalf of their members, it is extremely doubtful whether the statutory enforcement of an incomes policy is a practical proposition, except perhaps for a very short period in a crisis situation. On the other hand, voluntary policies do not appear to have met with much success. Where there is a large number of trade unions each representing sectional interests, it is extremely difficult to obtain general agreement on the guidelines for an incomes policy. There are many thousands of separate wage settlements and the effective policing of these agreements to make sure that they conform with the general principles of the incomes policy is a formidable administrative task.

Statutory rent control on privately owned houses can be imposed. Landlords can be required to satisfy a public rent tribunal before being allowed to raise rents. However, when this policy has been used to keep rents below the market price a number of disadvantages have arisen. In particular, supply has decreased with houses being sold rather than rented.

Effectiveness of incomes policies

Incomes policies have sometimes taken the form of a complete freeze on wages and prices. It is difficult to maintain a wage and price standstill for more than a few months, because supply and demand conditions will continue to change and hence relative prices must be allowed to change if the price mechanism is to perform any useful function. In addition, trade unions will strongly oppose any protracted wage freeze. While they have been in force, wage and price freezes have certainly slowed down the pace of inflation, but their effect has been like that of a temporary dam. Once the policy is relaxed, there is a flood of wage claims and price increases which very soon bring wages and prices back on their former trend.

It is very difficult to assess the effectiveness of the incomes policies which have been tried. It is not sufficient to discover whether wages and prices have risen faster in periods of controls than in periods without them. Incomes policies are normally applied when inflationary pressures have become very intense. The effects of the policies should be judged by the difference between what actually happened and what might otherwise have happened in the absence of any controls. As far as British experience is concerned, it seems that wage and price controls when firmly applied can work for a time, but they break down when prices are forced upwards by non-wage factors.

Incomes policies have been criticised because they bring the government into conflict with the unions and increase the extent of industrial unrest. For this reason the Labour government in 1974 introduced the idea of a *social contract* between unions and government whereby the government promised industrial and social legislation desired by the unions in return for union promises to moderate their wage claims. Incomes policies both statutory and voluntary were operated for 10 out of the 14 years between 1966 and 1979. These policies, however, did not reverse the trend to higher rates of inflation although, for short periods, they certainly reduced the rate of inflation. Although incomes policies are unpopular with the trade unions, the high cost of alternative anti-inflationary policies (e.g. demand-management and control of the money supply) in terms of unemployment have led many economists to the view that the government must give high priority to the task of devising an acceptable and workable incomes policy.

Since 1979 there has been no formal incomes policy. The conservative governments have stated they believe these do not address the real causes of inflation and they interfere with free market forces, for instance, making it difficult for firms which wish to expand to recruit labour. However, despite these views the government has occasionally suggested norms for pay rises and has often set cash limits on public-sector pay settlements.

Price controls

To many people, the obvious way to stop prices rising is to apply price controls. Such controls, however, attack the symptoms of inflation rather than the causes. Where the cause of inflation is excess demand, price controls will only lead to shortages and create a demand for a system of rationing. Another problem is that the size of the administrative task means that price controls and rationing can only be applied to a limited range of key commodities. Price controls, if maintained for any extended period, will distort the allocation of resources because price movements are the indicators which inform suppliers and purchasers of the extent and direction of the changes in supply and demand which are always taking place. Nevertheless, price controls may have a role to play in dealing with the problems of cost-push inflation.

Targets

A number of economists believe that expectations play a key role in creating and reducing inflation. If workers and firms become convinced that the government is committed to and able to reduce inflation, they will moderate their wage claims and rises in the prices of their products, thereby reducing inflation. It is thought by some that setting targets will increase people's and firms' conviction that the government is taking a firm line against inflation. A number of targets have been used in recent years including a target growth of the money supply and a target value for the exchange rate. The current target is the inflation rate itself. In September 1992 the government set the target for the underlying rate of inflation of between 1 and 4 per cent with the longer-term objective being to bring the rate down to 2 per cent or less. The rate is allowed temporarily to break the ceiling only if driven up by events outside the government's control, for example, a rise in commodity prices.

Index

abnormal profit 173–4
absolute advantage, international
    trade 434–6
accelerator theory 334
ad valorem taxation 227–9
aggregate demand 329, 339–49
    changes in 356–7
aggregate demand curve 339–42
aggregate supply 279–81
aggregate supply curve 342–6
aid, developing countries 495
allocation of resources 361
allocative efficiency 208–9
assets
    banks 395–404
    external 464
average revenue (AR) 170–1
    monopolistic competition
        179–80

balance of payments 461–9
    inflation 424
    policy 527–31
balancing item 465–7
Bank of England 390–1, 398–400,
    523
    assets and liabilities 395–7
banking mechanism 397–404
banknotes 385
banks
    assets 395–404
    clearing 389–90
    merchant 391–2
barriers to entry 190–2, 204
barriers to mobility 297–8
behaviour, non-collusive 187
benefits
    economic growth 362–3
    market failure 214–20
    trade 431
    unemployment 379
    wealth redistribution 313–14

bilateral monopoly 303
borrowing 98–9
budget 514–20
buffer stocks 235–6
building societies 388
Bundesbank, Germany 479
business cycles 365–70

capital 32–5
    economic rent 261
    movements 462
    types 99–100
capital-intensive production
        methods 14
capitalism 18
ceteris paribus 5
choice 2, 19
circular flow of income 334–5
circulation, velocity of 414–15
civil servants 501–2
clearing banks 389–90
coins 384–5
collective bargaining 290–3
collective control 16
collusion, oligopoly 185–7
command economies 15–18
Common Agricultural Policy
        (CAP) 451–2
comparative advantage 436–9
competition
    command economies 22–3
    government policy 237
    imperfect 223
    market economies 20
    monopolistic 179–83
    non-price 185
    perfect 168–78, 182–3
competitive demand 161–3
competitive supply 165
composite demand 163–4
conglomerates 81–3
conservation 30–2

consumer surplus 121–2, 210–11
consumption 330–1
contestable markets 213
cooperatives 95
cost curves 71–2, 192
cost-benefit analysis 220
cost-push inflation 419–22,
    541, 542
costs
    economic growth 362–3
    market failure 214–20
    production 56–63
    unemployment 380–1
cross elasticity of demand 132–5
crowding-out effect 526
currencies 480–1
current account 464, 468–8
cycles see business cycles
cyclical unemployment 374

debt
    international 488–9
    national 517–19
deficits 464–5, 468–9, 531
deflation 530–1
demand
    changes in 123–6
    definition 113
    elasticities of 127–42
    inflation 416–19, 421
    management 533
    relationships 161–4
    wage detemination 288–9
demand curve 114–16
    elasticity 130–2
    exceptional 122–2
    factors of production 252–4
demand-pull inflation 539–41, 542
demerit goods 25, 223
developing countries 490–8
differentials, wages 287
diminishing marginal utility
    117–21
diminishing returns, law of 47–52
Director-General of Fair Trading
    (DGFT) 238
discount houses 392–4, 400–1

discrimination 298–9, 305
diseconomies of scale 70–5, 77
disequilibrium
    national income 350–7
    unemployment 376–9
distribution
    command economies 17–18
    goods and services 15
division of labour 37–41
double counting 318–18

Eastern Europe 22–4
economic growth 358–64
economic rent 258–63
economic systems 14–21
economic unions 448
economies of scale 360
    external 75–6
    factors of production 54–5
    internal 64–9
education 304, 360
efficiency 24, 206–9
elasticity of demand 127–42,
    277–8
elasticity of supply 147–52, 283
embargoes 441–2
employer-employee relationship
    303
employers 296, 302
employment
    Eastern Europe 23
    part-time 284
enterprise, definition 87
entrepreneurs 24, 35–6, 85
    firms location 107
    market failure 224
    mobility 46
entry, barriers to 190–2, 204
environment 22, 24, 242–3
equal pay legislation 305–7
equilibrium
    balance of payments 467
    income 337–8
    long-run 346–9
    price 153–7
    short-run 346
    unemployment 375–6, 378–9

European Monetary System
    (EMS) 454–5
European Monetary Union (EMU)
    456–7
European Union (EU)
    firms location 107, 111–12
    restrictive practices 242
    trade bloc 448, 449–57
exchange rate mechanism (ERM)
    477–9
exchange rates 470–9
    balance of payments 527–30
    policy 542–3
    unemployment 535–6
expenditure
    national income measurement
        321–2
    switching measures 530
exports, goods and services 22
external assets 464
external liabilities 464
externalities, market failure
        214–15, 221–4

factor cost 318
factor markets 165–7
factors of production 27–55
    demand curve 252–4
    immobility 224
    supply 146–7
Fair Trading Act 1973 238
finance, industry 97–103
financial institutions 388–94
financial intermediaries 388
firms
    growth of 78–86
    internal economies of scale 66–9
    location of 104–12
    objectives 203–4
    perfect competition 169, 171–8,
        176–8
    profit maximisation 202–3,
        204–6
    regulation 242–3
    size 88
fiscal policy 503–20, 525, 534,
        539–41

fixed exchange rates 474–6
fluctuations, money supply
    367–8
forecasting, business cycles 369
foreign aid 495–8
foreign trade 335–6
fractional backing 385–6
free enterprise 18–21
free trade 446, 448
frictional unemployment 373
Friedman, Milton 413, 426, 427
full employment 532

games theory 188
gender, labour force 284
General Agreement on Tariffs and
        Trade (GATT) 446–7
gold 384, 480, 488
goods
    distribution 15
    exports 22
    output 27
    production 14
    public provision 237
    self-provided 317
    types 140–2, 221–3
government
    economic growth 363–4
    firms 72, 100
    intervention 237–43
    investment 336
    labour market 304–8
    market economy role 25–6
    market failure 225–36
    policy 499–502
    wage determination 296
Great Depression 443
gross domestic product (GDP)
    358–9
gross domestic product (GDP)
    inflator 410
gross national product (GNP)
    318–19, 358–9
growth 358–64

health and safety 243
horizontal integration 80–1

Human Development Index (HDI)
329, 490
hypotheses 3–4

imperfect competition 223
import controls 530
income
distribution 224, 309–15, 512
effect 116–17
equilibrium 337–8
government role 26
inflation 422–3
national 316, 329–38
see also national income
national income measurement
320–1
types 322–5
income elasticity of demand 136–9
incomes policy 543–5
index numbers 405–7
indicators, business cycles 369
indirect taxation 225–7, 229–30
industry
concentration 89, 90
definition 87
finance 97–103
location 104–12
ownership 244–9
perfect competition 178
structure of 28
UK 87–96
inequality 311–13
infant industries 444
inflation 416–24
Eastern Europe 23
policy 539–46
unemployment 425–30
information
lack of 223
market failure 243
national income 322–7
injections
changes in 350–7
investment 334–5, 337
innovation 209–10
profit 256
technology 368

integration, firms 78–81
interest, definition 264, 265–76
interest rates 522, 523
International Bank for
Reconstruction and
Development (IBRD) 497–8
International Development
Association (IDA) 498
International Finance Corporation
(IFC) 498
International Monetary Fund
(IMF) 481–9
international trade 431–9
intrapreneurs 36
inventory cycle 369
investment 333–4, 350–1, 360–1,
367
invisible trade 461

joint demand 161
joint stock companies 92–5,
397
joint supply 164–5
juglar cycle 367

Keynes, John Maynard
aggregate demand 329
paradox of thrift 351
skills 6–7
Keynesianism
crowding-out effect 526
government failure 500
inflation 422
interest 415
theory of interest 268–74
unemployment 532–5, 538
Kitchin inventory cycle 367
Kondratieff cycle 367
Kuznets cycle 367

labour 31–2
changes in 284–6
command economies 18
division of 37–41
economic rent 260–1
elasticity of demand 277–8
elasticity of supply 283

government 304–8
location 105–6
market 277–86
market failure 297–303
mobility 45–6
supply 281–6
labour-intensive production
    methods 14
laissez-faire economies 15, 18
land 30–2
    economic rent 261–2
    mobility 45
leakages
    changes in 350–7
    circular flow of income 334–5,
        337
least-cost combination 52–3
liabilities
    banks 395–404
    external 464
liquidity
    international 480–9
    preference 269, 271–3
living standards
    Eastern Europe 23
    measurement 316–28
loan capital 99
loanable funds theory 264,
    265–8
long-run cost curve 71–2
long-run equilibrium 181, 346–9
long-run supply curve 344–6

M0 387
M4 387
Maastricht Treaty 455, 479
macroeconomics 1, 500
management
    diseconomies of scale 70–1
    growth of firms 86
marginal product 250
marginal propensity to consume
    (MPC) 353–4
marginal propensity to save
    (MPS) 354
marginal revenue (MR) 170–1,
    179–80

marginal revenue product (MRP)
    250–4
marginal revenue productivity
    251–2
marginal utility, diminishing
    117–21
market
    definition 1, 113
    failure 214–315, 297–303
    firms location 105
    labour *see* labour market
    prices 153–60
    relationships 161–7
    structural comparisons 202–13
market economies
    Eastern Europe 22–4
    features 18–21, 24–5
market forces 18
marketable wealth 309
mass production 83–5
maximum prices 233–4
measurable economic welfare
    (MEW) 328, 490
merchant banks 391–2
merit goods 25, 222–5
minimum lending rate (MLR) 523
minimum prices 234–5
mixed economies 21
mobility
    barriers to 297–8
    lack of 23, 224
    types 44–6
models 5
momentary period, definition
    150
monetarism 414–15
    government failure 500
    inflation 421
monetary inflation 541
monetary policy 521–6, 535,
    541
money 382–7, 405–15
    income 322–5
    supply 367–8, 387
Monopolies and Mergers
    Commission (MMC) 238–40
monopolistic competition 179–83

monopoly 189–201
    bilateral 303
    trade unions 299–302
monopsony employers 302
multiplier 351–7
multiplier-accelerator theory 368

national debt 517–19, 524–5
national income 316
    determination models 329–38
    disequilibrium 350–7
national minimum wage 307–8
nationalisation 244–5, 249
near money 387
needs 1
new classical economists 536–7
non-accelerating inflation rate of
        unemployment (NAIRU)
        375, 427, 428
non-collusive behaviour 187
non-marketable wealth 309
non-price competition 185
normal profit 173–4
normative statements 2–3

oligopoly 184–8
oligopsony employers 302
opportunity cost 2, 56
    production possibility curves
        8–9
output
    costs 56–60
    goods and services 23, 27
    income equilibrium 337
    monopolistic competition 181
    monopoly 193–5
    national income measurement
        320
    optimum 216–17
    perfect competition 171–3
ownership
    command economies 15–16
    control comparison 245–6
    industry 244–9

paradox of thrift 351
part-time employment 284

partnerships 91–2
payments, balance of *see* balance
        of payments
peaks 366
perfect competition 168–78,
        182–3
Phillips curve 423–9
planned economies 15
plant
    definition 87
    internal economies of scale
        64–6
    size 88
politics 368, 501
pollution 22
population, developing countries
        494
positive statements 2–3
poverty trap 24, 315
power, firms 104–5
price elasticity of demand 127–32,
        157–60
price elasticity of supply 157–60
price takers 211
prices
    control 545–6
    determinationm 113–67
    marginal utility 121
    market 20–1, 153–60
    maximum 233–4
    minimum 234–5
    monopoly 195–8
    movements 410–11
prisoners' dilemma 188
private property 15, 19
privatisation 246–8, 249
producer price index (PPI) 410
production
    command economies 16–17
    costs of 56–63
    factor markets 165–7
    factors of 27–55, 146–7, 224
    goods and services 14
    inflation 423–4
    scale of 64–77
production possibility curves 8–13
productive efficiency 206–7

profit
  definition 255
  innovation 256
  maximisation 202–3
  types 173–4, 256–7
property, market economies 19
protectionism 440–7
public corporations 95–6
public expenditure 503–6
public goods 221–2
public interest 198–9
public ownership of the means of
      production 15
public services 316–17
public-sector borrowing
      requirement (PSBR) 515
public-sector debt repayment
      (PSDR) 516

quantity theory of money 411–15
quasi-money 387
quotas 441

raw materials 104–5
real income 322–5
regional policy 107–12
regulation, firms 242–3, 249
rent 258–63
Resale Prices Act 1964 241–2
resources 14, 15–16, 27–36, 361
Restricitve Practices Court 240–1
retail price index (RPI) 407–9
revenue, types 170–1
revenue curve, monopoly 192
risk 257
risk capital 99

saving 331–4, 350–1
scarcity 2
scientific method 3–6
seasonal unemployment 373
self-interest 19–20
shares 97
short-run cost curves 71–2
short-run equilibrium 346
short-run output 181
short-run supply curve 342–4

silver 384
Single Market 455
small firms 83–6
Smith, Adam 20, 37, 511
Social Chapter 455–6
social science 4–5
socially efficient output 216–17
sole proprietors 91
specialisation 37–46
specific taxation 227–9
stock exchange 100–3
stocks
  buffer 235–6
  flows 372
stop-go cycles 368
structural unemployment 374
subnormal profit 175–6
subsidies 230–3, 443
substitution effect 116–17
sunrise industries 444
supernormal profit 173–4
supply 144–7
  definition 143
  elasticity of 147–52
  labour 281–6
  relationships 164–5
  unemployment 536–7, 538
  wage detemination 288–9
supply curve 143–6, 176–8
surpluses 464–5, 468–9, 531

tariffs 440, 446–7
tax and price index (TPI) 409–10
taxation 227–9, 313–14, 506–14
  ad valorem 227–9
  economic rent 262–3
  indirect 225–7, 229–30
technology, change in 361, 368
terms of trade, definition 458
thrift, paradox of 351
time lags 501
Tinbergen's rule 500
total revenue (TR) 180
trade
  foreign 335–6
  international 431–9
  terms of 458–60

trade blocs 448–57
trade unions 290–6, 299–302,
    304–5
training 304
transfer earnings 258–60
troughs 365

underdevelopment traps 493
unemployment 315, 371–82,
    425–30, 532–8
United Kingdom (UK)
    ERM 478–9
    industry 87–96
    taxation 506–14
    terms of trade 459
    trade pattern 431–2, 433
Uruguay Round, GATT 446–7

value judgements 1
value of money 405–15
velocity of circulation 414–15
vertical integration 78–80
voluntary export restraints (VERs)
    442

wages 22, 23, 287–96, 305–8
wealth, distribution 224, 309–15
welfare 218–19, 229–30
World Bank 497–8
World Trade Organisation (WTO)
    447

X efficiency 207–8